T. S. ELIOT
A Life

Other books by Peter Ackroyd

London Lickpenny
Notes for a New Culture
Country Life
Dressing Up
Ezra Pound and His World
The Great Fire of London
The Last Testament of Oscar Wilde

T. S. ELIOT
A Life

Peter Ackroyd

Simon and Schuster
New York

First published in America in 1984 by
Simon & Schuster Inc.,
Simon & Schuster Building,
1230 Avenue of the Americas,
New York, NY 10020

This book was designed and produced by
The Rainbird Publishing Group,
40 Park Street,
London WIY 4DE

Library of Congress Cataloging in Publication Data

Ackroyd, Peter.
T. S. Eliot.

Bibliography: p.
Includes index.
1. Eliot, T. S. (Thomas Stearns), 1888–1965—Biography.
2. Poets, American—20th century—Biography.   I. Title.
PS3509.L43Z574 1984 821'.912 [B]   84–5333
ISBN 0–671–53043–7

Picture researcher: Anne-Marie Ehrlich
Indexer: A. D. Lecore

Text filmset by Wyvern Typesetting Limited, Bristol
Printed and bound by
Hazell Watson & Viney Limited
Member of the BPCC Group
Aylesbury, Bucks

Printed in Great Britain

Contents

List of Illustrations

Acknowledgments

I WOULD LIKE TO THANK the librarians and staff of the following libraries for making available to me the Eliot correspondence which they hold in their collections: the Humanities Research Centre of the University of Texas (Eliot to Mary Hutchinson, Richard Aldington, Ottoline Morrell, Leonard and Virginia Woolf, William Turner Levy, George Barker, Henry Sherek, Marion Dorn, Montgomery Belgion and many others); the Beinecke Rare Book and Manuscript Library at Yale University (Eliot to Ezra Pound, William Force Stead and others); the Manuscript Division of Princeton University Library (Eliot to Paul Elmer More, Allen Tate and others); the Berg Collection of New York Public Library (Eliot to Leonard and Virginia Woolf, Rupert Doone, and others); the Manuscript Division of the New York Public Library (Eliot to John Quinn); the Manuscript Department of the British Library (Eliot to Sidney and Violet Schiff); the Mill Memorial Library at McMaster University (Eliot to Bertrand Russell); the Huntington Library (Eliot to Conrad Aiken); the Department of Rare Books at Cornell University (Eliot to Wyndham Lewis and Ford Madox Ford); the Special Collections of the University of Victoria Library (Eliot to Herbert Read); the Brotherton Library of the University of Leeds (Eliot to Bonamy Dobrée); the Special Collections of the University of Arkansas Library (Eliot to John Gould Fletcher); the Alderman Library at the University of Virginia (Eliot to John Rodker and others); the McKeldin Library at the University of Maryland (Eliot to Djuna Barnes); the Pierpoint Morgan Library in New York (Eliot to E. McKnight Kauffer); the Rosenbach Museum and Library in Philadelphia (Eliot to Marianne Moore); the Manuscripts Section of the University of Sussex Library (Eliot to Leonard and Virginia Woolf, Maurice Reckitt and others); the Bodleian Library, Oxford (Eliot to Margot Coker, Helen Gardner and

9

others; also, the diaries of Vivien Haigh-Eliot); the Special Collections of the Morris Library at the Southern Illinois University at Carbondale (Eliot to Richard Aldington); Department of Rare Books and Special Collections at the library of the University of Michigan (miscellaneous correspondence); the Mugar Memorial Library at Boston University (Eliot to Osbert Sitwell). I would like to thank Miss Violet Welton for showing me the correspondence between Eliot and Philip Mairet.

I would also like to thank the staff of the following institutions for making available to me other information and material about Eliot: Brown University Library; the Missouri Historical Society; the library of Merton College, Oxford; the archives of Lloyds Bank, London; the Palaeography Room of the University of London library; the library of Milton Academy; the sound archives of the British Broadcasting Corporation; the library of the British Council; the Special Collections of the University of Keele Library; the Special Collections of the Library of the University of Canterbury; the Modern Records Centre at the University of Warwick Library; the Special Collections of the Library of Washington University in St Louis; the Manuscript Department of Duke University in North Carolina; the Special Collections at the University Library, University of Durham; Magdalene College Library, Cambridge; the Brynmor Jones Library at the University of Hull; the Special Collections at Stanford University Library. And my particular thanks are due to the staff of the British Library.

I would also like to thank the following people for agreeing to see me, or communicate with me by letter, on the subject of this book: Mrs I. A. Richards, Mrs Frank Morley, Mrs Anne Ridler, A. L. Rowse, Ronald Bottrall, John Lehmann, Constantine FitzGibbon, Peter Quennell, Lady Margaret Read, Leslie Paul, George Every, George Barker, F. T. Prince, C. H. Sisson, Geoffrey Grigson, G. Wilson Knight, Ann Lamb. I would also like to thank the following people for their assistance: Anne Olivier Bell, Lyndall Gordon, Michael Hastings, T. S. Matthews, Richard Shone, Humphrey Carpenter, and George Watson. Brian Kuhn and Jenny Smyer also offered me invaluable research assistance.

I am forbidden by the Eliot estate to quote from Eliot's published work, except for purposes of fair comment in a critical context, or to quote from Eliot's unpublished work or correspondence.

For Richard Shone

Prelude

THOMAS STEARNS ELIOT, in his last years, declared that there had been only two periods of his life when he had been happy – during his childhood, and during his second marriage.[1] This will be in large part an account of the years between, the years in which he wrote his poetry. The best of that poetry, he once confessed, had cost him dearly in experience;[2] the connection between the life and the work is here explicitly made, and it will be the purpose of this book to attempt to elucidate the mystery of that connection.

I

Origins
1888–1906

ELIOT WAS BORN in St Louis, Missouri, on 26 September 1888. In symbolic representations of such a birth, the forms of Tennyson and Poe, Browning and Whitman, might have been depicted as struggling for mastery over the eventual direction of the infant poet, America on his right side and England on his left; but there were other figures who pressed in upon him more closely. The family into which he was born makes its appearance in Burke's *Distinguished Families of America*; Andrew Eliot, of East Coker in Somerset, a Calvinist, left England in the late seventeenth century and sailed for America. He settled first in Salem and then in Beverley, Massachussetts where he was town clerk in 1690. Savage's *Genealogical Dictionary* of 1860 says this of the first American Eliot: 'He was of the juries, says tradit. wh. tried the witches, and had great mental affliction on that acc. in the residue of life'. There follow five pages chronicling the descendants of that apparently unhappy man and when, in 1887, the Eliots printed their own family tree it resembled a forest – displaying connections with the families both of John Quincy Adams and Rutherford B. Hayes. But America is only part of it; Eliot's mother informed Bertrand Russell that their ancestors were both English and French[3] and there was, it seems, a certain William de Aliot who was one of the conquerors of Hastings. Those who aspire to such a heritage only do so when they believe themselves to be worthy of it and, indeed, the Eliots were the aristocrats of nineteenth-century America (family motto: *Tace et fac*), part of that rising mercantile class which offered moral leadership to those who came after them; their self-imposed mission was to administer and to educate.

His place of birth, 2635 Locust Street, was a large, two-storeyed house; there would have been several servants here – a cook, a second maid, a nurse, a laundress, a gardener, and so on. It was a quintessentially late Victorian household, at least in the American fashion, and just as Eliot was born at the end of a century still populated by grand and dying figures, so he was raised in a household of people much older than himself. He was the last child, a little boy 'rather overwhelmed'[4] by his family. For some writers, the family is merely something from which to escape, but for Eliot it was the formative influence; no man, he was to write later, escapes from the culture which it imposes[5] and it became for him a model for both the private and public relationships which he felt obliged to establish.

His mother and father were in their forties, and had already been married twenty years, when he was born; he had four sisters of whom the eldest, Abigail Adams or 'Ada', was nineteen years his senior. His one brother, Henry, was nine years older. There had been another child – either Theodore or Theodora (the genealogies disagree) – who had died in 1886 after only a few months. The pervasive and dominant presence in the household, however, was that of his grandfather, William Greenleaf Eliot, who had died the year before Eliot was born. Eliot, even in old age, remembered his influence as that of one who 'rules his son and his son's sons from the grave'[6], a Moses upon whose tablets were engraved the laws of public service.[7] Eliot was always much possessed by the dead, and that sense of possession (or dispossession) was one which he learned early. William Greenleaf Eliot was a frail, hard-working man in whom duty was the central note: 'He wrote . . . in his student days, that principles were what his nature craved', or so explained Eliot's mother in a memoir of the man which she dedicated to her children 'lest they forget'.[8] He came from Boston, the seat of the Eliots, and travelled in the role of missionary to St Louis in 1834; he was a Unitarian minister who left Harvard Divinity School in order to establish that faith in the frontier wilderness. St Louis was then partly a French town, with a large population of Catholics, but the organizing piety of the Unitarian mind was set to conquer. Indeed, William Greenleaf Eliot's missionary zeal was matched only by his practical canniness in ordinary affairs. Not only did he build his own church but he helped to establish three schools, a university, a poor fund, and a sanitary commission. His work with the poor and the sick was debilitating but, although he possessed a naturally weak constitution, he drove himself forward as though some angel or demon were perched upon his shoulder, pointing out new territories to superintend. 'My time is all broken in little pieces,' he wrote – a complaint which his grandson was often to echo. Charlotte Eliot said of him in her memoir: 'I remember his fine presence and the earnest expression of his beautiful eyes, and the smile that had not only sweetness but intensity also'.[9] 'One feels rebuked in his presence,' a friend wrote in his journal in 1839 (when William Greenleaf was only twenty-eight), '. . . How can one be familiar with the Day of Judgment . . .?'[10] The fact that such observations were also applied to Eliot himself suggests that characteristics of this kind might indeed be inherited; like Aeneas and the Penates, he carried everywhere with him the image of his family, and it was one which weighed most heavily on those occasions when he felt that he had betrayed it.

This was most clearly the case with his abandonment of his grandfather's faith, Unitarianism, which he continued to discuss and describe long after he had rejected it as a bland and insufficient heresy. Although he had been baptised in his grandfather's Church of the Messiah, he did not, in later life, believe that he had been raised in the Christian communion.[11] Unitarianism is, in fact, from the perspective of orthodoxy, an heretical faith principally because it does not accept the Christian doctrine of the Incarnation – Christ becoming a sort of superior Emerson. It is essentially Puritanism drained of its theology, since it denies the central tenets of predestination and damnation; heaven and hell are of less account than the mundane space which we inhabit between them. The measure of Man is Man himself and a peculiarly American optimism, about the progress and perfectibility of humankind, is thereby given a quasi-spiritual sanction. Unitarianism is earnest, intellectual, humanitarian, part of that high-minded 'ethical culture' which Eliot in later years distrusted and mocked.

It has been said that the favourite prayer of the Unitarians begins, 'Paradoxical though it may seem, O Lord . . .' but that is perhaps unfair. At its best, after all, it is marked by a seriousness and integrity – a kind of 'emotional reserve', Eliot called it[12] – which made it the fitting instrument for the responsibilities which its adherents felt themselves to bear. And none more so than the Eliots themselves: their role in Boston Unitarianism was a powerful and pervasive one.[13] And indeed Unitarianism was uniquely fitted, with its optimism and social progress, to sustain the efforts of the American mercantile class which could now prosper with a good conscience. The symbols of its faith resided in the Church, the City and the University[14] since it is a faith primarily of social intent, and concerned with the nature of moral obligations within a society. It placed its trust in good works, in reverence for authority and the institutions of authority, in public service, in thrift, and in success. This was the air that Eliot breathed as a child.

It is not at all paradoxical, then, that despite his rejection of his familial religion, he was to embody in sometimes extreme form all of these characteristics – as a smiling public figure, as a businessman, and as, in the broadest sense, an 'educator', he could not have offered a better example of the Unitarian ethic of leadership and service. Certainly his parents were primarily concerned with his own social conduct – they taught him, he said, what was 'done' and 'not done', what was 'right' and 'wrong' rather than what was 'good' or 'evil'; he was never able to buy sweets because at an early age it had been impressed upon him that to do so was an example of needless self-gratification.[15]

The atmosphere of Locust Street, then, was one of duty and responsibility; his family, for the most part, took up careers in social service, in teaching, or in the Unitarian ministry. His father, Henry Ware Eliot, however, adopted the other course which leads from Unitarianism – he became a successful businessman. He had wanted to be a painter but the vocation of the artist, in such inhibiting circumstances, necessarily remained unfulfilled. His one act of rebellion against his father was to refuse to become a minister – 'Too much pudding choked the dog', he remarked later[16] – and he embarked upon a number of at first unsuccessful business ventures. He became a shipping clerk, then an acid manufacturer until finally he went into the making of bricks – a business quite suited to the needs of St Louis, which even then was being transformed into an urban and industrial centre. By the time Eliot was born, his father was President of the Hydraulic-Press Brick Company and had grown wealthy upon its proceeds. Henry Ware Eliot always placed great emphasis upon success in business, and was well known for his astute management of financial matters: he looked after the property holdings of the entire Eliot family, for example.[17]

Between 1910 and 1911, he wrote a memoir of his life which was entitled 'The Reminiscences of a Simpleton' – the self-description suggesting, perhaps, that he always felt a certain unworthiness in the shadow of his father. The most notable aspect of this little volume is the impression which it gives of St Louis, which in Henry's adolescence was still a 'frontier town' between white and Indian Americans, close to that border with the savage and primitive which was to be one of his son's own preoccupations. As a boy, Henry Ware Eliot would follow the troops of Indians to their camping places and there taunt them with renditions of their own 'war whoops'; they would endure it as long as they could, and then they would turn and 'make a dash' at him and his companions – Eliot feared that 'dash' all his life, in one guise or another. The memoir gives the impression of a placid but hard-working man, whose own imaginative gifts had been subjugated to the demands of duty. But he did draw – he made sketches of cats, the pictorial equivalent of his son's later verses.

It is impossible to gauge, of course, how much influence the father had upon the son: he was already growing deaf when Eliot was born, however, and there is a sense in which Eliot never seems to have felt close to his father. Certainly, in later life, Eliot felt that he had let him down, that he had left him unhappy and bewildered with the course of his son's life.[18] A more immediate influence was that of his mother, Charlotte Champe Eliot (her maiden name had been Stearns); of all the Eliot children he most resembled her in features, his brother once remarked.[19] Her influence never left him and, indeed, she made sure that it did not. Her ambition and care for her youngest son were all the more assiduous because they sprang from her own sense of failure. Although her testimonials on leaving school described her as possessing 'unusual brilliancy',[20] she did not go to university and was obliged to earn her living as a teacher, moving from school to school until she met and married Henry Ware Eliot in St Louis in 1868. She had wanted desperately to attend college, she once told her son, and in the absence of such opportunities she considered herself to be a 'dead failure'.[21] She was a poet or, rather, she wrote poems – most of them to friends or as contributions to newspapers. She pasted them into scrapbooks, like so many pressed flowers. But she received no early recognition, and her own frustration with her literary gifts was channelled into ambition for those of her son.[22] The burden of maternal longing can last a lifetime; even in his sixties, at the time of his greatest public triumph, he confided to a friend that he wished his mother had been there to share that success.[23] But her frustration also fuelled her interventions in the world which had denied her the full use of her gifts. She was very much in the militant mould of her generation of women in America. She joined organizations such as the Humanity Club, established to 'help the unfortunate', and throughout her life she was involved in various kinds of social work, particularly in the area of juvenile law reform. She was, to use a convenient analogy, a Fabian of American life.

Charlotte was not, according to one relative, 'particularly interested in babies',[24] and in fact Eliot's closest infantile relationship was with his nurse. But as soon as the stage of early infancy was passed, and he began to exhibit signs of that precocious intelligence which his contemporaries noted, she directed him towards the kind of literary culture of which she had so strong a sense. The family library was placed at his disposal, and Charlotte encouraged him to read Macaulay's *History of England* and other improving works. A shared preoccupation with literature seems to have animated their relationship as he grew older – for Christmas 1912, the young son gave his mother Bergson's *Introduction to a New Philosophy*. It has been said that she dominated her son, but the phrase hardly does justice to such a subtle commingling of temperaments. Many years later, and after his mother's death, Eliot was teaching a course in contemporary literature at Harvard; he told his students there that D. H. Lawrence had, in *Fantasia of the Unconscious*, written with more acumen about 'mother love' than any psychologist.[25] Lawrence suggests in this book that the idealized love of a mother for her son can nourish the intellectual and spiritual development of the child at the expense of his sensuality and independence. It is a possible interpretation of a most complex relationship.

He was genuinely devoted to his mother, however, and continued to write her long letters until her death – 'with infinite love', he signed one of them in December 1917. And it was no doubt more than an act of filial piety that prompted him, many years after he had left America, to arrange for the publication of her long poem *Savonarola*. In Charlotte's somewhat bloodless lines, there is a faint consonance with the work of her son:

> . . . and while my eyes
> Are closed I see it all. There is no hell
> More horrible than this. The shriek, the yell,
> The insult and the jeer . . . .

It is almost as if a certain rhythm had entered the blood of the child, a flatness of emphasis (related to the American accent which Eliot once had) used to conjure up fantasies of pain and martyrdom, of the well-dressed matron, Charlotte, crying 'Woe! Woe!'. Indeed, a fleeting image of the mother can be glimpsed in much of Eliot's own work, whether purged of physical association in the 'Lady' of *Ash-Wednesday* or in the strong-willed women of his drama. And so the father drew cats, and the mother wrote poetry on themes of prophecy and martyrdom. There is here, in outline, the makings of a most complicated writer: the late son of two parents who were thwarted artists, himself writing of cats and martyrs, both Old Possum and Saint Sebastian.

There were other women in Eliot's childhood; in fact, he was surrounded by them. His nurse, Annie Dunne, was someone to whom he said he was greatly attached.[26] She was a devout Catholic, who, when he was six, discussed with him the proofs of God's existence.[27] He remembered, in later life, one occasion when she took him with her to the local Catholic Church; he does not describe his feelings on that occasion, but the memory of the childhood event lingered with him. He was always susceptible to smells and noises, with an intensity which suggests hypersensitivity, and the entrance into a Roman church no doubt inspired a passage which he once wrote in an essay on Arthur Symons[28] – how the sensitive child may be entranced by the effigies, the candles and the incense. Here is a sense of wonder which may have hastened his later progress into another faith. When he was not in the care of Annie Dunne, his four elder sisters were also there to protect or comfort him – particularly Ada, who in some ways adopted an almost maternal role towards him. He was a frail child; he was born with a congenital double hernia which meant that he had to wear a truss for most of his life. The combination of a delicate infant and an household full of women is a potent one: he was surrounded by their protection and sympathy, all the more assiduous when they became aware of the gifts burgeoning within him.

It is difficult to gauge accurately the nature of any childhood, since it is that part of our lives which belongs to all of us equally. He described himself as a 'priggish little boy'.[29] His cousin, Abigail Eliot, has said that he was a 'thoughtful, bright, reserved, mischievous child'.[30] A childhood companion described him as 'diffident and retiring', a small boy who played by himself.[31] Only in the poems and the plays do the visions of this childhood reappear, perpetually lost and perpetually sought for. Eliot himself, on one of his last visits to his native land, addressed the girls of the Mary Institute, a school which had adjoined his house on Locust Street; it had been founded by his grandfather, and his sisters had attended it. Here, near the ground he had trod as a small boy, he told them a story. From behind the wall which divided his garden from the schoolyard, he could hear the voices of the girls, but he could not see them. But there was a door in the wall, and a key. When the girls had left in the afternoon, the little boy would sometimes open the door and enter the yard. He remembered an ailanthus tree within it. Occasionally, he would wander through the corridors of the deserted school. But once he arrived too soon, and the girls were staring at him through a window. And he fled.[32] The wall, the door, the key, the corridors, the sound of childrens' voices: echoes of these experiences appear in 'Burnt Norton' and elsewhere, just as other images return; he once half-planned to write a book of childhood reminiscences, to be entitled *The River and the Sea*,[33] but he hardly needed to do so – these two natural forces run through all of his poetry, remembered even when they are absent in the landscape of desert or dry rock.

Each summer, from June to October, the Eliots travelled to New England – at first to Hampton Beach, New Hampshire, and then from 1893 to Gloucester, a deep-sea fishing port off the Massachussetts coast. Here, in 1896, Henry Ware Eliot built a house (for the years before, they had stayed at the Hawthorne Inn), Eastern Point, from which could be seen the harbour of Gloucester and the Atlantic itself, the coast stretching up towards the Rockport Dry Salvages. From Gloucester Eliot went sailing (at first under the anxious tutelage of his mother) in a wherry and then, in his Harvard days, in a catboat or a small-boat cruiser. In later life he remembered those days with great joy, and the presence of the sea always instilled in him feelings of serenity and well-being.

He was a keen bird watcher, also. On his fourteenth birthday he was given a *Handbook of Birds of Eastern North America*, and there are pencilled checks beneath the birds he observed[34]– the quail, the plover, the song sparrow, the goldfinch and the waterthrush. But if he was entranced by the small, vivid beauty of birds he found that there was life to be observed, also, under the microscope: in one letter, in 1899, he lamented the fact that his slides had been shattered on the journey between Missouri and Gloucester.[35] He was a solitary, curious child peering at the beauty of small things – just as he himself once talked of a boy staring at a sea-anemone in a rock-pool, and how that might not be as simple an experience as it seems.[36] The intensity of these childhood experiences was one that he was able to recapture all his life: a sense of beauty combined with the invulnerability of the watcher, the experience of both wonder and isolation. Certainly, in adult life, his eye for detail remained extraordinary. When he was in his sixties, he could recall the appearance of the tins of devilled ham which his family ate on the journey from Missouri to Gloucester; a standing lamp reminded him of one he had had at Harvard almost fifty years before.[37] He always had a sharp eye for oddities of dress and physical carriage,[38] as if they too might be marked in a *Handbook*. And so, by indirection, a portrait of the young Eliot emerges – and of the child in the man.

But if New England represented a summer retreat into the calm associated with the sea, Eliot's principal environment was that of St Louis; even while he lived there, that area of the city in which he was raised was becoming shabbier and grimier until, as he said, it began to resemble a slum.[39] But there was also that other aspect of St Louis, the Mississippi, the great river. 'I feel,' he wrote in later life to a St Louis newspaper, 'that there is something in having passed one's childhood beside the big river which is incommunicable to those who have not.'[40] The river was within him, a source of imagery and of feeling – the river in flood, the river sluggish between two banks of yellow mud. Even the water coming from the taps of St Louis was yellow, as Theodore Dreiser noted.[41] Dreiser had come to St Louis as a journalist in the 1890s, and he described it as a rich and successful town but one that had grown dormant in a kind of soft decay. The fog of 'The Love Song of J. Alfred Prufrock' is the fog that blew from the factory chimneys across the Mississippi[42]– drab, an exhalation of urban squalor. Children who live in such places grow up amid dereliction and rapid decay – and for those of a sensitive nature, the first awakening impressions are associated with images that spring from such decay. Throughout his life, Eliot was to identify himself as an urban poet, and in his adolescent years he derived a strange pleasure from walking through the alleys and the slums. It is possible that the urban decay of St Louis had other connotations for him. When Eliot was fourteen, Lincoln Steffens published in *The Shame of the Cities* his account of the corruption, or 'boodling', which was rife in that city in the last years of the century. But if Eliot grew up amid stories of financial and political scandal in the city to which his family was so publicly attached, it would be unwise to suggest any particular effect which it might have had upon him – perhaps it did no more than to emphasize the uncomfortable fact that here was a place to which he did not truly belong.

To what territory or tradition he did belong is another question, and one which he himself found it difficult to resolve: in a letter to Herbert Read he described how he could not consider himself to be a Northerner in the United States because of his Missouri origins, and how because of his Northern ancestry he could not claim to be a Southerner. He did not believe himself to be an American at all.[43] He was a 'resident alien' – an appellation to which in various circumstances he attached himself. But the fact that he dated this letter 'St George's Day' suggests to what lengths he would go to find an identity and a home.

His sense of being an alien in America was by no means unique, however. Ezra Pound used much the same terms to describe his own position in the United States – he was, he said, brought up in a place with which his forebears had no connection.[44] But they were not simply aliens in one community or another; they were estranged from the country itself. They grew up in a time of great ethical and social confusion – the intercontinental railways were changing the shape of the country, just as the vast tide of immigrants from southern and eastern Europe was radically reforming the idea of what an 'American' was. This was a society which offered no living or coherent tradition, a society being created by industrialists and bankers, and by the politics and the religion which ministered to them. For those who feel themselves to be set apart, and who have found in their reading of literature a sense of life and of values not available to them in their ordinary lives, there is a terrible emptiness about such a country at such a time. The consequence was that both Pound and Eliot – and also near contemporaries, like Irving Babbitt and Paul Elmer More – sought for a tradition or order of their own. But they had to create it for themselves, going to sources as remote as Platonism, Buddhism or medieval literature. Until they found some centre, some kind of coherence or wholeness, they would remain like the character in *The Education of Henry Adams* – the passive, cynical or merely sceptical observer of an environment which seems meaningless and of other lives which seem absurd.

At the age of seven or eight, the young Eliot attended a local school run by a Mrs Lockwood. One St Louis contemporary, Thomas McKittrick, remembers that Eliot played very little part in the activities of the other children; he recalls also how difficult he found it to keep up with him in mastering the subjects of study.[45] From Mrs Lockwood's school, he went in the autumn of 1898 to Smith Academy, which was then considered to be the preparatory school for the local university, Washington (both institutions having close connections with the Eliot family). One of his contemporaries at Smith has described him as a 'rather dreamy, bookish, tousle-headed and very unobtrusive young classmate'.[46] When he came to lecture at Washington University many years later, he described his years at Smith as comparatively happy ones. Certainly he retained lasting impressions from the school since, even fifty years on, he could remember the names of his teachers and the subjects in which he was instructed.[47] While here, he studied Greek, Latin, French, German, Ancient History and English – which was then a proper discipline, taught as rhetoric. Although such an education resembles the classical kind found in an English public school, it is somewhat more diffuse. In his final year at Smith, for example, Eliot was studying Hill's *Principles of Rhetoric*, Shakespeare's *Othello*, the *Golden Treasury*, Milton, Macaulay, Addison, Burke's *Conciliation with America*, books III and IV of Virgil's *Aeneid*, Ovid, Cicero, Homer's *Iliad*, Racine's *Andromaque* and *Horace*, Hugo's *Les Misérables*, Molière's *Le Misanthrope*, La Fontaine's *Fables* as well as physics and chemistry. It may not go very deep, but it goes extraordinarily wide and confirms the American predilection for cross-cultural references on a gigantic scale. For the young Eliot of capacious memory and application, this canter through the centuries proved to be of inestimable benefit. At Smith, also, he no doubt learned the rewards, if not the virtues, of hard work.

'Work' is, of course, a relative term and Eliot was in any case a bookish child; books were his kingdom. He was barred from playing football or other strenuous games at Smith because of his hernia, and, as might be expected in such a case, his most evocative memories of early youth are implicated in the power of words – how they grasped and held him. Certainly he came to writing early; after his first term at Smith, in January 1899, he brought out eight issues of his own magazine, *The Fireside*. It promised 'Fiction, Gossip, Theatre, Jokes and all interesting' and is edited by 'T. S. Eliot, The T. S. Eliot Company, St Louis'.[48] Inside there are adventure stories, with characters like Rattlesnake Bob and Gabbie Talkers, rhyming verses and puns, a Kook's Korner: already the range of the young Eliot's concerns is considerable. For those of a psychological bent, it may be interesting to know that he wrote that George Washington wished to go to sea but that his mother would not let him; for those involved in literary scholarship, one might note the appearance of a 'Dr Sweany'.[49]

Up to the age of twelve his taste in poetry was the natural one for a child of his age and culture – the melodramatic 'thumpers' which rouse the blood and which even in later life he was able to recite. At that age, for example, he knew by heart Kipling's 'Danny Deever', a most melancholy ballad.[50] Then there seems to have been a period of abeyance, in which he read Milton and Browning as part of his school curriculum. But there came a moment at about the age of fourteen, which he clearly remembered, when he picked up a copy of *The Rubáiyát of Omar Khayyám*, as translated by Edward Fitzgerald. The entry into the bright world of the poetic line was, he said, 'overwhelming'; he compared the experience to that of conversion, since the world itself seemed renewed and painted with 'bright, delicious and painful colours'.[51] 'Painful', perhaps, because within the declamatory music of Edward Fitzgerald he glimpsed an image of the world, and of himself, larger than any he had known before. I suspect that he remembered the occasion of reading *The Rubáiyát* so well – it has the symbolic resonance of St Augustine's 'Tolle; lege' – because when he read those 'bright' lines he knew that he wished to become a poet.

One childhood incident, which he recalled in a radio talk many years later,[52] suggests the direction in which he was propelled. While he was a boy, he went to the dentist once a week or so to have his teeth straightened. In the waiting room there, he found a complete collection of the works of Edgar Allen Poe which he proceeded to read through. When he turned to Poe's story, 'The Assignation', he saw its epigraph taken from a poem by Henry King:

> Stay for me there, I will not fail
> To meet thee in that hollow vale . . .

Eliot described how the lines so affected him that he could not rest until he had read the poem entire. Here is a boy attracted to the melancholy cadence of the couplet, and to the sonorous low tone of its vowels. He was to describe this immersion in poetry as a sort of 'demonic possession',[53] since he began 'scribbling' verses of a similar tone and style. After he had read *The Rubáiyát* he began to compose poems in quatrain form, evincing equally gloomy sentiments.[54] This was to be the pattern of his early poetic development – within a year or two he was reading Byron and began producing Byronic stanzas – although it is not recorded if he copied Sir Edwin Arnold's *The Light of Asia*, a poetic history of the Buddha which he also read. That book was, perhaps, to have a different kind of influence.

There is nothing unusual, of course, about a young poet who adopts the formal organization and tone of the work he has admired – but Eliot had this gift of assimilation to a most unusual degree. In his early poetry he becomes charged with the style of the poet who 'possesses' him, as if he could only find himself within another. The earliest extant examples of his work, printed in the *Smith Academy Record* of February and April 1905, show diverse inspiration: one, 'A Fable for Feasters', is in a Byronic style and the other, 'A Lyric', in Jonsonian mould. The latter was written as a school exercise: his English master asked him if he had had any help in its composition and seemed surprised when Eliot denied this.[55] When his mother saw the poem, she told him that it was better than any verse she had written; they did not discuss the matter further.[56] His imitative skills were certainly astonishing and throughout his life he was able to adopt or parody the mannerisms of other writers – in verse pastiche, in fake letters, in the composition of publishers' 'blurbs'. And this element of comic pastiche, the angelic side of 'possession', makes an early entry into his prose writing as well. The short stories which he wrote for the *Smith Academy Record* in his last year at that school are, with the exception of one ghoulish item entitled 'The Birds of Prey', comic tales. One, 'A Tale of a Whale', concerns two shipwrecked sailors living on the back of a whale and the other, 'The Man Who Was King', about a sea captain who becomes lord of a desert isle. Apart from displaying Eliot's relish for the sea and the things of the sea, they are interesting for their ironic and parodic note – the author in one case claiming merely to be the 'editor'. If there is one quality which links these earliest poems and stories, it is the wit and discipline which spring from an apparently instinctive sense of tone and of form.

Eliot was always an efficient and practical worker: he received good grades at Smith, and was eventually awarded the Latin Prize. He could theoretically have gone to Harvard in the autumn of 1905 but because of their concern for his health his parents decided that, despite his academic prowess, he should wait another year.[57] They decided to send him to Milton Academy, a private school just outside Boston, which was considered to be the best preparation for Harvard. Mrs Eliot explained in a letter to the headmaster of that school how her son had been deprived of companions of his own age: she was used to talking to him as though he were a man, which was perhaps not good for him.[58] And so it was decided: he needed to 'grow up' in a more regular way and in the autumn of 1905 he travelled to Milton Academy, his first extended departure from the protective cocoon of his family.

This first step in what would be a long journey away from home had its difficulties; he was no longer *primus inter pares*, an Eliot in St Louis, and had been thrust into the company of other rich and intelligent young men. It was here that he first became self-conscious about his Missouri accent – it had a noticeable drawl[59] – and therefore proceeded to lose it.[60] In a speech to the graduating class of Milton, some thirty years later, he addressed the ghost of his seventeen-year-old self – a boy hopeless at science, indecisive, who by implication does not seem to be heading for the kind of conventional life which many of his contemporaries would have. He berates him for first setting out on a path which would prove to be an unhappy one: 'See what a mess you have made of things'.[61] Perhaps it was in this period, away from his family and in the company of putative equals or even superiors, that the first faint mosquito whine of private misery entered his life: he was to say later that he was quite aware how disagreeable early youth could be, and how difficult it is for sensitive men to be happy within it.[62] There are perhaps intimations here of the suffering of a young man who felt himself to stand apart, who cried out, 'I! I! I!' without yet understanding the meaning of that cry.

His cousin, Frederick May Eliot, records how the family thought that 'he was going to achieve greatness, but that they didn't know what form it would take'. Eliot's sisters, too, he said, were 'aware that their brother was going to make a name for himself'.[63] And, of course, Charlotte Eliot continued her anxious protectiveness. In September 1905 she wrote to the headmaster of Milton inquiring about her son's cold; she wanted to be informed immediately if he ever fell ill. In May 1906 she wrote again to the headmaster, informing him that 'Tom' had asked permission to swim in a quarry pond near the school. The Eliots wished to know the condition of the pond: was the water stagnant, were there sharp rocks near the edge, were there cold currents?[64] Nevertheless, despite his mother's best efforts, the secure world of childhood and early adolescence was coming to an end; even the home in which he had been brought up had gone: when he returned from Milton in the Christmas vacation, he went back to a new house which his father had bought in Westminster Place. It was the end of the first phase of his life – a phase marked both by discipline and learning, by absorption in reading and facility in writing. Such gifts can be wasted, of course: Eliot, however, never wasted anything.

2

The Pursuit of Learning
1906–1914

IN LATE JUNE 1906, Eliot passed his entrance examination to Harvard University. He was a tall, thin, rather handsome young man with that clean-cut listlessness which is characteristic of young and well-bred Americans. There is a photograph of him taken at this age: a soft shirt and tie, a watch chain, a handkerchief in the breast pocket of his jacket – what he would have called a 'natty dresser'. He is looking at the camera in a relaxed if somewhat wary manner. According to his cousin, Eliot was completely indifferent to Unitarianism by the time he reached Harvard[1] but nevertheless (like his grandfather) he had a 'great sense of mission'[2] – although, as we shall see, the mission was essentially to civilize himself. In his first year at the university he stayed at 52 Mount Auburn Street, an expensive private dormitory in a neighbourhood popularly known as the 'Gold Coast'; there was no sense in which he had to struggle to be recognized as a young man of note, at least in the social register. He always had, as Conrad Aiken noted, 'manners' and 'an enviable grace'.[3]

Although he could not properly be called a 'sport', and indeed came perilously close to being a 'grind', he was something of a dandy. 'Tom Eliot was always a bookish person,' one contemporary noted,[4] 'good looking and well dressed.' He was soon joining all the proper clubs – the Southern Club and the Digamma, and then later the Signet and the Stylus; in 1909 he joined the board of the Harvard *Advocate*. He went to see the latest melodramas, and to hear the concerts given by the Boston Symphony Orchestra. These are the kinds of things you do because you are expected to do them, an obeisance to custom which suggests a proper awareness of your fate; in later life, the Signet, the Stylus and the Digamma would be transmogrified into the Athenaeum, the Garrick and the Oxford and Cambridge. In his second year he roomed at 22 Russell Hall with Howard Morris, a friend and contemporary from Milton; for the next three years Eliot and Morris lived with, or near, each other. Morris was, according to his contemporaries, a somewhat plump and jovial young man with no particularly pronounced literary or intellectual interests. In fact throughout his life Eliot appreciated, and needed, the company of people who were more conventional, or at least less complicated, than himself – not out of any particular desire to conform but rather because there was a large element in his own character which was neither literary nor intellectual. At Harvard he liked comic strips such as 'Krazy Kat' and 'Mutt and Jeff'. There was, as Aiken noticed, a streak of buffoonery in his temperament, just as he sometimes displayed the characteristics of both a clown and an actor.[5] But he had other friends at Harvard besides Howard Morris: Harold Peters and William Tinckom-Fernandez knew him well enough to see him in the vacations, and both of them spent part of the summer with him at Gloucester. They would sail in Eliot's catboat along the coast of Massachussetts up to the Canadian border, and on one occasion he and Peters were stormbound on an island for two days and lived 'chiefly on lobster'.[6] On Peters's advice, also, he started to exercise in a gymnasium. But, as with most such undergraduate friendships, these relationships faded in adulthood.

No doubt that was inevitable, since for Eliot Harvard was essentially a place for work. One of his many complaints about American education – and Harvard in particular – was the indiscipline and laziness of the students; and it was precisely this lack of concentration and effort which his own university's 'free elective system' (by which students could choose their own courses) encouraged. Eliot himself worked, from the start, with an almost wilful intensity. In his early student poetry there is a preoccupation with the passage of time – time running away, flowers that wither . . . but the old *topos* is explored with renewed concern. His seems to have been a temperament acutely aware of waste, of the emptiness of passing days, of the need to *use* time, to put a stamp upon it. It was for this reason that, in his second year, he decided to complete his course for a bachelor's degree in three years rather than the conventional four; and then to spend his fourth year reading for his master's degree. His courses, at the beginning, were marked by an eclectic severity.

In his first year, 1906–7, he studied German Grammar, Constitutional Government, Greek Literature, Medieval History and English Literature. The emphasis is again upon width rather than depth – in the two succeeding years of his bachelor's course French Literature, Ancient Philosophy and Modern Philosophy, Comparative Literature *et al* would be added to the list. It is perhaps worth noting that the knowledge which he acquired from studying such subjects would be subtly redeployed in later life – even medieval history, albeit in an attenuated form, makes an appearance in his play, *Murder in the Cathedral*.

How, then, did this somewhat paradoxical character, well dressed but bookish, partly a 'sport' and partly a 'grind', appear to his contemporaries? 'Eliot was so widely read by the time he came to Harvard,' one of them writes, 'that he could correct one's misquotations and tell you what you meant to say.'[7] Tinckom-Fernandez, in a Harvard *Advocate festschrift*, has said, 'He was always the commentator, never the gutsy talker and seemed even then to cultivate a scholarly detachment . . . a quiet, subtle humour'.[8] Leon Little, in the same compilation of hindsight, remarked that, 'Everyone liked Tom but except for his extraordinary brain power he seemed rather ordinary'. And William Chase Greene told Herbert Howarth[9] ' . . . he was recognized as able and witty; not influential, at the time; rather aloof and silent'. And so already the lineaments of his personality can be discerned: laconic, witty, with a hint of asperity, clearly very intelligent but also somewhat reserved and detached.

If there is a suggestion of pride here, it is the pride that comes from self-reliance. Ezra Pound was later to describe Eliot as the poet who had modernized himself '*on his own*'[10] and that is the key, also, to his studies at Harvard: he was finding his own path, although as yet unsure of the direction in which it would take him. He once declared himself to be a 'descendant of pioneers'[11] and there is no doubt that he saw the body of inherited knowledge as territory to conquer on his own terms. There would, in any case, have been few to help him at Harvard: it was, according to one critic, 'a glacial era'[12] and although Eliot was always, in later life, respectful of his undergraduate teachers, he was never more than that. Some of them, in their turn, were less than enthusiastic about him. Charles Copeland, whose course in English composition he took in 1908–9, wrote in the margin of one of his essays, 'As usual, you lean to the unduly harsh . . . you must now be on your guard against becoming pompous, orotund and voluminous'.[13]

But if there were few intellectual models upon which he could draw, there were certainly no literary ones. He characterized the American poetry of this generation as representing for him a 'complete blank';[14] the acceptable standard verse appeared in volumes like *Poems for Travellers, Birds of the Poets* and *Poets on Christmas*. The only nourishment he obtained was from the work of the English 'Nineties' poets – particularly Davidson, Dowson and Symons – and in the slightly earlier *City of Dreadful Night* by James Thomson. Here he found what might be called the poetry of urban romance, in which the gratification that the poetic protagonist derives from his own gloom is matched by the significance which he attaches to the quotidian detail of contemporary urban life. They looked upon the face of their own civilization and were able to transform it into the material of poetry, as each generation of poets must do. John Davidson's 'Thirty Bob a Week' was the work which, by Eliot's own account, had the most powerful effect upon him.[15] The element of drama which he always looked for in poetry is most important here since it was the 'personage' in that poem who haunted Eliot:[16] a character who combines resignation and anger; imprisoned within a narrow round of struggling days, he is both weary and eloquent, able to cry out in his distress while at the same time noticing 'curious items about life'.

Eliot saw the point, and then moved on. In his second year at Harvard – perhaps as a result of taking the course in French Literature in that year – he started reading Baudelaire. Here, too, he confronted a 'personage' who combined morbidity with extreme self-consciousness, a poet who raised the imagery of the metropolis to a high degree of intensity and then wrapped it around himself so that it became an echo chamber for his own suffering. But it was not simply this spectacle of dramatic anguish that affected Eliot. The sound and cadence of the words held him, just as they did in his reading of Dante and the Elizabethan dramatists. He would recite Dante in bed or on a railway journey, even when its meaning was not entirely clear to him,[17] and the 'strong lines' of the Elizabethans were constantly to occupy his critical attention as he tried to locate the source of their clamour and their grace.

Then, in December 1908, he picked up in the library of the

Harvard Union Arthur Symons's *The Symbolist Movement in Literature*. It was a book, he was to admit later, that influenced the course of his life,[18] principally because here he encountered the work of Jules Laforgue. In Symons's chapter on the poet, he said, he discovered a temperament very close to his own[19] – he could see himself clearly from the outside, as it were – and in that act of self-identification he learned how to speak freely for the first time. And what was it that Symons had said of Laforgue? That he was reticent, scrupulous, correct both in dress and manner, confronting the world with a posed demeanour that he never abandoned. He was a poet 'terribly conscious of daily life' and the 'possibilities of art which come from the sickly modern being, with his clothes, his nerves'. Almost at once Eliot ordered the three volumes of Laforgue's *Oeuvres Complètes* which arrived in the following spring. Now the quickening process began. He was attracted primarily to the denial of conventional feeling in that poetry, both in its ironic scepticism about romantic passion and Laforgue's refusal to reveal or even to take seriously his own. Eliot had already appeared to his more percipient contemporaries as something of a wit and an actor, someone who, in other words, understood the artificiality of feeling; but he was also extraordinarily intelligent. He saw through everything, as very clever young men often do, and he was quite unable to be serious about those matters which other people took more solemnly. Now, in Laforgue, he discovered a tone and a formal technique which allowed these characteristics of his own temperament to be expressed. He was changed utterly[20] – recognizing himself through someone other, he became the person whom he had wished to be.

There is a marked alteration in his undergraduate verse as a result. Where before he had expressed conventional themes in allusive and decorative style, after the assimilation of Laforgue he writes poetry which satirizes conventional sentiments and the predilections of the (Boston) bourgeoisie. This ability to grow by the acquisition of another man's language is, of course, the sign of a highly refined literary sensibility, which finds meaning in words and words only. When he takes a line almost directly from Laforgue – ' . . . oui, divins, ces yeux! mais rien n'existe Derrière' becomes 'I could see nothing behind that child's eye' – the words precede the perception, and any 'feeling' associated with it. But his immersion in the French poet did not last very long. Already in the undergraduate poems modelled upon him there is a colloquial forcefulness and dramatic energy of movement that lead away from Laforgue's rather brittle melodies. The point is better made, perhaps, by noting that within a year Eliot had started writing 'Portrait of a Lady'.

In June 1909 he received his AB (or, in England, BA) – his grades (4 As, 3 Bs, 2 Cs and 1 D) were good although not exceptional. But he proceeded, in his fourth year, to his studies for a master's degree in English literature. Although he had roomed with Howard Morris for the previous two years, in his final year he took his own rooms at Apley Court and, according to his friend Tinckom-Fernandez, 'to his classmates and the *Advocate* Board he became a recluse'; he used to have to 'run him to earth' in his rooms.[21] He had entered a period of arduous and anxious scholarship (Tinckom-Fernandez noticed how supportive Eliot's mother and sisters were), and withdrew from the company of those he knew – setting the pattern for what others in later years would call his strange social behaviour. But it would be wrong to suggest that he was entirely isolated; it was in this year, for example, that he met Conrad Aiken, a young poet who was also on the board of the *Advocate*. They actually first came together when Eliot staggered, the worse for drink, out of the Lampoon Club and embraced Aiken. 'And that, if Tom remembers it tomorrow, will cause him to suffer agonies of shyness,' an acquaintance remarked to Aiken.[22] The shyness was soon mastered, however, since he and Aiken struck up a friendship which was to endure, with certain lacunae, to the end of their lives.

While studying for his master's degree in this final year, Eliot worked with two eminent teachers. With one of them, George Santayana, the poet and philosopher who was eventually to leave Harvard and become a 'wandering scholar' in Europe, he investigated 'Ideals of Society, Religion, Art and Science in their Historical Development' – the fact that he took such a course is perhaps a reflection of his consistent urge towards the systematization and organization of knowledge. But he never 'got on' with Santayana, and although Pound once in his hare-brained way tried to bring them together, Santayana himself was always somewhat dismissive of Eliot's 'thought'. His other teacher, Irving Babbitt, exercised a more powerful influence upon him. They were to correspond until Babbitt's death (Eliot sometimes addressing him in letters as 'Dear

Master', an appellation which Babbitt took *cum grano salis*). His course was 'Literary Criticism in France' but it was the man as much as the subject which appealed to Eliot; he was unpopular in the university because of his open scorn for the teaching methods then in vogue and his reputation, Eliot said, was preserved by a few 'discerning' graduates and undergraduates.[23] In his *Literature and the American College*, published the year before Eliot began to study with him, he had reviled those notions of progress dear to the American (and indeed the Unitarian) mind, just as he attacked the obeisance of colleges like Harvard to the egalitarian and industrial culture which America was in the process of developing. His was a call for 'standards' and 'discipline' as opposed to the conventional demands for growth, prosperity and success. This was the man for Eliot.

Although the lectures Eliot attended were primarily on the subject of French literary criticism, Babbitt tended to range widely over the whole field of his scholarly concerns. He placed in opposition to the ideals of 'the classicist' those of the 'emotional sentimentalist' – in this particular course (although it had larger ramifications) he suggested the limitations of 'Rousseauism' and its debilitating effects upon literary theory. His thesis was that Rousseau had created a climate of emotional anarchy in which the claims of the individual artist were considered greater than those of the literary tradition, and in which the 'romantic imagination' had risen like a serpent from the sea in order to obliterate the principles of classical order; this had been the work of sentimentalists who had derived from Rousseau the appealing but dangerously false notion that the human personality was innately good. But, for Babbitt, order and authority were necessary to check man's equally innate tendency to evil or the brutishness of appetite. And although Eliot was later to criticize Babbitt's humanism, with its reliance upon the 'inner check' and 'ethical strenuousness', he was profoundly affected by Babbitt's formulations. The distaste for sentiment, emotionalism and narrow self-expression was to become a permanent aspect of his own criticism and, although the origins of that distaste can never be fully elucidated (a psychologist might try and fail), they derive in part from the reserve and the integrity of his family's Unitarian ethic and in part from his own defensive and self-absorbed character.

Since it was Babbitt who first directed Eliot's attention to the study of Sanskrit and Oriental religion, that distrust for 'personality' no doubt played a large part here also. As Babbitt wrote in one essay, 'Buddha and the Occident', 'the temper of the Buddhist is more impersonal than that of the Christian'; Eliot's flirtation with Buddhism in his later Harvard years (and perhaps beyond – Stephen Spender recalled a conversation in which he claimed that he was thinking of becoming a Buddhist at the time he was writing *The Waste Land*)[24] may well be connected with the aloofness and invulnerability which Babbitt's notion of 'impersonality' suggests – an aspect of that shuddering disaffection towards the ordinary world which was to emerge in Eliot's early poetry. But although many of Babbitt's interests and attitudes are repeated in Eliot's own essays, it would be too easy to draw firm lines from one to the other. A teacher does not dominate a young man as clever as Eliot – he simply provides the framework, or language, in which he can develop and serves to confirm the direction which he is already instinctively taking. Certainly Eliot did not adopt these concepts in a theoretical or scholarly manner; and the fact that, in late 1909 and throughout 1910, there was an acceleration of his poetic activity suggests that here, if anywhere, the centre of his interests is still to be found.

In the summer of 1910, while staying with his family at Gloucester, he bought a notebook and began painstakingly to transcribe the poems which he had been writing. He called the book 'Inventions of the March Hare'; before that he wrote, 'Complete Poems of T. S. Eliot' which, since they include none of the verse written before the inspiration of Laforgue, suggests an ability to abandon the past. He was to continue adding to the notebook until his journey to England in 1914 and it is the only direct, if ambiguous, record of his private experience during these years. A number of the early poems transcribed are concerned with scenes of urban squalor and dilapidation – 'Caprices in North Cambridge' and 'Preludes in Roxbury' (which become the first two 'Preludes' in the published work) among them. Since he had come across versions of this theme in the poetry which most attracted him, it might be assumed that he was simply using a literary model – the urban scene, as opposed to the pastoral scene of the Georgians. But that would be to mistake the nature of his creativity: he needed the model before he could explicate his own experience, just as in later life he would read Ibsen before he wrote *The Family Reunion* and Dante before *Ash-Wednesday*. He did not imitate the previous work; he used it as a rough sketch which helped him to order and to understand his own experience.

These are poems which attempt to recreate the observations of a solitary wanderer through dilapidated streets; the images are of broken glass, of doorways and alleys, of the sound of children's voices, all of them gaining their power from a note of sexual adventure or sexual arousal which fills the observer with unease. There is both an attraction towards such experience and a withdrawal from it, but this is a difficult tone to control: at its worst, the poetry is ragged in execution. He can only master this ambiguous attitude when he objectifies it – when he creates drama out of it and assumes another voice (the first passages of 'Portrait of a Lady' were written in the early months of 1910), or when he controls it with an insistent rhythm which comes from a deeper source than the observing eye (as in the 'Preludes').

But in the same notebook there are more formal and mannered poems, much closer to the tone of Laforgue. They characteristically introduce the figure of the mandarin or marionette and the key word, repeated often enough to become a refrain, is 'indifferent'. One of these, 'Opera', dated November 1909 by Eliot, seems to have been written after he had seen a performance in Boston of *Tristan und Isolde*. When he was in his sixties he discussed this opera with Stravinsky, and from that conversation Stravinsky inferred that it must have been 'one of the most passionate experiences of his life'.[25] But there is none of that response in the early poem, and indeed any such passion is discounted or satirized; the mood is one of scepticism and weariness. Such a tone could only be called 'adolescent' if Eliot outgrew it – but he never did ('Why should the agèd eagle . . .').

Certainly there is in this early poetry a consistent preoccupation with retreat, with withdrawal into seclusion. Sometimes this self-absorption seems to be the condition of poetic vision itself, a 'moment out of time' which in the unpublished poem 'Silence' (June 1910) stills the waters of experience and creates a terrifying peace. But the pressures of the external world are insistent ones; in a sequence of poems entitled 'Goldfish (Essence of Summer

Magazines)', he describes in an ironical manner the routines of bourgeois life – the flannel suits, the cakes and tea, the outings, the circumspect conversations. This was the life of Boston, among people who came close to stifling him altogether.[26] It is the atmosphere in which he wrote passages which were later to be incorporated into the two great poems of his early maturity, 'The Love Song of J. Alfred Prufrock' and 'Portrait of a Lady'.

Just as the fog of 'Prufrock' is the St Louis fog, so the interior landscape of the poem is that of Boston. Van Wyck Brooks described that city during this period as 'congested with learning . . . hyper-critical, concerned, self-conscious . . . filled with a sad sterility, the fruit of emotional desiccation'.[27] Eliot, in a review some years later of *The Education of Henry Adams*[28] described the Bostonian mind as one that combined scepticism and doubt, also the manifestations of a desiccated society. Even before he had completed his master's degree, he wanted to get away. The poetry he was writing at this time was impaled upon its own self-consciousness, fit only to be neatly transcribed in a notebook and then forgotten; his solitary walks through the slums of the poor were taken on a lead which drew him back to Harvard and his family. He was protected every step of the way and although his family expected great things of him, these were to be attained only within the confines which they understood. It is a familiar story and the imperative is familiar also: to get out.

In his review of *The Education of Henry Adams*, he remarked that Adams was aware of the fact that he had not been perfectly educated at Harvard and that he recognized, as most Bostonians did, the narrowness of the horizons there: a sensitive but still immature young man would sense that there were other things he ought to experience and to understand.[29] This was very much Eliot's own situation, and he was in no doubt where to go in order to remedy it. His reading of Laforgue and Babbitt's own enthusiasm directed him towards France which at this time, he said, represented for him 'la poésie'.[30] He must have informed his family of his decision to spend a year in Paris in the early months of 1910, since Charlotte wrote to him in April expressing her distress at the idea of his being alone in that city: 'the very words give me a chill'.[31] She added that he might know better what he wished to do in June, since this would be the time of his graduation.

The pressures were now building up on him. Not only did he have to face an academic test, but he was about to make his first move against the wishes of his mother. In May he was taken into hospital with a suspected case of scarlet fever, and Charlotte went at once to Boston to see him. (The thread of illness will run through his life, sicknesses which often descended upon him at points of crisis.) And it was in June he wrote 'Silence', the poem of withdrawal. He was unable to take his final examinations, but he was not seriously ill and he attended the graduation ceremonies at the end of June. He spent the summer of 1910 in Gloucester, where he persuaded his family to allow him to venture beyond their own backyard: his father, at least, agreed to subsidize the trip. And then, in October, he sailed to Europe.

It was his first visit to that continent; to be immersed in the atmosphere of Paris, having only previously tasted the excitement offered by Harvard professors, was akin to the experience of a drowning man who is suddenly plucked up into the air. His arrival might have been celebrated by Henry James – this carefully dressed, nervous young American (he was always an anxious traveller) with his precise, bookish French, announcing himself in a self-conscious fashion at the *pension* where he was to stay – 9 rue de l'Université, close to the Sorbonne and in the cultural centre of the city. Eliot was to call it a 'romantic year'[32] although his own official account of the effect which Paris exercised upon him is couched in characteristically intellectual terms. He had travelled to the city drawn by that ineluctable sweet thread which connects poetry and place, but 'la poésie' was not a dominant presence there in the early years of the century. Paris had, instead, reassumed its role as a centre for conflicting ideologies and it was intellectual activity, as much as anything else, which animated Eliot during this period. He listed some of the eminent figures who were influential in Paris at this time and who were, for the most part, new to him: Durkheim, Janet, Remy de Gourmont, Anatole France, Henri Bergson and others.[33] He retained the habits of his undergraduate days; he studied French literature at the Sorbonne and French conversation with a private tutor, and in the first two months of 1911 he attended Bergson's Friday lectures at the Collège de France. He later recalled the packed lecture hall, and the atmosphere of excitement which the philosopher generated. Indeed he suffered a 'temporary conversion' to Bergsonism.[34] Bergson was an effective teacher because, like Babbitt, he admitted no doubts, and it was his dogmatism which attracted Eliot's more diffident temperament. He affirmed the relativity of all conceptual knowledge, and his descriptions of the flux or chaos which lay beyond the reach of such knowledge would have appealed to the young poet of the 'Preludes'. Certainly his notion of 'real time', 'la durée', affected the poems which Eliot wrote in Paris – he was a Bergsonian when he composed 'The Love Song of J. Alfred Prufrock', he told one inquirer[35]– but it is possible that he was drawn to the philosopher because he seemed to understand also the experience of poetic composition: 'intuition attains the absolute' was Bergson's phrase, affirming his belief that reality can only be grasped by an act of 'intellectual sympathy'.

But the allegiance passed; it had disappeared by 1913, and a less credulous Eliot was to criticize Bergson for being fundamentally fatalistic.[36] It could not have been otherwise. The notion of 'ideal duration', of immersion in time, of the flow of consciousness, is clearly an analogy for Eliot's own sense of experience and its claims. But he always withdrew from such experience, in the same manner that he withdrew from Bergson: he reverted to his need for order, for discipline, for tradition. That is why, although the influence of Bergson wore off quickly, the effect of Charles Maurras, whose work he also encountered at this time, was to last a lifetime. This is the Maurras, after all, who in 1913 was described as the embodiment of three traditions – 'classique, catholique, monarchique'. This trinity was ascribed to him in the *Nouvelle Revue Française* of March 1913 at precisely the time when Eliot was reading that magazine. Fifteen years later Eliot was to describe himself in turn as a classicist, royalist and anglo-catholic.[37]

Maurras was a man of deeply authoritarian temper, who espoused the principles of classical order and hierarchy in every field of human activity. His anti-Rousseauist and anti-republican ideology obviously suited a quondam student of Babbitt, but Maurras had never suffered the civilizing influences of Harvard and pursued his principles with the violent assiduity which seems endemic in French intellectuals. He was anti-democratic and rabidly anti-semitic (later to be incarcerated for his association with the Vichy regime). His organization, the Action Française, encouraged student riots (through offshoots like Jeunes Filles Royalistes and the

Camelots du Roi) against free thinkers and Jews – the year before Eliot's arrival they had demonstrated against a lecturer in pedagogical method, M. Thalamas, who had happened once to criticize Joan of Arc. Eliot himself remembered one such demonstration when the Camelots du Roi cheered the cuirassiers who had come to disperse them.[38] Here we have the excitement of the timid or hesitant man watching the violence of others (Eliot liked boxing matches also), just as his thirst for absolutism found nourishment in Maurrasien doctrines. Throughout his life, Eliot would continue to support Maurras, and his philosophy was to enter the fabric of Eliot's own concerns.

But Paris was a place of friendship as well as theory. He practised French conversation with Alain-Fournier, a young writer who had stolen a march on Eliot simply because he was in a country which took its literature seriously. He introduced Eliot to the work of Dostoyevsky, Gide and Claudel – although only the first of these 'took' – and they shared an enthusiasm for Laforgue; some of Alain-Fournier's own verses have as their epigraphs lines from Laforgue's *Derniers Vers*. Eliot struck up a friendship, also, with a fellow lodger in his *pension*, Jean Verdenal. Since Verdenal was acquainted with Jacques Rivière, the editor of the *Nouvelle Revue Française*, whom Eliot had also met (if for no other reason than that he was the brother-in-law and close friend of Alain-Fournier), it seems likely that Eliot and Verdenal were introduced and did not simply meet by chance. Certainly they had shared interests for although Verdenal was a medical student, his real preoccupations were literary ones and in his library there were copies of Laforgue's *Poésies* and *Moralités Légendaires*. One of Verdenal's closest friends remembers how he also 'took a small interest, literary and political, in Charles Maurras and the Action Française'.[39] It is legitimate to speculate, then, that Verdenal himself introduced Eliot to the work of Maurras. The two young men were, in any event, in close intellectual and imaginative sympathy. They visited galleries together, discussed the latest books, and corresponded after Eliot's return to America. It was the kind of friendship which, established upon youthful enthusiasm and in the absence of those constraints which afflict young men coming from the same background or country, Eliot had never experienced before. (He was to say later that there had been very few people at Harvard whom he could tolerate,[40] and even his friendship with Conrad Aiken was marked by a jocular uneasiness.) Jean Verdenal became an army medical officer in November 1914, joined the 175th infantry regiment in February 1915 and then three months later was killed in the Dardanelles: the first, but not the only, friend of Eliot to be lost in the war. Nevertheless he was on the way to a marginal immortality when Eliot dedicated to him his first book published in England, *Prufrock and Other Observations*, as well as the first American edition of his poems. His handwritten notebook of poems is also similarly dedicated: we see here the consistent wish to memorialize and to mourn, to celebrate a friendship which burned brightest because it was arrested in mid-career.

Despite Verdenal's presence, however, Eliot gives the impression that he suffered from loneliness in the foreign city. Certainly he went to the trouble of looking up a Harvard contemporary, Gluyas Williams, whom he hardly knew,[41] which suggests either boredom or desperation. Some years later he explained to a friend that, when he had lived in Paris, he had known nobody – and that the best way to take that city was to remain isolated and independent of the people who were mostly 'futile and time-wasting'.[42] This isolation made him more aware of his private desires, however. The sexual instinct was of considerable importance to him, despite the impression he seemed to give in later life, and in his twenties he wrote, in his studiously impersonal manner, that a child who has been starved of beauty may find in sexuality the only possible liberation from a constricting world.[43] But it was not as simple as that: although, as he explained to Conrad Aiken, he was invaded by sexual longings in Paris his own inhibitions were such that he could not, or would not, act upon them.[44] It is clear that there were such sexual opportunities if he had chosen to take them: one book which exercised a profound fascination for him, and which he described as 'a symbol' of Paris for him at this time, was Charles-Louis Philippe's *Bubu de Montparnasse*,[45] the story of the pimps and prostitutes of that quarter of the city. This resurgence of sexuality away from home, although or perhaps because it was held in strict control, had the effect of lifting other restraints, and between 1910 and 1911, he completed the two great poems of his youth, 'The Love Song of J. Alfred Prufrock' and 'Portrait of a Lady'. Even his handwriting changed in that year abroad, becoming larger and spikier, until once more back in America he reverted to his correct, smaller hand – although, in this latter hand, the 'I' has a lower loop.[46]

There were other poems, of course, which have remained unpublished and are, indeed, unpublishable. They are characteristically visions of the urban wanderer, given a darker shade as the images of Paris, of bars and nightclubs, supplant those of Boston. In the majority of them there are hints and whispers of female sexuality: the woman whose consciousness is invaded by sordid images (dated 'July 1911' with an epigraph from *Bubu de Montparnasse*: it became the third 'Prelude'), the women who stand uncorseted in doorways (from an unpublished section of 'Prufrock'). In 'Entretien dans un parc', dated February 1911, a dramatically personified 'I' walks with a girl; he is irresolute, exasperated, fearing ridicule. And in another poem, dated March 1911, the 'Absolute' (shades of Laforguian irony) is depicted as a female, syphilitic spider. Even in the more achieved poetry, the images of women are of those who destroy his self-possession and elicit from him feelings of self-disgust. There is the now notorious lady in the 'Portrait', conventionally associated with a Bostonian *grande dame*, Adeleine Moffat, whom both Aiken and Eliot used to visit. And the original title of 'Prufrock' was 'Prufrock Among the Women'. The middle section of this poem, 'Prufrock's Pervigilium', was apparently dropped at Aiken's urging;[47] its date is uncertain, although it seems likely that a rough draft of it was composed in 1911 when the rest of the poem was completed. Here there are whispers of children, women in hallways; such sensations arouse experiences of peculiar horror in Prufrock: the houses themselves seem to be pointing and laughing at him, and there are intimations of madness as the world itself falls apart. It would be absurd to find here only the material of private confession – much of the poetry is established upon literary models and is invested with a dramatic tone that precludes facile identification. But just as Eliot found in *Hamlet* obscure and inexpressible emotions which could not be dragged 'to light',[48] so we are able to recognize in the tone and preoccupations of his poetry during this period a brooding dislike, or fear, of women.

It has often been noted how paradoxical that reaction is in a young man who from his first years had been surrounded by the affection of mother, sisters and nurse. But the fact that he had close relations with women who supported or nurtured him makes it all the more likely that he found it difficult to accept their sexual nature also. His sexual instincts were, as he said, nervous in origin because they were implicated in his fear of ridicule and associated with feelings of guilt and self-disgust. Even by late 1914, in his twenty-sixth year, he was still referring to himself as a virgin,[49] although this was perhaps not unusual in an over-refined and over-cautious young man of the period, especially one brought up in a Unitarian household where the father thought of sex as 'nastiness'.[50]

What is unusual is not the fact that Eliot was preoccupied by such matters but that he was able to order or to 'place' those feelings within a larger dramatic or tonal organization. 'Prufrock', 'Portrait of a Lady' and to a lesser extent the 'Preludes' were originally fragments, composed at scattered intervals over a relatively long period. The isolated passages are often intensely lyrical in inspiration, and it is almost as if he was unsure of, or distrusted, his lyricism – his music. And so they are placed in a larger order where their fragility or temporariness – the imminent sense of loss which accompanies their appearance – becomes one aspect of the beauty of the whole poem. Eliot could, as it were, pick up a poem where he had left off. He had an extraordinary gift of synthesis so that what seems to be one poetic persona, or one melodic shape, is in fact the result of compression and the selective rendering of otherwise disparate materials. The identity of the poem, and indeed of the poet, is in that sense factitious but in this constant dialogue, between his sensitivity towards experience and his instinct for organization, can be discovered the roots of Eliot's poetry.

Paris was not the only city he visited on this first trip to Europe. He apparently travelled to London in April 1911 – there is, at least, one short poem 'Interlude in London' bearing that date in which, with that melancholic lyric music which Eliot seems able to summon at will, a damp and apathetic life is evoked. (This may not have been his first trip; since he had a Baedeker guide, *London and the Environs*, which has the date 14 October 1910 written in it, it is possible that he passed through London en route to Paris six months before.) Then in the summer of this year he travelled to Munich, where he completed 'The Love Song of J. Alfred Prufrock'. He transcribed it into his notebook and then forgot about it. Conrad Aiken said that he had been 'heartlessly indifferent to its fate'.[51]

At one point, Eliot recalled, 'I had at that time the idea of giving up English and trying to settle down and scrape along in Paris, and gradually write French.'[52] It was a romantic idea, to suit his sense of a romantic year, but it was one he quickly abandoned; in the summer of 1911 he told Conrad Aiken, who had come to visit him, that he had decided to return to Harvard and become a philosopher.[53] Aiken recalled Eliot's phrase that poetry perhaps 'could do no harm'[54] – a somewhat dismissive attitude which even in later life he would adopt from time to time. Why did he decide to leave Paris? The call towards philosophy is the call towards order, and no doubt the idea of 'scraping along' quickly loses its charm for someone who has visions of madness and a disintegrating world: such natures are not meant for restless drifting because they are destroyed by it. Perhaps also for the more mundane reason that he had run out of money, and his family were unlikely to subsidize further adventures in an alien and iniquitous city. Family pressures were indeed very strong upon him at this period in his life, and there is no doubt that his mother in particular had decided that he should adopt a profession within the American university system. He was still too young and too unsure of himself to withstand such pressures: the real confrontation would come later, when he would present his parents with a *fait accompli* and there were sympathetic friends to support and advise him. As it was, familial and institutional demands drove him once more back into the shelter of Harvard where he would remain for the next three years.

He returned in time for the autumn term of 1911 and enrolled as a graduate student in philosophy. Of course, he tried to bring back with him the atmosphere of Paris. He subscribed to the *Nouvelle Revue Française*, he pinned a reproduction of Gauguin's 'Yellow Christ' upon his wall (he was very fond of crucifixion scenes) and sported a malacca cane (in later life replaced by an umbrella). Conrad Aiken describes him with 'exotic Left Bank clothing, and with his hair parted behind . . . it had made a sensation'.[55] In his comic memoir *Ushant*, he calls Eliot 'Tsetse', with its suggestion of a bite – he was shy and often witty, Aiken said, but he could be waspish and on occasions was capable of 'icy fury'. He also penned a caricature of his friend in which he describes his pose as that of a 'decadent';[56] it was the first of a number of roles which he was to observe in Eliot's career. Self-aware but also filled with self-doubt, evincing a kind of narcissistic vulnerability, Eliot was always concerned with the correct appearance, the correct manner through which to project himself. He was also able to act in a more straightforward manner: at an evening of amateur theatricals which his cousin, Eleanor Hinkley, arranged, he played the role of Mr Woodhouse from Jane Austen's *Emma*.

But his return to Harvard also inaugurated a period in which he was beset by worries about his future.[57] And although his outward existence seemed to follow the conventional pattern of a young graduate – operas, concerts, parties, amateur theatricals – he was suffering from doubt and indecision about the eventual shape of his life. He decided first to study Sanskrit, enrolling in C. R. Lanman's course in Indic philology, and in his second year he read Indian philosophy in the classes of James Haughton Woods. In the original language he tried to master the Pancha-Tantra, the Bhagavad-Gita, the Jatakar (the sacred books of Buddhism) and, in addition, he attended a full year course on Buddhism given by Masaharu Anesaki. He was following the path which other American intellectuals had taken, towards the exploration of Eastern (specifically, non-European) religion, as if the American experience could only find a resolution in a philosophy quite different from that of the now fatally compromised Christianity of their forebears. Babbitt and Paul Elmer More, for example, had already travelled in this direction.

But Eliot's attraction to Buddhism was not simply a philosophical one. *Nirvana* is extinction – the annihilation of desire, the freedom from attachments – and there was, as can be seen in his poetry, an over-riding desire in the young Eliot to be so free. The absolutism of Buddhism is quite as relentless as anything he had found in Maurras and, although he was perhaps attracted to it for much the same reasons, the Eastern religion had more romantic affiliations for someone who wished to break free of the familial bonds which otherwise held him. Certainly Eliot did not enter any of his academic studies in the spirit of disinterested enquiry and, when he ceased to need such studies, he abandoned them. That is perhaps why he confessed later that his years under Lanman and Woods had left him only with a sense of 'enlightened mystification'.[58]

In this uncomfortable state, he started courses in the more conventional realms of philosophy and comparative methodology. In June 1913 he bought a copy of F. H. Bradley's *Appearance and Reality* and then from September until May of the following year he attended Philosophy 20 c, a course by Josiah Royce in 'A Comparative Study of Various Types of Scientific Method', in which problems of description and interpretation were investigated. In this course he wrote one paper, 'The Interpretation of Primitive Ritual', the content of which was so important to him that he was able to remember it more than twenty years later.[59] His stance in that paper might be characterized as one of inspired doubt: no ritual, he said, can be properly interpreted because our own values and sense of 'fact' are implicated in a quite different system of belief. Even the religious 'belief' of those who participate in such a ritual may simply be a rationalization of the ritual itself, the origin of which has been forgotten. What Eliot seems to be working towards here is the impossibility of discovering any objective 'meaning' in even the most significant patterns of human behaviour, and this opens an abyss into which all of us might fall. 'Meaning' exists in human activities only if those who participate in such activities wish or believe them to have meaning; the 'truth' of such things is relative. In his classes of 1914 he was also asserting the epistemological value of illusions and hallucinations – for who is to claim that they do not have meaning also, for those who believe in them? On 5 May, he gave a paper on the empirical classification of different types of objects. His work at this juncture gives the impression of a highly refined and sceptical intelligence investigating its own patterns and its sudden leaps without finally being convinced that its conclusions are valid. Perhaps his characterization of Henry Adams should be recalled here – of a man who is interested in many things but who could believe in nothing, who has inherited a Bostonian or Unitarian scepticism which 'is not destructive, but . . . dissolvent'.[60]

But the impossibility of finding inherent meaning points in two directions. Eliot declared at one of the seminars, 'You can't understand me. To understand my point of view you have to believe it first.'[61] This comes close to pure subjectivity, and to the failure of communication in a world which is interpreted and shaped by the individual consciousness: that is why he seemed indifferent to the poems tucked away in his notebook. And is it not also the cry to be taken up by Sweeney in 'Fragment of an Agon': 'I gotta use words when I talk to you'? The only way out of this subjective trap is in the idea of system and order: there is, on the one hand, the invasive power of subjective feeling which cannot be communicated and, on the other, the need for order and ritual which may counteract that subjective consciousness. Indeed the notion of ritual permeates both Eliot's work and the meticulous routines of his adult life.

It was not, then, by accident that he picked up Bradley's *Appearance and Reality* in 1913 since that book in elegant and subtle form examines those doubts which Eliot had already investigated in Josiah Royce's seminars. He was in later life to describe himself as a 'Bradleyan' – it was an influence which, unlike others, he never wished to discard and in order to understand Eliot's prose writings it is also necessary to understand Bradley. Since Eliot came to him by way of Bergson, the last great European philosopher by whom he had been affected, he felt an immediate affinity with Bradley's own scepticism about the uses of conceptual intelligence in either recognizing or defining 'reality'. For Bradley 'Reality is One', a seamless and coherent whole which is 'non-relational' – that is, it cannot be divided into separate intellectual categories. And in his subversion of such orthodox categories as 'space' and 'time', which reflect only a partial comprehension of reality, Bradley is pushed back towards a larger description which can only be expressed as the Absolute. Without such a concept, the world becomes literally meaningless. The Absolute holds together Thought and Reality, Will and Feeling, in a sublime whole.

We live in a world of 'appearances' which partake of the Absolute without fully containing or representing it. And yet this Absolute can only be approached from the perspective of a number of 'finite centres' – not quite the same as the 'self' or the 'soul' but equivalent to them. And although 'finite truth must be conditional' it is only through such experience and through 'appearances' that we can begin to have any knowledge of the Absolute. This consorts very well with Eliot's own scepticism, and his awareness of the limitations of conceptual knowledge which he emphasized in Royce's seminars, but it provides also the comfort of an absolute reality or order which, however elusive it remains, is that unrealized whole in which we move and have our being. There is one other point to be made here: since all forms of knowledge and experience are conditional or relative, the only way of reaching towards the Absolute is by a steady enlargement of our knowledge and a continual search for system, unity and coherence. The shattering and divisive nature of ordinary thought and experience – 'You can't understand me' – can only be healed if placed within the search for an ever-increasing unity: 'Perfect truth in short must realize the idea of a systematic whole'[62] – rather like the 'tradition' which confirms the 'individual talent'.

Such a position is, as Richard Wollheim has stated in his analysis of Bradley, 'the last refuge of a sceptical and critical mind'[63] which has dissolved all other conventional ethical and epistemological notions. And are we not seeing here, a little more clearly, into the movement of Eliot's own thought and sensibility? To combine scepticism with idealism, to recognize the limitations of ordinary knowledge and experience but yet to see that when they are organized into a coherent whole they might vouchsafe glimpses of absolute truth – there is balm here for one trapped in the world and yet seeking some other, invaded by sensations and yet wishing to understand and to order them.

It is not surprising, then, that in a later conversation Eliot should claim that during this period his philosophical studies *were* him.[64] And in fact it seemed that his life was going to be that of an academic philosopher. By 1913 he was a teaching assistant in the philosophy department, giving courses to undergraduates, and in his last year at Harvard he became President of the University Philosophical Society. This was an association composed primarily of graduate students from the various philosophical disciplines, and Eliot's main job was to select speakers and persuade them to visit the society.

One of the teachers whom he impressed was Bertrand Russell, whose course in symbolic logic he took with eleven other postgraduates in the spring of 1914. Russell described his students to Lady Ottoline Morrell: 'One, named Eliot, is very well dressed and polished' but the class 'obviously had not been taught with the minute thoroughness that we practise in England. Window-dressing seems irresistible to Americans'.[65] Eliot himself seemed 'very silent' but he surprised Russell during one seminar by comparing Heraclitus to Villon[66] – whether this was an example of window-dressing or not, Russell does not say. He characterized Eliot in terms that will become after a while familiar: ' . . . altogether

impeccable in his tastes but has no vigour or life – or enthusiasm'.[67]
Here in Russell's description of the well-dressed and impeccable
young man, we have a glimpse of the philosopher as dandy. It is not
that the principles or ideas which he affirmed were not genuine
ones, or even that they did not significantly affect him, but rather
that he could both understand, and distance himself from, them. He
could play with them, in that intense but wilful way we play with the
things we hold most dear.

Eliot told Virginia and Leonard Woolf, some years later, that he
suffered a 'personal upheaval' after writing 'The Love Song of J.
Alfred Prufrock' which prevented him from developing in the
manner which he intended – the manner was to be that of Henry
James.[68] His natural instinct was to write poetry which was as close
to fiction as possible – to depict externals, to anatomize social life by
a process of selection and concentration. The 'upheaval', at its most
mundane level, was his retreat from Europe and his return to a
routine existence which he had blithely thought he might leave
behind for ever: the prospect of another life had been given to him
and then snatched away. He was unsure of himself now, aware that
the philosophical studies to which he was supposed to devote his life
were of no permanent value, hating the academic world to which he
had been consigned but unable to see any way out of the course
which had been planned in advance for him.

The fruit of this 'upheaval' is to be found in the poems which he
wrote on his return to Harvard and which have remained
unpublished. They are confused poems, often clumsily written,[69] in
which the desire to make a statement is stronger than the ability to
formulate that statement in a melodic or convincing way. One poem
(undated but written after his return from Paris – probably 1913) is
in the form of a monologue delivered by a character who bears some
resemblance to Prufrock; he is not sure if he knows what he feels or
what he thinks, and impaled upon his own lacerating self-consciousness he has fantasies of suicide. In another poem, the persona is lost
in a maze of 'appearances' from which he cannot break free. It has
been suggested that Eliot, trapped in just such a manner, was
already inclined towards some kind of escape in religious belief.
Certainly the student notes of his reading show that his predominant
interest during this period, outside his conventional studies, was in

the literature of mysticism and the psychology of religion. That would be one way of shaking off the Unitarianism of his family and the sterility of Harvard. But the poems which he wrote in his last year at university, and in the months after he left, employ the themes and language of religious belief in a morbid or declamatory manner and are primarily concerned with the meditations of the martyr or putative visionary. They would have had a certain appeal for a young man trapped in an environment which he did not care for, but it is as if Eliot's consciousness of his own power, fulfilled in 'Prufrock' and 'Portrait of a Lady', was now frustrated, turning inwards and creating images of self-absorption and self-disgust. In 'The Love Song of St Sebastian', the speaker imagines the experience of self-flagellation and the strangling of a woman. In 'The Death of St Narcissus', which Ezra Pound wished to publish but which Eliot 'killed' in galley form, the saint welcomes the arrows of his assailants. Eliot's sense of the religious life is one in which he is the central figure, both supplicant and saint, tormentor and martyr. The anxious sexuality of the early poetry has now been transformed into a general violence directed primarily against himself – perhaps he was attracted to Gauguin's 'Yellow Christ' because the artist painted his own features on the sallow and shrunken body on the cross. But you cannot make poetry out of suffering and pain without in some way enjoying the experience of doing so – a tormented man speaks in sighs and monosyllables, not in iambic pentameters. These 'religious' poems read like attempts to work up feeling or imagery in the way that an actor might work up a part: that is why they are not successful, and why Eliot wisely refrained from publishing them. Just as we have glimpsed the philosopher as dandy, here we have the religious poet as dandy also.

Indeed at the same time as he was completing these poems, he was also engaged on an epic, 'King Bolo and His Great Black Queen', which was to occupy his attention for rather longer. These are comic verses which are consistently pornographic in content, with allusions to buggery, penises, sphincters and other less delicate matters. He seems to have derived a certain satisfaction from the description of sexual excess, and for at least another fifteen years he would send extracts from this unfinished (and as yet unpublished) work to friends – sometimes posing as its editor, in the manner of his schoolboy stories. Eliot confessed many years later that he was afflicted with the sense of the emptiness in all human affairs;[70] severe religious discipline or gross sexual indulgence are, for the self-obsessed, ways of alleviating that meaninglessness – here, in the contrasting images of St Sebastian and King Bolo, we have both in rampant growth.

3

Into the Vortex
1914–1917

BY THE TIME Eliot was attending Bertrand Russell's seminars in early 1914, he had decided to take up the option of a Sheldon Travelling Fellowship which Harvard offered him and to return to Europe: it was, at least, a temporary escape. He planned to continue his philosophical studies at Merton College, Oxford, where he could also complete his thesis on F. H. Bradley under the tutorship of Harold Joachim who was himself a Bradleyan. The fellowship would last initially for one year, although he could be renominated for a second. It was a journey of which his family could hardly disapprove.

Instead of going straight to England, he decided to spend some time on the European continent. He journeyed through Belgium and Italy, visiting the galleries and inspecting the 'sights' although he was somewhat disdainful of the more conventionally picturesque aspects of these cultures.[1] By the middle of July he had arrived in the German town of Marburg, where he was to attend a summer programme in philosophy. After his fatiguing European tour, made more tiring because of the heat, he relaxed here; he ate a great deal, went swimming or walking, and did some studying – although, in the company of the German bourgeoisie, he thought of himself as being in exile.[2] The position of the alien was one, however, that always appealed to him and his sardonic powers of observation can be seen in the drawings of the Berliners and Marburgers which he included in his letters to Conrad Aiken. He was still working, in a self-conscious and uninspired way, upon his religious poems – he was planning to write a long poem called 'Descent from the Cross'. It would contain an insane section, a mystical section, a love song and a Fool-house sequence in which the protagonist goes to a masquerade ball dressed as St John of the Cross. But he was worried

54

about his poetry, since it still seemed too forced and contrived.[3] Although in these letters to Aiken there is a tone of general dissatisfaction, both with his life and his writing, there is no doubt that these two young men were buoyed up with a sense of their own possibilities; Aiken recalled how they were full of plans for 'the immense, the wonderful future', a future which was 'theirs to create'.[4] The approaching war, however, was to suggest that other forces might also be at work which would affect such plans.

Eliot left Marburg hurriedly, having only been there for a fortnight; he arrived in London in August 1914 and took lodgings at 28 Bedford Place. At first, he disliked the city: he felt out of place[5] and, during these first months in England, he suffered once more from various small worries about the future; there were different aspects of his life – philosophy or poetry, Europe or America – to which he had a wavering attachment, and he was not at all clear which would be the most profitable for him. But if he was unhappy and nervous about his own work, there were others whose faith in his abilities was more marked. Conrad Aiken had his own copy of 'The Love Song of J. Alfred Prufrock'; he had come to England the year before and, with touching loyalty, had shown the poem to anyone he thought might be interested. Rupert Brooke had introduced him to Harold Monro, the owner of the Poetry Bookshop, but Monro handed the poem back to him saying that it was 'absolutely insane'.[6] Indeed those of a markedly English taste found it quite odd: its mingling of the dramatic and the demotic, and its insistent but broken rhythms, would have seemed merely perverse. But Aiken also spoke about his friend's work to Ezra Pound, a fellow American who took an interest in such things, and Aiken urged Eliot to contact Pound when he came to London. Eventually Eliot visited Pound and his wife, at Holland Park Chambers, on 22 September. He had seen some of Pound's verse while he was at Harvard, and thought very little of it; he must also have known the public activities in which Pound was currently engaged since, in a letter to Aiken from Germany in July, he had parodied the Vorticists' use of 'BLAST' and 'BLESS'. Pound had already been in London for more than five years and, although only three years older than Eliot, had published five volumes of poetry; the fact that Eliot took almost two months before visiting him suggests that he had to nerve himself for the ordeal of meeting a more successful contemporary. Eliot said later that Pound reminded him of Irving Babbitt, by which no doubt he meant that slightly hectoring manner which came from enthusiastic conviction. Pound said, in turn, of Eliot's own Americanness, that he 'has it perhaps worse than I have – poor devil'.[7] Here were two young Americans, discerning in each other the lineaments of the country which they had left behind, both of them more alike than they perhaps cared to admit. They were both mid-Westerners; they had both educated themselves on their own; they were both seeking traditional cultural authority, and a sense of their own worth, in Europe. There is something most poignant, then, about this first meeting – not least because it was to have such extraordinary consequences.

Pound asked Eliot to send him some poems. 'Prufrock' and 'Portrait', along with some others, arrived and Pound told him, 'This is as good as anything I've ever seen. Come around and have a talk about them'.[8] Pound then wrote almost at once to Harriet Monroe, the editor of the Chicago magazine *Poetry* for which he was 'foreign correspondent', and informed her that Eliot 'has sent in the best poem I have yet had or seen from an American . . . . He has actually trained himself *and* modernized himself *on his own*'.[9] On the same day, Eliot was writing in decidedly less enthusiastic terms about Pound's work,[10] which, at this stage in their association, he thought of little merit. And so the strange collaboration of the two men began, with wariness on the one side and enthusiasm on the other; Pound was extrovert, eccentric, enthusiastic and Eliot cool, reserved, sardonic (although in human relations, as opposed to poetical proselytizing, Pound was in fact much colder and more egotistical). When Wyndham Lewis met Eliot in Pound's small triangular flat he encountered a 'sleek, tall, attractive, transatlantic apparition – with a sort of Gioconda smile, *moqueur* to the marrow . . .' and, at this stage at least, he still had a 'ponderous, exactly articulated drawl'.[11] Lewis was one of the first contemporary artists to whom Pound introduced his newest protégé. Pound had, by a potent mixture of posturing and talent, placed himself at the centre of the really interesting cultural activities in London at this time; he knew, or thought he knew, who was worth knowing and who was worth attacking. He had marshalled together the Imagists and was now promoting the Vorticists. Almost by accident, Eliot had arrived during a unique period in twentieth-century English literature, when there seemed a chance that a literary revolution might be effected.

Pound also introduced him to other American writers, like Hilda Doolittle ('HD') and John Gould Fletcher, who had made the break with their own past. Perhaps more importantly, he lectured him about his own enthusiasms. And although Eliot knew as much as he did, if not more, about contemporary French poetry, it was Pound who sharpened his appreciation of Dante and the medieval Italian poets. It seems probable, also, that Pound emphasized to him the importance of the work of Remy de Gourmont whose *Problème du Style* affirmed the need for clear and exact presentation through the medium of the poetic image. There was, in addition, the influence of T. E. Hulme, whom Eliot never met but whose notions of a 'new classicism' in a hard and rigorous poetry were even then being embodied in the poems Pound himself was writing. Eliot was more influenced by such ideas in his criticism than in his poetry, but they demonstrate, if demonstration were needed, that his preoccupations were not unique. A number of people, starting from different points, had decided that on the debris of an old romanticism a hard-edged and rigorous classicism had to be reconstructed. It was Eliot, however, who in the end rendered such ideas respectable.

And so, for the first time, he found himself in an environment in which art and literature were taken seriously as a living force, and where he need not be as defensive or dismissive about his own poetry as he had been at Harvard. But although the conditions were appropriate, he was unable to make full use of them since he was still most uncertain about the development of his work. Pound told him that he was interested in bringing out a book of his poetry, but 'Prufrock' had been his last good poem and for some months to come Eliot was to lament his apparent inability to write new work of equal value; he had the vague notion of going to Paris, where four years before he had found inspiration, but the idea came to nothing.[12] Nevertheless, he had indeed come to London at the right time. If he had arrived earlier, he might conceivably have been lost in the scramble of other Americans trying to make an impression; as it was, he arrived with a formed style of his own and, as Pound's influence began to fade, Eliot became the predominant 'voice' in contemporary English poetry.

He went up to Merton College for the autumn term of 1914. It would be easy to say that, even after his relatively brief exposure to Poundian London, philosophy began to bore him; but this is unlikely. It remained a bolt-hole for him, a discipline into which he could escape and which might provide him with a career if he wished for one. Oxford, also, offered a retreat into a more familiar and settled existence, albeit of a somewhat dreary kind. Because of the First World War, the majority of undergraduates had been enrolled into the Officer Training Corps or were already on their way to the trenches; most of those who remained were Commonwealth students, Rhodes Scholars from America, and others who for various reasons had not yet enlisted. At first the change suited him, and he found the university peaceful and agreeable; he was attending to his studies, but he was also playing tennis, rowing in a four oar, and smoking (in later life he generally smoked French cigarettes, which suggests that he had adopted the habit when he was in Paris). He was happy, and reasonably indolent.[13] His tutor, Harold Joachim, was Philosophical Tutor in the college. He was a disciple of Bradley, and 'stood in considerable awe of the great man'.[14] Bradley was himself a member of the college – he was rarely seen, however, and Eliot never met him – and on one occasion, when an undergraduate was reading out an essay criticizing certain aspects of his philosophy, Joachim closed the window in case the master should hear it.

As well as continuing work on his thesis, Eliot studied Aristotle under Joachim; indeed, practically the only book which he borrowed from Merton library was a copy of Zabarella's *Commentary*, which he was taking out constantly from October 1914 to February 1915. He also borrowed Westermark's *Origin and Development of Moral Ideas*, but that may simply have been to prepare a talk which he gave to the Moral Sciences Club. His lessons were not only of philosophical benefit, however: from Joachim, Eliot said, he learned how to write good English prose.[15] As a respite from his academic studies, he joined the Bodley Club and the Nineties Society, a gathering of aesthetes whose members included Aldous Huxley and Raymond Mortimer – he would have shared their interest in the poetry of that period, if nothing else. After he had met E. R. Dodds at a lecture, Dodds invited him to join a small literary circle known as the Coterie, and it was here that Eliot recited 'Prufrock' – the first 'poetry reading' he gave in England.

But Eliot's friends at Oxford were not altogether literary: the undergraduate closest to him was Carl Culpin,[16] a young historian who was five years his junior. Nothing is known of this gentleman, except that he was called to the front and died in May 1917. But despite the distractions of university life, it was still an existence with which Eliot had been all too familiar at Harvard. He was always most susceptible to the atmosphere of places, and it seems that in Oxford he did not feel properly alive at all.[17] He confessed to Aiken that he relied very much on the company of women (an apt evocation of his childhood years), and in this university town there were none.[18] One of the words he often used to describe his reaction to unpleasant or constricting circumstances is 'numbness', and this was essentially the mood which invaded him at Oxford.

After his first term, he went for a brief vacation with two other Americans to Dorset. One of them, Brand Blanshard, has left a memoir of that trip.[19] Eliot, he wrote, was 'reserved, shy, economical of speech, rather frostily formal of manner'. Blanshard felt that Eliot remained apart from them, and examined them 'with feelings that were singularly disengaged'. They discussed their academic studies, of course, and Eliot said of symbolic logic that '. . . it gave me a sense of pleasure and of power manipulating those curious little figures'. But Blanshard also noticed that there seemed to be an element of laziness in his speculations, in the sense that he was too content with his own generalizations (a criticism to be taken up by others in succeeding years). After Dorset Eliot went back to London and in late December he rented a room off Gordon Square. He was now quite disenchanted with Oxford, and seriously considered the idea of removing himself to the capital for the remainder of his stay and studying at the Reading Room of the British Museum (a reader's ticket was issued to him at the end of the month). After his exile in the university, London certainly came as a relief; but although he was invaded by the same sexuality which had affected him in Paris, he was still unable to conquer that anxious reserve which had consigned him to a virginal existence.

He went back to Oxford for a second term and immediately felt ill at ease there (apart from anything else, he was suffering from constipation, indigestion and a chest cold). When in February a telegram arrived from Harvard, notifying him that he had been renominated for his fellowship for a second year, he was plunged into deeper uncertainty. Although London had its attractions in comparison with Oxford, the wartime atmosphere was oppressing him and he did not think he would ever really care for England. Should he stay there or go back to America? Should he adopt an academic career and raise a family? Or should he plan eventually to live in Paris? What was he to do? These were some of the worries which he poured out in his correspondence.[20] They were further compounded by the knowledge that the poetry he had been writing, while studying philosophy, had not been at all satisfactory. His earlier work now seemed to him less convincing, and he was expressing doubts even about 'Portrait of a Lady'.[21] But he was considerably more sanguine about his development as a poet than he was about his immediate choices of residence or career and, indeed, he had every reason to be sanguine, since Pound was working energetically on his behalf. Even while Eliot was at Oxford, they kept up a continuous correspondence. Pound was sending him poems and manifestoes to which Eliot responded in his cautious and meticulous style – pointing out platitudes, warning against excessive generalization and suggesting the need for concreteness in statements. Pound was meanwhile distributing Eliot's poetry to anyone who cared to look at it. He had already sent 'Prufrock' to Harriet Monroe, and was in April 1915 nagging her to publish it: '*Do* get on with that Eliot,' he wrote.[22] Reluctantly she did so, and it appeared in the Chicago magazine, *Poetry*, in June 1915. Then in August he sent her a group of poems which Eliot had written at Oxford – they are short and somewhat satirical verses which have been called the 'Bostonian poems' because they deal with aspects of American life which he knew at first hand. 'Cousin Nancy', 'Aunt Helen' and 'The Boston Evening Transcript' are seen slowly sinking in the West, but without the roseate glow, as Eliot watches with amusement. It has been suggested that their brevity and compression owe something to Pound's influence, but they possess a melancholy flippancy which was never quite Pound's style: as if to say, the poetry does not matter. While he was at Oxford, and unable to feel his way through to any consistent design in his own work, he was content with what is essentially occasional verse.

Nevertheless, for the first time Eliot's poetry was being introduced to the world – or at least that part of it which read little magazines. In July, Wyndham Lewis published 'Preludes' and

'Rhapsody on a Windy Night' in *Blast* – although he refused to print extracts from the Bolo saga, 'Bullshit' and 'The Ballad of Big Louise', a folly which Eliot ascribed to his puritanical principles. In September 'Portrait of a Lady' was printed in Alfred Kreymborg's *Others*, again at the instigation of Pound; then, in November, five of his poems appeared in Pound's *Catholic Anthology*. This marks the first appearance of Eliot in volume form, and almost all of his good early poetry was now in print.

If 1915 was the year which marked the beginning of his career as a poet, it was also the year in which his private existence was altered radically: he met a young woman and married her. Her name was Vivien Haigh-Wood (originally 'Vivienne' but she abbreviated it, although Eliot when exasperated would stretch it out to its original pronunciation). The actual circumstances of their first meeting are not clear, but it was through the agency of Scofield Thayer, an American whom Eliot had known both at Milton and at Harvard and who was now also at Oxford. His sister, Lucy, had established a friendship with Vivien after meeting her in Switzerland six years before. She and Vivien would go up to Oxford from time to time, and it seems that Vivien and Thayer were engaged in some kind of affair – that was Pound's guess, at any rate.[23] The romantic theory is that Eliot and Vivien met on the river during the Trinity term, and although in those few weeks they certainly went punting together,[24] it is more likely that they met in Thayer's rooms in Magdalen.

What kind of woman was Vivien when he first encountered her? She was vivacious rather than beautiful, according to Osbert Sitwell[25] when he met her three years later. She was self-conscious, alert to the point of over-sensitivity. She liked to go to plays and to dance to the music on the phonograph; she always dressed well, although sometimes in a startling manner. And, to judge by her later stories, she had a gift for expression and an instinctive sharpness of wit which was close to cruelty; her voice was rather high – like that of a parrot, someone said. 'Please don't laugh,' she would say if someone misinterpreted her, 'There's nothing funny about that!'.[26] Abigail Eliot described her as a 'delightful person, charming, interested, sensitive to beauty',[27] and Osbert Sitwell said that she must have seemed to Eliot the embodiment of the carelessness and audacity of youth[28] – although she was, in fact, six months older than Eliot.

Vivien's diary entries for the year before she met him[29] show her to have been rather nervous, subject to worry and depression but with sudden changes of mood that would release in her an exuberant and unexplained high spirits. Her favourite adjectives were 'rotten' and 'awfully nice'. During that year she had a rotten time with a young man she called 'B' – it was in fact a schoolmaster whose name was Charles Buckle – and the stresses in that relationship gave her headaches and general 'neuralgia'. When Bertrand Russell met her shortly after the marriage he described her as 'Light, a little vulgar, adventurous . . . .'.[30] By 'vulgar' he meant brash and high-spirited rather than 'common' – she and her family could hardly have been less 'vulgar' in that sense of the word. Her parents, Rose and Charles Haigh-Wood, were an exceedingly respectable upper-middle-class Edwardian couple, representing the kind of Englishness to which Eliot in succeeding years would be most susceptible. Her brother, Maurice, eight years her junior, was already an officer in the army (he had attended Malvern College and Sandhurst). Charles Haigh-Wood was a landscape artist and portrait painter, but he derived much of his income from his estates. He had a second house in Anglesey (the family house was in Hampstead) and owned several properties in Dublin. Vivien was, in other words, affluent and respectable. Eliot was no doubt soon apprised of all this; what he did not know, and what he did not discover until after the marriage, was that she had a history of illness from her earliest years: as a child she had suffered from tuberculosis of the left hand. Her problems were largely nervous in origin, however, and the symptoms included headaches, cramps and from the age of twelve an irregular and over-frequent menstrual cycle – as a result of the latter complaint, she had an obsessive habit of washing her own bed linen even if she was staying in an hotel.[31] Although now her condition would probably be diagnosed as one of hormonal imbalance or deficiency, she was given morphine-based depressants in order to control her moods, and her mother was always fearful that she had inherited what was then known as 'moral insanity'. Because of this fear, Rose had been instrumental in the breaking up of the relationship between Vivien and Charles Buckle.

And what of Eliot, faced with this bright and vivacious young woman who was filled with that strange gaiety which unstable people often possess? The idea of marriage in America did not really appeal to him, as he had already explained to Aiken[32] – he may not have had any specific partner in mind, but he had been engaged in an elaborate and innocent courtship with a girl he had known at Harvard, Emily Hale. He acted with her in 1913 at the evening of amateur theatricals at his aunt's house in Cambridge, Massachussetts; in the following year, when he was ensconced in Oxford, he asked Aiken to send her some roses after another dramatic performance.[33] But a relationship conducted across the Atlantic by means of flowers could not, of its nature, be a passionate one.

Vivien was, in any case, quite unlike the women he had known at Harvard or at Oxford. In the months before he met her Eliot had been complaining about both his virginity and his shyness – and also about the lack of female society upon which he depended. He was worried about the future, and did not know what kind of life he wanted after Oxford. Now this virginal, perplexed, intellectually over-refined but emotionally immature young man encountered an adventurous and vivacious young woman. She was for him a revelation of sexual and emotional life, and one in which he might lose all his doubts and anxieties. Aldous Huxley believed it to be 'almost entirely a sexual nexus' between them: 'one sees it in the way he looks at her . . . she's an incarnate provocation'.[34] But I believe that he went towards her with a kind of child-like trust, with a sudden upheaval of emotions which was able to overwhelm all the refinements and hesitations which had previously paralysed him. And what would she in her turn have seen in Eliot – apart from a very clever young man who flattered her self-regard by becoming infatuated with her? He was good-looking, and shared her own quick-wittedness, a foreigner who might extricate her from the world of Edwardian respectability, and a poet for whom friends like Scofield Thayer predicted a great future. She complained later to Bertrand Russell that he had 'tricked her imagination':[35] it is more likely that, in these first months, her own impulsiveness and gaiety were adopted by Eliot so that he seemed much more vivacious than in fact he was. And here are the makings of their unhappy life together: from the beginning, they quite misunderstood each other's characters.

He was in later life to discourse upon the frightening nature of choice – how some decisions are irrevocable, and can lead to a lifetime of misery. This was to be one of them. He came down from Oxford and found lodgings in Greek Street, Soho. He and Vivien were married a week later, on 26 June 1915, at Hampstead Register Office. On the marriage certificate it says, next to Eliot's name, 'of no occupation' – which suggests that his ties to academic life were now slowly being loosened. Neither of them had informed their parents in advance about their intentions – both families, after all, would have had good reasons to prevent or delay the marriage. (Vivien's aunt, Lillia Symes, was present at the ceremony, but she was more of a *confidante* than a family representative.) For Eliot it was the visible sign that at last he was about to decide something, to change his life – such a step would have to be taken quickly, if it was to be taken at all.

After the wedding, they went on honeymoon to Eastbourne, which lasted only for six days rather than the two weeks which had been planned. Vivien's brother, Maurice, was sent by the Haigh-Woods to pick up the Eliots at the railway station: he remembered how happy they seemed, although there was an air of forced cheerfulness in his new brother-in-law's demeanour which he did not then understand.[36] He drove them back to the family house at Compayne Gardens in Hampstead. The Haigh-Woods had just returned from Lincolnshire, where they had received news of the marriage in a telegram from Vivien, and Maurice was expecting a bitter family row. But it did not materialize. Eliot's perfect manners and natural 'breeding' must have been reassuring, and no doubt in his measured way he explained his position – that he had no 'immediate' prospects, but that he loved their daughter and would take his responsibilities seriously. It may have been on this occasion also that Rose Haigh-Wood described to him Vivien's nervous and physical history. Certainly some kind of understanding was reached, since the Haigh-Woods gave Vivien an annual allowance of £50. It was also necessary, of course, for Eliot to notify and placate his own parents. And such was his nervousness that he enlisted others to help him in the task. Only two days after the wedding, Ezra Pound was writing on his instructions to Henry Ware Eliot, and in the letter he attempted to justify the 'literary life' and suggested that the prospects for Henry's son were very hopeful.[37]

But Eliot feared his parents' disapproval, and now no doubt he knew about Vivien's history of illness: the first adventurous impulse of the marriage was being dissipated. Some of the evidence for this comes from Bertrand Russell. He had met his ex-student quite by chance in New Oxford Street soon after Eliot's arrival in England, and he began to take an active and almost paternal interest in the young man's affairs. Eliot introduced his new wife to him in July, about two weeks after the wedding, having been somewhat mysterious about her in advance. 'He is ashamed of his marriage,' Russell told Ottoline Morrell, 'and very grateful if one is kind to her'; Russell reported also that Vivien had told him on this occasion that she had married Eliot in order to stimulate him but found that she could not do so. 'I think,' Russell added, 'that she will soon be tired of him.'[38]

Eliot's problems, however, were only just beginning. In late July he did what he had to do: he sailed to America in order to face his parents. He went back to Gloucester, not as a promising graduate student with the world before him but as a married man with few prospects. His parents urged him to return to America with his new wife and continue his philosophical studies at Harvard,[39] but Vivien had refused to leave England, partly because of the danger from German 'U' boats. They asked him not to abandon, in any case, his dissertation and to this he agreed. Although Henry Ware Eliot thought that his son had taken a wrong course in life, he was not particularly severe with him: he did not, for example, cut off the allowance which he had already made. The reaction of Charlotte Eliot was no doubt more agitated: Eliot was the child in whom she had placed her hopes, and in whom she recognized abilities that she had done her best to nurture. From this point on, she began to worry much more about him and confessed to his brother, Henry, that at night she suffered from nervous anxieties about 'Tom'.[40] It was not a happy family reunion; he left America after a visit of about three weeks, and never saw his father again. For a young man of such strong familial loyalties, acutely aware of his parents' ambitions for him, it was tantamount to an act of betrayal – the significance of which never faded from his memory.

He and Vivien had been staying with the Haigh-Woods in Compayne Gardens, but when Eliot returned from America they travelled down to Eastbourne for a while. It was from there that

Vivien wrote Bertrand Russell a despairing letter which sounded to him not far from suicidal[41] – the date of this letter is unclear, but since Russell describes them as being on a 'pseudo-honeymoon', and he did not know Vivien until two weeks after the wedding, it was probably sent by her during this second visit to the Sussex coast. Russell does not dwell upon the nature of Vivien's 'despair' but all the evidence suggests that it was of a sexual nature. In Eliot's own poetry the sexual act is described in impersonal and characteristically violent terms; it is implicated in an awareness of sterility and leaves only guilt or resentment in its wake. In a strange 'Ode', printed only once, in 1920, a bridegroom sees blood upon the bed and confronts a 'succuba eviscerate'; in 'Hysteria', a prose poem written in 1915, the 'I' feels that he is being engorged by a woman – thus confirming the images of threatening and salacious females which had appeared in Eliot's earlier poetry. There is no doubt that throughout his life he suffered from low physical vitality – a doctor once told him, 'Mr Eliot, you have the thinnest blood I've ever tested';[42] and there is also his wife's testimony that she could not 'stimulate' him. His own fastidiousness and anxiety must have been greatly compounded by Vivien's menstrual problems, however, and the sexual failure, if such it was, cannot simply be blamed upon him. Russell characterized Vivien as possessing mental passion but not physical passion, that she wished for male devotion but did not particularly enjoy any physical expression of it.[43] Is this not another description of a 'succuba eviscerate'? Here, then, were two anxious people who had been carried away by the idea of marriage rather than the reality of it – both of them ill at ease or unenergetic in sexual relations. That it was a terrible disaster, there can be little doubt. Eliot was unnerved by the physical failure of his marriage, but he covered up the fact and never talked about it with his friends (except, according to Maurice Haigh-Wood, with Ezra Pound).

The plight of the couple seems to have touched Russell, and while they were still at Eastbourne in September he renewed an offer that they should share his flat at Russell Chambers in Bury Street. In his *Autobiography*, he described it as 'two-bedroomed', but in fact the bedroom which the Eliots occupied was a tiny closet room – Eliot himself slept in the hall or in the sittingroom, which suggests a certain lack of married intimacy.[44] Eliot wrote back accepting his offer and although Russell had questioned the propriety of staying the night at the flat with Vivien when her husband was away, Eliot readily acquiesced in the idea.[45] It was a strange ménage: there is no doubt that Vivien flirted with Russell, as she was in later years to flirt with other men, and Russell in turn bought many and expensive presents for her. He was consistently generous to Eliot himself, however, and gave him £3,000 in engineering debentures, a debt which Eliot repaid in 1927. Russell insisted in later years that his relationship to both was simply a paternalistic one, and at the time he explained to Ottoline Morrell that he only wished to be useful to them. He wanted to help them in their troubles, he said in his memoirs, 'until I discovered that their troubles were what they enjoyed'[46] – but he was being less than frank about his association with Vivien.

The fact that he wondered about Eliot's absence from Bury Street on certain nights was based upon the prospect of Eliot taking up a job in High Wycombe, some way out of London. After his return from America, it was clear that it was now in his hands alone to make a new life. He said, many years later, that the fact that he had to earn his own living came as something of a surprise to him.[47] But the obvious employment for a graduate student was that of schoolmastering, and during the summer he applied for, and was offered, a post at High Wycombe Grammar School for the coming term. To Eliot, as to all those who have never experienced it, schoolteaching seemed an easy option: the teaching of subjects long since mastered, the long vacations in which he could write poetry, and an income which although not large was regular (£140 per annum, plus one meal a day). Soon after taking up his appointment, he discovered that, apart from his regular duties, he was called upon to do occasional jobs like supervising games or taking scripture class.[48] But the Eliots badly needed the money, and he was also eager that his parents should know that he was taking his financial responsibilities seriously.[49] In her own diary, Vivien records how, in the early days of marriage, they walked together about the streets of London at night and discussed the future.

But even as they were planning the life ahead of them, she became ill, the first taste for Eliot of the sickness which was to haunt him. She was already unwell when he returned from America, and by the winter she was suffering from 'nerves' or 'acute neuralgia', a condition of prostrate sickness in which it becomes impossible to disentangle the mental and physical elements. She complained of stomach cramps, headaches and faintness. There were also problems with her teeth, although on at least one occasion the dentist seemed to think that Eliot needed to be calmed down more than she did:[50] it was during this period that Russell told Ottoline Morrell that Eliot was 'devoted' to his wife.[51] And it is possible that in her sickness she reverted to the helpless condition of a child, that in nursing her Eliot could escape the inflictions of the sexuality which so unnerved him. In any case, Vivien's condition was now serious and Russell offered to take her to Torquay at his own expense while Eliot was teaching, so that she might have the benefit of sea and air. Eliot agreed, although it was at best naive of him to leave his wife with so notorious a philanderer. He replaced Russell after a week or so (Russell also paid his expenses there); husband and wife would walk to the shore together, and Eliot described in poignant terms the tranquillity which the sea brought to him always.[52] Although Vivien was slowly recovering, she still suffered from various aches and from exhaustion – she found it difficult to sleep at night – and he remained most anxious about her health as late as the spring of 1916.

Since there were now doctors to pay, and medicines to buy, Eliot needed to earn as much money as he could; so he began that punishing ritual of work which he was to maintain for most of his life. After one term he resigned from High Wycombe school and moved to Highgate Junior School – it was closer to home, and the post paid him an extra £20 per annum. Here he taught, among other subjects, Latin, French, German, mental arithmetic (he had difficulty in mastering the system of pounds, shillings and pence), drawing and swimming. He tried to teach the smaller boys baseball, but that was not a success.[53] His was a nature, however, quite unsuited to the demands of schoolteaching – he was not able to project his personality in a forceful enough manner, and he found the demands on his time and patience exhausting.[54] One of his pupils there was John Betjeman, who recalled 'the American master' as 'much quieter than the other masters . . . a remote, quiet figure'.[55]

Despite his exhaustion, the need for money prompted him to look for additional work. He thought of tutoring boys privately, and also applied for work as an extension lecturer. He became a reviewer of books as well: Bertrand Russell introduced him to the *International Journal of Ethics*, and by the end of 1915 he was criticizing studies on

Theism, Nietzsche, and assorted philosophical subjects. He enjoyed the work and took it rather seriously – it would impress the Harvard authorities, in any event, and his family would be able to see that he was not altogether wasting his time; although he was nervous about not concentrating on his thesis, he felt it was work which he was justified in doing.[56] Again through Russell, Eliot was introduced to the literary pages of the *New Statesman*, and it was for this journal that he most enjoyed reviewing. For the first time he was able to write upon a wide variety of subjects – from Paul Elmer More to Giordano Bruno – and there was an eclecticism in his temperament which such activity both satisfied and encouraged. He was learning to compose upon the typewriter as well – as a result, his sentences were becoming shorter and sharper – and he was acquiring a taste for book reviewing.[57] But even while engaged in such work he was still, as he had promised his parents, preparing to finish his thesis. He completed his revision quickly; he mentioned in one letter in January 1916 that he was about to start upon it and it was actually sent to Harvard in April (it can be assumed that the larger part of the work had already been written by the time he had left Oxford).

'Experience and the Objects of Knowledge in the Philosophy of F. H. Bradley' (later published under an abbreviated title) is a difficult work, and to the layman it is in some places quite unintelligible. What the thesis does display, however, is Eliot's extraordinary ability to create a synthetic discourse; he is able to employ over an extended space a certain form of language while simultaneously remaining quite detached from it: even as he was completing this elaborate and learned study, we know that he had become bored with, or had decided to abandon, academic philosophy. When the writing does acquire an independent life and momentum, it is in those passages where Eliot draws out Bradley's implications and animates them with his own concerns or obsessions. He begins with immediate experience: lived truths are 'partial and fragmentary' and the experiences of the Bradleyan 'finite centres' are 'mad and strange' but, paradoxically, they are all that can be known to be real: 'All significant truths are private truths.' But we are compelled to think and behave as if this is not so and, in order to combat the extreme relativity of such a position, Eliot postulates 'degrees of truth' which help to create an objective world in which 'the cruder and vaguer, or more limited, is somehow contained and explained in the wider and more precise'. The purpose is to reach beyond the miasma of private experience and construct a world, or rather an interpretation of the world, 'as comprehensive and coherent as possible'. And so it is that throughout Eliot's work the idea of pattern or order becomes the informing principle – he finds it everywhere, in literary tradition, in ritual, in political myth and in English history.

The hypothesis which supports this attempt to find a larger context is that of a 'world of absolute order', the Bradleyan 'absolute truth'. But Eliot affirms – and this is where his own scepticism is most corrosive – that the 'Absolute' is established only upon an 'act of faith'. And what if that faith vanishes? The intellectual framework of knowledge and perception collapses because it is built on sand, or less than sand, and we are left only with what can be definitely known – those 'mad and strange' experiences which are private and incommunicable. That is, I believe, the situation in which he found himself at this time: one contemporary remembered 'his inability to express himself conversationally, to enter into personal relationships'.[58] Everything boiled secretly within him until that time when he found his own 'Absolute' to make sense of his experience. Aiken recalls in *Ushant* the period when Eliot had begun writing at Harvard, and describes his 'brilliantly analytical and destructive thesis in epistemology . . . that magnificent vision, into the apparent chaos which blazed and swarmed and roared beyond the neat walls of Eden'. It was a vision, he said, from which Eliot was gradually to retreat into 'the security of conformity' – a miracle of transformation but also a surrender, 'perhaps the saddest' that he knew. We have here the North and South, the twin poles of Eliot's creative and critical work – the vision of chaos and the attempt to deny or defend himself against it, the scepticism about 'order' and 'truth' and at the same time the need for such order and such truth.

The dissertation was complete by the spring of 1916, and in April he was about to sail for America to deliver it to Harvard and to take his *viva*. At Pound's urging he was to carry in his luggage a large number of works destined for a Vorticist show in New York. But at the last minute the ship was taken off, and Eliot did not sail. He sent the thesis to Harvard instead, and in June the philosophy department wrote back to tell him that they had accepted it without hesitation (probably, Eliot said later in a Harvard Class Report, because it was 'quite unreadable'). The university, then, offered him the option of returning, but he had already decided to abandon his doctorate: he was writing in the *New Statesman* in July of this year about the 'laborious dullness' of the American student, and how fatal the academic atmosphere was to any kind of intellectual development. In May Mrs Eliot, worried about the fact that her son had not come to America as expected, wrote a rather desperate letter to Bertrand Russell hoping that his influence would confirm her son's choice of philosophy – she had faith in that, but not in his 'vers libres'.[59] When the family learned of his decision not to leave England they were greatly disappointed and blamed Vivien; indeed it was partly her decision: Vivien said in a later letter that she had struggled desperately to keep her husband from returning to America.[60] Despite his decision, however, the Eliot family still supported him financially (up to a certain extent) and he continued to write optimistic letters to them – explaining, for example, how after the War there would be more opportunities for him to explore.[61]

The Eliots had definitely decided now to 'settle down' in London. They had left Russell's flat at Christmas, as had been previously arranged with him, and in the early months of 1916 returned to Compayne Gardens. But they wanted a place of their own, despite worries about the cost of rents in the capital, and by early summer they had moved to a small flat at 18 Crawford Mansions – situated in a not particularly salubrious area just south of Baker Street, about which Eliot was continually to complain over the next few years. But why did he stay, then, and reject the professional university career which his family was urging him to accept? The choice was all the more strange in the conditions of wartime London – a city which seemed like some vast and gloomy cavern, in which people hurried to their work and then back to their homes. It was in a state of suspended animation, the young and the best gone, silent, blacked out at night (in fact on 2 October Eliot was summonsed for showing too much light through the curtains in Crawford Mansions). The explanation, I think, lies in his letters. His life in London, he said, was quite different and much more interesting than any which he had previously anticipated for himself; it had been filled with work and worries, but it had not been dull.[62] This last sentiment is expressed more than once and the refrain suggests what he had escaped from: from dullness, from the rewards of academic labour and the anticipation of preferment, from the social and familial duties of New England. Tinckom-Fernandez has suggested, in fact, that Eliot came to England precisely to escape from the academic career to which his family seemed to have consigned him: on one occasion, when he was leaving Harvard for St Louis, Tinckom-Fernandez noted that he had a 'hunted' look.[63] Well, he had escaped and had entered the area of actual and struggling life. He had made a commitment to another person, he was working for his living (becoming 'more of a man', as Russell noted) and he was among people who believed in him as an artist. The influence of Pound cannot be over-emphasized here: it ought to be remembered that he, too, had abandoned an academic career in the United States (albeit under other circumstances) and he was urging Eliot to follow his example. He was already actively engaged, by April 1916, in planning a book of Eliot's poetry and had told Harriet Shaw Weaver, one of the editors of the *Egoist*, that, along with Lewis and Joyce, Eliot was the best of the younger men.[64] That kind of support, and the prospect of a first volume, had a bracing effect upon him. Not that he was at all sanguine about the future of his poetry: he had been too anxious, and indeed too busy, to write any since his marriage. He told his brother in September that he feared that 'Prufrock' might be his last good poem,[65] and Maurice Haigh-Wood remembered him sitting in the garden at Compayne Mansions and lamenting the fact that he could not write.[66] But Vivien had great faith in her husband's work, and harboured large ambitions for him; he did not want to disappoint those ambitions, and in one letter to his father, he expressed in fulsome terms his indebtedness to her.[67]

Of course, there were other attractions in London as well, which were quite lacking in Boston or St Louis. He was at the centre of a literary culture which, although it was suffering from the privations of war, was as varied as anything he had encountered since Paris. And more importantly, unlike Paris, he was afforded social entry into it. Pound had prophesied to Henry Ware Eliot that Eliot's progress would be smoother and swifter than Pound's own, and in this he was to be proved right.[68] Pound himself had already introduced him to the younger artists and writers, but men like Wyndham Lewis and Richard Aldington hardly formed a 'group' – they were much too suspicious of each other for that. His first real experience of 'social' life was in fact arranged by Russell. Russell introduced him to Ottoline Morrell in 1915, and by the end of that year Eliot was visiting her at Garsington Manor, near Oxford. Lady Ottoline Morrell was married to a Liberal MP, Philip Morrell, who was a militant pacifist during the First World War – Garsington itself became the home for a number of their friends who, as conscientious objectors or 'conchies', worked on the farm there. Ottoline Morrell was a hostess and 'patron' of the arts who, first at Garsington and then in Gower Street, entertained a large circle of writers – among them Aldous Huxley, Lytton Strachey and D. H. Lawrence. Her extravagance of manner and somewhat startling appearance were often cruelly parodied, even by those closest to her, but her generosity to her friends was equally remarkable. Vivien Eliot, in later years, used to express her reliance upon her and Eliot himself often requested her help and advice. Her first impressions of him were not altogether favourable, however: 'I found him dull, dull, dull. He never moves his lips but speaks in an even, mandarin voice . . . I think he has lost all spontaneity and can only break through his conventionality by stimulants or violent emotion'.[69] She added that he did not seem to understand English society, and apparently believed that it depended upon decorous politeness and the meticulous observation of conventions. This is a very good description of Eliot in his frozen state, when embarrassed or nervous – no doubt the atmosphere of Garsington and cultural 'society' was unnerving for a young man who had only previously participated in university clubs. But with Ottoline Morrell he eventually broke through his anxious stiffness, and sustained a long although sometimes turbulent friendship.

It is not clear whom he met on his first visits to Garsington, but when he was there in December 1916 the other guests included Katherine Mansfield, Clive Bell, Mark Gertler and Aldous Huxley. Huxley himself wrote to his brother Julian, 'You ought to read his things. They are all the more remarkable when one knows the man, ordinarily just an Europeanized American, overwhelmingly cultured, talking about French literature in the most uninspired fashion imaginable'.[70] It was through such at first inauspicious meetings that Eliot became associated with 'Bloomsbury' (although he did not meet Virginia and Leonard Woolf until late in 1918). It was a continuing connection, mocked by Pound and Lewis and treated with suspicion by Vivien who never felt at ease in such company. But it was one he seemed to need. Although he always kept a certain distance from writers like Lytton Strachey and Clive Bell, and was never an integral part of 'Bloomsbury' itself, certain members of that group played a large part in his ordinary social life. No doubt he was interested in them because they were writers and artists who were much more rooted than Lewis or Pound in the English life which Eliot himself wished to join – although they were, at this stage, less publicly successful than those other friends (Lewis published *Tarr* in this year and Pound never stopped publishing, whereas Strachey's *Eminent Victorians* had not yet appeared, and Virginia Woolf had only *The Voyage Out* to her credit). But their social and sexual candour, as well as sometimes unorthodox behaviour, were such that they were in some ways outcasts from conventional Edwardian society: their wartime conscientious objection, for example, would have been viewed with the greatest distrust by the Haigh-Woods. It was their nonconformity within a culture to which they nevertheless firmly belonged which attracted Eliot: it was a position, after all, which he had already occupied in the United States.

That is why he and Vivien took a cottage in Bosham, near Chichester, for the summer of 1916 – Bosham was an area much favoured by some of the people whom he had already met at Garsington. Mary Hutchinson, who was Clive Bell's mistress, had a house at Wittering, nearby, and during the period when the Eliots stayed both Roger Fry and Lytton Strachey were in the vicinity. But there were other reasons for this summer retreat, since here Vivien could recuperate steadily from her illness of the previous winter and spring. Eliot worked in the mornings, and then bicycled or boated in the afternoons. On occasions, he would come up to London and spend his days in the Reading Room of the British Museum. He was studying there in order to prepare for the extension lectures which he had been engaged to deliver in the autumn. In fact the Eliots' financial problems were such that, despite his teaching and reviewing, he had contracted to deliver two separate sets of lectures. Under the auspices of the University of London Extension Board, he gave tutorial classes on Modern English Literature, from Tennyson to George Meredith (no longer 'modern' for him). These classes were held at Southall on Mondays, for twenty-four weeks during the winter months. Each class lasted two hours, the first devoted to Eliot's lecture and the second to questions and free discussion; essays were set fortnightly. He was to continue these classes at Southall for the next three years, although he does not seem to have been a particularly good teacher. When in January 1917 he applied for a 'lectureship' – the next grade up – and offered twelve possible courses ranging from Tendencies of Contemporary French Thought to Social Psychology, the Board postponed a decision until January 1918. At that time, it was suggested that his name be added to the Supplementary List of University Extension Lecturers 'subject to a satisfactory report on his lecturing'. On 27 February, a Dr Chesser was accepted but, 'Not such a good report on that of Mr Eliot' and he was turned down.[71] In his last year at Southall, the number of students was fewer than that required by the Board, but in the minutes of the committee concerned with such matters it was reported that 'the tutor [Eliot] had written asking whether the Committee would allow him to continue the Class for a reduced fee if the Board of Education refused to pay grant on it. In view of all the circumstances, the Chairman has authorized the continuation of the Class . . .'.[72]

While teaching at Southall in the winter of 1916, he was also giving a course of six afternoon lectures on Modern French Literature in Ilkley, Yorkshire. The prospectus for this course has survived, and it demonstrates the facility with which he was already able to organize his knowledge and reading into a coherent framework. The lectures take as their theme Romanticism and the reaction against it, a reaction formulated in terms of a new classicism (opposed to 'Rousseauism'), nationalism, royalism and the Catholic Church. Eliot defines the classical view as 'essentially a belief in Original Sin – the necessity for austere discipline'. And he also anticipates his own development: 'The present day movement is partly a return to the ideals of the seventeenth century. A classicist in art and literature will therefore be likely to adhere to a monarchical form of government, and to the Catholic Church.'[73] Despite the studiously dispassionate tone, the framework of his lifelong concerns is already apparent. He did not develop as a 'thinker': he merely elaborated on the implications of his previous convictions.

His notion of 'Original Sin', and the need for 'discipline' to curb it, is one that he could have adopted entire from T. E. Hulme; in a series of essays in *The New Age* of 1915 and 1916, Hulme described his essential conviction that 'man is by nature bad or limited and can consequently only accomplish anything of value by disciplines, ethical, heroic or political. In other words, it [the new sensibility] believes in Original Sin'.[74] For a young man who had rejected the bland optimism of his familial Unitarianism, and who was aware of the shuddering chaos of private experience, such a formulation would have seemed profoundly convincing: Hulme's notion of 'sin', in particular, affected him.[75] But Hulme merely helped to crystallize what he had already gathered from Babbitt and Maurras in his student days, and the abiding influence upon his thought is really that of Maurras. He once planned to write a book on him, and in 1928 he was still addressing him as 'Cher Monsieur et Maître':[76] as late as 1948, in *Hommage à Charles Maurras*, he described him as a Virgil who led some to the very gates of the temple. And although Eliot criticized certain aspects of Maurassien doctrines – primarily because of their secularism – there is no doubt that he was predisposed to favour them.

Thus, by his twenties, Eliot had attached himself to an intellectual movement which existed in America, England and Europe, the main tenets of which were an attack upon humanitarianism and liberal democracy, the espousal of a hard classicism after the flatulence of Rousseauist 'self-expression', the affirmation of absolute and objective values, and the recognition of the need for order and authority to discipline man's fallen state. In his thesis on Bradley, he had postulated the existence of an 'absolute order' which transcends the 'strange' and limited experiences of the individual; here that order is given an ideological and historical context. As an intellectual model it has the virtues of simplicity and wide applicability, but nevertheless it represents only a part of Eliot's mind. His pervasive and sometimes corrosive scepticism was not to be easily overcome – just as, in his private existence, he was soon plunged into the disorder which he most feared.

4

Mr Eliot, the Banker
1917–1918

ELIOT RESIGNED from Highgate Junior School at the end of 1916, hoping that he would be able to earn his living by lecturing and by obtaining more review work. The first months of 1917 were in fact the only period of his life when he was entirely self-employed, living off his wits as it were, and the experiment was not a success. For one thing he was quite unable to do any sustained poetic work of his own – he had 'dried up', in a manner that became characteristic of his writing life – and, to judge by the evidence available, he was not able to earn his living as a reviewer: indeed, he seems to have done less reviewing in January and February of 1917 than he had in October of the previous year. It was a bad period, especially for a young man trying to make his way in London and persuade his parents that he was able to succeed there. He was stuck in Crawford Mansions and, just as he had been worrying about Vivien's health, so she now became anxious about his.[1]

Perhaps she appealed to her parents for help – in any event, a friend of the Haigh-Woods, Mr L. E. Thomas who was chief general manager of the National Provincial Bank, recommended Eliot for a position at Lloyds Bank. He was to say later that he was accepted because of a false reputation as a linguist – he did, however, speak French and Dante's Italian. In March 1917 he joined the Colonial and Foreign Department at Lloyds at 17 Cornhill, at first on the 'temporary' staff from which he graduated to the 'supplementary' staff. His first job was to tabulate and interpret the balance sheets of foreign banks so that their development could be charted. (His salary, in 1918, was £270 per annum – well above the general level of a clerk.) He had, as it were, gravitated to the job through a combination of chance, economic necessity and desperation; certainly his primary concern was his writing and at least bank work was less exhausting than teaching had been.[2] But that is not the whole story. Although he was soon to start complaining about the bank, and about its demands upon his time, there is no doubt that at first he enjoyed the work. He found the 'science of money' fascinating[3] and if he enjoyed manipulating the little figures of symbolic logic, how much greater enjoyment was to be had in handling the larger figures of finance. The routine of the banking day also gave a rigour and formality to his life, and such formality was always important to him. One contemporary remembers his 'Immaculate black jacket and sponge-bag trousers, and his large tortoise-shell rimmed glasses which, at the time, were a new thing and not generally worn, even at managerial level'.[4] Although he often professed not to understand the complexities of financial affairs, he was at least engaged in useful 'business' as his father had been: for the rest of his life, in fact, his public career was that of a prosperous and successful businessman. It may simply be coincidence but it is worth noting the fact that he also began writing poetry again at the time he entered Lloyds – as if he needed the discipline, or protection, of a 'proper' occupation before he could feel at ease with his own creative instincts.

He seems to have got on well enough with his banking colleagues, who remember him as being pleasant but somewhat puzzling. One has recollected a 'rather aloof man, slightly stooping and dark-eyed with . . . a sallow complexion'.[5] Another recounts that he 'often seemed to be living in a dreamland . . . he would often in the middle of dictating a letter break off suddenly, grasp a sheet of paper and start writing quickly when an idea came to him . . .'.[6] The same colleague remembers how Eliot and another bank employee started reciting the Greek alphabet for fun – Eliot became stuck in the middle, and had to be prompted. But Eliot was not altogether unknown as a poet in his bank: one employee even ventured to show him some verses, which he said were 'quite nice'.[7] He was to remain here for the next nine years, arguably the most important years in his creative life. The man who wrote *The Waste Land* was a man behind his desk, a bank official indistinguishable from other such officials except perhaps for the absolute decorum of his dress, arriving at 9.30 and leaving at 5.30, working one Saturday in four, taking his luncheon at Baker's Chop House with its curved front windows, visiting the wine shop in Cowper's Court with its dusty

shelves and corners,[8] a little cog in the machine of Britain's commercial empire. Here are the makings of a truly remarkable double
life. And, just four months after he entered his bank, *Prufrock and
Other Observations* was published.

The guiding spirit behind Eliot's first book of poems had been
that of Pound. He first broached the idea and, because of the
worries and fatigue which preoccupied Eliot, organized and collected the material which is contained within the volume – more or
less everything publishable which had been written to date, from the
'Preludes' composed at Harvard to the shorter poems completed at
Oxford. It was not easy to find a publisher. Pound had taken it first
to Elkin Matthews, with whom he had had troubled dealings in the
past. But Matthews insisted upon an advance payment, in case sales
were disastrous. Then Pound took the typescript to Harriet Shaw
Weaver of the *Egoist*. He told her, in confidence, that he would raise
the money for the printing of the book if she would allow him to use
her imprint. She agreed (in fact, the money came largely from
Dorothy Pound although Eliot was not to know this). Five hundred
copies of the slim, yellow pamphlet were printed, and although it
caused a sensation at Garsington when Katherine Mansfield read it
aloud to the assembled company, it aroused little reaction
elsewhere: according to the *Egoist* receipts, it did not 'sell out' until
early in 1922. The reviews in the English press were characteristically short and dismissive, the major complaint being that this was
verse rather than poetry because it had no conception of 'the
beautiful'. It was 'amusing' but no more.

The little volume provoked such a response in part because of its
unappealing or at least 'unpoetic' subject matter, but also because
the poetry had no identifiable single voice behind it. Even the
dramatic or 'prosy' monologues of Meredith and Browning seemed
to bear the weight of a powerful poetic personality; and in late-
nineteen- and early-twentieth-century English poetry the idea of a
sustained 'tone' was still central. That is precisely the reason why
the poetry of the years before Eliot seems so insubstantial or simply
decorative: the steady attenuation of the romantic 'personality' had
caused in turn an attenuation of the outward reality to which it
clings.

The poems of *Prufrock* are examples of dramatic virtuosity,
conceived in terms of monologue and dialogue, 'scene' and charac-

ter. Eliot's unpublished poetry – in other words, the poetry which he knew could not be published – had been of a more private kind, but it had collapsed under the weight of morbid self-consciousness. In this volume, even when the poetry seems to be most personal, as in 'Rhapsody on a Windy Night' and 'Preludes', it is curiously objective and 'pointed' – manifesting a highly sensitive but also highly conscious deployment of cadence and image to produce the required effect. The pain is announced in a stage whisper:

> Every street lamp that I pass
> Beats like a fatalistic drum,
> And through the spaces of the dark
> Midnight shakes the memory
> As a madman shakes a dead geranium.

The geranium is Laforgue's,[9] but the colour of the poem is Marlowe out of Webster. Even in an ostensibly lyrical poem like 'La Figlia Che Piange', where the poetry of incantation holds together a most disconcerting double image, the incantation itself is so evidently concocted that it deliberately invites scepticism about its nature. When the poet seems most himself, he is an actor watching his own performance. Because of this dramatic virtuosity, it would be unhelpful and indeed impossible to locate the true voice of Thomas Stearns Eliot except as a principle of literary organization. The longer poems are a number of heterogeneous fragments held together under enormous pressure, to which the insistent cadences and the consistent rhymes contribute – pressure like a headache, like a tight suit, bearing down upon a number of displays, retreats and evasions. Aiken, who understood Eliot's poetry best (Pound often missed its point because he had no real dramatic sense), described *Prufrock* in *The Dial* as the work of a 'bafflingly peculiar' man.[10]

Eliot had been, up to the beginning of 1917, 'rather desperate' – 'At that period I thought I'd dried up completely'[11] – and when Mary Hutchinson wrote to congratulate him on *Prufrock and Other Observations*, he expressed doubts both about its reception and about the prospects of new work.[12] But the confidence derived from a published volume had helped to break his period of dryness; he was always economical in his habits, and may unconsciously have been waiting for one thing to be 'evacuated' – one of his favourite words – before beginning another. By March or April he had begun the experiment of writing in French as a way of lifting his 'block' (perhaps exercising that language in his new banking work prompted him): the mental discipline and the tonal distance involved in foreign composition seem to have ambushed his conscious mind and released the poetry within him. By April Pound was writing to Joyce that Eliot has, 'burst out into scurrilous French'. Perhaps by 'scurrilous' Pound meant Eliot's account of a waiter's infantile sexual experience in 'Dans le Restaurant', but that poem is more notable for a passage on 'Phlébas' which was transposed four years later into a more famous work.

In default of poetry, Eliot had also been experimenting with prose in two short pieces entitled 'Eeldrop and Appleplex' (they were printed in the May and September issues of the *Little Review*). They are strange and murky pieces, written in that stilted and rather compressed style which is characteristic of a poet attempting to write fiction, in which the two figures of Appleplex and Eeldrop are defined and contrasted. Appleplex is a materialist and a sceptic, and is generally thought to represent Pound (although there is a shade of Russell hovering somewhere) and Eeldrop represents Eliot himself – passive, reflective, with a taste for theology and mysticism, musing on the moral fate of a man who has murdered his mistress. (Eliot enjoyed reading about murders and at a later date even wrote to the *Daily Mail* about one particularly macabre example.) Eeldrop also meditates on the strange double nature of the artist – both the drifter to whom things happen and the sharp-eyed creature coldly looking on. It is as if Dostoyevsky had been rewritten by Thomas Love Peacock.

The writing block was, at any rate, beginning to disappear. The French poems had helped, and with Pound Eliot began to study the quatrains of Theophile Gautier: in the meditation of rigorous form, his imagination might once again free itself. 'We studied Gautier's poems,' he recalled, 'and then we thought, "Have I anything to say in which this form will be useful?" '[13] And indeed he did, albeit only a small amount. Through the remaining months of 1917 and into the following year, he wrote his own quatrains. He would send copies of the poems to Pound to see if they were any good; Pound would scribble his comments in the margin. At the same time, Pound was in turn showing his poetry to Eliot – he was the only person, Pound said, who criticized rather than simply objected to the Cantos which he was now beginning to write.[14] And of course it was Pound who made sure that such work was published. He had already told Margaret Anderson, the editor of the *Little Review*, that he, Pound, knew what was the real stuff and, perhaps in shock, she appointed him foreign editor. 'The Hippopotamus' and three French poems appeared there in July; other quatrain poems were published in the following year. 'Eliot has thought of things I had not thought of,' Pound told Anderson, 'and I'm damned if many of the others have done so.'[15] Eliot returned the compliment in an anonymous pamphlet, *Ezra Pound: His Metric and His Poetry* (the title was Pound's) which was timed to coincide with the American publication of Pound's *Lustra*. It was anonymously written partly to camouflage the effrontery of two poets engaged in an attempt to 'boost' each other but partly because, at this stage, Eliot's name was not fashionable enough to have any *cachet* of its own. As by degrees he established himself in London, of course, that situation would be remedied.

And, in fact, the process had already begun. At Pound's instigation, Harriet Shaw Weaver offered Eliot the job of assistant editor on the *Egoist* in June, the month in which under her imprint *Prufrock* was published; his salary was £9.00 per quarter, part of which was financed by Pound's benefactor, John Quinn, an American lawyer and patron of contemporary artists, whose efforts on behalf of Pound's friends were nothing short of heroic. It marked Eliot's first entry into the editorial world, which included the commissioning of articles as well as more important matters such as the editing and correcting of proofs. In one form or another, he was to continue with this kind of work for the rest of his life. Apart from his editorial responsibilities, he was also contracted to write articles on a regular basis. In his first year he reviewed the letters of J. B. Yeats, Noh drama, Turgenev, and wrote a number of 'Reflections on Contemporary Poetry'. They are not so much reflections as animadversions, and he was, in fact, highly skilled as an occasional journalist. The pieces in the *Egoist* are some of the funniest and sharpest he wrote, quite without that note of orotundity which appears in his criticism published in volume form. He was still, at this stage, a young man with nothing much to lose and his high-spiritedness is evident in the 'spoof' letters which he wrote in the *Egoist*, no doubt to fill up space. He signed each letter with a different name – Charles Augustus Conybeare was one – and, as always, he was a good ventriloquist; an inveterate *moqueur*, as Wyndham Lewis had said.

In the first six months of 1917, he had published a book, acquired a job and joined a magazine; after this hectic period he and Vivien went in July to Bosham again, although since the bank only allowed him two weeks' holiday each year they could not spend as much time together there as they had in the previous summer. And as soon as he returned to London, he had to accustom himself to the routine which he had only recently established. He was now fully engaged for something like fourteen or fifteen hours a day. He would try to rise two hours earlier than was strictly necessary in order to concentrate upon his own writing, and then he would travel to the bank. On his return home in the evening, he would get on with his literary reviewing, his *Egoist* duties, and the preparations for his lectures: not only was he still conducting his Monday evening tutorial classes at Southall but he was also now contracted to give a course of twenty-five lectures at Sydenham on Victorian literature. In October 1918 he joined the London Library and, on Saturday afternoons, he would visit it in order to collect the books which he needed for these multifarious studies. And although the lectures seemed to expend more of his energy than his work in the bank, it was the daily routine of office work which clearly took up most of his time. Pound thought it a great waste[16] but it is doubtful if, at this stage, Eliot would have agreed. Much later in life, he told a friend that those activities which other people considered wasteful often proved useful for his own development.[17] He enjoyed his bank work, in any case: it assuaged the guilt which he felt towards his family, and it provided a refuge also from the increasing difficulties of his marriage.

Vivien was still in poor health, and suffered from nervous head-aches and sleeplessness – no doubt aggravated by the fact that, while her husband was actively and continually engaged in work of some kind, she had very little to do and was becoming bored. She had tried to get a job in the Civil Service but she was turned down on the grounds that she was married to an American and therefore could not work for the government in wartime. Her life was much emptier than her husband's – always a potent source of dissatisfaction and anxiety in a marriage. She took dancing lessons when her health permitted it, since dancing was still her passion; she and her husband would sometimes visit the dance halls together, and Queensway on a Sunday afternoon was a favourite 'haunt'. These lessons were being financed by Bertrand Russell who, although no longer sharing the same flat as the Eliots, still took an almost proprietorial interest in their affairs; often he would have lunch or dinner with Vivien when Eliot was working. This was to prove a less than ideal arrangement, however, since, on one occasion in the autumn of this year, Russell broke his self-imposed vow of paternalism and (acceding, perhaps, to her requests) made love to Vivien – at least this is what he claimed in a letter to his mistress, Lady Constance Malleson. The experience, however, was 'hellish and loathsome. He disguised his antipathy and she seemed satisfied, but since then he had awful nightmares that strip his self-evasions.'[18] He did not explain why it was quite so 'loathsome', although no doubt Vivien's own physical problems had something to do with it. It was the pointless and messy end of what had been an intense but 'platonic' relationship, and the intimacy between Vivien and Russell came to an end. She told Ottoline Morrell that, although she had been fond of Russell and perhaps still was, she would make no attempt to see him again.[19]

It is an open question whether Eliot knew what had happened. It was a situation with which he was not yet used to dealing, and no doubt, given his own reticent and defensive temperament, he would have found it peculiarly difficult to respond in an active or decisive manner. It seems likely that he did know, or came to suspect, but that he preferred to 'forget' what had happened and to remain silent. The fact remains that, in the following summer, the Eliots stayed at a cottage in Marlow, Buckinghamshire, in which Bertrand Russell had a financial stake, and there is no sense in which they broke off relations with him immediately. Later, however, Eliot was to accuse him of further damaging Vivien's already frail health.[20] He confessed to Virginia Woolf that the thing he most feared was 'humiliation',[21] however, and this, rather than jealousy or anger, would be his own kind of suffering after such an incident.

But it ought to be remembered that sexual infidelity was no great matter among the people whom he and Vivien both knew, and indeed there were some women who would gladly have lured Eliot away from a wife whom Ottoline Morrell described as a 'frivolous, silly little woman':[22] Nancy Cunard was one such, according to Maurice Haigh-Wood.[23] It is not known how he reacted to such advances, although his inexperience, close to naivety, would have been the deciding factor. Nevertheless he possessed a kind of coquettish gallantry: he told Edith Sitwell that he had once visited a fortune teller who described him as 'flirtatious and obstinate'.[24] Certainly he seemed most at ease in the company of women, as his letters to Mary Hutchinson, Ottoline Morrell and Virginia Woolf testify. Mary Hutchinson was a particularly close friend during this period; a cousin of the Stracheys, she was married to an eminent barrister, St John Hutchinson, and was also the mistress of Clive Bell – she had a foot in both camps, as it were, and combined the conventional role of an Edwardian hostess with the less restricting one of a writer associated with 'Bloomsbury' (the Hogarth Press published a volume of her short stories). Eliot understood that double role very well, and became attached to her as a result. She was intelligent and witty, but she also possessed the confidence of her class and social position: it was an enviable mixture, and one under which he could shelter from the social and physical strains of his own marriage.

But it would be wrong to underestimate the bonds between Eliot and Vivien even in the midst of their difficulties. Brigit Patmore knew them both in the early days of their marriage, and has left a remarkable account of their behaviour towards each other.[25] They were, by her account, exhausting company because they treated everything with a 'terrible seriousness'. On one occasion Vivien told her what a 'frightful time' she had with her husband, but Brigit Patmore noticed how she could sometimes enliven him and arouse in him a schoolboyish humour. One has the impression of a couple who at this stage relied upon each other, in the sense that they lived off each others' nerves, and were able to amuse each other also – accomplices against the world. But Brigit Patmore's memoir is interesting not only because it records the exasperated affection which obtained between them, but because it also provides some testimony to Eliot's character as a young man when he was trying to make his way in the world. He was, she said, 'pleased with nobody' – he could 'pounce on one' and 'speak sharply'. He was not only 'critical of people, but also of their class and position in the world' – he was, in other words, a bit of a snob. 'Never had I met a less humble man. And pain – he loved not only his own but the pain of others. . . .' There was certainly a note of asperity in his character – he had a tendency to 'put down' people who said foolish or annoying things – which suggests that dissatisfaction with others which springs from dissatisfaction with oneself. It is not the happiest aspect of Eliot's behaviour as a young man, although it is one that was mollified by the time he reached middle age and had ceased to be quite so vulnerable.

The war, of course, exercised its own form of attrition even upon those who, like Eliot, watched from the sidelines. It was in Britain the time of great economic and political discontent, with shortages of fuel and food. The nature of this conflict, in which Europe itself might be destroyed, dwarfed ordinary personal problems as Eliot explained to his father.[26] And by the time of the German offensive in March 1918, only Lewis and Pound seemed unaffected by the horror around them.[27] Certainly Eliot found the strain of earning his living under these conditions increasingly hard to bear and, when he had gone to the house of Lady Colefax to read poetry in December 1917, Aldous Huxley described him as 'haggard and ill-looking as usual'.[28] In fact, poetry-readings of this kind were small comfort to a man who was working too hard to concentrate his mind upon new production, and by March he had only completed some half-dozen short poems.[29] His own father was very ill, and Vivien's health was so precarious that she was now an invalid.[30] The strain of this uncertainty compounded his own exhaustion, and during the winter he was in a very shaky state. He consulted a doctor, who advised him and his wife to rest in the country during the summer months as much as possible.

In May 1918 they went down to the cottage in Marlow which Russell had arranged for them. From here Eliot commuted to the bank during the week and he spent the weekends in the garden writing and reading. Vivien grew attached to the cottage and its garden, which offered her some distraction from her ill health, and by June Eliot was telling his mother that he felt much happier and healthier;[31] when Aldous Huxley visited them in the same month he found Eliot 'in excellent form, and his wife too'.[32]

This more contented life was not, however, to last. America had entered the war in April 1917 as an 'Associated Power', and the Allied misfortunes of early 1918 seem to have persuaded Eliot that it was his duty to join the American army – if he could enter it at a rank high enough to be able to provide for himself and Vivien. Although he was still of draft age, he had already been pronounced unfit for active military service because of his congenital double hernia, and tachycardia – an abnormally rapid heart beat generally induced by nervous strain. Army records state that he was five feet eleven inches in height, and weighed 137 pounds – 15 pounds lighter than he had been at Oxford, suggesting the physical toll which the last three years had taken on him. There then ensued a succession of mistakes, delays and confusions which would be comic were it not for the fact that he felt himself to be placed in constant anxiety because of them.

At first he tried to join the United States Naval Intelligence Service – because of his linguistic abilities and his knowledge of Europe, that seemed the most appropriate department – but the 'red tape' involved proved insurmountable. He sent a telegram to his family from Marlow, asking them to inquire about the possibilities for a commission in the army or navy if he returned to America. Then the Quartermaster Corps was suggested to him; then Political Intelligence; then Army Intelligence. While obtaining testimonials for the latter from various eminent citizens, he was again sent for by Naval Intelligence who asked him to leave the bank. They had heard that he was the most suitable man for their purposes, and offered to give him the post of Chief Yeoman within a few months. So he left Lloyds, only to discover that the naval officers were not ready to enrol him and then, later, that they did not have the authority to do so in any case. He was most distressed, and attempted to meet various authoritative figures, like Admiral Sims (through the agency of Nancy Cunard) who might be able to help him. He waited for two weeks, and then at the beginning of November returned to the bank where his employers signed an appeal for his exemption from service. To judge by his correspondence, the uncertainty and strain had had a paralysing effect upon him ('paralysing', like 'numbing' was one of his favourite adjectives), but fortunately, by the time Eliot had reached the end of his patriotic efforts, the armistice had been signed. He was relieved, and he had the satisfaction of knowing that at least he had tried his best:[33] he had, after all, been willing to abandon his career, and so no doubt incur Vivien's displeasure, for the sake of his country.

Despite these endeavours, however, his attitude to America was now a somewhat ambiguous one. Although he referred to Americans as 'us' in a letter to John Quinn,[34] he was also in the same year referring to the English as 'we'.[35] In one letter, undated but on *Egoist* notepaper, he described his unhappiness at the fact that he no longer had any real connection or sympathy with Americans, and yet in the *Egoist* itself he also described the density and stupidity of the English environment,[36] an awareness compounded by his sense of the spiritual degeneration of English life.[37] That sense never left him, and his attitude is one of pervasive ambiguity: he was never completely at home anywhere and, even after he adopted British citizenship, he would sometimes sign himself 'metoikos', the Greek for 'resident alien'. He cultivated such distance and detachment as if by not fully belonging, or wholly participating, something of himself was preserved – something secret and inviolable which he could nourish. The idea of isolation and invulnerability was clearly very important to him, and in letters to friends such as Conrad Aiken and Mary Hutchinson he sometimes conjures up images of submarine depths – of their coolness and remoteness. Sudden withdrawal into himself – in silence and in 'avoiding' people – was also a mark of his adult life, just as for many people a quality of detachment or remoteness was his most visible characteristic. In the *Athenaeum*,[38] he wrote of the 'true coldness, the hard coldness' of the real artist; in the same way, he admired in Massine's work its 'unhuman' quality.[39]

Certainly by now he was well on the way to losing his American identity. Another expatriate who knew him during these first years in London has reported that 'There was nothing, either in his speech, his dress or his demeanour, that proclaimed the former middle-westerner,' and one noticed instead, 'his pale ascetic face, his correct manners, his blend of deliberate reserve and intellectual arrogance.'[40] You may be sure that this 'arrogance' emerged in the company of compatriots rather than at places such as Garsington; there he was learning the manners and methods of a world new to him. He moved carefully, watching, understanding, incorporating anything that might be of use, taciturn, an economist of style as well as of words in whom the instinct to conform and the instinct to stand apart merged in a subtle, almost ironic, imitation of those around him. If he sought for any definite identity, it was closer to the 'European' one which he recognized in another American expatriate, Henry James. James was a European, he said, in a way that no person born in Europe could be: it was a consciously created identity, nourished by a peculiarly American sense of the past.[41] In the same period he had written of Turgenev's exile in Paris that the Russian knew how to make use of his transplantation – how, by maintaining his role as a foreigner, he could acquire authority.[42]

This is close enough to Eliot's situation to suggest that he was consciously meditating upon his own fate. Such a sense of life requires deliberation, however: to turn one's personality into a made thing, a construct. And although, when closely observed, his life seems to move from crisis to crisis there was clearly that within him which encouraged people to believe that he behaved in a deliberate and premeditated fashion. Richard Aldington, an early and for a while close friend, suggested that it was in this very period, when he was buffetted by circumstances and deterred by accidents, that he was 'laying the foundations of his future influence by cultivating the right people'.[43] This is in part the asperity of hindsight from a less successful writer, but certainly more than most young men, Eliot was meeting the rich, the powerful and the clever. His friends and acquaintances in these years were people quite dissimilar from each other: Ezra Pound and J. C. Squire, Conrad Aiken and Mary Hutchinson, Wyndham Lewis and Clive Bell, Charles Whibley and Leonard Woolf. It suggests, at the very least, a profound ability to 'get on' with men and women – of some of whose work and opinions he had no very high regard and about whom, in letters, he was sometimes scathing.

He had met the Sitwells, for example, at the Lady Colefax reading in December of the previous year (in a letter to Pound, he added an 'h' to the first part of their surname[44]). Edith Sitwell was rather taken with him – she found him slim and elegant, although a little pale.[45] Osbert Sitwell has said that: 'Though he was reserved, and had armoured himself behind the fine manners . . . his air, to the contrary, was always lively and jaunty'.[46] He observed, also, the control and ease of his physical movements which, perceptively, he related to similar qualities in Eliot's poetry. After that event, the Eliots and Sitwells saw a great deal of each other. They would attend

Edith Sitwell's Saturday afternoon tea parties in Bayswater and, in his memoir of the Eliots, Osbert Sitwell recalled how they would sometimes take tea in a café near Marble Arch, Eliot arriving from the bank somewhat later than the rest.[47]

Other literary friendships followed. During this period, he met Sidney and Violet Schiff – a wealthy literary couple (Schiff wrote novels under the name of Stephen Hudson) who invited the Eliots to evening gatherings in Cambridge Square and for weekends to their house in Eastbourne. And then, in November 1918, Eliot for the first time visited Leonard and Virginia Woolf at Hogarth House in Richmond. He brought and read some of his newly composed quatrain poems, which they were soon to decide to publish, and they discussed contemporary literature. He struck Virginia Woolf as being enormously slow and elaborate of speech but underneath the orotundity she suspected intolerance.[48] 'That strange young man,' she called him.[49] Leonard Woolf was rather disappointed – Eliot seemed formal and cautious, with a much slower and more rigid intelligence than he had suspected from the poetry.[50] Other contemporaries saw him quite differently: Middleton Murry took to him at once, believing him to live in the same kind of isolation as Murry himself. Herbert Read, who had dinner with him and Lewis in the October of this year, commented that 'He has brains'.

After the struggles over the American military, he and Vivien were both ill in November and December of 1918. Eliot was perplexed by his wife's migraines,[51] and Pound was describing to John Quinn how Eliot's own health was in so shaky a state that his doctor had ordered him not to write any prose for the next six months.[52] Eliot had told his father, a year before, of his ambitions for his own writing. And so there was a struggle going on, between those ambitions and his unfortunate circumstances, the outcome of which was still uncertain.

5

Toil, and Troubles
1919–1920

ELIOT'S FATHER died at the beginning of January 1919; Vivien wrote in her diary that it was a terrible ordeal for him. Eliot had already been planning to visit his family later in the year[1] and hoped, in addition, that he might be able to publish a book in America which would persuade them that his decision to settle in England had not been a mistake – that he had not, as they suspected, squandered his life and talents. The book he had in mind was one that he had been working on during the previous year – a collection of verse and prose in which Pound's publisher, Alfred Knopf, had professed himself interested. By the end of 1918, Knopf had the manuscript but Eliot had heard nothing further.

Now his father was dead. He had died without seeing any evidence of his son's capacity except for a few strange poems in a slim volume. For a young man who had been trying so hard to win his father's approval, the loss was extraordinarily great: not least because Henry Ware Eliot represented the American aspiration towards success, thrift and practicality which exerted so powerful an influence throughout Eliot's life. He always had a strong sense of familial pride: Osbert Sitwell remembered how, in the little flat in Crawford Street, Eliot kept a corner of family photographs and silhouettes;[2] he also wore an Eliot family ring. Such things reminded him of the people whom he had left behind, and, in the loss of his father, he also lost part of himself.

His unhappiness was compounded by the fact that, at the end of January, Knopf decided to turn down the book. John Quinn, who was acting as his unpaid agent, then offered it to Boni and Liveright but, when their tactics seemed to be those of protracted delay, he withdrew it and offered it instead to John Lane. Lane also turned it down, in early August: 'Mr Eliot's work,' he wrote to Quinn, 'is no doubt brilliant but it is not exactly the kind of material we care to add to our list'.[3] In April, however, Knopf agreed to publish his poems separately. This worked in the end to Eliot's advantage; it got into print his most enduring work, and gave him more time to consider and refine his journalism in a way that Pound's 'pushing' had not encouraged. In addition, the Woolfs had agreed to print Eliot's most recent work under the imprint of the Hogarth Press. Such an arrangement suited his meticulous and economical nature: his new work was, as it were, 'mopped up' and he could move on.

Poems, which the Woolfs published in June 1919 in a marbled jacket, contains most of the verses Eliot had written in French and the majority of his quatrain poems; three of the latter, 'Sweeney Erect', 'Burbank with a Baedeker: Bleistein with a Cigar' and 'A Cooking Egg' were written too late in the year to be included in the Hogarth pamphlet but they were added to the Knopf volume which was published nine months later. The quatrain poems are some of the most original and inventive of Eliot's work. They are sharp, tight, hard, ironic, manifesting exactly the kind of 'coldness' which he believed to be essential in the work of a genuine writer. But he himself was at pains to distinguish between the poems which were not really 'serious' – he included 'Whispers of Immortality' and 'The Hippopotamus' in this category – and those which were. Poems like 'Burbank with a Baedeker: Bleistein with a Cigar' and 'Sweeney Among the Nightingales' were very much so.[4] The former are essentially poems of satirical argument, the latter tend towards dramatic and verbal intensity.

The poems in this volume are marked by great shifts of tone also, and by the rapid succession of images. There are constant modifications of thought and emotion, moving from half-comic expressions of regret or nostalgia to cruel or simply impersonal observations. Wide-eyed intimations of horror – the sharpened razor, the arched epileptic – are placed alongside flat and lethargic sounds of indifference, 'sprawls', 'yawns', 'exhales', as if any possible violence was continually being vitiated by mental and physical passivity. Eliot's extraordinary rhythmic intelligence is manifested throughout, of course, and the tight form which he has adapted from Gautier holds in place even the most recondite or alarming perceptions: they are literally 'cut down to size'. Like the practical jokes of which he was so fond, the implicit assault upon the reader's consciousness is excused or justified by the faultless use of an orthodox form.

The quatrain poems are, in certain sections, almost impenetrably obscure – an ostensible piece of 'light' verse, 'A Cooking Egg', has provoked reams of critical controversy about its meaning, a pursuit which Eliot himself found quite futile.[5] These poems are difficult principally because although they seem to work in objective or dramatic terms – with the titles setting the 'scene', as it were – their transitions and imagery come from some private source of feeling which is either concealed or obscure and unarticulated. It ought to be remembered that Eliot was writing them at a time when he was over-worked, sick, demoralized and uncertain about his future as a poet. In an article in *The Monist*, he suggested as an hypothesis that his emotions were more likely to be understood by someone other than himself, as an optician knows his eyes.[6] And yet, as he knew from his reading of Bradley, the whole world is private to oneself. I see everything and I cannot tell you: explain to me how I must feel.

While he was completing the last of the quatrain poems, he also reverted to what was for him a more familiar form: during May and June he was writing 'Gerontion', a dramatic monologue in which he assumes the persona of the 'little old man'. When he takes on such a persona, his poetry loses the constriction and the wilful obscurity of more private work like the quatrain poems; there is an immediate sense of release into an expansive, elaborate and allusive mode of address. Here we have the character of an old man who has not engaged in the martial or creative activities of his contemporaries, who is so lost in the contemplation of the futility of history and the worthlessness of action that he remains immobile and alone. Eliot had in fact been re-reading the Elizabethan dramatists for his extension lectures, and the images and cadences of that poetry are exposed upon the surface of 'Gerontion':

> I that was near your heart was removed therefrom
> To lose beauty in terror, terror in inquisition.

But the language is borrowed, drained of meaning, a form of rhetoric which disqualifies itself because it does not provoke action. There is no despair or agony in the movement of the poem – only a calm and considered vision of its own emptiness. The strength of 'Gerontion' lies in its dramatic recreation of such a vision; and, in a perspective longer than any of us can possess now, it may emerge that Eliot's poetry was the real English drama of the early twentieth century.

Copies of the poem were sent to Mary Hutchinson and Sidney Schiff (and no doubt others) for their comments before Eliot got down to revising it – this was a typical procedure on his part, since he was self-confessedly hesitant in his judgments. He knew, however, when his work was bad or incomplete, and there were some verses which he kept entirely to himself. During the years 1916–19 he had written sketches and fragments which were to appear later, in much revised form, in *The Waste Land*. In their original state pieces like 'Death of a Duchess' and 'London' were unassimilable; they contain ragged and often enervated poetry, material not 'worked up' because it is too close to its source in Eliot's private experience – these are poems concerned with the hell of living with another person, and the hell of the city itself.[7]

Vivien's diary for 1919 records a social life of a conventionally convivial kind. There were dinner parties for the Pounds, for Aldous Huxley, Harold Monro, Richard Aldington, Ottoline Morrell and others. The Eliots visited, or were visited by, the Schiffs, the Hutchinsons, and the Sitwells. There were outings to the ballet and to the dance halls, although they sometimes went separately to such places. In March, Vivien spent an evening dancing with three Canadian 'flying men', and in the following month Eliot asked Mary Hutchinson to accompany him to a dance hall near Baker Street.[8] And yet even in the midst of these happy activities both husband and wife seemed to be suffering from the effects of acute strain. Vivien recorded migraine, a swollen face, tiredness and depression. 'Tom' himself was often depressed as well, staying in bed with various ailments, sometimes sick in the night and looking altogether ill. And in April he was complaining of his exhaustion[9] – a consistent note in his correspondence over the next decades.

The flat at Crawford Mansions was, according to Vivien, in an 'awful condition'. Osbert Sitwell remembered it as being cramped and sparsely furnished[10] – he noticed that Vivien's own tastes were not shown in the decoration, and that the flat seemed to be pervaded by Eliot's personality (an apt indication of who most influenced whom). The neighbourhood was also run down. The building in which they lived had several flats, and the windows of their own looked down upon a pub on the other side of the street which, at closing time, would have been raucous. Eliot's hypersensitivity was another reason why domestic life was becoming intolerable for him: he was, for example, highly susceptible to noise, and he found no peace in such surroundings. Osbert Sitwell recalled two of his neighbours: sisters who lived above the Eliots and had a habit of shouting down from the window to friends in the street, as well as playing the phonograph very loudly. They were, it seems, 'actresses' and when Eliot complained to the landlord about the commotion they made, the landlord replied, 'Well you see, sir, it's the artistic temperament: we ordinary folk must learn to make allowances for artists. They're not the same as us'.[11]

The cramped surroundings and the sordid environment in which husband and wife lived threw them too closely together, and confirmed the emotional dislocation from which they both suffered: he was in this year writing about the 'indestructible barriers' which exist between human beings,[12] and proximity gave rise to mutual depression and sickness. When worry and exhaustion made Eliot ill, his own condition affected Vivien's already highly nervous disposition. As a result, they were beginning to spend a great deal of time apart – perhaps they came to an agreement, if only unspoken, that it was best to do so. They rented a cottage in Bosham again for the summer, and in June Vivien travelled down: she was there until September, with Eliot generally coming only for weekends. The time was spent in bathing, picnics with neighbours like the Hutchinsons, long walks in the country. It was a respite which both of them needed. And of course Eliot's own work took him away from Vivien; apart from his daily absence at the office, in May he was sent on an extended business trip to the provinces: he was gone for some time, returning to London once a week or so. He explained to Lytton Strachey how his mind was then filled with commercial considerations only – the appreciation of the rupee, or the reasons why it was cheaper to buy steel from America rather than from Middlesbrough.[13] But all of this took up a great deal of his time, and such waste preoccupied him since it meant that he could not get on with any sustained work of his own.

And yet the fact that he was forced to lead a life continually under pressure was at least in part the result of his growing reputation and success. During the late spring and early summer of 1919 he was working out the contents of a collected book of poems which John Rodker wished to produce. Sir Algernon Methuen and Martin Secker conveyed an interest in publishing books of his prose, and Harriet Shaw Weaver suggested a book of essays – later in the year, the *Egoist* announced a forthcoming volume, *The Art of Poetry*, to be published in the spring of 1920. He had also begun in April of this year to write for the *Athenaeum*. Its editor, Middleton Murry, had originally asked him to join the staff as an assistant editor, with a putative salary of £500 per annum, but Eliot turned down the offer. The job did not seem to be a secure one (in this he was proved right) compared with that of the bank, and he disliked the idea of earning his living primarily by writing journalism.[14] Nevertheless Murry used Eliot as a regular contributor, and the long articles which he wrote for the *Athenaeum* assured him a larger readership than he obtained in the *Egoist*. Some of these pieces, such as those on Swinburne and *Hamlet*, were to be reprinted later in volume form.

But the constant accretion of work, as well as the long hours and the difficulties involved in labouring in the impersonal institution of a bank, bred in Eliot an attitude of exhausted contempt towards urban life. He regarded London with disdain, he told Strachey, and divided human beings into 'supermen', 'termites' and 'wireworms' – he was living with the termites.[15] So it was with a certain personal asperity that he wrote in April of the essential isolation of the great American figures,[16] just as he had spoken of the isolation of an exilic writer like Turgenev. And there is no doubt that he felt a certain intellectual superiority to most of the writers and artists whom he encountered, an attitude compounded by the fact that he found it difficult to persuade most of his contemporaries of the worth of men like Joyce and Lewis (Vivien admired them, however – a sign that she was not lacking in literary judgment). Virginia Woolf was one of those who did not care for Joyce's work; and although Eliot was now her friend (and author), there is a sense in which neither of them really understood or appreciated the other's writing. It seems from Virginia Woolf's diary entries for April of this year that she also suspected him of abusing her behind her back on some occasions, and elaborately praising her on others. She was determined to 'draw the rat from his hole'.[17]

The competing pressures were too much for him. He had already

been ill in February, and in June he was anticipating a period of
seclusion.[18] In July he felt too ill to get on with his own writing; he
took to his bed and was recuperating in August. There was,
however, relief at hand. He decided to take a three-week holiday in
France, part of which he would spend with Ezra Pound in the
Dordogne; it was the only proper rest he had had in two years.
Pound was prepared to act as a male nurse: he told Quinn he was
about to put Eliot through a course of 'sun, air and sulphur baths'.[19]
Eliot was greatly relieved to be getting out of London; he set off in
mid-August, and told Mary Hutchinson that he was not sure if he
would ever return:[20] that, however, was just a dramatic flourish. He
spent his time walking and sight-seeing; the stimulus of being in
different surroundings and speaking a different language seemed to
have done him good.[21] Certainly he was able to relax for once, and
that alone made him feel much better: he had even grown a beard.
Vivien does not mention this in her diary entry for the day of his
return; she was much more concerned with his moods: 'Tom' was
agreeable at first but rapidly became depressed.[22]

But if he was depressed by the amount of work he had to return
to, he made no effort to decrease it. As a result of his *Athenaeum*
pieces his criticism had come to the attention of Bruce Richmond,
the editor of *The Times Literary Supplement*. It was Richard
Aldington, already a reviewer for that paper, who brought the two
men together – for the reason, as he explained later in his autobiography,[23] that it would help to curb the opposition against Eliot in
metropolitan circles if he was in a 'powerful' position. After a
somewhat difficult meeting, which was not helped by the French
beard – it made him 'look awful', according to Aldington – Richmond hired him. His 'brief' was to review studies of Elizabethan
and Jacobean drama, and his first article appeared in November on
Ben Jonson's plays. The anonymous role of a *Times* reviewer in fact
suited him very well: it allowed him to adopt the role of the scholar,
and thus employ the tone of established authority. And so the path
was being made straight for him: within five years of his arrival in
England, he had risen to the first ranks of literary journalism, at the
same time as his prose and poetry were finding permanent expression in volume form. A good deal of this early success can be
attributed to good fortune and the efforts of friends, but the chances
could only have been seized and exploited by a most ambitious

young man. He was not, however, entirely happy with his journalistic productions and tended to denigrate them in letters to his friends. But if these were trifles, they were the ones which he depended upon both for his living and his critical reputation. Nevertheless it is important to realize that Eliot knew they were trifles, and understood that he had to keep a firm hold upon what was his important work. In October 1919 he gave a lecture for the Arts League of Service on 'modern tendencies in poetry'; then, in the following month, he began work on a long poem which was tentatively entitled, 'He Do The Police In Different Voices'.

Conrad Aiken used to have lunch with him during this period. 'Tom Eliot is here for life,' he wrote.[24] And, in *Ushant*, he described him as being by now 'rootedly established'; he had 'built the splendid ramparts . . . and behind them he had become all but invisible'. Aiken called this a 'tragic metamorphosis'. Eliot, in a letter to Pound, in turn accused Aiken of stupidity.[25] There were few people by this stage, however, who could have reasonably claimed that he had made the wrong choice by deciding to stay in England. By the beginning of 1920 his poetic work could be seen entire, both in England and in America. *Ara Vos Prec* (it was originally entitled *Ara Vus Prec*, a mistake in Provençal which Eliot made) was published by John Rodker; *Poems* was published by Alfred Knopf. Both books contained all of the poems which Eliot thought fit to print, from 'Prufrock' to 'Gerontion'. In addition, Harriet Weaver had already asked Eliot to collect his essays, and he was now intending to turn such a volume into a definitive statement about standards in modern poetry, with his lecture to the Arts League of Service at its heart. Among its themes would be the technique of poetry, the public for poetry, and its possible social employment. He wanted it to be a small book, to make it all the more effective and, when discussing the subject with Sidney Schiff, he demanded secrecy[26] – as if he were preparing for an assault.

In the end, the idea came to nothing: throughout Eliot's career, there are examples of books planned in advance, announced, and then never written. It is not clear why this book was abandoned: it may be that the practicalities of writing it outweighed his desire to complete the task, since such a volume would have required the kind of sustained concentration and thought for which he did not have the opportunity. In the end, he never wrote anything longer than his undergraduate thesis: his talent was for concentration and elimination, rather than for expansion and divagation. Nevertheless he was determined to be associated in the public mind with work other than occasional journalism and, in April, he signed a contract with Methuen to produce a book of essays. He wanted something more substantial than his first attempt, although in fact he signed the contract without quite knowing what was going into the book, and a large number of essays which appeared in this volume, *The Sacred Wood*, were written at high speed during the early months of 1920. The manuscript had been promised to the publishers for the end of June, but it was still far from ready by the end of May. He went down to Marlow and there, in July, he finally completed it.

And yet it was the simultaneous publication in England and America of his informal 'collected' poems which proved to be the most significant event. He was already known as a critic, at least in England, and at this stage his reputation as a journalist was higher than that as a poet. He was known only as a 'satirist', a writer of mordant and witty verses. Other poets like Osbert Sitwell had been copying his quatrain style and were rather better known for it – Eliot was at great pains to emphasize that he had done it first.[27] But the publication of *Ara Vos Prec* and *Poems* made it clear that he was a more considerable poet than the early slim volumes might have suggested: what precisely he was doing, however, was still not apparent to the reviewers. There were long pieces on *Ara Vos Prec* in the *Observer, New Statesman, The Times Literary Supplement* and elsewhere, in which his cleverness and difficulty were discussed without being explained.

In fact the most enthusiastic response to Eliot's work came not from the metropolis but from the academy. I. A. Richards, a young don at Cambridge and a member of the only recently established 'English school' there, bought a copy of *Ara Vos Prec* and was so excited by it that he determined to meet the poet and, if possible, persuade him to join the Cambridge faculty in some capacity. When Richards actually did meet him, and suggested that he take up some kind of academic work, Eliot refused – he was not at all sure, Richards remembered him saying, that academic life was the one he would choose to adopt.[28] That choice had, after all, been offered to him by Harvard only five years before. He was happier in the bank, despite its more lugubrious aspects: when Richards visited him there on one occasion, he found him in a basement 'stooping, very like a dark bird in a feeder, over a big table covered with all sorts and sizes of foreign correspondence';[29] above him were the familiar thick green glass squares which separate pavements from basements, and Richards could hear the endless clicking of heels a few inches from Eliot's head.

Although he had refused Richards's suggestion, they became close acquaintances, thus establishing his first connection with academic 'English studies'. Richards took upon himself the role of critic and explicator of his poetry so that, within a very few years, his name became closely associated with that of Eliot. Eliot never felt comfortable close to anyone, however, and before long he was at pains to disassociate himself from Richards's theoretical pronouncements. Nevertheless the academic enthusiasm for, and espousal of, his poetry was a formative factor in the steady advancement of its reputation. It was an accidental liaison at first, but it came to be a most significant one. Eliot was defining the idea of a 'tradition' in his prose criticism, and offering a formidably complex range of literary associations in his creative writing – both of these fitted absolutely the needs and demands of burgeoning English studies, which needed contemporary material to 'interpret' and to 'place'. But just as once Eliot needed academic attention in order to further his claims of respectability, so in the end it was his status as a cultural magus which seemed to justify in part the study of 'English literature' as an intellectual and even moral discipline.

Despite the evident fact that a bank seemed preferable to a university, it was still for Eliot a source of anxiety. It provided him and Vivien with a living, but it also wasted his time in an egregious fashion. By this year he had moved to the information department at Lloyds' head office, where he dealt with the complicated matter of pre-war debts between the bank and the Germans. Although he told his mother he found the work interesting,[30] he often complained about the effects it had upon his life and work. In fact, he was to keep on worrying about these matters until he finally left Lloyds. In May 1920 he again wondered out loud whether he should leave the bank and take up a post in journalism if one should be offered to him,[31] but then a year later he congratulated himself for not having done so.[32] And yet he did not have the time or energy to write that long poem . . . and so it went on, with Eliot impaled upon his own

cautiousness and uncertainty. Other people were of a less complicated mind in such matters. Ezra Pound wrote to Quinn, 'It is a
crime against literature to let him waste eight hours per diem in that
bank',[33] and in July he initiated a scheme in which four or five people
would raise between them £400 per year to subsidise Eliot and allow
him to leave the bank. But the scheme, like later such attempts to
rescue him from something which he did not really want to leave,
came to nothing.

If Pound worried about Eliot, so in turn did Eliot worry about
Pound. Eliot explained to Quinn that Pound was alienating too
many people in England, and contrasted his literary prestige
unfavourably with that of Osbert Sitwell.[34] Almost from the beginning Eliot had a clear understanding of the mechanics of making a
literary reputation; he understood the importance of being mentioned regularly in the newspapers,[35] just as in his own criticism he
was always aware of the need to make the right impression: hence
his air of scholarship which was, in part, only assumed. Certainly he
had read much less than his admirers imagined, although at this
stage in his career he did not attempt to disabuse them.

Pound did, in fact, abandon England in September, having
decided that he would be less neglected and better understood in
Paris; when Lewis contemplated following Pound, Eliot advised
against the move because in that city he would be in the company,
and ambiance, of much less talented artists. It was better to remain
in isolation than to be marked by such associations. That is why, for
example, he would not contribute to *Wheels*, the annual anthology
of new writing edited by Edith Sitwell.[36] There is an element of
justifiable pride, and a respectable ingredient of self-preservation,
in such an attitude, but it did lead Eliot to a most extraordinary
caution in both private and public affairs. No doubt he recognized
the fact: in one letter to Mary Hutchinson, he accused himself of
suspiciousness and pusillanimity in human relationships.[37]

If Eliot was to continue successfully with the punishing routine
which he had established, it was necessary for him to 'refresh'
himself with occasional trips out of England. The visit to France in
1919 had been a great success, but just before Christmas of that year
he had a bronchial attack – the harbinger of much misery to come
and related, perhaps, to the habit of smoking which he had picked

up in earlier years – and although the Eliots spent a week's holiday with friends in Wiltshire he was still feeling quite ill in the middle of January. In addition, the strain of nursing her husband had affected Vivien's health and she, too, was not at all well. Since she had not been out of the country for six years, he decided to take her to Paris: but, on their brief visit there, he contracted influenza. It was a catalogue of woes.

Nevertheless, he was planning another walking tour in France for the summer of 1920. Vivien was worried about his health, however, and the prospect of his travelling so far by himself – as a result, Wyndham Lewis was persuaded to accompany him. They set off in August, travelling first to Paris, which came as a great relief after London,[38] then down to Saumur on the Loire – here they hired bicycles and, when Lewis's handlebars fell off, propelling him into the road, he imagined he had contracted lock-jaw from the graze. They followed the river down to Nantes, and then went to the north of Brittany. They sketched and walked and rode; they lived frugally, although Eliot listed each day's expenses in a little notebook which he carried with him.

It was in Paris that Eliot and Joyce met for the first time – at Pound's instigation, since he had entrusted a parcel to Lewis and Eliot which they were ordered to hand to Joyce. When it was opened in Joyce's presence, it contained, embarrassingly, a pair of old boots which Pound had decided to donate to the apparently impoverished novelist. Joyce, according to Lewis,[39] paid very little attention to Eliot and referred to him continually as 'your friend'. Eliot found him arrogant and, when Lewis disagreed, he spoke in his usual meticulous fashion: ' "He may not seem so," Eliot answered, in his grim Bostonian growl. "He may not seem arrogant, no." "You think he is as proud as Lucifer!" "I would not say Lucifer." ' And then, Lewis recorded Eliot's conversation later: ' "Oh yes. He is polite, he is polite enough . . . I should be better pleased if he were less polite." Eliot was very grim.' Nevertheless, he was despite himself impressed by Joyce's manner:[40] Joyce's artistic self-confidence was a quality which he noticeably lacked.

The holiday had been a great success. Eliot felt much improved by it and was as usual reluctant to leave France. But he was worried about Vivien – on the day he had left England, she had seemed tired and ill. One of the major problems which provoked such tiredness was the atmosphere of Crawford Mansions, of course; they had already begun flat-hunting before the visit to France, and had both been appalled at the cost of renting even an only reasonably decent place in London. When in October they did find one that seemed suitable, they became involved in tortuous negotiations with the previous tenant, and Eliot was so overwhelmed by it all that he felt unable to arrange any dates for the future;[41] when their attempts to move seemed about to fall through, he was close to desperation.[42] Once again, the common experience of life's problems seemed to induce in him a reaction far in excess of the facts. But the matter was finally settled and at the end of October they moved to 9 Clarence Gate Gardens – a little north of their previous address and close to Regents Park. It was part of a large Victorian mansion block, and the Eliots were to move to different apartments in the building over the next ten years.

Vivien Eliot, in one of her own compositions, has described the 'Mansion' with its jangling lifts, its wide and dark carpeted stair-cases, the beetles and crickets in the kitchen. The story,[43] apparently composed in the mid-nineteen-twenties when she began seriously to write fiction, concerns two characters, Ellison and Anthony, who as in much of Vivien's work seem closely modelled upon herself and her husband. Anthony returns from work and quietly hangs up his coat and hat – he has a book with him, which he has been carrying around all day in case he gets an opportunity to read it. He lingers in the hallway: Ellison might have a headache, or be irritable, or in a state of despair . . . he creeps towards his study, and finds Ellison lying upon the little bed which he keeps there. He bends over her and kisses her tentatively. Silence. Ellison asks, in a tired voice, if anything has happened. He replies, almost apologetically, that nothing has. Here we have the portrait of what is perhaps a fictional relationship, but one which suggests that Vivien quite understood the weariness and emptiness which can invade two people left alone together. One senses in this little sketch, however, the affection which she believes the husband still to possess for the wife. When the Eliots visited Katherine Mansfield in May of this year, she recorded the scene: 'They are just gone and the whole room is quivering. . . . Mrs E's voice rises, "Oh don't commiserate with Tom. He's *quite* happy".' But although Katherine Mansfield is rather dismissive of Vivien, she noticed how attentive and considerate Eliot was towards her. Despite the fact that they often lived apart there seems little doubt that at this stage Eliot was a kind husband – Lewis even accused him of having a 'wife obsession'.[44]

Vivien's father was taken ill with appendicitis in October, and it seemed so serious that she was afraid he might die at any moment. She was nursing him, and was herself on the edge of collapse. Throughout the latter months of 1920, Eliot's letters are full of depressed complaints: he was about to have an operation on his nose;[45] he had seen hardly anyone, and did not believe many people wished to see him;[46] he was unable to write;[47] his brain did not seem to be functioning;[48] the strain of caring for her father had given Vivien terrible migraines.[49] In fact, Charles Haigh-Wood seemed to be recovering, and then relapsed again at the end of December. The pressures were mounting upon Eliot, pressures which were to lead eventually to a nervous collapse.

His life was not entirely one of unassuaged woe, however. In September of this year, for example, he spent the weekend with the Woolfs at Monks House in Sussex. In her diary[50] Virginia Woolf noticed how his eyes shone out in what was otherwise a cramped and inhibited face (the brightness of his eyes was noticed by many people). She suspected him of a vanity which he tried hard to conceal just as, on a later occasion, she intuited a driving will beneath his somewhat diffident exterior.[51] Eliot relaxed as the weekend progressed, and started to talk about his own work. His main interest was in people and the creation of caricature; he wanted, he said, to compose a verse drama in which the characters from the 'Sweeney' poems would appear. This is an interesting remark, not only because it suggests Eliot's natural affinity with drama and the fact that he saw his poems in this context. He was, he told Virginia Woolf, interested in externals; it is possible that his detachment, of which so many contemporaries spoke, is simply the effect of Eliot looking at himself from the outside, arranging himself with his slow and infrequent gestures as an actor might. For a highly intelligent man with a sense of 'the Void', life itself might seem to be drained of inner significance and meaning – it thereby becomes a spectacle merely, a 'drama'. There are photographs of him with Virginia Woolf at Monks House, perhaps taken during this visit. The hair is neatly slicked back, the handkerchief in his top pocket carefully folded, and he has what Wyndham Lewis called his 'Gioconda smile'.

His interest in drama was not, at any rate, purely theoretical. He went to the theatre often and regularly attended, for example, the Restoration and Jacobean revivals of the Phoenix Society. With Lewis he would visit the London music halls, the brightly lit world of Marie Lloyd and Little Tich where sentimentality and grotesquerie, brutality and gracefulness, were the predominant notes. The 'halls' were also the halls of his imagination; he would attempt his own kind of performance in 'Sweeney Agonistes', and throughout his life he was fond of singing music-hall lyrics and was able to quote extensively from them. With Lewis, also, Eliot went to boxing matches – he had taken lessons at Harvard, and retained the interest of a timid man in that stylized but aggressive sport.

The problems of moving flats meant that he could not give his whole attention to the volume of essays which was even then going through the press, and, when he returned from his French holiday, he had to ask Vivien and Pound to assist him in reading the proofs. *The Sacred Wood* appeared in November and represented the apotheosis of Eliot's literary journalism. The essays, taken from the *Egoist*, *Athenaeum*, *The Times Literary Supplement* and *Art and Letters*, were concerned with criticism, poetry and drama (with the emphasis upon the latter). They were, in other words, occasional pieces, but with Eliot's genius for structure and order he turned them into something which is much more than the sum of their parts. He used to say that he had learned how to write prose from the example of F.H. Bradley and the instruction of Harold Joachim; in his journalism, he had adopted their manner, having abandoned their matter, and so brought to his literary criticism an air of clarity and logic. He characteristically begins with a judgment – that is to say, his perceptions seem instinctively to take that form – and then casts around for evidence which might support it. But where the assertions of judgment seem magisterial and final, the actual process of justifying, or elaborating upon, them is often vague or inconsistent. Critics have noticed how often, and with what ease, he will contradict himself, even in such key matters as the nature of 'belief' or poetic 'personality'. His tone of certainty and assurance, however, carries him over these difficulties – he exhibits a kind of

wilfulness, an extraordinary faith in his own perceptions and judgments which he does not feel it necessary properly to justify. There
is, of course, also an element of subtle bluff as he had once confessed
to Richard Aldington[52] – he has a habit of making recondite
references which are meant to impress rather than to inform. For
these essays are in a way performances – Eliot is contemplating
himself playing the role of critic, and there is a tone of oblique irony
evident in many of them. They are, as it were, dramatic monologues
no less rigorously 'worked up' than his poetry. But although his
generalizations succeed one another too rapidly and do not escape
inconsistency, his specific analyses of an individual writer or a single
passage are unerring. In these detailed judgments he spots lines
which he will later redeploy himself, or he unearths problems and
complexities which are intimately related to those of his own work –
the absence of coherent traditional ideas marring the work of Blake,
the lack of sentiment in Jonson, the weakness of a creative mind
which has to exercise itself in criticism. He found himself
everywhere, transforming sometimes dull or inexplicable lines into
plangent mirrors of his own preoccupations; that spontaneous
genius with which he dramatized his experiences also allowed him to
transform his private preoccupations into persuasive abstractions. It
is that which gives his critical essays their unity and their
consistency.

The Sacred Wood is perhaps best known for containing in handy
form some of his most potent generalizations – the 'objective
correlative' in the essay on *Hamlet*, and the entire argument of
'Tradition and the Individual Talent'. (The phrase 'disassociation
of sensibility' appeared a year later, although its presence is noticeable throughout this volume.) Such formulations were not new:
they had been implicit in all of his studies. In Babbitt's *Masters of
Modern French Criticism*, for example, he would have come across
the notion of tradition as 'the constant adjustment . . . of the
experience of the past to meet the changing needs of the present'.
And in Remy de Gourmont's essay on Laforgue there is the idea
that in living 'one acquires the faculty of dissociating intelligence
from sensibility'. Eliot had few original ideas, but he was immensely
susceptible to those of others – the act of creation was for him the act
of synthesis, both in his poetry and his prose. He brought to bear
upon such ideas a unique power of organization so that they seemed

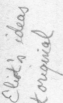

Eliot's ideas not original

to form a coherent and persuasive pattern. Simplicity, order, intensity, concentration are the principles he applied to that end, and from them emerged something very like (but not quite) a poetic creed. He differs from mentors like Babbitt and de Gourmont, however, in the apparent narrowness of his range; and yet this is also his strength. His attention is directed specifically and exclusively to literature, but he brings to its analysis all the moral and philosophical weight which he has borrowed or learned from elsewhere. As a result, in his exposition it becomes a larger and more significant thing. There is, for example, a strange oscillation in his vocabulary so that it possesses both a moral and critical weight – words like 'carelessness', 'decadence' and 'sensitivity' have a literary reference while being firmly established in an ethical context. This is the real importance of *The Sacred Wood*. Eliot provided literature with an order and certainty all the more potent because these were the qualities lacking in social and political life after the First World War: the older generation had lost its authority, and the younger had not found any way forward. His was not the first attempt to do so in England – T. E. Hulme had sketched out something of a similar kind, and in 1919 Clive Bell wrote a series of essays on 'Order and Authority' for the *Athenaeum*. But Eliot's stance was, in the end, more influential. He reaffirmed the status of literature, as a way both of understanding the larger culture and of disciplining private feelings and experience. His own need for order reflected that which existed among his generation; his own fears of fragmentation and meaninglessness ('the Void') were also theirs. He had, I believe, a clairvoyant sense of his time – clairvoyant because he found its preoccupations within himself.

But he was not happy with the book – he was never happy with anything he had just completed. A great deal of it ought to have been extensively revised, he thought,[53] and only five or six essays would ever be worth reprinting.[54] There were mixed reviews, and Eliot looked 'pale and ill'.[55] He complained to Virginia Woolf that although the critics described him as 'learned and cold' he was in fact neither.[56] The accusation of coldness seems to have bothered him: he explained on another occasion the difficulty of interpreting coldness and emotion in literature.[57] In imaginative work, of course, the discipline of steadily regarding an object and eliciting its central features can by the sentimental be mistaken for 'coldness'. On a private level, also, 'coldness' is often erroneously attributed to those who have a fervent desire for self-possession, for composure in the face of life. Conrad Aiken, who was seeing him regularly during this period, noticed only the occasional 'glint of guarded humour' in Eliot's manner.[58] Virginia Woolf noticed a twinkle in his eye when she made fun of him.[59] These are descriptions of a man labouring under a weight of self-restraint; it is not at all clear what was being restrained, but he sometimes speculated about the nature of 'the savage' and even its presence within himself.[60] He was similarly preoccupied with the artist's reaching down into the 'dark embryo' of the unconscious: poetry itself probably began with 'a savage beating a drum in the jungle'.[61] Certainly he was himself capable of violent emotions, and in her diary Vivien remembered an instance of his sudden and violent ferocity.[62] Charlotte Wolff, a palmist, discerned in him 'a seething, easily provoked temperament which may explode at any moment'.[63] His conventional demeanour concealed this, just as it concealed his rapid, nervous heart beat – rather in the manner of the truss which restrained his hernia, the intrusive mark of physical weakness and disorder.

Conrad Aiken has recounted one incident of this period which instigated the 'icy fury' of which Eliot was capable. He told Aiken that he was finding it impossible to write. He would come home in the evening, thinking that he might begin, and nothing happened. Aiken discussed Eliot's 'block' with a friend who in turn asked a psychiatrist for his opinion. The latter's message, relayed by Aiken to Eliot, was that it was the fear of not achieving perfection which was inhibiting him: 'He thinks he's God.' 'When I told Eliot . . . he was literally speechless with rage. The *intrusion*, quite simply, was one that was intolerable.'[64] Nevertheless it was this intrusion, Aiken believed, which broke the ice of his self-consciousness and instigated the extraordinary poem which transformed him into the leading poet of his generation.

6

The Collapse
1921–1922

As A RESULT of nursing her father through the last months of 1920, Vivien became ill, and after he had been declared out of danger she collapsed. She went first to a nursing home in March but, because of the expense involved, she returned to her bed in 9 Clarence Gate Gardens where she was in April. In May she retired to the seaside. Her major complaint seems to have been that of severe stomach pains, but her symptoms were only partly of a physical nature: she was suffering from general nervous exhaustion, which manifested itself as a self-consciousness close to panic or delirium. There were periods when only her husband and their maid, Ellen Kellond, were able to minister to her, and the flat became a kind of sanatorium. He would leave gatherings early in order to return to his wife, and he seemed 'tired and overworked'.[1]

Although they could hardly afford the expense, Eliot had decided that a country cottage would again be the best place for Vivien to recover her health, and he asked his friends to look out for one. Lytton Strachey met him at an Anglo-French poetry recital in June, and noticed that he seemed 'very sad and seedy'.[2] And Pound insisted to Wyndham Lewis that he must somehow get Eliot out of England.[3] But Eliot's distress was not caused by private matters alone, since he told Aldington that public events had provoked in him a mood of despair.[4] The year in which *The Waste Land* was written was one of intense political and economic discontent: the post-war 'boom' had collapsed, there were two million unemployed and the economic chaos was exacerbated by the indecisiveness of the coalition government. Eliot despised democracy, he explained to Aldington in the same letter, and he described in vivid terms the feelings of loathing and repugnance which the contemporary situation induced in him.

Eliot despised Democracy

It was precisely while under the strain of these difficult circumstances that he began consistently to work on the poem which he had entitled 'He Do The Police In Different Voices'. The actual chronology of the writing of this poem, which was later retitled *The Waste Land*, remains obscure. But certainly he must have started serious composition by the beginning of 1921 at the latest since, on 7 February, Wyndham Lewis told Sidney Schiff that Eliot had shown him a new and long poem in four parts which was a departure in his style.[5] In March Eliot saw *Love for Love* with Virginia Woolf, and she recorded part of their conversation: ' "We're not as good as Keats," I said. "Yes, we are," he replied, ". . . We're trying something harder." '[6] He already knew that his poem would be the longest he had ever attempted. By the beginning of April, he had enough of it written to contemplate the need for revision; he was also preparing to do more work upon it, and wanted to have something close to a final revision by the end of June. On 9 May, he told Quinn that he had a long poem partly written and wanted to finish it.[7] It was at some point in this period that he visited Richard Aldington in the country. They went to a churchyard in Padworth, Berkshire. Eliot inspected the graves, and then started to discuss Thomas Gray's 'Elegy Written in a Country Churchyard': 'Eliot said that if a contemporary poet, conscious of his limitations as Gray evidently was, would concentrate all his gifts on one such poem, he might achieve a similar success'.[8]

The fact that Eliot wanted to complete the poem by June may have been influenced by his expectation that he would be able to benefit from his wife's absence in May. And no doubt he also wanted to finish it before his mother arrived in England. He had already written to his brother, in the previous year, saying that he did not think he could ever be happy again until he could see his mother – the 'see' is underlined, as if to emphasize the physical proximity which he desired.[9] He suggested in this letter that she might come to him, since he could not afford to travel to America. The suggestion was taken up, and in June 1921 Charlotte Eliot arrived with Marian, Eliot's sister, and Henry himself. (Henry may have arrived a little earlier: certainly Eliot was looking for a separate bed sittingroom to accommodate him.) He had not seen his mother for six years, since his return to America with news of his precipitate marriage. It was a delicate situation – he knew that

Charlotte blamed Vivien for his decision to stay in England and, indeed, in his previous letter to Henry he had admitted that she would not want to see his wife. And so while the family were ensconced at 9 Clarence Gate Gardens, the Eliots moved to temporary lodgings at 12 Wigmore Street. Vivien was for a large part of the time safely away in the country but, despite Eliot's belief, it does seem likely that Charlotte would have insisted on meeting her daughter-in-law on this first visit to England – out of curiosity, if nothing else.

That Vivien did meet Charlotte, on this or a later visit, is evident from Osbert Sitwell's memoir in which he described her request to him and Sacheverell to help her set tea for Mrs Eliot. It seems, according to Sitwell, that Vivien very much resented Charlotte's treatment of her son and blamed her for the penury in which they were both forced to live. However, Sitwell says that on meeting Charlotte it was impossible to think ill of her – she appeared to be quite conventional and straightforward. She and her daughter seemed to be the quintessence of New England – sombrely clad, and polite to the point of stiffness.[10] Since Charlotte was then seventy-seven, Eliot was worried about the strain on her health which an extended visit would exert. But, as it turned out, she was extraordinarily energetic. He showed her around London, took her to the country, and was at pains to introduce her to those more respectable people who might demonstrate to her that he was well established in the country of his choice – there was, for example, a visit to Garsington to see Ottoline Morrell. But the inevitable tensions involved in such meetings were exacerbated by the fact that he was forced to adapt himself to a family to whom he no longer felt so close.[11]

There were other distractions throughout the summer. Through Sidney Schiff, Eliot had been introduced to Lady Rothermere; her husband was a newspaper proprietor who owned the *Daily Mail*, and it seems that she wanted something similar, although on a much smaller scale, of her own. She raised the possibility with Eliot of a literary review based in London. In July he discussed with his friend, Scofield Thayer, the possibility of an international review, partly financed by Lady Rothermere and with himself as London editor: Thayer had some experience of such matters, since in November 1919 he had become editor of the *Dial*, partly as a result of 'backing' it financially. In the previous year, Eliot and Pound had also contemplated starting their own magazine. But both schemes had, in the way of such things, come to nothing. Lady Rothermere's plan for a literary review established in London alone was much more definite, and she promised Eliot that he would be given a free hand as editor; she also agreed to subsidize the venture although she set definite limits on the amount of money available. There were, of course, difficulties involved: as an employee of Lloyds bank, he was not allowed to accept an outside salary so that, although he could be paid for his contributions to the magazine, he could not receive any payment for his editorship. The editorial work involved would be substantial, however, and leave him little time for his own writing. The negotiations with Lady Rothermere were complex, and Eliot called Vivien back from the country in order to assist him with them.[12] The plan seems to have been to bring out the first issue at the beginning of 1922, but it was going to be altogether a hard year for him and the first issue did not appear until October 1922.

All of his plans were going awry: by May the long poem was still in an inchoate shape and he was not able to complete it in June as he had once anticipated. But that may have been just as well, since certain unrelated events of that spring and summer helped him to crystallize the kind of work which he had in mind. The game of source-hunting is a barren one; it is only possible to suggest the general direction which Eliot himself was signalling in the course of the poem's composition. He was writing essays on Marvell, Dryden and the Metaphysical Poets. He was reading the later chapters of *Ulysses* and was explaining to Joyce that, although he wholly admired the achievement, he rather wished, for his own sake, that he had not read it.[13] In a later review, he noted that Joyce's great conception had been to use myth as a method for bringing order to the contemporary world.[14] The presence of a book which, in the same review, he described as 'the most important expression' of the present age was no doubt one that prompted his own ambition to create in poetry something similar: to make that large statement towards which all of his previous poetry seemed to be leading. In the summer he attended a performance of Stravinsky's *Le Sacre du Printemps* and at the end he stood up and cheered. Here again was an emblem for him of the way in which the complexities and even trivialities of contemporary existence, all that abruptness and dissonance which Stravinsky introduced into the texture of his music, could be rendered significant by an artistic vision which made use of the primeval drum beat. He was interested in those contemporary artists who simplified 'current life' and transformed it into 'something rich and strange'[15] – to purge it, perhaps, of the accidental complexities which rendered it unbearable. He had already been introduced to the Tarot pack – despite Eliot's animadversions on the subject, 'psychic' phenomena held a certain fascination for him. He liked, for example, to hear and to tell ghost stories. And, in the previous year, he had attended séances which had been organized by Lady Rothermere, at which P. D. Ouspensky, the 'mystic', presided.

But the burden of ordinary life was still very much with him. When his family left England towards the end of August, he suffered a severe reaction; the strain of their visit had exhausted both him and Vivien – she was ill, and the after effects had paralysed him also.[16] It had been a summer of drought – no rain fell for six months, and in his 'London Letter' for the *Dial* in August he recorded the incidence of a new type of influenza which left sensations of extreme dryness and a bitter taste in the mouth. By the beginning of September Eliot himself was experiencing severe headaches,[17] which seem to have been the symptoms of acute mental distress. His temperament was such that, in almost literal fashion, he lived 'off his nerves'. When he was exhausted or worried, as he then was, he suffered from a constant if undirected feeling of anxiety and dread.[18] Certainly his condition was alarming enough to convince Vivien that he needed help and, at her insistence, he visited a London specialist who promptly diagnosed some kind of nervous disorder. The specialist told him that he had to get away at once, for at least three months, and to regulate his life according to the doctor's regime. He had not expected such an alarming diagnosis of his condition, and the idea of such an abrupt change in his life filled him with apprehension.[19] He had at first been undecided whether to accept the doctor's verdict, since it was possible that he simply needed a holiday, but he felt his condition was deteriorating and his anxiety was heightened by the fact that the Americans were pursuing him for income tax. He really had no choice but to accept the doctor's advice, and he discussed the matter with his employers at the bank. They were willing to give him leave of absence for three months from 12 October ('nervous breakdown' is the reason given on his staff card).

He had decided to go to Margate, on the Kent coast, for a month, and then to rest in a cottage which Lady Rothermere had offered him, situated in the mountains behind Monte Carlo. Although the doctor had advised him to be on his own for a while, he could not bear the thought of such solitude and asked Vivien to come with him to Margate. They travelled down in the middle of October; by 22 October, they had moved into the Albemarle Hotel, from where Vivien wrote to Sidney Schiff on the 26th that her husband was improving quickly and was already looking 'younger and fatter and nicer';[20] he was keeping regular hours and was staying out in the air. At least Eliot was better able to turn his mind to the much delayed poem, and by the beginning of November he had written a draft of one portion of part III. This section was, in the final version of *The Waste Land*, 'The Fire Sermon'; since Eliot had told Schiff that he had been able to complete only about fifty lines in Margate,[21] it seems likely that he was referring to those which are written in pencil in the manuscript version, and which begin 'The river sweats'. These fifty lines were written while sitting in a shelter on the front ('On Margate Sands./I can connect/Nothing with nothing . . .'). He read nothing, and spent his time drawing people (in his characteristic fashion), or practising scales on the mandolin which Vivien had bought him.[22] There have been suggestions that by this time their marriage was in ruins, and that as a consequence 'A Game of Chess' sequence in the poem can be read as chronicling the death of the relationship. But this is clearly not the case. Not only did Eliot need Vivien with him in Margate (apart from anything else, she was writing letters on his behalf), but he was also eager to have her opinion on the poetry which he had managed to complete: at this stage, her approval was the prime consideration.[23] This is not a marriage soured by mistrust or antipathy, but one in which closeness (and even collaboration) is the dominant note.

This surely affects any reading of 'A Game of Chess' (and, by extension, the other supposedly autobiographical sections of the poem), since the element of artifice and fictional creation must play a large part in the creation of the anxious, harried woman in that section – 'What shall I do?' Indeed in the margins of the typewritten copy (which Eliot may have sent to Vivien when she was away in

May) Vivien has written 'Wonderful'. No nervous, anxious woman who saw herself mirrored in such a passage would write in this manner, and it is more likely to be the case that Eliot and Vivien were quite aware of their nervous predicament, recognizing the effect which it had upon themselves and others, and were at this stage inclined to make a kind of game out of it. They both possessed a strong theatrical streak and the element of willed drama in their relationship was not entirely negligible.

While at Margate, Eliot sought advice upon his next move. Ottoline Morrell had already suggested that he needed, not a 'nerve specialist', but the same kind of psychological therapy which she had undergone under the care of a Dr Roger Vittoz in Lausanne. She half-persuaded him of the efficacy of such treatment, and while at Margate he wrote to Julian Huxley – who had also been under the care of Vittoz – to elicit his opinion. Huxley wrote back recommending it. It is in this context that Eliot wrote to Aldington, on 6 November, explaining that he was not afflicted by 'nerves', as his original doctor had thought, but rather from 'aboulie', an emotional disorder that he had suffered all his life.[24] 'Aboulie' itself can be defined as a withdrawal into negative coldness, with an attendant loss of mental vigour and physical energy. In other words, as he said, his 'emotions' rather than his 'mind' were at fault – it has to be remembered, of course, that it was always his emotions which he feared and distrusted. He was the passive sufferer, the Tiresias who could not act.

After consultations with Vivien, he changed his plans. He decided not to take up Lady Rothermere's offer of a cottage in the Alpes Maritimes, and made arrangements to go instead to Lausanne and begin Vittoz's treatment. He travelled back to London from Margate in the middle of November (Vivien had gone back separately about a fortnight before, as soon as her husband was properly 'settled') and then, after a brief stay in London, they went together to Paris. Here he left Vivien (she was going to her own sanatorium just outside the city, and stayed with the Pounds for a period) while he travelled on to Lausanne. Before he left, he met Pound and showed him the long poem which was still incomplete.

At Lausanne he booked into the Hotel Ste Luce, which had been recommended by Ottoline Morrell, and began his treatment under Vittoz. Dr Vittoz was an analyst who had been in practice since 1904

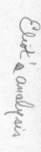

and was pre-Freudian in his training. His method of treatment was an unusual one in which the emphasis was on (in lay speech) taking the patient 'out of himself'. His patients were required to perform simple tasks over and over again, and were asked to solve puzzles. Vittoz also believed in a contemporary version of the 'laying on of hands' in which he would by physical contact and suggestion draw off the weight of nervousness or self-absorption which incapacitated or paralysed those like Eliot who came to see him. He appeared to understand Eliot's condition, and at the time seemed a far more appropriate doctor than the one Eliot had consulted in London. Certainly Eliot was pleased with the treatment – he liked Vittoz very much, and trusted his judgment.[25]

He was, in fact, given the same room as Ottoline Morrell had had on her visit – he was happy with the hotel, and Lausanne itself was a very quiet town in which banks and chocolate shops were then the most noticeable features. It was too foggy, in the period he was there, to see the mountains but he listened to the playing of the orchestra[26] and tried to relax. As a result of his treatment, he told his brother, he was learning to collect his thoughts and to cease worrying in his usual fashion; he hoped, as a result, he would be able to take some of the burden off Vivien who had had to do so much of the 'thinking' for him in the past[27] – again, one sees the extent to which he relied upon her still. Indeed there were times now when he felt calmer than he had for a long time – and, in an interesting aside in a letter to Ottoline Morrell, he compared this calmness to that which he had known as a child.[28] We have a picture of a neurotic and over-anxious man who for the first time was learning to release himself from formal restraints, to relax and depart from that strict order which he had imposed upon himself and which had caused so much suffering, to retreat from worldly cares into that amorphous sea which he had known as a child, to slide out . . . and now, in a trance as he was later to explain to Virginia Woolf, he wrote the final sections of *The Waste Land*. 'I wasn't even bothering whether I understood what I was saying,' he said in an interview much later;[29] and we see in the plangent rhythms of 'What The Thunder Said', which he wrote in this blessed state, a return to the music of Eliot – the music which he had otherwise suppressed or tightened into strict and undeviating shapes. Passages which he had written in his years at Harvard occur in this sequence, as though they had long been held in suspension and could only now emerge – in a shape which he did not attempt to control and which was in a sense 'inspired'.

The poem was now more or less finished. Eliot returned to London in January (by way of Paris, where once again he offered the manuscript for Pound's inspection) and on 24 January Pound wrote to him, 'Complimenti, you bitch. I am wracked by the seven jealousies'. (Indeed the ambitious scale of the poem seems to have prompted Pound to begin serious work again on his Cantos.) Pound had now been working on the original bundle of manuscripts and typescripts for some time. 'The thing now runs from "April . . ." to "shantih" without a break,' he wrote in the same letter, although in its earlier versions the poem had not run from 'April' at all but from a dramatic pastiche in which the protagonist is a conventional man-about-town. That passage had now gone, as had much else, and the 'nineteen pages' which Pound praised were the result of his own 'Caesarian Operation'. Some further correspondence followed after Eliot's return to London, correspondence which revealed what a weak hold he had upon the poem at this point. He asked Pound if he should omit the verse on Phlebas, should he use 'Gerontion' as a prelude, should an epigraph from Conrad be used since it would help to elucidate the poem?[30] The answer, in each case, was in the negative. Where Eliot was distrustful or uncertain of what he had done, wishing to clarify it with other material, Pound found its very resistance to interpretation – the cold, hard images and rhythmic passages which he had first espoused in the principles of Imagism – to be the key to its power.

The original poem had been quite different, since it was one in which Eliot freely developed his gift for dramatic impersonation and stylistic allusiveness. Its first four sections had been introduced by poetry which is as close to parody as he ever got: the music-hall monologue of a rake, the stiffened replica of Elizabethan narrative which remains as the opening of Part II, a piece of misogynistic satire in the manner of Pope, and the seaman's yarn which began 'Death by Water' – the last reminiscent in tone of the stories which he wrote as a schoolboy in the *Smith Academy Record*. But if these passages veer close to parody or pastiche they are still not simply 'imitations' but rather the creative borrowing of another style and syntax which releases a plethora of 'voices' and perceptions. Observers like Auden and Edmund Wilson noticed the variety of

'characters' which seemed to exist within the personality of Eliot –
V. S. Pritchett described him as 'a company of actors inside one suit,
each twitting the others . . .'[31] – but they recognized something
which is displayed in a much more intense manner in poetry such as
this. Eliot found his own voice by first reproducing that of others – as
if it was only through his reading of, and response to, literature that
he could find anything to hold onto, anything 'real'. That is why
Ulysses struck him so forcibly, in a way no other novel ever did.
Joyce had created a world which exists only in, and through, the
multiple uses of language – through voices, through parodies of
style. The novel is, in that sense, the dramatic epic of the word. Its
range encompasses the whole literary tradition which begins with
Homer and, presumably, ends with Joyce; just as he will place the
same scene in the perspectives of late romantic prose, scientific
description or conventional journalese, so he also parodies the
history of prose style from Anglo-Saxon to Romantic narrative.
Joyce had an historical consciousness of language and thus of the
relativity of any one 'style'. The whole course of Eliot's development would lead him to share such a consciousness. His early
philosophical investigations had been concerned with the primacy
of 'interpretation' and the irrecoverability of any original 'meaning'
which is being interpreted. And in this year he defined 'wit' as the
recognition 'implicit in the expression of every experience, of other
kinds of experience which are possible'.[32] In the closing sequence of
The Waste Land itself he creates a montage of lines from Dante,
Kyd, Gérard de Nerval, the *Pervigilium Veneris* and Sanskrit. Eliot,
a thoroughgoing sceptic and relativist as he himself claimed to be,
understood exactly what Joyce was trying to do and in *The Waste
Land* achieved something of a comparable order.

Why, then, did he wish to introduce the entire sequence with
'Gerontion' and with a quotation from Conrad's *Heart of Darkness*? The quotation from the latter which Eliot found helpful in
elucidating the poem occurs just before Kurtz's death when, at the
moment of 'complete knowledge' he cries out, ' "The horror! The
horror!" '. For the complete knowledge is, in this novel, also the
knowledge of emptiness – both his own and that of the world. There
is no meaning to be found, anywhere. And similarly in 'Gerontion'
we have a persona which exists within broken phrases and half-
remembered cadences, and the poem embodies an attempt to create

meaning which fails. Siegfried Sassoon heard Eliot insist, in the summer before he travelled to Lausanne, that 'all great art is based on a condition of fundamental boredom – passionate boredom'.[33] And in the same year Eliot pointed out to Virginia Woolf how Joyce had demonstrated the 'futility' of all English literary styles.[34] Some years later he explained that past and present were used in *The Waste Land* as different versions of 'futility' also.[35] There is no 'truth' to be found, only a number of styles and interpretations – one laid upon the other in an endless and apparently meaningless process. This was the vision of the world which he had had as a student of philosophy, and it was the informing principle of the original version of *The Waste Land*.

But that is neither a tragic nor even a particularly lugubrious view of the world: in a paper to the Harvard Philosophical Club, he stated that pessimism of this kind encouraged a kind of 'cheerfulness'.[36] A world of 'appearances' is the material for parody, drama and wit. And so the poem in its original state is dramatic, highly stylized, working by contrasts and depending upon the resources of comic invention. When Ezra Pound began working on it, he removed most of the elements of stylistic reproduction – he considered the sequence in the manner of Pope to be simply parodic – and curbed the tendency of the poem towards dramatic and fictional exposition. Pound was, perhaps, the purer poet of the two; certainly he was never much interested in Eliot's skill as a dramatist ('oh them cawkney woices . . .' he said of *Murder in the Cathedral*)[37]. And it might fairly be said in retrospect that he quite misunderstood the essential nature of Eliot's genius: on a private level, it was Pound's very lack of scepticism and relativism which destroyed him. But Pound had an extraordinarily good ear, and he located in the typescripts of *The Waste Land* the underlying rhythm of the poem – the music of which Eliot was so distrustful and which he surrounded with more deliberate and dramatic kinds of writing. Pound heard the music, and cut away what was for him the extraneous material which was attached to it. It had emerged freely only in the last section, 'What The Thunder Said', which Eliot wrote at Lausanne – the part which Pound approved practically without comment. And it was surely the music of the poem which affected its first readers; like Swinburne's poetry sixty years before, *The Waste Land* was sung and chanted by undergraduates – they heard the music, too.

In other words, Pound mistook or refused to recognize Eliot's original *schema* and as a result rescued the poetry. Eliot's most significant feelings, as opposed to his conscious intentions, are attached to a certain kind of rhythm derived from his earliest reading (all his life he could quote the 'thumpers' of his youth) and to certain literary texts which have been transformed in memory. His feelings cluster around literary cadences; the images and themes of *The Waste Land* are both his own and not his own, a continual oscillation between what is remembered and what is introduced, the movement of other poets' words just beneath the surface of his own. This accounts for the strange echoic quality which his poetry has; and it is related, also, to its peculiar flatness of emphasis, so that the reader must lend to the poetry the inflections of his own voice in order to give it shape.

This quality of intervention or interpretation on the part of the reader marked, on another level, the history of the reception of the poem. Pound imposed an order on it which it did not originally possess; as a result of his removal of the original context of the poem, it has become much easier for readers and critics to provide their own – to suggest a 'theme' which the abbreviated sequences might be claimed to fit. *The Waste Land* provided a scaffold on which others might erect their own theories; so it is that it has been variously interpreted as personal autobiography, an account of a collapsing society, an allegory of the Grail and spiritual rebirth, a Buddhist meditation. Thus *The Waste Land* began a process of which Eliot has been the principal beneficiary, or victim. In the absence of philosophical or religious certainties, his poetry has been invested with a gnomic or moral force which it can hardly carry. A thin wash of 'great truths' has been placed over *The Waste Land* and over Eliot's succeeding work. The poet himself was to be treated as a kind of seer, a position most unsuited to him.

Part of his unsuitability for such a role can be recognized from the fact that he allowed Pound to change the poem in so radical a manner. He was always timid or cautious in his judgment of his own work, of course; but there were other factors at work: after his return to London, he was too sick, tired and harassed to concentrate upon the matter. But his compliance with Pound's recommendations suggests a somewhat cavalier attitude towards something which he had, as it were, finally got out of his system. Despite his

reputation for precision and meticulousness, this is, in fact, characteristic of his attitude towards his work: when it was completed, he
simply did not want to have any more to do with it (the peculiarly
eccentric nature of Eliot's texts, which vary from edition to edition,
and his inability to date his own work correctly suggest the sense in
which he removed himself from what he had accomplished). But in
the final version of *The Waste Land*, he could see at once the point of
Pound's revisions since it was one which conformed to Eliot's
characteristic demands from his own work: it was sharp, economical
in its effects, and made a definite assault upon the preconceptions
and conventions of the audience of the period. Certainly he was
aware of the worth of the poem in this final form – he told both John
Quinn[38] and Virginia Woolf[39] that he thought it the best thing he had
done so far, and Virginia Woolf sensed that he felt more secure and
happy as a result.[40] He was also anxious to get it into print as soon as
possible and shortly after his return from Lausanne he wrote to
Scofield Thayer, his friend and editor of the *Dial*, offering it to him
for his magazine.

The stay in Lausanne had been a happy period when he was able
to abandon the daily life which so much oppressed him; but, as is
often the case, his return to the same conditions marked a redoubled
awareness of the burden which they placed upon him. Dr Vittoz's
treatment acted in this sense only as a palliative, and when back in
London he caught influenza and was very depressed.[41] His wife had
returned from France, and had again contracted the feverish
neuralgia of which she was so often the victim. In addition they had
decided to let their flat at Clarence Gate Gardens and move from
March to the end of June to the flat in Wigmore Street which they
had occupied in the previous year. Under these combined strains,
he once more began to retreat into the horrors of the previous
autumn. Life once again became an ordeal through which he had to
pass.[42] On Eliot's urging, Vivien went back to Paris, but her
condition seemed to be deteriorating there and she returned to
London in April still very weak; then he fell ill again, and Vivien had
to nurse him as well. The situation was that of *maladie à deux*, in
which the constant cycle of illnesses exhausted both of them. He was
getting behind in his work (not least of which was the responsibility
of negotiating with Lady Rothermere over the new magazine). In a
despairing letter to Sidney Schiff, he described how sickness and

exhaustion were destroying his time and energy, and speculated about the possibility of giving up writing altogether.[43] Richard Aldington told Pound that Eliot seemed to be 'going to pieces',[44] and Pound explained to William Carlos Williams that since Eliot was 'at the last gasp' something had to be done for him quickly.[45]

And so Pound revived an idea which he had floated in the previous year, that of arranging an income for him which would relieve him of his time-wasting duties at the bank. In March he initiated the Bel Esprit scheme, under the terms of which thirty people would guarantee Eliot £10 per year. The three initial subscribers were Pound, Aldington and the novelist, May Sinclair. A circular was sent out to likely guarantors, emphasizing that the plan had been drawn up without Eliot's knowledge: 'The facts are that bank work has diminished his output of poetry, and that his prose has grown tired. Last winter he broke down and was sent off for three months' rest. . . .'[46] John Quinn pledged some money, but few other subscribers came forward to make the scheme work and it quietly collapsed – Pound did, however, manage to get an 'emergency grant' of two hundred dollars for him from the Authors Club in New York. Although the scheme was not formally abandoned for many months, part of the reason for its failure was no doubt the fact that Eliot himself disapproved of it. For one thing, he had been raised in the Puritan tradition of 'self-help': Bel Esprit seemed too much like charity.[47] And, for another, he was not at all as anxious to leave the bank as others were on his behalf: he was now earning £500 per annum, with a bonus, and the income at least afforded him a measure of independence as well as security.

But his health continued to run down and Vivien described, in retrospect, to Aldington how he was close to a state of collapse: although he was under contract to write a 'London Letter' for the *Dial*, he could write nothing and asked Vivien what he should say; he was in too much despair to care what he said.[48] It seems that Vivien appealed to her father for help, and in May he invited Eliot to take a holiday in Lugano at his expense. The offer came as a great relief, and indeed rescued him from the second nervous breakdown which he believed to be hanging over him.[49] He was anxious in advance about the journey – he derived no advantage from such trips if there was the slightest difficulty with travelling arrangements,[50] the sign of a most nervous character – but the vacation was a great success. He was in Switzerland for two weeks, and went walking, bathing and boating; the weather was very good, and he made small excursions on the lake. He also visited Ezra Pound at Verona, and spent about two days with him. At the beginning of June, he returned to London feeling in good health – in much better health, in fact, than on his return from Lausanne in January.

Shortly afterwards, he and Vivien made preparations to move out of Wigmore Street and back to Clarence Gate Gardens – as always with the Eliots, the process was 'hell'; they quarrelled with the landlord of Wigmore Street and tried to get money for damages from their tenant at Clarence Gate Gardens. Vivien was exhausted by the move, and her condition was not materially assisted by the medical treatment she was now receiving. Part of the therapy consisted of a strict regimen of her diet, and the near starvation which it induced seemed to provoke other symptoms in her, such as colitis. Their faith in doctors was, as a result, rather undermined.[51] But they managed to rent a four-roomed labourer's cottage at Bosham for the summer and, despite the cramped conditions and the bad weather, Vivien's health seemed slowly to improve. Eliot came down each weekend, if he could; he did not like to leave her for more than a fortnight. With Vivien safely in the country, and his own health improved, he set to work again on all those matters he had been postponing. The most important unfinished business which he had to pick up was that of Lady Rothermere's review; he had kept her waiting for almost a year and now he had to face the matter seriously. There were some difficult negotiations, the result being that the paper would be financed and administered by Lady Rothermere and that Eliot would take charge of the contributors and their work. It was her paper rather than his, but nevertheless he would be the editor. He had already been planning the shape and size of the magazine – he wanted it to look simple and austere, and it was to be a quarterly.[52] There had been some problem in deciding upon an appropriate name, and Vivien suggested calling it the *Criterion*: that was, incidentally, the name of a restaurant where she used to dine with her former lover, Charles Buckle. In fact, Vivien actively collaborated with her husband on the editorial preparations for the magazine – she wrote from Bosham to Ottoline Morrell that she was devoting a great deal of time to it.[53] Nevertheless by July he had to hire a shorthand typist two evenings a week in order to deal with the correspondence involved, and by late summer he was mailing circulars to prospective subscribers. Eliot was also concerned to gather around him a number of sympathetic acquaintances who might help him to plan the contents of the magazine. These included Herbert Read, F.S. Flint and Harold Monro (friends like Bonamy Dobrée and Frank Morley joined the gathering later) and over the next few years they started to meet regularly – first at the Commercio, a restaurant in Soho, and later at the Swiss Hotel; lunches were held at the Cock public house in Fleet Street and then at the Grove public house in South Kensington. Richard Church, another member of what inevitably became known as the 'Criterion group', recalled that Eliot seemed always to be the centre of attention despite his characteristic reticence and taciturnity. He spoke with an 'old-fashioned precision', and there was always a cutting edge to his conversation which suggested, if it did not exhibit, 'merciless satire'.[54]

From the start, Eliot was concerned to employ the best critics, and not only those in England.[55] He did not want the magazine to become lodged in an English provincial tradition, but saw it rather as a magazine for Europe. The nucleus of writers was indeed English (he found many of them from the pages of *The Times Literary Supplement*), but he also took the opportunity which his editorship offered him of establishing relations with eminent men of letters throughout Europe – among them Valéry Larbaud, Ortega Y Gasset and Ernst Robert Curtius. He took his responsibilities very seriously indeed. If he failed, he told Aldington (who was to become assistant editor), he would lose a great deal of prestige.[56] Vivien shared his anxieties – he would 'stand or fall' by the *Criterion*, she said.[57] Eliot's fears were exacerbated by his suspicion that he was disliked by a large number of 'literary people'[58] – 'shits' was how he once described them to Conrad Aiken – and that there were many people who were waiting for him to fail. His suspicions were not entirely unjustified, although he tended to exaggerate the extent of his isolation or alienation in letters to genuinely isolated figures such as Wyndham Lewis or Ford Madox Ford; his critical opinions – that English poetry stopped around 1800, for example[59] – were indeed designed to outrage conventional sentiment. Siegfried Sassoon has recalled how Edmund Gosse dismissed Eliot as 'a conceited literary humbug' for having condemned *Hamlet*.[60]

Certainly the enormity of the task he had set himself with the *Criterion* was something of a strain. He had to mediate between Lady Rothermere, who really wanted a fashionably 'cultivated' magazine, and contributors like Lewis whose work he wished to publish. And it seems that on occasions he felt it necessary to consult Lady Rothermere's preferences in such matters – in September of the following year, he reassured Lewis that she would like the 'Zagreus' episodes of the novel Lewis was then writing.[61] Since Eliot was working all day at the bank, he could devote only his evening hours to the magazine. That additional burden of work may have been the reason why Charlotte Eliot was so opposed to his taking on the editorship and hoped he would give it up.[62] He attempted to reassure her by telling her that he was planning another long poem which would be of a more optimistic nature than *The Waste Land*.[63] But that may just have been whistling in the dark: it is possible, after all, that he loaded himself with banking, journalistic and editorial tasks in order not to have to think too much about his own creative work: he distrusted himself too much to rely upon its regular appearance. But in the end, as he explained many years later,[64] the *Criterion* gave him more freedom for his creative writing and changed the whole course of his life. The first issue was published in October 1922. The contents included an essay by George Saintsbury on 'Dullness', an essay on *Ulysses* by Valéry Larbaud and a piece by Herman Hesse; and sandwiched between a short story by May Sinclair and an article by Sturge Moore, there also appears *The Waste Land*.

Negotiations had in fact been continuing throughout this year over the publication of the poem. Eliot had, as we have seen, asked Scofield Thayer how much he would offer for its publication in the *Dial* as far back as January, when it was still being pressed into final shape. Thayer proposed 150 dollars, which Eliot considered to be a reasonable price until he heard that Thayer had offered twice that sum to George Moore for a short story. Eliot, in turn, demanded, by wire, £856. Thayer was furious, and there was a rancorous exchange between the two men. Pound had already introduced Eliot to the publisher, Horace Liveright, in Paris; he offered to print the poem in volume form, with an advance of 150 dollars and a 15 per cent royalty. Eliot already had a contract with Alfred Knopf, however, and was supposed to offer his next two books to that firm. And so in

April he wrote to Knopf explaining his situation.[65] Knopf agreed to waive his rights to the poem, and Eliot raised the possibility of another prose book within a year.

In spite of the difficulties with Scofield Thayer, Thayer was still anxious to acquire *The Waste Land* and the managing editor of the *Dial*, Gilbert Seldes, came to an arrangement with Liveright: the *Dial* would print the poem and also give Eliot the magazine's annual award of two thousand dollars; they also agreed to take 350 copies of Liveright's book. It was, under the circumstances, an ideal arrangement and for the success of the negotiations Eliot had to thank John Quinn. Since the middle of 1922 he had been in correspondence with Quinn over questions of translation, anthology and periodical rights: he was not an author who professed no interest in, or understanding of, the commercial matters involved in the publication of his work. In gratitude for Quinn's help – the man was, in fact, working himself to an early death on behalf of a number of artists and writers – he sent the original manuscript of *The Waste Land* to him, as well as the manuscripts of his early poetry (for the latter, Quinn paid him). Eliot explained that he did not expect these manuscripts to have much literary value – a great many of the poems had never been published, and he appealed to Quinn to ensure that they never were.[66] His wish has been fulfilled.

The Waste Land appeared in the November issue of the *Dial*, just one month after its publication in the *Criterion*. Eliot had originally suggested to Thayer that the poem might be spread over four issues of the magazine – he was not sufficiently convinced of its organic coherence, in other words, that he wished to insist upon single publication. He had even originally thought of splitting it into two issues of the *Criterion*, in the hope of bringing in a few more readers, but Pound objected to that arrangement. And although Pound had referred to *The Waste Land* as a 'series of poems' in the prospectus for Bel Esprit, it was he who finally persuaded Eliot that it should appear as one sequence. Liveright published the American edition in December 1922, of 1,000 copies (it quickly went into a second edition, also of 1,000 copies). And in September of the following year, the Woolfs published the poem under the imprint of the Hogarth Press. Eliot preferred the smaller size of their edition, although it was still affected by misprints as a result of his poor proofreading.

The published editions of *The Waste Land* were distinguished from the magazine versions by the addition of Eliot's notes. He had originally included them in order to avoid the charges of plagiarism which had been levelled at his earlier poetry. But the poem still did not seem long enough to 'make' a book, and he expanded them. As a result there emerged what he called his 'remarkable exposition of bogus scholarship'.[67] Certainly there is an air of bravura about it which, as in his critical allusions, comes close to posturing. He quotes, for example, a passage from Bradley's *Appearance and Reality* – '. . . the whole world for each is peculiar and private to that soul.' – although in the *Monist* of October 1916 he had said of the same passage, 'Never has it been put in a form so extreme'. And yet such dramatic gestures paid off: according to Pound, it was the presence of the notes which provoked the attention of the reviewers. They were, of course, also to provide much needed fodder for academic critics since they seemed to lend thematic or structural coherence to a poem which was otherwise obscure.

To Eliot's contemporaries the poem came as a profound shock, although not always a pleasant one. Pound wrote in July of this year that it was 'the justification of the "movement" of our modern experiment since 1900'. William Carlos Williams, on the other hand, considered it to be a blow against the 'new art' which was about to emerge in America: 'I felt at once that it had set me back twenty years',[68] in what seemed then to be an unequal struggle with the European tradition. The reviews in the English press were variously baffled and respectful, although some of the less fashionable critics, like Squire in the *London Mercury*, pronounced it incomprehensible. They were probably right: Conrad Aiken, who reviewed it in the *New Republic*, believed the poem to succeed 'by virtue of its incoherence, not of its plan; by virtue of its ambiguities, not of its explanations'. He called it the work of an 'intensely literary consciousness'.[69] Most of the poem's celebrants saw it as a public statement, an expression of the 'malaise of our time', while its detractors considered it to be the expression of a wholly private sensibility and a kind of literary game. Already we see the makings of that ambiguity which has always surrounded the poem. Eliot himself thought the reviews on the whole unfavourable, although some of the critics were too cowardly to say that they did not like it.[70]

It was not with the reviewers, however, that the reputation of *The*

Waste Land was first made but rather with undergraduates and young writers who saw it as the revelation of a modern sensibility. With its 'jazz' rhythms, its images of urban and suburban life, its fashionable use of anthropological myth, its introduction of quotation and parody – this was, as Edmund Wilson said, 'the great knockout up to date'.[71] Cyril Connolly recalled 'The veritable brainwashing, the total preoccupation, the drugged and haunted condition which the new poet produced on some of us . . . of whom one could find out nothing but that he was poor and unhappy'.[72] A cult of 'The Waste Landers' developed. Peter Quennell read the poem to guests at a Conservative party fête and, in Evelyn Waugh's *Brideshead Revisited*, the aesthete Anthony Blanche recited it from the window of his college rooms. The poem was widely imitated by young or aspiring poets, and Brian Howard said that, 'It became such a plague that the moment the eye encountered, in a newly arrived poem, the words "stone", "dust" or "dry" one reached for the waste-paper basket'.[73] Within less than a decade, *The Waste Land* had attained a kind of eminence from which it has never been dislodged although, in later life, Eliot felt himself to have been imprisoned by its success.[74]

By the middle of 1922, however, such success was merely hypothetical: the poem had been written, but it seemed unlikely that he would have the time, energy or enthusiasm to work again on anything of such ambitious proportions. Ezra Pound was still collecting money for his Bel Esprit fund and then, in July, Ottoline Morrell established a complementary scheme called the Eliot Fellowship Fund. On its committee were Leonard Woolf, the Cambridge mathematician Harry Norton, Richard Aldington and Ottoline Morrell herself, and almost at once Virginia Woolf was writing to people who might be willing to donate £10 each year in order to rescue Eliot from the bank. Although she complained that Aldington was suggesting that Eliot was 'very ill' when he was, in fact, clearly not so,[75] she emphasized in her letters to putative subscribers that he had 'broken down' once already and had now to care for an invalid wife. The peculiar aspect of both rescue bids is that the participants did not seem to know, or understand, Eliot's own views on the matter – indeed, it is possible that he himself was unsure of them. One of the major reasons for his disapproval of Pound's scheme had been that at least bank work allowed him a

Top left Charlotte Champe Eliot.
Top right T. S. Eliot.
Above Henry Ware Eliot.
Right William Greenleaf Eliot.

5. **Above** Eliot with his mother, his sister Margaret and cousin Henrietta outside 2635 Locust Street, St Louis, 1896.   6. **Below left** With his nurse Annie Dunne.
7. **Below right** In the schoolyard of the Mary Institute, 1896.

Above With Thomas McKittrick, 1896.   **9. Below** Eliot with his cousins on the beach at Gloucester where his father had built a summer home, Eastern Point in 1896.

Opposite At Eastern Point, Gloucester, aged about twelve. **11. Above left** Eliot, 1899.
Above right Photographed at the piano by his brother Henry, 1899.
Below Photographed with his cousin Frederick by his brother Henry in 1903.

14. **Above left** Eliot sailing. He retained a deep feeling for the sea all his life.   15. **Above right** Eliot in his first year at Harvard.   16. **Below** Eliot, 1910.   17. **Opposite** Eliot as a young man. It was probably during his year in France that he started to smoke French cigarettes and he remained a consistent smoker until his last years.

18. Above The guests at a house party at the home of W. S. Blunt in 1914. (*left to right*) Victor Platt, Sturge Moore, W. B. Yeats, Wilfred Scawen Blunt, Ezra Pound, Richard Aldington, and F. S. Flint.   **19. Below** Eliot at Garsington, the home of Lady Ottoline Morrell (*left*), with A. N. Whitehead (*centre*).

. **Above** In the garden at Garsington. Inscribed on the back of the photograph in Eliot's
ndwriting ' "left to right" Lord David Cecil, Leslie Hartley, Anthony [Asquith], TSE,
dward Sackville-West. At Garsington.' **21. Below left** Percy Wyndham Lewis by G. C.
eresford. **22. Below right** Lytton Strachey and Virginia Woolf.

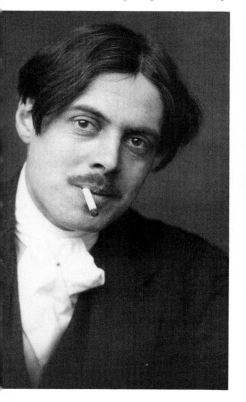

23. **Top** Vivien Eliot at Garsington.
24. **Above** The Eliots in Sussex, 1919.
25. **Right** Vivien Eliot, 1919.

26. **Left** Photographed outside Faber and Gwyer in 1926 by his brother Henry.
27. **Above** Vivien in the Eliots' London flat.
28. **Below** Eliot's mother and sister Marian with Eliot photographed by his brother Henry on their visit to England in 1921.

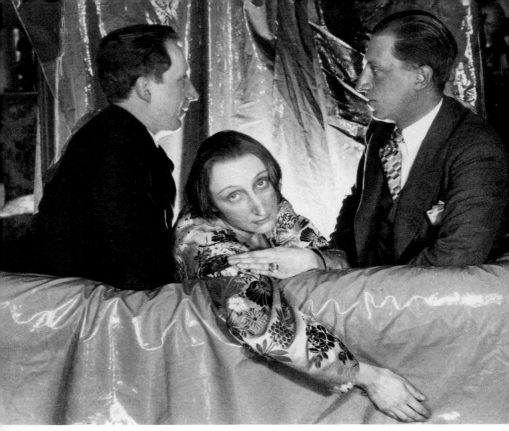

29. Above Sacheverell, Edith and Osbert Sitwell by Cecil Beaton. **30. Below left** W. H. Auden, Christopher Isherwood and Stephen Spender in 1937. **31. Below right** Richard Aldington by Howard Coster. **32. Opposite** Lady Ottoline Morrell by Cecil Beaton.

33. Above T. S. Eliot at his desk at Faber and Faber.
34. Below At a meeting at Faber and Faber with Frank Morley and Geoffrey Faber in 1948.

36. Above Eliot in the garden and with George the cat at 57 Chester Terrace, 1928.
Below Vivien Eliot, Ahmé and Maurice Haigh-Wood and T. S. Eliot in Rome.

38. Eliot with his sister Marian and sister-in-law on a visit to New Hampshire, 1936.

measure of independence, and he did not want to become an object of charity to his friends. But he prevaricated. He allowed the Eliot Fellowship Fund to go ahead with its target of finding £300 per annum, and then in September told Virginia Woolf that he could not leave the bank unless he received £500 per annum, although he would accept less if receiving the money did not carry with it a moral obligation to give up banking;[76] Virginia Woolf wondered why he had not told them this in the first place. Throughout these negotiations he seemed shy and awkward, covered with embarrassment when money was mentioned. His psychology, she told Roger Fry, 'fascinates and astounds'.[77] The month before, Conrad Aiken had said, 'He, poor devil, cries out for analysis. . . .'[78] Certainly his fear of life was such that he was subject to panic in difficult situations. But the problem was mainly one of indecision: should he keep the security of the bank and remain, as it were, a model of Puritan probity or should he rely upon the charity of others? The choice of the former was in the end inevitable for a man such as Eliot, but it is clear that he did not wish to disappoint or alienate those who were working so assiduously on his behalf. Prevarication combined with fear of humiliation left him frozen in indecision; his only thought was to escape from the whole situation.[79]

But there was no escape – 'There never is . . .', he wrote later;[80] the demands upon him were increasing, and within them one can see him twist and turn. Despite her summer of recuperation and her regime of diet and exercise, Vivien's improvement was only temporary. She collapsed again in September, and Eliot once more found himself acting as nurse and comforter. He could not concentrate on his other duties,[81] however pressing they were. Vivien herself was acutely conscious of the strain she imposed upon him, and had already offered to leave him if her constant illness prevented him from working:[82] she was, she told Aldington, a constant burden upon him.[83] And she explained to Sidney Schiff how the *Criterion* was a considerable achievement for a man who had to minister to a sick wife.[84] It is clear that she had great respect and admiration for her husband's work, but it was an admiration not without pain for someone so vicariously involved: the publication of *The Waste Land*, she said in the same letter to Schiff, had been rather terrible for her since it seemed so much a part of her, and she of it.

Eliot went for a fortnight's rest to Worthing in October but, almost as soon as he returned, another blow fell upon him. In the *Liverpool Daily Post* of 16 November, an article appeared on the Bel Esprit scheme which stated that the sum of £800 had been collected for him. It continued, 'The joke was that he accepted the gift calmly and replied, "Thank you all very much, I shall make good use of your money, but I like the bank".' The article then went on to describe Eliot's 'nervous breakdown'. He immediately took up the matter with a solicitor, and frantically asked for the help of friends such as Bruce Richmond in dealing with this calumny. The effect upon him and Vivien was devastating: not only was his nervous collapse trumpeted to the public – which for such a proud and reticent man was an intolerable intrusion – but he also believed his position in the bank to be jeopardized by this account of his supposed double-dealing. He drafted a letter of complaint and sent it to the newspaper and, when it did not appear, he telephoned them for an explanation. They denied that any such letter had arrived and so he wrote a second which was eventually published on 30 November. 'I have not received £800 or any part of such sum,' he said. 'Nor have I received any sum from Bel Esprit, nor have I left the bank. The Bel Esprit scheme . . . is not in existence with my consent or approval.' He added that the circulation of such false rumours astonished and annoyed him, and could do him great harm.

Although he did not wish to sue the newspaper, because of the extra strain involved and the fact that the time wasted upon legal matters would interfere even more with his own work,[85] there is no doubt that the affair exhausted and unnerved him. He was also in danger of appearing merely ridiculous: someone sent him a gift of four 1½d stamps subscribed 'Your Well Wisher'. He had got the worst of everything: the repercussions of his friends' doomed charitable endeavours had possibly damaged his standing at the bank and had severely affected the chances of Vivien's own recovery. He asked Lewis not to telephone him at the flat;[86] he expected fresh assaults to be made upon him; he was exhausted and wanted to rest.[87] He had so little time, and had been able to see so few people, that it felt almost as if he was in prison.[88] This was the year of *The Waste Land* – the year, he said later, which marked the beginning of his adult life.[89]

7

A Sense of Failure
1923–1924

AT THE BEGINNING of 1923, Eliot and his wife were planning to change their way of life, in an effort to manage a situation which had threatened to become unmanageable. They were partly prompted to do this because of the fact that the lease on their flat in Clarence Gate Gardens was about to expire[1]: if they left that flat, and were able to reduce their living expenses generally, they would at least have more room for manoeuvre. He was at this stage investing as much as he could. He had placed the *Dial* award in a special account, as well as £50 which Virginia Woolf and Ottoline Morrell had given him. He thought of this as a trust fund, not to be touched for ordinary expenses but used as a way of accumulating capital for the time when he should leave the bank. That he was now actively considering such a departure is clear. He told Virginia Woolf that he would have left it already if it had not been for Vivien's bad health,[2] and with Mrs Woolf he was now considering alternative forms of employment. He certainly did not want to return to teaching, but librarianship or some kind of secretarial work were possible. Virginia Woolf then conceived the idea of his becoming the literary editor of the *Nation*. It was a job he said he would like, and she wrote to Maynard Keynes, who was on the board of that magazine, and asked him if he would put forward his name. Keynes did so, but objections were raised by his fellow directors who had never heard of Eliot. Keynes told Virginia Woolf that it would be easier to back him if he could have testimonials of his worth from some important writers.

Now that negotiations were going ahead, however, Eliot began to have second thoughts. Virginia Woolf recognized what a scrupulous and complicated man he was but wished nevertheless that he had more 'spunk' in him.[3] The major reason for his tentativeness and indecision, however, was the fact that Vivien strongly disapproved of the idea. She wrote to Mary Hutchinson that she would take it very badly if he accepted the *Nation* job and left the bank. Since the inheritance from his father reverted to the Eliot family on his death, she would be ill provided for. If he went to the *Nation* they would be reduced to living in an attic and would be unable to afford her medical treatment.[4] When she thought that friends, such as Ottoline Morrell and the Sitwells, were also urging him to leave the bank she wrote to them and accused them of disloyalty[5] – the first evidence that her physical condition was also provoking mental instability.

And so Eliot faced a dilemma: his natural ambition pitted against his responsibilities towards his wife, the risk of a new job against the security of an established one. Once more he could not decide what to do. He spun out the situation into endless complexities – he was, according to Virginia Woolf, 'peevish, plaintive, egotistical'.[6] It was not, however, an easy choice to make even under the best of circumstances. For one thing, his career at the bank was prospering. He was about to move from the head office to the Colonial and Foreign Department, where with another man he was placed in charge of the Foreign Office Information Bureau, of which he eventually became sole head. Part of this job consisted of compiling a sheet of extracts each day from the foreign press – to begin with, he set this up in type himself; he also wrote a monthly commentary on foreign exchange movements although this was a subject, he said later, about which he knew nothing.[7] But, on the other hand, it left him too little time to devote to the *Criterion*. There were monthly dinners and weekly meetings, quite apart from the fact that he had rapidly to learn how to deal with mutually antagonistic contributors like Aldington and Pound. Slowly, however, he was learning how to delegate responsibility[8] and concentrate upon the really important task of creating an interesting magazine. Indeed, in the first year of its existence, he had gathered together a number of extraordinarily able contributors – Luigi Pirandello, Virginia Woolf, E. M. Forster, Paul Valéry and W. B. Yeats among them. Such was his enthusiasm, in fact, that he had commissioned too many articles – by January 1923 he had enough for the next two or three issues.[9] He even proposed to Lady Rothermere that books ought to be published under the *Criterion* imprint, but the idea came to nothing. He was also fortunate in having Richard Cobden-Sanderson as his publisher. Cobden-Sanderson kept the accounts and reported on the finances of the magazine to Lady Rothermere, but he also dealt with most of the publishing and administrative details: he did the lay-outs for the magazine, dealt with authors' corrections, looked after payments and sent out the copies.

Nevertheless, Eliot felt that the dual responsibilities of banking and editorship were crippling him. On 12 March he wrote a long and unhappy letter to John Quinn, in which he expressed the wish that he had never become involved with the *Criterion*. The situation, in summary, was this: he would either have to give up the bank and find another and less strenuous source of income, or he would have to relinquish the editorship of the *Criterion* before his health broke down. The literary editorship of the *Nation* was one possibility, which is why he had been originally so eager to take it, but it paid £200 less than his bank salary. He was, he told Quinn, at a point of crisis and he added at the end of the letter, 'I am worn out. I cannot go on'. He telephoned Virginia Woolf and said that he could only take the *Nation* job if he was also given a five-year guarantee – he was, she thought, on the edge of collapse.[10] In fact the *Nation* was only able to offer him a six-months' guarantee, and at the end of March he finally turned down the job. The primary reason, as he explained both to Pound and Quinn, was that the post did not offer sufficient security for Vivien: at least with the bank his wife would be given a year's salary with a pension on the event of his death. Nevertheless his inability to take up the literary editorship severely depressed him and he told Quinn that if any position like it was offered to him in the future, he would accept it.[11] He was determined to leave the bank, in other words, although the precise circumstances in which he could do so were still most unclear. Vivien had for the first time actively impeded his literary ambitions, and it is likely that he felt a certain amount of resentment as a result. Since she was also showing signs of mental instability in her accusatory letters to his friends, that resentment might well have been mixed with fear.

Certainly her illnesses now were taking on a malign pattern of dependence – her health broke down again in the early spring, and Eliot blamed his own indecision over the *Nation* for her collapse.[12] Vivien herself could not bear to think about what she termed the 'fiasco'.[13] They had found a cottage at Fishbourne in March and travelled there at the beginning of the following month: it was only a few miles from Bosham, where they had stayed in previous summers. Just before they started moving, Vivien had a severe attack of colitis and by the time she arrived in Fishbourne she was very ill indeed. She had what was described as 'catarrh of the intestines' combined with enteritis, and this was followed by a septic influenza which threatened to turn into pneumonia. The main cause of these disorders seem to have been a form of malnutrition induced by the severe diet which her doctors had ordered for her, and by the end of April she was reduced practically to a skeleton and had almost died on several occasions.[14] Eliot had taken his three weeks' holiday from the bank in order to be with her in the country: even in advance of that trip he had felt like going into a sanatorium to recuperate, and now he felt even more ill than before. In May he went back to the bank in order to request sick leave, and then returned to Fishbourne for a further fortnight. Vivien seemed to improve but suffered a relapse in June.

On the recommendation of Ottoline Morrell, Eliot sought the help of a German physician who was also a 'lay psychologist', Dr Marten; he specialized in a treatment which combined near starvation of the patient with the injection of animal glands and it seems that, in July, some cultures were sent over from Germany in order to help Vivien. She was well enough in this month, however, to visit Virginia Woolf who described her as 'very nervous, very spotty, much powdered'.[15] Vivien was certainly acutely aware of her position – in a letter to Virginia Woolf in April, she had expressed anxiety about the fact that she had ruined her husband's holiday.[16] Her own sense of isolation was acute; when Eliot returned to London in June she told Virginia Woolf that she hated the cottage but, although she wished she could accompany 'Tom', she knew that she had to stay in comparative retirement.[17] In fact, Eliot himself was at great pains to be with her as much as possible: he was travelling between London and Fishbourne throughout the summer, generally at the weekends but also on average taking one day's leave each week from the bank (he had altogether two months' leave apart from this).

One very serious problem was his lack of money. In response to his despairing letter during the *Nation* negotiations, Quinn had sent him 400 dollars and promised to do so annually for three years. But his expenses were still heavy: apart from the two rents which he was now paying, Vivien's medical bills were very large. Her London doctor came down to Fishbourne twice a week, and a local doctor came twice daily. Vivien's mother, or sometimes another relative, was there for a large part of the time – she had to be looked after, and there were also bills for Vivien's special food. Despite his attempts at financial prudence, he had been living beyond his income for five months already, and now his savings were being quickly used up.[18] The only way he could earn money was to settle down and write as many reviews as possible for the magazines with which he was associated, but even if the will was there the energy and concentration required were not.[19] Nevertheless he did manage to write ten articles between April and December, a not inconsiderable amount for a man who was also editing his own magazine. But his difficulties were not solely with his journalism. Even by the end of 1922 he considered *The Waste Land* to be an achievement now past, since he wanted to work upon something in a different form,[20] and six months later he was describing his ambition to write something on a larger scale than he had attempted before.[21] The work he had in mind was his play, *Sweeney Agonistes*; some of it was certainly written by September 1923, because in that month he wrote to thank Lewis for his encouragement over it.[22] But his ambitions were frustrated by the fact that he was suffering from one of his regular and characteristic 'dry' periods, an unhappy state in which he was tempted to believe that he would never write anything again. It was a condition which induced in him a somewhat acerbic deprecation of poetry itself: he was asked to reply to questions in the July *Chapbook*, one of them being 'What in modern life is the particular function of poetry as distinguished from other forms of literature?' Eliot's answer: 'Takes up less space'.

This was a kind of defence. He thought it necessary, as he once explained to Sidney Schiff, to attempt to insulate his mind from unpleasant or trying circumstances and, when he visited Virginia Woolf in May, he discussed Vivien's condition in a way that although extremely considerate also seemed to her to be 'detached'.[23] Sassoon referred to his 'cold-storaged humanity',[24] and one of his nicknames (apparently given to him by Ottoline Morrell) was 'the undertaker'. It was this quality of detachment which Conrad Aiken also noted in his friendship with him – Eliot seemed always to be keeping him 'at arm's length'. 'He is a strange creature,' he wrote in June, 'full of protestations of friendship, not to say affection; but makes no move to see me . . .'.[25] The characteristic rhythm of Eliot's friendships does seem to have been one of involvement and then of abrupt withdrawal – as if he did not want anyone to come too close. It was a quality which emerged also in the secretiveness with which he conducted some of his affairs. Aiken complained of this, and no doubt he was one of the many friends who did not know that Eliot had taken rooms in Burleigh Mansions, on the Charing Cross Road, in this year. There was nothing particularly unusual about this: he needed somewhere quiet and secluded where he could work undisturbed, and he slept here sometimes. But what is odd is the manner in which he guarded himself. When Mary Hutchinson was preparing to visit him, he told her to ask the porter for a 'Captain Eliot' and then to knock at the door three times.[26] When Osbert and Sacheverell Sitwell were invited to Burleigh Mansions for dinner, they were told simply to ask for 'the Captain'.[27] This nautical persona which Eliot adopted has its jaunty aspects, but it is more bizarre than comic.

The strangeness is compounded by the fact that the Sitwells noticed, while dining with him there, that he was wearing face powder: ' . . . pale but distinctly green, the colour of forced lily-of-the-valley'.[28] Their observation confirmed what Virginia Woolf thought she had seen – green powder on his face. The year before she suspected that he painted his lips,[29] and in March 1922, Clive Bell told Vanessa Bell that Eliot 'has taken to powdering his face green – he looks interesting and cadaverous'.[30] Osbert Sitwell's explanation for this use of make-up was that he wore it in order to accentuate his look of suffering, so that he might more easily provoke sympathy. This would undoubtedly conform with Eliot's strongly realized sense of drama, contemplating himself as a romantic or dramatic figure, as he once said of Cyrano de Bergerac,[31] and thus enjoying his situation all the more keenly – as if only by displaying his suffering could he actually experience or even deal with it. But it is significant that the only people who noticed his make-up, and probably the only ones in whose company he wore it, were writers and artists; it is unlikely he powdered his face before going to the bank, for example. His sensitivity to atmosphere was such that he may have wanted to live up to it – wearing face powder

Eliot the dandy wearing lipstick + face powder

made him look more modern, more interesting, a poet rather than a bank official. He was too intelligent not to realize the effect which he had upon others – that slightly chilling and aloof quality of which we have read the descriptions – and this was one way in which he mitigated it.

But he was also living in a state of intense anxiety, and such minor eccentricities are quite explicable. A more conventional expression of his strain occurred at a party which he gave at Burleigh Mansions in December; he invited, among others, Lytton Strachey and the Woolfs. Vivien, apparently, was not present and Eliot proceeded to get very drunk; he was eventually sick and then sank into a stupor from which he was barely able to rise to speak to his departing guests.[32] Throughout his life, in fact, he drank a good deal (although rarely showing signs of inebriation – part of his remarkable self-control), and he confessed to Elizabeth Bowen on one occasion that he needed alcohol to get himself into the mood to write.[33] The morning after the party at Burleigh Mansions, he telephoned Virginia Woolf and spent ten minutes apologizing for his behaviour. It was the first time this had happened, he said[34] – and we can see here the effects of what had been the most unpleasant and difficult year of his life.

On the cover of *Time* magazine of 6 March 1950 which was devoted to Eliot, there was a picture of one hand holding a champagne glass and another holding a crucifix; the caption read, 'No middle way out of the Waste Land'. Since humiliating drunkenness seemed to offer no escape, it was perhaps fortuitous that in this year he met a young man who was able to assist him in his progress towards the Christian faith. William Force Stead was an American poet who had been ordained in the Church of England: Eliot met him through Richard Cobden-Sanderson, who published his poetry. Stead remembered Eliot in this period as 'perennially middle-aged': 'Even in 1923 he had an air of weariness, like a man who worked and carried his burdens patiently with only a small reserve of vitality . . . He was never the man to accept life with a carefree enjoyment'.[35]

Eliot's sympathetic attitude towards the religious life was already well known to his friends, although he tended to treat it in a semi-jocular manner. In one letter to Virginia Woolf in 1924, he explained how the company of clergymen always appealed to him and, in discussing a proposed visit to her, intimated that he might attend Sunday service.[36] But what might be called a religious sensibility, as opposed to religious conviction, had already been apparent in his graduate reading in the literature of mysticism and Buddhism. Although it is likely that his youthful interest in the martyred saint or visionary was a dramatic extrapolation from his own sense of uniqueness and thwarted power, he was instinctively attracted to the spectacle of the organized Church: his extension lectures of 1916 had suggested that a 'classicist in art and literature' (the sphere in which he placed himself) would be likely to 'adhere . . . to the Catholic Church'. In other words, his conversion was not the dramatic or unexpected reversal of interests which some have claimed it to be, but rather the culmination of a lengthy and consistent process which at least in hindsight seems inevitable. In 1919, he discussed the sermons of John Donne and Lancelot Andrewes – 'a writer of genius', he called the latter[37] – but at this stage he was objective about the claims of Christianity itself and compared the work of these two eminent divines with Buddha's 'Fire Sermon'. In March 1921 he described the human wisdom of certain Elizabethan and Jacobean poets which leads towards and is only completed by 'the religious comprehension'[38] – an insight which is strengthened in a later essay where he wrote of the wish to surrender to 'something outside oneself'.[39] Such a sensibility may explain his fascination for the peace to be found in the churches of the City of London, where 'the solitary visitor' (not yet a worshipper, clearly) can escape 'the dust and tumult' of the world outside.[40] On his visits to these churches he was deeply impressed by the spectacle of men and women on their knees,[41] an experience quite unknown in the Unitarian services of his youth. Peace, stillness, withdrawal: these are some of the characteristic qualities which Eliot associated with the religious life. In the same way he described, long before his conversion, the necessity for an allegiance to an external order which will silence what he called the 'inner voice', a relic of the Rousseauism or Romanticism which he professed to despise and which he associated with 'vanity and fear and lust'.[42] And yet his was still the expression of aesthetic preferences or psychological needs (it is impossible to separate the two) rather than the formulation of any religious belief as such. V. A. Demant has recalled Eliot's conviction in later life that 'religious emotion without God as the object of faith was really a pathological condition';[43] we shall see, in the account of succeeding years, how he attempted to escape from that condition.

Vivien's health seemed much improved during the winter of 1923, after the crisis of the previous months, but the weather in February 1924 was exceptionally cold and she became feverish, succumbing to a form of influenza. Eliot contracted the virus from her which was exacerbated by his general fatigue. He stayed in bed for a period during February, and did not even bother to answer the door.[44] Those who enjoyed good health, he once said, scarcely realized how much bravery was required from those who did not.[45]

They had been trying to find another country cottage because of their dissatisfaction with the cramped conditions of the one in Fishbourne (there was a garage beside it, which made matters worse) but nothing suitable had become available and they were obliged to return to 2 Milestone Cottages. They were established there by April, although Eliot now found the country unendurable: they both had to struggle to keep warm and, in addition, he had a suitcase full of letters and manuscripts with which he had not found the time to deal.[46] Everything seemed to be going wrong: in June he had an abscess under his fingernail, which then became infected.

In the periods when Vivien felt well enough to concentrate, she was working very hard upon the *Criterion* and in March of this year, having recovered from the worst of her illness, most of her time was taken up in preparing the next issue.[47] Not only was she helping her husband in editorial duties, but with his encouragement she was also beginning to write her own prose sketches for the magazine, which were published throughout 1924 under assumed names. Eliot had a very high opinion of his wife's literary abilities, and wished her to have some kind of proper instruction.[48] Vivien herself was more diffident about her work – she described it to Schiff as a 'flash in the pan' and, in any case, she did not think writing was a real substitute for living:[49] perhaps an implied criticism of her husband's unequal talent for both.

Eliot would go over her work with her, sometimes adding phrases or changing sentences. From an examination of Vivien's note-books,[50] it seems likely that he wrote certain passages himself (even some lines from an excised section of *The Waste Land* appear in one of her pieces), but on occasions their handwriting is so similar that it is difficult to be sure. Vivien herself suggested that they collaborated in the stories, together with Eliot's secretary, Irene Fassett.[51] They are social sketches, which contain harsh accounts of literary parties and *thés dansants* as well as caricatures of the people who participate in such events – apparently they gave offence to friends like Mary Hutchinson and Ottoline Morrell who believed themselves to be parodied in them, and Eliot had to go to some lengths to placate them. The rhythm of the dialogue is the most original feature of Vivien's work, and it reflects, interestingly, the kind of writing with which Eliot was experimenting at this time: 'Excuse me, it's perfectly all right, there isn't a hole' in one of Vivien's stories has the same ring as 'Excuse me, they don't all get pinched in the end' from 'Fragment of an Agon'.

Another significant feature of Vivien's work is the way in which she satirizes a figure who seems to be very close to Eliot himself. In a story in the *Criterion* of July 1925 we find a poet who is 'thickly powdered' with 'long hooded eyes, unseeing, leaden-heavy' and who speaks 'in a muffled, pedantic and slightly drunken voice'. When an enthusiastic young woman describes him as the 'most marvellous' poet in the world, Sibylla replies that he might be, if he ever wrote anything. He wanted too much: the devil had taken him up the mountain and shown him the kingdoms of the earth. ' "He's still up on the mountain, so far as I know," said Sibylla indifferently.' This caricature of her husband (at least it sounds very much like one) and the fact that he published it, suggest the element of malign comedy which they were still self-conscious enough to invest in their relationship. But, in general, the impression derived from Vivien's work is of a woman acutely sensitive to the external world but also nervous and withdrawn, aware of 'my savage and rebellious conduct'. Social constraints and the people who observe them are the subjects which claim her attention, but there is also an abiding wish to be free of such things: the narrator of her stories and sketches is always sharp, nervous and in the end solitary. In one of them, the narrator is left standing on the Quai Voltaire, staring at the bridges and the water until, cold and weary, she is forced to turn away.[52]

In Vivien's notebooks at the Bodleian, there are also certain small pencilled notes which seem to be in Eliot's hand. One is a rhyme attacking his friend, Charles Whibley; there is an account of the Bloomsbury Group which describes them as failures and compares them to miniature Japanese trees; a distinction between Puritanism and Catholicism drawn upon the fact that the latter has an awareness of Sin; and another note on the sterility and crudity of the relationship between a man and a woman as opposed to the subtlety of the relationship between man and cat. They are curious items.

Between bouts of illness, for both Vivien and her husband the *Criterion* was the major preoccupation. He told Virginia Woolf that he was tired of important people coming up to him and congratulating him on having a magazine with which he could do as he liked,[53] although one could hardly blame them for not being aware of all the anxieties with which he deluged his friends. There were practical difficulties, of course: he had no proper office and was forced to work at home where there were continual interruptions. All he had was a part-time secretary and a second-hand desk. But there were, of course, advantages also. The editorship had given him a position and an authority which he would not have been able to acquire in any other way, and the fact that he would continue with it for the next fifteen years suggests that he knew as much. Already, in these first two or three years, he was establishing relations with people who in the ordinary course of events he would scarcely have encountered. He lunched with Hugh Walpole – 'Enjoyed it very much,' Walpole wrote afterwards, '. . . he is a very quiet man and of course I'm a little afraid of him, but he was awfully kind . . .'[54] – and in the autumn of this year he visited Gertrude Stein in Paris. He gave the impression of 'A sober almost solemn, not so young man who, refusing to give up his umbrella, sat clasping its handle while his eyes burned brightly in a non-committal face.'[55] Eliot asked Gertrude Stein to contribute to the *Criterion* and then, not surprisingly, sat upon the piece for several months. Of much more importance is the fact that in this year he began to print extracts from Wyndham Lewis's *The Apes of God* – despite the fact that his relationship with Lewis was continually being soured by mutual mistrust and financial arguments, he told Lewis that it was worth editing the paper just to be able to publish it.[56] He did not seem perturbed by the fact that Lewis's novel brutally satirized most of his literary friends, the Sitwells and the Bloomsbury Group among them.

Criterion gatherings were now regular occurrences, and were known to the participants as the 'Criterion Club' – 'messy affairs', Conrad Aiken called them, in which literary reputations were the target for assassination and which revealed a 'deliberate and Machiavellian practice of power politics'.[57] Certainly there was an element of hardness in Eliot's judgments – in letters to Richard Aldington, for example, he asked him to deal harshly both with Katherine Mansfield and Carl Sandburg.[58] Even the work of friends such as Virginia Woolf and Ezra Pound was coldly anatomized in his critical discourses. But if he was sure of anything, it was of his literary judgment – in that area of his life, if in no other, there was no confusion or disorder, and he was never one to suffer gladly those whom he considered to be literary fools. He in turn expected severe criticism of his own position, although sometimes it came from unexpected quarters. Both Lewis and Pound criticized the magazine for its apparent lack of commitment, and it is true that Eliot used contributors like Hugh Walpole and George Saintsbury who were not exactly in the vanguard of contemporary literature. Herbert Read, himself a contributor, expressed doubts of a similar kind, and Eliot excused himself on the grounds that he needed a certain number of fashionable or respectable 'names' to placate Lady Rothermere, who often accused the magazine of being dull. He also wanted the cooperation of a number of people in what he planned to do, and to publish them was the best means of achieving this.[59]

But he was also convinced that the *Criterion* was at last acquiring a kind of internal coherence. Because he had been willing to accede to Lady Rothermere's requests, at least in part, she in turn had given him a large measure of freedom: he was, after all, publishing work in which she could have no possible interest. Since it was his customary belief that there were some people who were always ready to criticize him, and to suspect his motives, he was never in these years willing to explain in detail the kind of magazine, and the kind of group, which he wished to establish. But it is clear that he wanted to have around him people who shared those assumptions which he had first borrowed from men like Babbitt and Maurras – who believed, for example, in clarity of dogma and precision of statement. He told Herbert Read that he wished to publish those who in some degree adhered to a faith which was not essentially at odds with his own.[60] What Eliot's 'faith' consisted of is not clearly stated,

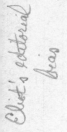 Eliot's editorial bias

although he announced himself elsewhere as a firm 'Tory'.[61] In this year, he introduced an editorial commentary – signing himself 'Crites' – and the first of them contained a panegyric on the work of T.E. Hulme; Hulme was 'classical, reactionary and revolutionary' as opposed to the 'eclectic, tolerant and democratic' mind of the late nineteenth century. And in a circular which he sent out to attract new subscribers in December, he explained that the *Criterion* represented pure Toryism which, in its espousal of 'reaction' and 'revolution' as opposed to old-fashioned 'suburban democracy', would attract the younger generation.

Here is a hardness of attitude which is compatible with the characteristic hardness of his literary judgments, and it is one that informs many of his other opinions. In a peculiar letter which he wrote to the *Daily Mail* in January 1923, for example, he congratulated the paper for a series of laudatory articles by Sir Percival Phillips on the rise of Mussolini – one such article, on 1 January, had described the Black Shirts' 'triumphal march' through Rome. In the same letter, he then turned to the *Daily Mail*'s coverage of the notorious 'Ilford Murder'. Edith Thompson and her young lover, Edward Bywater, had been sentenced to death for the murder of her husband. There had been a public outcry at the prospect of hanging a woman and a very young man, but Eliot clearly disapproved of this liberal distress and praised the paper's unsentimental attitude in its demand that the pair should be executed. Murders always seem to have fascinated him, in fact – according to Herbert Howarth, he was 'haunted' by the Crippen case.[62] And on one occasion he went to a fancy dress party disguised as Dr Crippen himself.[63]

It was Eliot's dogmatism and idealism, evinced in his plans for the *Criterion*, which marked him off from his contemporaries and ensured that he became, as Herbert Read put it, 'our undisputed leader'.[64] But this was not only because of the personal authority which Richard Church had noticed in his manner (and it must be admitted, also, that none of the *Criterion* group were in any sense his equals – fellow writers like Lewis or Virginia Woolf would never have considered him any kind of 'leader') but also because of the fact that there were few people in England able or willing to acquire that kind of intellectual authority – who wanted to form what Eliot called a phalanx. But if he had all the advantages of an 'outsider', an American who saw more clearly the principles of European civilization than the Europeans themselves, he also suffered from the disadvantages of that position. He recognized the fact that he gave to many people the impression of pride or intellectual vanity,[65] and his characteristic mode of dealing with the larger world became one of patience and reserve. He was always recommending caution, Herbert Read remembered, 'caution in showing one's hand, caution in speech and correspondence, caution in the small exchange of literary life. "Always," he would say, "acknowledge the gift of a book before there has been time to read it: if you wait you have to commit yourself to an opinion." '[66] And so slowly he made his way.

In the summer Eliot's mother again travelled to England to see him, and his time was taken up in looking after her. Charlotte still strongly disapproved of Vivien – it was not an 'eugenic' marriage, she told her brother-in-law[67] – and during the period of her stay Vivien spent a great deal of time in Eastbourne. The strain of dealing with such familial matters again affected Eliot, and he too went down to Eastbourne where he was confined to bed with illness. He saw his mother off from Liverpool at the end of August, and shortly afterwards complained that he had been unable to write anything for some weeks.[68] This was in any case a time of great uncertainty about his work, since he had produced nothing of any consequence since *The Waste Land* more than two years before. His was the fate of any serious writer who feels thwarted: he was dissatisfied with his own writing and envious of that of others.[69] Virginia Woolf wanted to print a selection of his essays, and in his mock-facetious tone he explained that he had not yet finished those on Church Reunion and other topics.[70] Despite their ostensibly friendly and professional relations, Virginia Woolf was still somewhat wary of him – she described him as very vain, in a diary entry in May of this year, as well as 'suspicious, elaborate and uneasy'.[71]

Although he could not send the Woolfs any essays on Church Reunion – he was to expatiate on that topic later – he did offer them three essays, on Dryden, Marvell and the Metaphysicals, he had written for *The Times Literary Supplement* in 1921, and which they published in pamphlet form as *Homage to John Dryden*. Eliot himself did not think very highly of these pieces;[72] since in any case they were written at the time he was composing *The Waste Land*, and are in part concerned with the kind of poetry he was then attempting to write, they were in a sense for him out of date. He was now involved with something quite different.

He was discussing his plans with Arnold Bennett in the September of this year. 'He said he didn't mind what I said [about *The Waste Land*] as he had definitely given up that form of writing,' Bennett wrote, 'and was now centred on dramatic writing. He wanted to write a drama of modern life (furnished flat sort of people) in a rhythmic prose, "perhaps with certain things in it accentuated by drum beats".'[73] This notion of the drum beat was one he had explored the year before in an article 'The Beating of a Drum',[74] where he emphasized the importance of rhythm and ritual in artistic performance. All of his interests pointed in this direction – the ballet, the music hall, and the work of the Elizabethan playwrights prompted him towards a redefinition of what the drama was and what it was capable of becoming. In an essay published in this year, 'Four Elizabethan Dramatists' (which he described as the 'preface of an unwritten book') he drew together his assumptions and concerns. He wanted a drama established upon firm theatrical conventions, not one messily engaged in 'realism' – ritual rather than life, actors rather than people. He was interested in a hieratic and formalistic approach to performance, which he had already noted in Marie Lloyd and in the work of Massine – Eliot had seen him dance at the Coliseum in 1922 and had been captivated by him. He wished to create something impersonal, inhuman almost, and to construct a dramatic dialogue which was itself intensely ritualistic. This was precisely the kind of work he was engaged upon with *Sweeney Agonistes*, the play that he had been writing slowly and painfully since 1923.

The problem he had set himself was this. He wanted to move quite away from the manner of *The Waste Land* – a work which depended to a large extent upon its literary echoes and its deliberate 'difficulty'. Just as he had created a new form of poetry there, he now wished to create a new form of drama. The reason why he consulted Arnold Bennett, who was derided by many of the younger writers who thought of themselves as 'serious', was that Bennett understood public taste and the craftsmanship necessary in order to appeal to it successfully. Evidently, from Eliot's conversations with

Bennett, he wished to refashion contemporary life (he knew all about 'furnished flats') into a disciplined and ritualized mode in the manner of Noh drama, with masks and light drum taps as part of the effect. In the form of incantation, strange sins and desires might come to light which the quotidian details of ordinary living effectively concealed.

He was trying to write the play through the autumn and winter of 1924, but it did not seem to be working out as he had anticipated. He sent a draft to Arnold Bennett in October, and started to reconstruct it on Bennett's suggestions at the end of the same month. But he was writing only fragments and although he had a grand plan of action in his head, the play was not emerging in a coherent form. In 1925 he told Bennett that he had abandoned it because of several basic problems. One of them was, I suspect, that he did not yet have a fully developed theatrical sense. He said, many years later,[75] that one of the difficulties with the play was that it would have to be spoken too quickly to be possible on stage. His writing abilities had outstripped his dramatic conception, in other words, and he had written non-theatrical drama – something very close to the Senecan drama of recitation. But we can see from the little of it that he chose to publish – in the *Criterion* of October 1926 and January 1927 – that he had indeed been trying for something akin to popular theatre (as he would try again in later life). Doris and Sweeney have been taken out of the quatrain poems and put upon the stage, which is where Eliot's cold, bright vision properly belonged. Snatches of music-hall dialogue and song are here raised to a pitch of intensity by the use of insistent rhythms and by the incantatory repetition of certain key words and phrases: the gaiety which this releases transcends any conventionally 'tragic' or 'comic' mood. Eliot himself believed that *Sweeney Agonistes* was the most original of his compositions,[76] but he was never able to complete it and, characteristically, refused to speculate on what it might have been like if he had done so.

He once told F. T. Prince that in his own work there would generally come a moment of 'despair', when he would have to abandon it and then return to it later. It was the same with his critical responses which after a certain point 'went dead':[77] one is tempted to think of his mind as a piece of elaborate machinery run on a very rare and expensive fuel. And that fuel was often derived from the work of other writers. When he was engaged on *Sweeney Agonistes*, he complained to Virginia Woolf that, in the absence of illustrious models, the contemporary writer was compelled to work on his own[78] and that was, perhaps, the essential problem with *Sweeney Agonistes*. He could not work easily upon the play because there was no literary context for such writing from which to draw energy or inspiration. Throughout his published work, there is evidence of an imagination which received with full force the impression of other writers' forms and language, and which was then able to assimilate them within an original design. He always needed a safety net, as it were, before he indulged in his own acrobatics. An analysis of his prosody, for example, shows that he took conventional metrical units as his essential pattern – he departs from, and then returns to, them. The major form can support irregularities, which are justified and ultimately controlled by the underlying order. But there was no safety net beneath *Sweeney Agonistes*: no one had done anything quite like it before, and he did not seem able to trust himself sufficiently with only the non-literary material derived from the ballet or the music hall. And so the project slowly disintegrated in front of him.

What he could do was to work on something much tighter, more disciplined and therefore more manageable. And it was during the period of frustration over the play that he began writing some short poems which over a number of months took the shape of a sequence known as *The Hollow Men*: poems which, he said, were related to *Sweeney Agonistes*.[79] Certainly in their incantatory measure, and their eschewal of the allusive poetic modes of *The Waste Land*, they manage to achieve something of the directness which he had been attempting to bring to the play. The third poem in the sequence was in fact originally one of 'Doris's Dream Songs', published in the *Chapbook* of 1924, thus affirming its connection with *Sweeney Agonistes*. His preoccupation with drama had materially altered his attitude towards poetry itself, as it would in later work, and in *The Hollow Men* we see for the first time his use of clear and simple images, of repeated statement and of an uncomplicated accentual metre much closer to speech than any of the poetry he had composed before. It is very much a bravura dramatic performance, and could easily have found a place within *Sweeney Agonistes* itself – these poems, too, might be read to the sound of a light drum beat.

When he finally completed what he called the 'suite' of poems – they were not put finally into shape until the late autumn of 1925, after appeals to Pound to inspect them – Eliot felt that he had come to the end of his poetic life.[80] The failure of *Sweeney Agonistes* clearly unnerved him. Even Pound thought that it might be now 'too late' for him – that he had written too little, and what he had written was not as good as it might have been.[81] These fears were unjustified, but they were part of what seems to have been a chain reaction of distress in his own life. In November, he had taken Vivien to a sanatorium in Paris and returned alone. She came back soon after, however, and by the end of that month they were both ill at 9 Clarence Gate Gardens – Vivien had contracted bronchitis, and Eliot was suffering from a particularly virulent form of influenza. He was still ill in January and his doctors advised him to get away to the country for several weeks. But in February he had a high temperature and felt unable to use his mind at all. He felt empty, using an image of a shell to describe himself which might have come out of *The Hollow Men*,[82] and permanently weakened.[83] And yet the worst was still to come.

8

In Search of Faith
1925–1929

IT WAS IN 1925 that Eliot began openly to discuss with his friends the possibility of a separation from Vivien – for her sake as much as for his own. They had been looking for a place in the country – anything would do, since they were so desperate to get away from London. Apart from an attack of influenza Vivien seemed to have survived the rest of the winter well; but then in March, just as Eliot was recovering from his own protracted bout of 'flu, she became very seriously unwell. She seemed to be suffering from a combination of rheumatism and neuralgia, so that any physical movement became agony for her. She could not sleep at night, and she was in such pain during the day that the exhaustion seemed to be killing her. Throughout the spring, she had recurrent and violent bouts of neuralgia: and, in addition she was the victim of most peculiar after-effects from these attacks: she would become entirely numb and prostrate, unable to move. Her liver and intestines were severely affected, and only her mind seemed still to be working,[1] although, for a woman of such frantic self-consciousness, 'thought' itself must have induced bewilderment and panic. Throughout these months, she needed constant and exclusive attention: the flat was hushed and darkened; they saw nobody; they accepted no invitations; Vivien had fallen into what she called a 'fearful abyss'.[2] They hardly felt themselves to be alive.[3]

Vivien's numbness or paralysis seems to have been largely nervous in origin, much of it induced by the treatment she had received from Dr Marten. She had reverted to infantile terrors of loneliness; it was a loneliness compounded by the fact that her husband spent much of his time away from her. Now, if he did leave her, he found her in a desperate and half-fainting state on his return.[4] Vivien did not like him out of her sight: she was clutching at him. He told his friends he was desperate, and that he did not know what to do. Now, in his own fearful state, he was watching her closely for signs of disturbing behaviour. She was clearly suffering from what was then called a 'neurasthenic' rather than a 'mental' collapse, and it seems that she was trying to make some effort towards resuming a regular routine. For one thing, she wanted to get back to her writing. He asked Leonard Woolf if he should encourage her, and how he should regularize such activity.[5] Leonard Woolf had nursed his own wife through much worse crises, and was in a position to advise Eliot. But the fact that he was now relying upon the recommendations of friends suggests that the situation had become too overpowering for him alone to cope with. And once more he appealed to Bertrand Russell, despite the fact that he blamed Russell for affecting Vivien's stability after the incident eight years before. In letters written in April and May, which Russell published in his *Autobiography* no doubt in self-extenuation, he explained to him that matters had turned out just as Russell had anticipated; living with him had harmed Vivien, and perhaps it would be best if she lived alone. But he in his turn found her puzzling and misleading: he mentioned, in particular, that he could not escape the compelling force of her arguments.[6] Osbert Sitwell noted how Vivien was often able to turn her husband against friends or acquaintances by accusing them of often imaginary faults and betrayals. 'As to Tom's *mind*, I am his mind,' she once wrote.[7] She had encouraged and advised him, but now that closeness and mutual dependence were beginning to threaten him. Eliot was a man of complicated and in part uncertain identity: living in close proximity to a woman who was becoming unstable would have made him fearful of the contagion of that instability – that 'fearful abyss' was one into which he might also fall, in a kind of *folie à deux*. He did, in fact, suffer some kind of breakdown[8] and in May he asked Leonard Woolf if he knew of a doctor with psychiatric expertise who might minister to him rather than to his wife.[9] Certainly his behaviour was on occasions bizarre. Conrad Aiken has recalled how, at the end of this year, he sent a complimentary letter to Eliot about a new volume of poetry. A few days later he received through the post a page torn out of the *Midwives' Gazette*. Eliot had underlined the words *Model Answers*, which came at the top of a column which was describing various forms of vaginal discharge.

Within that column he underlined the words *blood, mucus* and *shreds of mucus* as well as, further down, the phrase *purulent offensive discharge*. There was no other comment, and Aiken said, 'I still shudder when I think of it'.[10] Aggression, and the brooding on female sexuality, are here strangely compounded and perhaps it ought to be recalled that part of his wife's 'neuralgia' manifested itself in an irregular menstrual flow. In an equally strange letter which Vivien wrote to Sidney Schiff at some point during this year (she mentioned Eliot's poems in the *Dial* of January 1925), she described in an oblique fashion those people who perplex or enrage Schiff – the problem is that Schiff has energy where 'they' have none, and that such people are so ashamed of their low vitality that they try to conceal the fact.

Eliot blamed much of their unhappiness and ill-health upon the fact that he was compelled to spend so much of his time working – that was no doubt one reason for Vivien's loneliness, at least. Even before the onset of her serious illness, he had been wondering whether Lady Rothermere might pay him a salary so that he and Vivien might get away from London for a while. He had now been a bank employee for eight years, and the situation had become unendurable for both of them. He must have explained his predicament to Charles Whibley, a Tory journalist, who introduced him to Geoffrey Faber. In 1923 Faber had gone into partnership with a firm of scientific publishers, Gwyer, and under the imprint of Faber and Gwyer had launched a general publishing house in 1925. Faber had been consulting Whibley about the choice of a literary adviser for the new firm and, over dinner at All Souls, Whibley had recommended Eliot. Eliot then went, rather nervously, to see Faber. Faber had really only wanted to employ a part-time adviser, but he was so 'impressed and charmed'[11] by Eliot that he asked him to join his Board of Directors. Frank Morley had suggested that, since Eliot's literary reputation was not at this period such that it commanded universal respect or admiration, Faber really wished to acquire his skills as a businessman and financier.[12] But that can only be partly true: Faber really wanted to hire someone who had a certain reputation among the young and would as a result be able to attract promising new writers who would enhance the standing of the firm. Eliot also had experience as an editor and it was a combination of all these qualities – businessman, editor and 'talent scout' – that made him perfectly qualified for such a job. And so it proved.

Negotiations were being finalized in April – he was to begin work at Faber and Gwyer in the autumn, with a five-year contract and four-fifths of the salary which he had been earning at the bank. Faber also wished to publish Eliot's own work. He was to be given an advance on his salary so that he might leave the bank and, together with Vivien, get away from London, possibly to France, for the summer. At the end of April, he visited the Woolfs in an excited state to tell them the news. It was, indeed, a 'new start' and one that was to change the whole course of his future life. The immediate advantages for him were obvious: the only alternative to banking had seemed to be journalism, but now he was given the chance to enter another 'business' which his familial training rendered so important to him. He would be able to retain that routine world of 'the office' which rescued him at least temporarily from Clarence Gate Gardens. But apart from affording him economic security within congenial surroundings, the new post meant that he had secured a home for his work where he would be free from the exigencies of editors and from that difficult combination of luck and perseverance which marks the ordinary course of a writer's publishing career. With his own magazine, and with his own firm, he was in a unique position to determine the nature, and the timing of his own writing. Now, at thirty-seven, he entered the middle course of his life.

But if Fabers in one sense 'made' Eliot, so did Eliot 'make' Fabers. He was in a position to publish in permanent form the work of the writers whom he admired – among them Joyce, Lewis and Pound. With his own strong convictions, he was able to form the literary taste of a generation, and under his aegis Faber and Faber (as it was later called) were until the mid-nineteen-sixties the pre-eminent publishers of twentieth-century poetry. But were there not disadvantages for Eliot, to be gathered in hindsight? His professional life, and indeed much of his social life, would be in the company of men professionally involved in the retailing of books – for the most part respectable, middleclass Englishmen who were, of course, interested in literature (Geoffrey Faber himself was a minor poet, whose work Eliot had reviewed in a non-committal fashion some years before) but whose understanding of, and assumptions about, contemporary writing were very different from those of Eliot's peers. And it is possible that Eliot himself became over-comfortable with such assumptions, although no doubt he was aware at least in part of the dangers of that position: there is a photograph of him, taken after he joined Faber and Gwyer, leaning jauntily against the wall of the office, with bowler hat, buttoned up double-breasted suit, and tightly rolled umbrella with a malacca handle. He looks almost too perfect to be entirely serious – as if he were posing in fancy dress.

But the prospect of new employment seemed to galvanize him and by June he was actively planning to edit two periodicals at once. He had in mind the publication of a new quarterly, in which four or six writers from different countries would concentrate upon the same theme for each issue. He wanted such a magazine to be broadly European in tone, not only because the English seemed ignorant of continental thought but also because the 'European' writers themselves were now, in contrast to the position in the earlier years of the century, becoming divided on local or national lines. When Lady Rothermere learned that he was planning such a magazine, she wrote and asked him if he would continue to edit the *Criterion* for at least another year and, because he felt in her debt, he agreed to do so. It was clearly absurd for him to edit two different magazines, however, despite the differences in their style. It was decided to launch the *Criterion* as a new magazine, edited by Eliot and, after some difficult negotiations which were still going on in October, it was agreed that it should come under the joint patronage of Lady Rothermere and Faber and Gwyer.

Clearly there was a great deal that Eliot wanted to do, and as soon as he had entered his new job in September he was beginning to commission books from his friends. One of his first ideas was to edit a new series of critical studies of foreign writers. He suggested to Herbert Read that he should write a short book on *Bergson and His Critics* (he also asked him for some poems); he wanted Richard Aldington to work on de Gourmont, John Gould Fletcher on Rimbaud, while he himself planned to write a book on Charles Maurras. There were difficulties, however. Although he had already explained to Virginia Woolf that he did not believe his new firm to be in any kind of competition with the Hogarth Press, he did in fact persuade Herbert Read to leave that press and place his work with Faber and Gwyer. Virginia Woolf called it 'poaching'[13] and became even more annoyed when she saw in *The Times Literary Supplement* an announcement that Faber and Gwyer were about to bring out a collected edition of Eliot's poetry – together, of course, with *The Waste Land*. The Woolfs had already offered to reprint that poem, and Eliot had not informed them of his decision to give it to his new employers – although he had, only a week before, written to Virginia Woolf about other matters. She was convinced that he wished to get by on worldly methods and accused him of being 'shifty';[14] judging by her diary entries, his character was also being unflatteringly dissected by other people. And in a harassed letter to Wyndham Lewis in September Eliot discussed the enmity which some people felt towards him.[15]

He and Vivien had, in fact, been planning to move to a house in a more agreeable area near Sloane Square; but there were various difficulties and they went back temporarily to Clarence Gate Gardens. Vivien had by now almost recovered from her terrible illness of the spring, although she had contracted shingles in the summer and was still subject to nervous collapse. Eliot was ill partly as a result of an infection of his teeth and gums: this caused him persistent pain and irritation throughout the year until in September he was compelled to have an operation on his jaw. It was an unpleasant business, according to Vivien,[16] and he felt very ill afterwards – the problem being exacerbated by the fact that he needed to have daily injections from his doctor.

In the last weeks of the year he went to the Savoy-Hotel in the Alpes Maritimes in order to recuperate in the sunshine, and he remained here until Christmas. While there, Faber and Gwyer published *Poems 1909–1925*, a compilation of his work to date including the new sequence, *The Hollow Men*, of which he was still somewhat doubtful. He told Leonard Woolf that he was not happy with the book.[17] This might have been an attempt to placate Woolf and his wife after moving publishers, if it were not for the fact that *Poems* simply afforded him the opportunity to clear away all his previous poetry and to begin again. In a summary of this period some fourteen years later, he remarked that 1926 was the year in which the features of the post-war world emerged and that the intellectual and artistic work of the previous seven years 'had been the last work of an old world, not the first one of a new':[18] it may be that he was contemplating here the progress of his own writing, also.

Although he found the reviews of the new collection disappointing – the critics now all agreed that his poetry had something vaguely to do with 'the sordidness of reality'[19] – there was one article about it which looked ahead to that 'new' world which Eliot would attempt to create for himself. In the *Adelphi* John Middleton Murry described Eliot as a nihilist who espoused classical principles because they represented a certainty 'he longs for and cannot embrace'. 'The intellectual part of him desiderates an ordered universe . . . the living emotional, creative part of him goes its own disordered way.' One means of resolving that conflict, Murry suggested, 'is that he should make a blind act of faith and join the Catholic Church: there he will find an authority and a tradition'.[20] It was perspicacious of Murry to see Eliot's progress in that light, although a careful study of his work might have suggested it, and it was precisely in this period that he began to formulate his own position in terms not dissimilar from those that Murry had outlined. In fact one of the reasons why he went to the South of France was to prepare a series of lectures on a related topic, which he had been asked to deliver at Cambridge University at the beginning of 1926.

While resting in France, he had been reading the work of Jacques Maritain since he was interested in the possibilities of some kind of neo-Thomism: to make the work of St Thomas Aquinas intelligible to a contemporary public in much the same way as Aquinas himself had reinterpreted Aristotle.[21] Eliot's concern was not simply a theological or philosophical one: Aquinas's work embodied the unity of European culture in the thirteenth century, and he believed an examination of that culture to be the best possible training for the contemporary mind.[22] A new form of Thomism offered at least the possibility of re-establishing the principles of order and lucidity, just as in his Cambridge lectures he wanted to demonstrate how that original unity had disintegrated. This notion of order, which reaches its culmination in the work of Dante and Aquinas, is one that had preoccupied him since his first acquaintance with the work of Babbitt and Maurras. And indeed his notion of a medieval Europe in which literary, religious and philosophical activities were all broadly in accord is not very far from Maurras's own idealization of seventeenth-century France and the rule of *le roi soleil*. What Eliot has done is to introduce a specifically Christian dimension and so to enlarge Maurras's secular and nationalistic myth, without losing the Maurrasien sense of discipline and hierarchy.

In his review in the *Adelphi*, Middleton Murry had compared Eliot's putative conversion with that of Huysmans, suggesting that such an act of faith would be the work of a dispossessed romantic or decadent. There was indeed in the late nineteenth century a tradition of poetical conversion, and certainly the circumstances of Eliot's life and the nature of his personality would impel him in his search for order and authority. But it would be unwise to forget the presence of genuine intellectual inquiry in his concerns. Here was a man who had witnessed in his lifetime the beginnings of the disintegration of European culture, but who saw the sources of that disintegration as lying much deeper than did those, for example, who thought it might be repaired by the political manoeuvres of such bodies as the League of Nations.

Between January and March 1926 Eliot gave the Clark Lectures at Cambridge, spending most of the Tuesday and Wednesday of each week there. This was the first sign of his steadily increasing academic respectability, and by the late nineteeen-twenties his influence at that university at least was, according to one contemporary, 'paramount'.[23] The lectures were entitled 'The Metaphysical Poets of the Seventeenth Century', and his purpose was to criticize that poetry from the perspective of thirteenth-century Europe, using Dante as his exemplar and tracing in broad terms the disintegration of thought as manifested in the movement from ontology to psychology, from objective values to subjective truth. The lectures (which remain unpublished) were to form part of a book, *The School of Donne* which itself would be one of a trilogy entitled 'The Disintegration of the Intellect'; the other two volumes were to be called *Elizabethan Drama* and *The Sons of Ben*. It was an ambitious undertaking (although, as it turned out, only an ambition) and it suggests the path which Eliot now wished to tread. After *The Hollow Men* and the abandonment of *Sweeney Agonistes*, it was conceivable that he would never write poetry again, and he was outlining a possible future career as an intellectual historian in the European mould – an Anglo-Saxon Maurras, perhaps.

That was at least in part the inspiration behind the *New Criterion* which resumed publication in January 1926 under its joint patronage. In a leading article for the first number Eliot explained that what he still called a 'literary review' would espouse the principles of classicism which embraced 'a more severe and serene control of the emotions by Reason'. He listed the books which were in this context important, and included the work of Maurras, Benda, Hulme, Maritain and Babbitt – a familiar list, except for the inclusion of Maritain. The rigour of his position, and what at first glance seems to be an odd amalgamation of source material for it, was one that would further isolate Eliot from his contemporaries, and during this period he was sometimes treated with suspicion and distrust – 'cultural exhibitionism' and 'affected integrity' were two of the phrases about him which Virginia Woolf reported. The essential problem was the peculiar ambiguity of his work and personality: he seemed too radical to conservatives, and too conservative to radicals. He appreciated Massine and Diaghilev and jazz, but he also respected the work of Maurras and Hulme. Two effects of this ambiguity may suffice. When Geoffrey Faber in the early months of 1926 proposed him for a research fellowship at All Souls, in Oxford, Eliot submitted for consideration to the Fellows his essays on Elizabethan drama (no doubt he planned to use his fellowship to continue work on 'The Disintegration of the Intellect'). But after they had seen his latest volume of poetry, they decided that he was not quite what they were looking for: *Poems 1909–1925* was too modern, too iconoclastic. And what was the poets' own reaction to him? William Carlos Williams described how he had seen him in Paris, two years before, wearing a top hat and striped trousers at the Café La Dome – Williams interpreted this as a gesture of 'contempt'.[24] Eliot later denied the charge, if such it is, but it is indicative of the suspicion which his Anglicized manners provoked in some of his contemporaries.

After the abortive attempt of the previous year, Vivien and Eliot moved to their new house at 57 Chester Terrace, near Sloane Square, in March 1926. Their maid, Ellen Kellond, had left them in order to get married (the Eliots gave her and her new husband a reception at Frascati's), and they tended to eat out in the evenings – often dining at a restaurant by Victoria Station, a short walk away. Certainly Vivien was not able to take care of any kind of household without help. In a letter to Ada Leverson at the beginning of that year, she explained that she was both worried and unhappy.[25] Both Edith Sitwell and Ottoline Morrell have described the strange and sometimes incoherent letters which they received from her. In April, for example, Vivien wrote to Ottoline Morrell that she was in terrible trouble and did not know what to do.[26] Aldous Huxley has described how her face 'was mottled, like ecchymotic spots, and the house smelled like a hospital'.[27] The smell would have been that of ether, which was then used as a tranquillizer for patients suffering from nervous disorders: Vivien would have rubbed it over her body. It has been said that she was an 'addict', but it is rather the case that she was prescribed morphine-based medicines to alleviate some of her symptoms.

Throughout the spring and summer she was travelling to various sanatoria in Europe, sometimes with Eliot and sometimes alone. It is difficult to disentangle their precise movements during this period, but in April they both travelled to Paris and then – in the company of their 'in-laws', Henry and Theresa Eliot as well as Maurice and Ahmé Haigh-Wood – they went on to Rome. Eliot seems to have left Vivien there because in May she wrote to the Sitwells, saying that she was involved in some kind of scandal and would not return to her husband unless they advised her to do so. The nature of this 'scandal' is not known – all that Maurice Haigh-Wood remembered was that Vivien took some sheets from the hotel bedroom (she and Eliot had separate rooms), washed them, and then later returned them to the hotel.[28] Understandably reluctant to offer advice on an affair about which they knew nothing, the Sitwells did not reply to her letter, and Vivien later told her husband that they had refused to help her in her distress – as a result, Eliot's friendship with them was temporarily suspended.[29] In June, Vivien was alone at a sanatorium in France, but in August and for some of September Eliot joined her at the Sanatorium de la Malmaison in Reuil, not far from Paris: such sanatoria were fashionable during this period, much closer to a 'health farm' than an asylum, and, for Eliot at least, they offered an opportunity simply to rest. In September they moved on to the Grand Hotel, Divonne-les-Bains, near the Swiss border, which was a centre for nervous disorders. Another patient there has described Vivien's appearance: '. . . she walked almost as though in a trance along the wooded path. Her black hair was dank, her white face blotched – owing, no doubt, to the excess of bromide she had been taking. Her dark dress hung loosely over her frail form; her expression was both vague and acutely sad'.[30] This was Eliot's companion; this was the shape his life had taken. He was now in his late thirties, approaching middle age. He believed that he had achieved very little so far, and wanted to accomplish more.[31]

They had been married for more than ten years: each of them a disappointment to the other, both of them aware of what they had become in each other's company. Eliot had told Bertrand Russell that living with him had harmed Vivien, and in turn she knew that she was a burden to her husband. When they were about to visit Garsington in this year, she wrote in advance to Ottoline Morrell suggesting that they took two rooms in the village – so that she would not have to see Vivien unless she wanted to.[32] It was a pitiable situation, but what was Eliot to do? He had already thought of separation, and in an informal way they spent much of their time apart. It was only by treating her in a detached manner that the situation became bearable: when she was no longer part of him, clutching at him in the frantic manner of her last illness, she did not threaten him in the insidious form which had brought him near to nervous collapse. He had written in her copy of *Poems 1909–1925* a dedication which declared that only she would really understand the contents of the book. But that poetry was of the past; the work which followed was not to have the same resonance for her. The *Criterion*, on which she had laboured, was now being edited in the offices of Faber and Gwyer and she played a much smaller part in it. Eliot was by degrees withdrawing from her, and his growing religious belief could only serve to confirm and even encourage that detachment. In an epigraph to the fragments of *Sweeney Agonistes*, he quoted from St John of the Cross: 'Hence the soul cannot be possessed of the divine union, until it has divested itself of the love of created beings.'

On his visit to Rome in this year, Eliot surprised his relatives by falling to his knees in front of Michelangelo's *Pietà*. But he was not to enter the Roman communion – for one thing, it smacked of republicanism and the Boston Irish – and already, before his formal conversion, he was undergoing regular training and attending early morning services in the Church of England. In an essay on Lancelot Andrewes, published in this year, he described the virtues of what he called the 'English Catholic Church',[33] and indeed his confessor has recalled how Eliot saw his conversion as a return to the religion of his English ancestors.[34] But it was by no means a purely atavistic retreat, and in his essay he saw the principles of that Church, exemplified in the writings of Hooker and of Andrewes, as deriving from a broadly European tradition – expressive of the finest spirit of English culture but not as a result parochial or provincial.

He became attached to the Anglo-Catholic movement within the Church of England, precisely because he saw in it the continuation of such a tradition. Its emphasis upon the apostolic mission of the Church, and upon the importance of sacramental worship, afforded (for those who wished to look for it) the kind of historical and ritualistic continuity which were for Eliot the essential elements of faith. Furthermore, the ties of the English Church with the political and social life of the nation, as well as with the monarchy, encouraged him to believe that here, if anywhere, a formal synthesis was to be found. Eliot, in fact, brought with him a sense of tradition and an instinct for order which the English themselves rarely possess, and it may seem something of a sophistry to locate the glories of the Tudor polity within the Church of England of the nineteen-twenties. Eliot himself was quite aware of the fact, but that did not prevent him from making his own act of faith. His genuine desire for a national church which retained its Catholic inheritance led him to do so and, if this seems to be the work of deliberation rather than instinct, that is because in part it was.

Three years after his conversion, he described himself as even in religious matters a disciple of Bradley – in other words, he chose that which was in philosophical terms the 'less false'. He discovered the least incredible belief and grew slowly to understand and accept it,[35] since the highest goal of civilized man was 'to unite the profoundest scepticism with the deepest faith'.[36] He was aware of what he called 'the void' in all human affairs – the disorder, meaninglessness and futility which he found in his own experience; it was inexplicable intellectually (his own scepticism had taught him that) and could only be understood or endured by means of a larger faith. The shadow of his grandfather can be glimpsed here: 'Principles were what his nature craved . . .'. He began with rational assent and, although the emotional discipline encumbent upon that assent was to be a later and more difficult task, the two elements cannot be easily distinguished. V. A. Demant has suggested that 'in his religion, and probably in his conversion, he found himself under compulsion, chosen rather than choosing',[37] and there is a sense in which this must be so. In the *Criterion* of this year, he described the appeal of churches to the 'passing penitent',[38] and if it were necessary to locate those elements of the Christian faith which impressed Eliot most deeply, they would surely be those of prayer and confession, balm and absolution for a soul deeply conscious of sin.

He told Constantine FitzGibbon that prayer can give to misery an apparent meaning;[39] Stephen Spender has described how once, in the company of Virginia Woolf, Eliot tried to impart the significance of prayer, the attempt 'to concentrate, to forget self, to attain union with God'[40] – the rapt concentration of thought and emotion upon an external force or presence, so rapt that they become absorbed in this presence. But, paradoxically, the attachment to something outside oneself can create a sense of the self as whole again, united in the act of worship. He wanted an object for his intense feelings which was not human, in order to heal a personality which threatened to shatter apart. In a later essay, he described dogmatic religion as one means of learning how to train and discipline the emotions – but, he added, such discipline can only be talked about by those who have peered into 'the abyss'.[41]

Early in 1927 Eliot asked his friend, the American chaplain William Force Stead, for advice and help in becoming confirmed in the Church of England. He demanded the utmost secrecy:[42] it did not concern, for the time being, even those closest to him. He was already preparing the ground: in the *Enemy* of January 1927 he refuted I. A. Richard's suggestion that in *The Waste Land* he had effected 'a complete severance between poetry and *all* beliefs', and in the *Dial* two months later he affirmed that the chief distinction of Man is to glorify God.

In February he was with Vivien at St Leonards on the Sussex coast: she was helping to nurse her father, who was dying, and was as a result herself excessively depressed. Eliot stayed with her for a few weeks, commuting to London on most weekdays; his hours at the publishing house seem to have been flexible, and often, even while in London, he would work at home in the morning and travel to the office in the afternoon. Charles Haigh-Wood died on 25

March and Eliot's time was taken up as an executor with Maurice, Vivien's brother. Maurice has recalled how, at Charles's funeral, Eliot had a 'vision' – it was a bright, sunny day and the concatenation of light and death seemed to affect him profoundly.[43] (In her father's will, Vivien was left with some shares in a trust fund which yielded a modest income – enough for them to be able to return to Bertrand Russell the debentures which he had given them during the First World War.) In order to rest after the ordeal of her father's death, in April Vivien took a brief holiday with her husband in France; then, in May, they went back to Eastbourne where they settled for a month or two. He commuted between London and Eastbourne, spending three or four days a week at Faber and Gwyer. He told Virginia Woolf, at the beginning of June, that he would bring some 'jazz' and dance records when he next visited her.[44] This was the age of 'flappers' and 'bright young people', that irruption of the pleasure principle between the Great War and the Depression, but there were no doubt times when Eliot knew that he was dancing in the dark.

And then, on 29 June, having completed his training, he was baptized and received into the Church of England at Finstock Church in the Cotswolds. William Force Stead, who performed the ceremony, was chaplain of Worcester College, Oxford, and Eliot's two sponsors, or godparents, were also members of the university. It was, as in so many of the major events of his life, performed in great secrecy. The front doors of the church were locked, and a verger was posted on guard at the vestry: Stead explained that the precautions were necessary in order to avoid anyone being embarrassed by the sight of an adult at the font.[45] Vivien was not present at the ceremony. After dinner that evening, Eliot, Stead and the two sponsors walked through Wychwood, an ancient wood close by (Eliot was later to set *The Family Reunion* in a house called 'Wishwood'), and Stead remembered Eliot pacing among the oak trees in a suit and bowler hat.[46] The next day he was driven to the palace of the Bishop of Oxford, Thomas Banks Strong, where he was confirmed in the Bishop's private chapel.

The news of his conversion, when he finally announced it to the world in the following year, came as a revelation to those who did not know him well and who still thought of him as the poet of *The Waste Land*, the iconoclast who had overturned the marble temple of his elders. 'What does Mr Eliot believe?' then became the question. When he was asked it directly, he would answer in a straightforward manner that he believed exactly what he was obliged to believe – the Creed, the Invocation of the Blessed Virgin and the Saints, the Sacrament of Penance, and so on. As a man, he gave his intellectual assent to the propositions of the faith which supported him. But we shall see that the ritual observances of that faith – in the devotional discipline of confession, Mass and communion – were of equal if not greater significance to him. In a preface to his mother's long poem *Savonarola*, for which he had arranged publication the year before, he reasserted the perception of his days as a student with Josiah Royce, that a rite may be established without any concept of 'meaning' being attached to it: that the series of acts themselves may be the only justification required by those who perform them. The rite *qua* rite may be the significant thing, in other words, and in the same essay he goes on to compare the religious service and its liturgy with conventional drama.[47] It may seem odd to distinguish between his doctrinal allegiances and his Christian observances, but it is likely that his need for the latter came from a much deeper source. In an essay on Bertrand Russell which he wrote in this year, he remarked that, 'Mr Russell believes that when he is dead he will rot: I cannot subscribe with that conviction to *any* belief'[48] – and this was just before his conversion. In a discussion with Hugh Sykes Davies about Marxists, he said, 'They seem so certain of what they believe. My own beliefs are held with a scepticism which I never even hope to be rid of'.[49] When Paul Elmer More asked him if his Christianity meant that he had abandoned poetry, he replied 'in that "I am absolutely unconverted" '[50]. Which is another way of saying, 'That, at least, I *know* to be true'. For in poetry, belief need play no part; and, within Eliot's own work, the structure of orthodox faith and the language of devotion are broken apart in order to make room for something much stranger and more tenuous, like the sound of someone crying in an empty church.

Eliot had been attempting to break the writing 'block' which he suffered after the composition of *The Hollow Men* by exercising his faculties in a conscious and painstaking manner: in the latter half of 1926 he was working on a translation of St John Perse's *Anabase*, a

ritual or pattern is valuable even if it doesn't mean

poem which he much admired. He had finished a draft by the end of the year, but in January 1927 St John Perse returned it to him with many emendations and suggestions – as a result, the translation did not finally appear until 1930. His 'block' was not successfully lifted, in fact, until in this year Geoffrey Faber asked him to write one in a series of 'Ariel' poems – single poems published as illustrated pamphlets for Christmas. It was the first poem written since his student days on an ostensibly religious subject, and its theme was 'Journey of the Magi'. In this poem he elaborates on that accentual measure he had first used in *The Hollow Men*, which gives the illusion of a single, spoken voice. The poem begins with an abbreviated quotation from one of Lancelot Andrewes's sermons, 'A cold coming we had of it . . .' and then draws out the implications of that journey itself in a series of direct but not unambiguous statements and images. This directness of statement and lucidity of structure derive at least in part from his recognition of the 'ordonnance' of Andrewes's own writing – an internal agreement of words which encourages precision, relevance and intensity. It is rhetoric in the best sense, and informs much of Eliot's poetry after the dramatic experiment of *Sweeney Agonistes*. But this fluently structured and quasi-conversational poetry is marked by a certain loss of power – the brilliant obliquities of the earlier work have gone. The energy has given way to a kind of plangency; the lines no longer flash and gleam, they reach a conclusion.

'Journey of the Magi' is the poem of a convert, which takes as its theme (and, for the first time in his poetry, we can talk of 'themes') the painful necessity of rebirth which is itself a form of 'Death', creating weariness and suffering – as well as a sense of alienation among men which is not very different from the agonies suffered by the martyrs of his Harvard verse. It was succeeded by another poem, 'Salutation', which was published in December of this year but eventually became part of a sequence entitled *Ash-Wednesday*. In this poem he employs Biblical references as well as passages which are strongly reminiscent of Anglo-Catholic liturgy, just as much of its imagery and symbolism derive from his reading of Dante, but these elements are pressed into the service of a narrative expressing dryness and solitude. Eliot evokes the tone of 'religious verse' without any faith being articulated or convictions expressed. Belief falls away, and what we find is the expression of an unattached religious sensibility – the instinct for belief. Eliot is thus able to create a devotional language out of his own preoccupations:

> Speech without word and
> Word of no speech
> Grace to the Mother
> For the Garden
> Where all love ends.

Here a peculiarly private vision is given the force of religious feeling, because it is presented as being equivalent to it. Since much of the inspiration for the poem, and for the sequence in which it finally found a place, comes from Dante, it is perhaps instructive to note that Eliot was finding the same kind of transformation in the work of the Italian poet. In 'Shakespeare and the Stoicism of Seneca', published in this year, he described Dante's attempts in *Vita Nuova* to construct something 'permanent and holy' out of his 'animal feelings', out of 'private failures and disappointments': religious belief plays its part in such a construction only as surface material, employed to provoke recognition and assent from the reader while the obscure or at least unclarified substance below does its own work.

Certainly, in letters to Bonamy Dobrée during this year, he was somewhat detached from what in neutral terms he called 'Religion'.[51] He was still elaborating upon the Bolovian culture which he had invented in his student verses, and with Dobrée he discussed the minutiae of Bolovian theology and religious practice, with its fundamentalists and its modernists. He was also sending to Dobrée further Bolovian stanzas of an obscene character, in which words like 'pricks', 'fucking', 'penis', 'bunghole' and 'Jewboy' were used for light relief. This was perhaps an example of what I. A. Richards described as Eliot's persistent concern with sex'.[52]

His formal attachment to the Anglican communion was extended when, in November, he became a British citizen. It was really only the legal recognition of an evident fact: 'In the end I thought: here I am, making a living, enjoying my friends here. I don't like being a squatter. I might as well take the full responsibility'.[53] Virginia Woolf saw him, just before he adopted citizenship, wearing a white tie and waistcoat – very much the man of the world.[54] His dress and demeanour were indeed now of the English type, and on occasions he went to theatrical lengths in order to proclaim himself one. Mary Colum related how Eliot once dined with her in a typically English restaurant, how they drank sherry before the meal and port after: 'He loved,' she said, 'the whole English civilization'.[55] As early as 1923, Eliot was explaining to Charles Whibley and Richard Aldington that if there were another war he would join the British Army – but then, when they strolled home together, Aldington was shocked when Eliot lifted his hat to a sentry outside Marlborough House.[56] It was the wrong gesture to the wrong person, suggesting that he did not yet understand the society which he wished to join. In addition, it became his practice to wear a white flower, and to hear Mass, on the anniversary of the Battle of Bosworth – he supported the Yorkist cause and wore the flower in memory of Richard III whom he considered to be the last English king. In other words, as one of his close friends admitted, 'He wasn't a bit like an Englishman'.[57] Since his commitment to English life and history was self-willed and therefore artificial, it is not difficult to see why he should get it wrong. But probably he understood that fact, and played upon it: it was his way of fitting in and yet not fitting in, the external sign of his own sense of himself as a 'resident alien'.

Yet he was also becoming a recognizable part of English letters and, when the *Criterion* became a monthly in May 1927, the cover announced that the magazine was 'edited by T. S. Eliot'. Its more regular appearance meant, however, that he had to work harder on its preparation while, in addition, he was writing a great deal of journalism: in 1927 alone, apart from preparing his regular Commentaries in his own paper, he wrote some thirty long reviews or articles for magazines like the *Dial*, the *Nation and Athenaeum*, and *The Times Literary Supplement*. Then, at the end of the year, the future of the *Criterion* seemed to be in doubt. On 5 December his secretary and occasional contributor, Irene Fassett, wrote to other contributors that, 'owing to differences of opinion between the proprietors on a matter of policy', publication of the magazine was to be suspended. What seems to have happened, quite simply, was that Lady Rothermere had had enough and wished to withdraw her support: she apparently disliked the *Criterion* very much,[58] and the extra costs incurred in running a monthly rather than a quarterly no doubt hastened her decision. At first it seemed that the magazine would simply have to end, and Frank Morley reported how Eliot would not take an active role in appealing to his fellow directors at Faber and Gwyer for financial help.[59] The truth was, though, that he had been convinced that his editorship would last only for another year or so[60] and he might, in any case, find it easier to express his opinions by writing for other papers.[61] But a number of contributors objected to the sudden disappearance of the magazine and, apparently at Frank Morley's instigation, a fund was established. Enough money was collected to pay for the issues of January and February, at which point Eliot intended to stop; nevertheless various eminent people pledged further support and, with Faber and Gwyer as sole proprietor, the *Criterion* did manage to continue, although once more on a quarterly basis. But it seems likely that Eliot was already feeling some of that weariness and lack of interest to which he confessed at the end of the magazine's life: as so often happens in such ventures, the good intentions and the high aspirations tended to be diluted or only mechanically adopted because of the exigencies of regular publication.

One of the most interesting aspects of Eliot's work on the magazine during this period was of a less serious kind, however: in the issues of January and June 1927, he reviewed some twenty-four detective novels. He also wrote a long essay on Wilkie Collins in this year. Detective fiction was his passion – he could quote long passages of Sherlock Holmes from memory (this was one of his party tricks), and in later years he liked to discuss with friends the work of Georges Simenon and Raymond Chandler (he particularly appreciated the latter's grasp of Californian law). It may seem an odd enthusiasm for a poet who generally professed uninterest in fiction, but it is not really so. He himself characterized 'thrillers' as being on one level a sort of melodrama,[62] and his own interest in the Jacobean drama suggests the nature of his preoccupation: these, too, are narratives of crime and punishment, of guilt and detection, evoking in crystalline form his own preoccupation with such matters. His fascination with murder trials has already been mentioned and, in his own work, the theme of murder plays a powerful role – from the anatomy of a murderer in 'Eeldrop and Appleplex' to the haunted and guilt-ridden protagonist of *The Family Reunion*.

Unlike her husband, Vivien Eliot was not able to cope successfully with her own obsessions and anxieties. In the year of his

[margin note: Detective fiction + Jacobean drama]

conversion, she was unhappy and often distraught. She was no longer really 'normal'[63] and Eliot had to persuade her in September to return to her sanatorium near Paris. Osbert Sitwell has given an account of her behaviour after her return from just such a period in a sanatorium: although he does not date the occasion precisely, it is at some point in 1927. A dinner party had been arranged to celebrate Vivien's return and, with the Joyces and Fabers as fellow guests, she proceeded to pick arguments with her husband across the table. She had a somewhat 'twisted' smile and the look in her eyes was one of 'consternation and suspicion'. At the end of the meal, Mrs Faber thanked her: 'It's been lovely, Vivienne.' 'Well it may have been lovely for you, but it's been dreadful for me.' 'Nonsense, Vivienne, you know it's been a triumph.' 'A triumph! Look at Tom's face.'[64]

Throughout this period, in fact, she was going from one sanatorium to another. In January 1928 she was back at the Malmaison, from where she wrote to Ottoline Morrell that her husband hated the sight of her, and she repeated what was by now her constant cry – she did not know what to do.[65] She was well aware that her behaviour was alienating Eliot still further, but she no longer seemed able to control it: it was an instinctive cry for attention and for help. When she returned to London in February, she began to suffer from the delusion that he was having an affair with Ottoline Morrell. She caused scenes at parties, shrieking at him, 'You're the bloodiest snob I ever knew!'[66] – she always knew how to wound and to anger him. He was, it seems, drinking[67] and a rumour went round which Anthony Powell records in his memoirs: 'Someone remarked, "They say Eliot is always drunk these days . . ." '[68]

For a man who was peculiarly attentive to manners and to the formal courtesies of 'society', the behaviour of a deranged wife would inevitably lead to anxiety and a sense of shame not far from panic. He often refused invitations to dine; to those who did not know him well, and who invited him and Vivien to social gatherings, he sometimes excused himself on the grounds that he and his wife were too busy to attend evening parties. But he could not disguise the situation from his friends: Virginia Woolf refused to visit him,[69] although her own mental balance was so precarious that Leonard Woolf might well have forbade her to have any contact with an apparently 'mad' woman. To Ottoline Morrell Eliot wrote that, although he wished to see her, he could not do so because of Vivien: he suggested that she write to Vivien and explain that, as she was sick, she could only see one of them at a time.[70] There are photographs which he and his wife took of each other in the garden of Chester Terrace in this year. Eliot, seated in a chair with their dog, Polly, on his knees, smiles cautiously at the camera (and at his wife behind it). Vivien stands at the back of the garden, looking elderly and frail and worn.

These were the unhappy months in which he placed his new faith around him like a carapace. By the beginning of 1928 he was communicating three times a week, and in March of this year – with Vivien ill in bed with influenza – he made his first confession. He had taken the first steps on what he now believed to be an irreversible journey – he did not know how much further he could travel, but he was quite sure that he would not return.[71] He was redeeming the time with prayer and the regular practices of devotion; but he wanted something else – he wanted discipline, and in one letter to Stead he described in powerful terms its importance to him.[72] This craving for discipline is not unknown in Christian practice, but it is rare in the Church of England. The significance which it held for Eliot is in part elucidated in a series of letters which he wrote to Paul Elmer More. He explained that Christianity reconciled him to human existence which otherwise seemed empty and distasteful and, in this context, he contrasted the sensual and the ascetic life.[73] Certainly libertinism, in the manner of de Sade, is one way of assuaging or defying the meaninglessness of human existence; and for those instinctively drawn to it, severe discipline or asceticism would be the only way of holding it in check, of averting the 'evil'.

This is, of course, close to the classic position of the saint who mortifies his flesh in order to silence its insistent demands – that self-imposed martyrdom which Eliot had dramatised many years before in his Harvard poetry. It is the particular fate of those who associate the senses with sin and guilt; such an association is formed early in life, and its origins are not susceptible to investigation. But it is at least clear that Eliot's instincts and preoccupations had not changed, only the context in which he placed them. He remained a Calvinist or perhaps even a Gnostic in Anglican clothing.

Of course his contemporaries could not see the peculiar and private aspects of his religion. In the public mind he had merely

the discipline of religion

attached himself to a Church which was even then in the slow process of decline as a force in national life. It was a time, also, when political and social discontent were propelling the young 'intellectuals' of England – who were in a sense Eliot's natural constituency – towards the espousal of more extreme forms of political belief and action. In succeeding years he was concerned to defend the fideistic position which he had adopted, but he did so only obliquely. He did not think of himself as a leader and made no attempt to win converts. In fact he rarely asserted the positive merits of his faith, but characteristically exposed the flaws and follies in other competing ideologies.

From the mid-Twenties to the late Thirties, in fact, his contributions to the *Criterion* were less concerned with literary or critical matters than with an analysis of the various claims of humanism, fascism and communism. Although he was not to announce until the issue of October 1933 that he approached public affairs as a 'moralist' rather than as an 'artist', there is no doubt that the original literary direction of the periodical was now of less importance to him than what he described as the 'problems of contemporary civilization'.[74] As he had once said of Matthew Arnold, 'he saw something to be done and no one else to do it'.[75] His first concern was humanism which, in the late Twenties, was enjoying something of a renaissance among American intellectuals. It was opposed to conventional scientific naturalism, and the humanists – with Eliot's old teacher, Irving Babbitt, as their principal exponent – claimed that the measure of Man was to be found in the cultivation of those values and qualities which removed him from a deterministic 'natural' order. Reason, intuition and free will were all associated with the concept of the 'ethical imagination' and Babbitt's notion of the 'inner check'. Eliot was sympathetic to the principles of classical order and propriety which such a view encouraged, but he was unconvinced of the merits of humanism as a general system. Its primary flaw was that it provided a certain intellectual discipline, but no firm foundation for emotional discipline. And as soon as humanism tried to raise itself as a substitute for religion, the poverty of what were essentially borrowed ethical formulations became quite clear. The authority of the 'inner check', for example, could in the end only be established upon religious grounds – humanism, by itself, had no permanent validity.

The appeal of humanism was in any event a temporary one, and its decline can be dated from the Thirties when economic depression and social unrest seemed to emphasize the necessity for specifically political and economic ideologies. And it was at this stage that Eliot began seriously to attend to the competing claims of communism and fascism. His intellectual respect for communism was far greater than for fascism; in fact in his commentaries in the *Criterion*, he suggested that it was the only practicable alternative to the Christian faith. By this he meant that it had a coherent set of principles, and offered a convincing explanation of the human order; in addition, it demanded from its adherents a certain kind of intellectual and moral discipline: '. . . as it is the faith of the day, there are only a small number of people living who have achieved the right *not* to be communists'.[76] There were, in other words, very few who could answer the claims of communism with coherent principles and values of their own.

His position on fascism is more complicated. Although his attachment to the work of Charles Maurras might have inclined him towards that political creed, he was quite aware of its intellectual shortcomings as an ideology. It also represented a form of populism, a political phenomenon of which he entirely disapproved. Perhaps he might have contemplated his own interest in the early activities of Mussolini: fascism offered a temporary emotional stimulus, especially for someone of Eliot's temperament, but unlike communism it could not provide any set of objective values or principles. In distinction to Lewis and Pound, whose aesthetic view of politics was such that they embraced the discipline and authority of fascism without properly understanding its implications, Eliot recognized very well that the reliance upon order and 'the state' alone was a form of escapism, a cover for unprincipled militarism and nationalism. He was as sceptical of 'order' as he was of 'liberty'.

The central element of his reactions to political events was to move to the higher ground of religious authority and tradition: that was the 'less false'. His essential point was that political beliefs are vicious when they are adopted as a substitute for religious belief, and when they pretend to offer what religious faith alone can provide. It was not a position designed to impress his contemporaries, but even those who would take issue with his espousal of orthodox Christianity might admit that the contemporary alternatives – represented by Auden on one side and Pound on the other – seem now to be vapid and debilitating ones. Eliot was so far removed from the preoccupations of his period that if he shirked its transient battles he also avoided its egregious follies.

In his commentaries in the *Criterion*, his characteristic method in dealing even with local and temporary matters – such as the standard of living or the problems of literary censorship – was to raise the issues to a level at which he could deal with the principles that animated them, and concern himself with questions of right language and right definition. His assertion that the *Criterion* was 'quite disinterested' in its general stance[77] was one that infuriated his more combative contemporaries, and there is an element of disingenuousness in his description of himself as a 'political ignoramus'[78] But the notion that he was interested in 'political ideals, but not in politics'[79] was one that suited his temperament very well: his refusal fully to commit himself to a definite position was part of that invasive scepticism which led him to doubt the final validity of any belief. He withdrew; he watched; he noted where one political statement might lead, and from what another derived. His training as a philosopher helped him to adopt a tone of enlightened observation, but his conviction as a Christian that the world was entering the 'dark ages'[80] gave force and animus to his new role. He was trying, with a very few others, to create a social and political ideology informed by Christian principles and he was interested in the possible emergence of a new kind of intellectual – a Christian intellectual who would try to combine both thought and feeling within a devotional spirit.[81]

Such a stance did not alienate only his readers and admirers; some of those who knew him well now felt that he was moving out of their reach, into a world with which they had little sympathy and less connection. Virginia Woolf said that he had less credibility than a corpse[82] – it is a measure of Eliot's secrecy over his conversion that she did not know of it until six months after it occurred. Lewis derided him also; and when William Force Stead visited Ezra Pound many years later, the poet told Stead that he had been responsible for 'corrupting' Eliot. Pound wrote a couplet on the matter:

In any case, let us lament the psychosis
Of all those who abandon the Muses for Moses.[83]

But if his old friends were suspicious of his Christian allegiance, he was beginning to make the acquaintance of those who, although they may have distrusted or failed to understand his poetry, shared his new faith and saw him as a respectable and eloquent spokesman for their own concerns. It was in this year, for example, that he met Paul Elmer More. More had already written to Eliot from America, suggesting that he come to Princeton, More's university, in order to lecture there. Eliot had turned down the invitation, since he did not have the time. His mother's health was, in any case, so fragile that when he next travelled to America it would be to stay with her. But More himself came to England in the summer of 1928; he had heard rumours from Irving Babbitt that Eliot was about to 'go over' to the Church of Rome but when they met Eliot assured him that he was a 'strong High Churchman and an enemy to Rome'.[84]

In fact Eliot and More had a great deal in common; they had both been born in St Louis (More twenty-four years before Eliot) and More had taught Greek to his brother, Henry, at Smith Academy. Having abandoned his family's Calvinism he took a course in Sanskrit in Harvard, where he met Babbitt who had a similar enthusiasm for Eastern religion. After studying Hinduism, More became attached to a platonism derived from his classical reading, and then finally made Eliot's leap into Anglo-Catholicism. Eliot's own development was not entirely unique, in other words, since it sprang from a common dissatisfaction with the culture in which he had been raised. In an America marked by a vague spirituality and an inchoate civilization, many young men had looked both to the East and to Europe for the tradition and authority they lacked at home. But the important fact for Eliot was that More was a theologian who had wrested from his American experience attitudes and conclusions very similar to his own. In a later tribute[85] he explained that More was quite unlike the English theologians who did not understand the pressures of 'barbarism' and 'infidelity' which now surrounded the Church. The two men were to correspond a good deal over the next decade, although like others More was to find Eliot on occasions baffling. He told one friend that he believed Eliot's conversion to have been profoundly affected by Charles Maurras and the Action Française – although he was convinced that he was sincere in his religious faith, he was not at all sure what it meant to him.[86] Another American visitor during this summer, Irving Babbitt, was in a similar spirit urging Eliot to 'come out into the open' about the nature of his religious commitment.[87]

But Eliot was pleased to have seen both Babbitt and More.[88] They were the only American 'thinkers' for whom he had any respect, and it is significant that he was attracted in both cases to their 'isolation' within their own country, just as he felt isolated in what was now his own. He was no stranger to intellectual solitude, however – indeed he had always in a sense welcomed it, as a sign of his own especial destiny. It exhilarated him.[89] He embraced it with the passion of a man who is used to being misunderstood and, more importantly, is quite happy to be so. For just as he realized that he sometimes gave the impression of arrogance, so, too, he knew himself to be one jump ahead of his critics: he understood the dangers of appearing to be an escapist, in his Christianity, for example, long before his detractors pointed them out.[90]

The most recent critics had been those who condemned his volume of essays published in this year, *For Lancelot Andrewes. The Times Literary Supplement*, for example, considered that he had committed a kind of treason[91] and even an old friend, Conrad Aiken, said that the book was filled 'with the presence of a spirit which is inimical to everything new or bold or generous'.[92] There was an element of provocation in Eliot's own stance, however, and in his preface to the collection he announced his new allegiances in a somewhat dramatic fashion. He had decided, he said, 'to refute any accusation of playing "possum".' (Pound had, in fact, given him the nickname, 'Old Possum', as a way of describing his ordinary tactics of evasiveness and caution – the opossum being an animal which shams death in order to escape predators.) But on Babbitt's urging, he emerged into the 'open' and here declared himself to be a 'classicist in literature, royalist in politics, and anglo-catholic in religion'. It reads as an aggressive statement, as if he were saying, 'There now. I have told you something about myself. Make what you can of it, but do not expect me to help you.' He also announced that he was preparing three books – *The School of Donne, The Outline of Royalism* and *The Principles of Modern Heresy* which, since they were never written, suggest a self-assurance which is putative rather than actual.

The essays in *For Lancelot Andrewes* were taken from his journalistic work of the preceding years and, despite the polemical preface, do not constitute a thematic whole. If there is any common ground between them, it is the manner in which Eliot's most powerful and persuasive passages are always delivered *ad hominem*; his criticism of Donne, Ruskin or Hobbes seems to spring not from disinterested inquiry but from exasperation or dislike. He confronted them on an emotional rather than an intellectual level – Donne's sermons are the work of a man who 'seeks refuge in religion from the tumults of a strong emotional temperament which can find no complete satisfaction elsewhere', and Hobbes was 'one of those extraordinary little upstarts . . .'. The subtitle of the collection is 'Essays on Style and Order', and the ostensible subjects of the essays – Bramhall, Bradley, Andrewes, Machiavelli – are those writers whose personalities are so free of confusion or disorder that they can be readily subdued in the pursuit of principles of right thought and right action; they have, as Eliot said of Machiavelli, an 'impersonality and innocence'. And yet his most interesting criticism is directed against those who, like Donne, employ style as a protective device or who, like Hobbes, adopt theories in part out of 'the weaknesses and distortions' of their own temperament. Hobbes was 'a revolutionary in thought and a timid conservative in action'; Ruskin's style was 'partly a deflection of something that was baffled in life'. Herbert Howarth has suggested that many of Eliot's judgments on other writers were autobiographical in character[93] and can we not see in such passages the outline of the author himself, bending over the images of others and seeing there something of the mystery of his own being?

One of the characteristic features of this volume, also, is the way in which Eliot will establish pairs of opposites – Donne against Andrewes, Bradley against Ruskin, Bramhall against Hobbes – in order to formulate his judgments. This is a technique which became a dramatic device in his 'A Dialogue on Poetic Drama' which was published in this year as a preface to Dryden's *Of Dramatick Poesie*. This kind of dialogue in fact suited him very well, not only because of its theatrical form but also because of its literal equivocation. And when he enters the more controversial areas of social and political inquiry, an oscillatory movement – to and fro – becomes characteristic of his prose. A typical statement will be of this kind: something too extreme will encourage us to move towards something less extreme, something weak will impel us towards something energetic. Democracy will persuade us of the advantages of elitism but, then, the triumph of elitism will suggest the virtues of democracy. And so it goes. It is one measure of his profound intellectual scepticism: not declaring any fixed position, but demonstrating how any particular one can be arrived at.

But that which in intellectual terms can be described as scepticism can also manifest itself in other areas as uncertainty. He told Virginia Woolf that he was in doubt 'about his soul as a writer',[94] and in a letter earlier in the year he had explained to John Gould Fletcher that he often entertained severe doubts about his poetry.[95] But he had suffered such doubts all his life, and now knew that it was best to ignore them – or, even better, to incorporate them within the poetry itself. Certainly he was continuing work on a new sequence of poems; 'Salutation' and 'Journey of the Magi' had lifted his 'block' and out of 'Salutation' came the complete sequence of *Ash-Wednesday*: it emerged like *The Hollow Men*, he said, 'out of separate poems. . . . Then gradually I came to see it as a sequence. That's one way in which my mind does seem to have worked through the years poetically – doing things separately and then seeing the possibility of fusing them together, altering them, and making a kind of whole of them.[96] As always, he took the precaution of sending typescripts of the new poems to friends, asking them for their comments. In the autumn of this year, the Woolfs, Mary Hutchinson and E. McKnight Kauffer, an American artist and commercial designer who illustrated many of Eliot's 'Ariel' poems, were summoned to Chester Terrace to hear and discuss what he had written so far. Virginia Woolf expected cocktails and music since that was his conception of the fashionable thing to do.[97] And Leonard Woolf has described how he read the poems in his 'curious monotonous sing-song'.[98] He was, Woolf added, rather 'severe' in his dismissal of some of the group's criticism. But perhaps at last his reputation was such that he had earned the right to be severe – in the following year, for example, the first book devoted to his poetry was published, the harbinger of many. George Williamson's *The Talent of T. S. Eliot* is a slim volume, and is perhaps most interesting now for the way in which Williamson discussed his work in terms that Eliot himself had already outlined: he was seen as the poet presiding over the disintegration of modern culture, and was compared with Donne whom Eliot had previously described in similar terms. A

1st critical work on T.S. Eliot

176

process was beginning here which is unique in twentieth-century poetry: of a poet setting the context and the principles for the description and critical evaluation of his own work.

And indeed external recognition of this kind was all the more important when his private life seemed daily to harass and diminish him. Early in 1929, his face became swollen and two teeth had to be removed – one of a number of dental operations which he was to suffer over the years. His main concern, however, was still with Vivien; he was reading the clinical notes compiled on her in the French sanatorium and consulting with her doctors. He was on the telephone to Virginia Woolf in April, talking in what she called his 'sepulchral' voice about Vivien's swollen legs and their humiliating difficulties with servants. 'We have been deserted. Nobody has been to see us for weeks. Would you really come – all this way? To see us?'.[99] Then, three days later, he cancelled the proposed visit since circumstances were such that they could not see anyone.[100] Part of these 'circumstances' was the fact that once more the Eliots were moving house – throughout this year, in fact, they were plagued by meetings with surveyors, valuers and solicitors. They moved from Chester Terrace to 98 Clarence Gate Gardens, their old quarters, in June; a few months later, they moved on to 177 Clarence Gate Gardens, spending an unpleasant Christmas there. They disliked the flat so much that they did not ask friends to visit them. Then once more they moved, to 68 Clarence Gate Gardens; and this was to be the home where the last scenes of their marriage were enacted.

9

The Woes of Marriage
1929–1931

IN SEPTEMBER 1929, Charlotte Eliot died: Vivien wrote, in a later diary, that it had been a terrible and agonising time for her husband.[1] That agony no doubt sprang in part from Eliot's sense that he had failed his mother. One friend remembers his speaking in 'moving and unforgettable terms' about her, and how at the time of his greatest success he wished that she could be with him since 'she would have been so glad'.[2] Is there not guilt here, as well as love? Charlotte Eliot had died two years after her son had formally abandoned the family's Unitarian faith and his own American nationality, and before the time when he achieved the 'greatness' which she had suspected in him and which he seemed to have thrown away by a hasty and loveless marriage to an Englishwoman. She admired his poetry, but it is not at all clear what it meant to her; she once remarked to a friend that she did not understand her son's work.[3] So even in this, the one talent which she might have believed she had bequeathed to her son, she felt isolated from him.

Eliot had just been writing on Dante and in 'Animula', an 'Ariel' poem which was published a month after his mother's death, he takes his theme from the description of 'l'anima semplicetta'; in this poem, he contrasts the world of infancy with the world of time and experience which spreads slowly like a stain. His mother dead, his wife disturbed and unhappy: of all people he was the least fit in temperament to suffer the extremes of human experience, and yet he had been impaled on them. In the month before Charlotte's death, he had explained that, whatever his detractors might say, he was not settling for an easy life but was on the first stages of an arduous journey:[4] 'Because I do not hope to turn again' are the first words of the poetic sequence which was now taking its final shape. The line itself is a straight translation from Cavalcanti, suggesting

Eliot sees language as order — Williams sees language as disorder

once again that it was only in response to other poetry that Eliot could express his own deepest feelings. That self-revelation which the work of Laforgue had once afforded him was to mark the pattern of his development; his was an imagination which went to literature for that which life could not give – a sense of order and significance, and the possibility of dramatic intensity.

In *Ash-Wednesday*, which was published in its final form in March 1930, his literary borrowings are almost entirely from religious texts – the Bible and the liturgy of the Mass – and from the work of Dante. Apart from specific correspondences of imagery and language, Eliot had originally given Dantesque titles to five of the six poems in the sequence: 'Perch'io non spero', 'Jausen lo Jorn', 'Som de l'escalina', 'Vestita di color di flamma' and 'La Sua Voluntade'. In a similar spirit he revised the poem in order to render it more impersonal: an earlier version of Part III had 'my own shape' which he altered to 'the same shape', for example. In *Dante*, a pamphlet published in 1929 as part of 'The Poets on the Poets' series, Eliot emphasized the Italian poet's virtues of simplicity, lucidity and economy – as well as his use of allegory mediated by clear visual images – principally because these were the qualities which he himself wished to acquire. For he found in Dante the highest expression of that civilization of Christian Europe which he had been considering since the time of the Clark Lectures at Cambridge in 1926: Dante was for him the embodiment of a cultural and social order, and it is significant that his pamphlet should be dedicated to Charles Maurras and contain a Maurrasien epigraph: 'La sensibilité, sauvée d'elle même et conduite dans l'ordre, est devenue une principe de perfection'.

It is possible to understand from this conjunction of Dante and Maurras why Paul Elmer More believed the latter to have had such an influence upon Eliot's conversion; 'l'ordre' in *Ash-Wednesday*, after all, has become that of the trained religious sensibility. Eliot said that his poem was an attempt roughly to apply the *Vita Nuova* to contemporary life,[5] and explained that Dante's treatise was of great importance in the struggle to discipline feeling.[6] In his essay on Dante, he was more specific about the nature of that treatise. He explained that its source was in part biographical, and derived from a sexual experience of early childhood. This event, 'which no subsequent experience abolished or exceeded', was then transformed by Dante, partly by means of allegory, into an intellectual and spiritual reality. This is in fact very close to his own account of *Ash-Wednesday* as an elucidation of his most powerful emotions in the context of man's pursuit of God.[7] Although we cannot derive from this happy conjunction any theory that Eliot himself had an intense sexual experience at the age of five or six, it serves perhaps to corroborate Auden's belief that the inspiration for most of his poetry came from 'a few intense visionary experiences, which probably occurred quite early in life';[8] and *nostalgie de l'enfance* has been discerned in his work by many of his more perceptive critics.

Certainly some peculiarly private elements are smuggled into the poetry. Eliot told John Hayward, who was later to become a close friend, that the yew trees of the poem were in fact remnants from two or three of his dreams.[9] And at the close of the poem, images from Eliot's childhood return in a cluster of significant sounds:

> Sister, mother
> And spirit of the river, spirit of the sea,
> Suffer me not to be separated
>
> And let my cry come unto Thee.

The voice of the lost child is mingled here with lines from the Catholic liturgy. Eliot has borrowed the authoritative tones and cadences of religious texts in order to sustain images or sensations which are wholly personal and inexplicable. The language of *Ash-Wednesday* is disciplined and denotative, close to his idea of classical poetry in its simplicity and lucidity of statement; and yet the classicism is privately won and held. A language of order and belief is being used to stabilize an insistent sense of loss and emptiness, perhaps suggesting also the nature of Eliot's own faith.

He seemed gratified by the reception of *Ash-Wednesday*; it had pleased his Christian friends and at least been accommodated by those who were not Christian. The former were now a growing constituency. There were individual priests, like his spiritual adviser Father Underhill, and there were also Christian communities like that of Kelham Theological College, where Eliot would, on occasions, go on retreat. He was also acquainted with prominent Anglo-Catholic laymen, like Lord Halifax, as well as the ecclesiastical establishment: in December 1930, for example, he spent the weekend without Vivien at the palace of George Bell, the Bishop of Chichester. Here he read *Ash-Wednesday*, apparently to general bewilderment, and one of his fellow-guests recalled that 'Mr Eliot did not join much in the conversation among the ten people who made up the party'.[10]

In fact, his was not the kind of religion at home in bishops' palaces. Although he was to be embraced by the ecclesiastical establishment, and in manner often seemed more priestly than the priests, he was not himself of that establishment. His central position was an orthodox one, but his stance within the English Church was critical and combative – his *Thoughts After Lambeth*, published in this year, is marked by what is in places an ironic polemic against the fatuities of ecclesiastical utterance. His charac-teristic position remained the same: to adopt the tone and color-ation of his surroundings, while at the same time preserving a sceptical detachment from them. In any case, he knew too much to be impressed by the conventional formulations which he attacked in his pamphlet, just as his own religion was so haunted by private obsessions that he could not accede to a conventional piety.

It would not be too much to say, in fact, that at the centre of his faith was the belief in, and fear of, Hell: 'to be damned for the glory of God' seemed to him to be a literal truth.[11] This becomes dramatically apparent in his articles and letters of the period. In one essay on Baudelaire published in this year, he suggested that the prospect of damnation imparted significance to life which it otherwise lacked: the glory of man was in part 'his capacity for damnation'.[12] He was preoccupied with Hell – not just the Hell of eternity but that torment to which human beings are sometimes consigned on earth,[13] just as he felt himself to be thus consigned. The idea of Hell liberated Eliot; not only did it give significance to suffering, but the flames bore him aloft so that he could see the conventions and customs of the world from a great height: he had at last found a truth which resisted even his powerful scepticism. And so it was that when Paul Elmer More suggested to Eliot that God had not created Hell, he replied in vehement fashion. Eliot's was a temperament that might have succumbed to the onslaughts of acute personal misery. But he withdrew; he learned how to study his own anxiety and suffering, to see in it a divine pattern that gave even damnation a meaning.

More replied to Eliot's rebuke with the charge that the God he seemed to worship was 'an abortion sprung out of the unholy coupling of the Aristotelian Absolute and the Phoenician Moloch'.[14] What More diagnosed as the savage or primeval aspect of Eliot's faith was also discerned by Ottoline Morrell. When she showed him some photographs of Greek statues of the fourth and fifth centuries, he said that they gave him 'the creeps' and were akin to 'snake worship'. Ottoline Morrell felt that he had 'Demons – on the brain'.[15] In fact, his brain had very little to do with it. One of the reasons for his dismissal of humanitarianism and conventional liberalism was that he felt genuinely the presence of evil and darkness with which they could not adequately deal, just as he had a clairvoyant sense of chaos or disorder: Stephen Spender has recalled how he seemed to have a horror of places associated with murder or violence.[16]

In his own life during this period he imposed order wherever he could, and he confessed that he both needed a 'daily routine' and had a 'dependence upon work'.[17] He seems, in fact, to have had a lifelong compulsion – in spite, or perhaps because, of what he often called his natural tendency to sloth – to take upon himself more duties and responsibilities than an ordinary man would wish to carry. Frank Morley, a fellow director (and fellow American) at Faber and Faber – the name had been changed from Faber and Gwyer in 1929 – has recorded how Eliot became 'submerged' in 'menial tasks' like other employees, with the difference that the members of the firm would rely upon him to deal with authors or manuscripts which they found too difficult.[18] He was also adept at composing blurbs – one of his skills was in parody so close to the original that it is difficult to tell whether it is faked or genuine, and he was pleased enough with these to keep a number of Faber catalogues in which he marked the blurbs written by himself.

This solid daily work has largely gone unrecorded, being merely the environment in which he was able to lose himself, and in his professional life Eliot is now remembered only as a singularly successful publisher of poetry. It would not be too much to say, in fact, that, through his publication and support of certain judiciously chosen poets, he determined the shape of English poetry from the Thirties into the Sixties. The most interesting example is that of

W. H. Auden. Auden had submitted some poems to him in 1927, while he was still at Oxford, and Eliot replied some three months later, explaining that although the work was not 'quite right' he would be interested to follow his progress.[19] In the autumn of 1929 Auden submitted his charade, *Paid On Both Sides*, which was 'right' enough for Eliot to publish in the next *Criterion*. Then, in October 1930, he published Auden's *Poems*. Eliot was occasionally to express doubts about Auden's progress as a poet – in particular, the fact that his mastery of technique seemed to have outstripped his ethical or religious development – but the important point was that he had recognized Auden's abilities, and described him as the best poet he had found in several years.[20] Eliot's contemporaries, like Lewis or Pound, were generally quite unable to see the solid or objective merit in the work of the generation then emerging, but Eliot was able to get outside his own preconceptions and assumptions so that he could spot the real thing, even in work very different from his own. He did not neglect in the process, however, the writers whom he had been supporting long before he became a publisher. In July 1931 he contracted to publish Joyce's *Finnegans Wake* (he offered a £300 advance for a book of between 190,000 to 200,000 words), and was already printing selections from it: *Anna Livia Plurabelle* was published in 1930, and *Haveth Childers Everywhere* and *Two Tales of Shem and Shaun* in the two succeeding years. He was also Pound's publisher: *ABC of Economics* and *A Draft of XXX Cantos* were published by Faber in 1933.

A great deal has been written about Pound's formation of the 'modern movement' in English letters, and indeed the pioneering work was his; what Eliot did was to make that movement accessible and, in the end, respectable to a larger public. And although it would be rash to assume that, without Eliot, such work would have remained limited in its appeal there is no doubt that his patient advocacy shaped the literary taste of two generations – after Pound and Joyce, there came Auden, Spender and MacNeice, followed by George Barker and Vernon Watkins; the Eliotic mantle in later years fell over Ted Hughes and Thom Gunn, simply because they were published by Faber and Faber. Although Eliot did not participate in any of the 'gangs' or 'groups' which were established around the work he published – he always remained reserved and somewhat aloof from the internecine struggles of those attempting to gain recognition – he became a kind of 'godfather' whose praise or criticism was accepted as the final arbiter.

E. W. F. Tomlin has recalled how he met Eliot and Vivien in 1930, when Eliot lectured on John Marston at University College, London. Vivien was wearing a scarf across the lower part of her face, and was constantly plucking her husband by the sleeve; he paid no attention to her as he answered Tomlin's questions but eventually they went off together, 'a forlorn pair'.[21] There are many stories of Vivien Eliot at this time, all of them showing her to be an outcast in her husband's life and affections. One young man went to visit Eliot; Vivien opened the door and when she learned his business exclaimed 'Why, oh why, do they all want to see my husband?' before slamming the door.[22] When Auden visited his new editor at home, he politely told his hosts that he was glad to see them, whereupon Vivien replied, 'Well, Tom's not glad'.[23] Geoffrey Grigson remembered husband and wife, together with dog Polly, arriving for tea in their Austin Morris – a sardine can of a car which caused Eliot endless trouble. As he gravely and courteously answered Grigson's questions, Vivien kept on asking her husband 'Why? Why? Why?' Eliot by all accounts retained a composed demeanour in public, and often launched into laborious and protracted conversations in order to cover up his wife's nervous interjections, but there is no doubt that Vivien's behaviour humiliated and unsettled him.

When Conrad Aiken had dinner with both of them in the autumn of 1930, he recalled Vivien's furtive but intense examination of him; she looked like a scarecrow, 'shivering, shuddering' – this recalls Eliot's line on the apparently murdered wife in *The Family Reunion*, 'A restless shivering painted shadow' – and throughout the meal the Eliots directed streams of hatred at each other. When Eliot in the course of conversation declared that there was no such thing as pure intellect, Vivien interrupted with 'Why, what do you mean? You know perfectly well that *every* night you tell me that there *is* such a thing: and what's more that *you* have it, and that nobody *else* has it.' He retorted, rather lamely Aiken thought, 'You don't know what you're saying'.[24] Vivien was clearly trying to embarrass her husband in front of his friends. This is not a sign of madness, however, merely of desperation.

But more disquieting symptoms were seen by Virginia Woolf when they came to tea later in the same year. Vivien smelt of ether, and her conversation exhibited signs of what might broadly be described as paranoia. 'Tell me, Mrs Woolf,' she said, 'Why do we move so often? Is it accident? That's what I want to know.' And, 'Does your dog do that to frighten me?' When Virginia Woolf asked her if she kept bees for honey, she replied that she kept hornets – 'under the bed'. The Eliots then left precipitately when Vivien thought that their host was making secret signs for them to do so.[25] Maurice Haigh-Wood has also described his sister's aberrant behaviour – how, for example, she would run out of the flat at night and stay in a hotel.[26]

Part of her anxiety and restlessness may have been due to the fact that she was taking an assorted and not necessarily complementary range of drugs: alcohol-based items for her headaches as well as various morphine derivatives. But the trouble went much deeper than that: Rose Haigh-Wood's fear that her daughter might be suffering from 'moral insanity' seemed to be justified, and both Eliot and Maurice Haigh-Wood believed that she might do something desperate.[27] Maurice has suggested that, at some point, plans were made to have Vivien committed by a 'reception order' to a private mental home – the kind of place to which Virginia Woolf had gone during her bouts of madness – but that she 'pulled herself together' and nothing came of them.[28] There is no other evidence for this, but the general horror of the situation was such that it seems possible. For Eliot there seemed to be no escape: however often he spent weekends away, and however frequently Vivien visited sanatoria in England or Europe, her condition was the fundamental fact of his life. Virginia Woolf described him as looking 'leaden' and 'sinister';[29] Harold Nicolson, on a later occasion, said that he seemed 'very yellow and glum'.[30] He was also becoming more isolated from others – he saw no one during the summer of 1930, for example, except American relatives and business associates.[31]

But if Vivien's behaviour was a source of gossip and scandal, Eliot's own life and temperament were subjects of no less interest to his contemporaries. When Osbert Sitwell described the Eliot household as a tragic one but also 'tinged with comedy and exhaling at times an air of mystification',[32] a great deal of that mystification derived from Eliot himself. Contemporary descriptions of him are sometimes perplexingly various – where Herbert Read, for example, remembered that 'I always felt that I was in the presence of a remorseful man, of one who had some secret sorrow or guilt',[33] another friend, Robert Sencourt, had quite the opposite impression of a man noted for his humour and the fact that he chuckled 'whenever he showed up the seriousness of what he was saying'.[34] It is hard to believe on occasions that one is reading accounts of the same person, and yet how could he, who bewildered himself, not bewilder others? Again and again he returns in essays and private correspondence to the sudden and unforeseeable changes in individual emotion – how he had great difficulty in analysing his own emotions,[35] and how one can suddenly experience quite different feelings from any one has had before.[36]

Certainly by 1931 the interest in Eliot – as a phenomenon, apart from anything else – was such that Richard Aldington was able to write a novel, *Stepping Heavenward*, which was an elaborate and protracted caricature of him and Vivien. Geoffrey Faber tried to prevent the publication of the book, according to Aldington, by asserting that Vivien would be deeply hurt by the account of herself; and although Faber declared that Eliot knew nothing about it, Aldington suspected that he did indeed know.[37] The novel itself is clearly animated by spite and jealousy, but although it presents only a caricature of Eliot it was accurate enough to be immediately recognizable to his friends: Sidney Schiff approved of it, for example, and wrote to Aldington telling him so.[38] Eliot is caricatured under the name of Blessed Jeremy Cibber – taciturn, cautious, afraid to commit himself and yet 'everything forces us to see in him a man with a fixed ideal and ambition, one who foresaw and predetermined every step of his way'. He was 'characteristically unhappy' with a 'tart and acid' pessimism, but those who spoke against him found themselves the victims of his 'formidable sarcasm'. The most malicious part of the narrative concerns Cibber's marriage to Adèle. She had been one of the first to 'proclaim Cibber's genius' but became more and more unhappy in the marriage because of Cibber's treatment of her; he thought of the marriage as a 'purely legal contract, implying none but social obligations'. This was far from the case, but the publication of *Stepping Heavenward* hurt Eliot deeply: as a result, according to Robert Sencourt, he 'refused to allow any mention of his marriage even from the friends in whom he most fully confided'.[39] But there were those, of course, who still speculated in private, and Osbert Sitwell's unpublished memoir contains a suggestive portrait of their marriage. He believed Vivien to be devoted to her husband but, aware of her own unequal position, was uncertain of her hold upon his affections. Her 'flirtations' with men like Bertrand Russell were ploys to arouse jealousy in him, just as the occasions on which she wounded and humiliated him in front of others were attempts to engage his emotions in some way, even if those emotions were only of anger; at least such anger might prove that she had some influence over him still. In addition, she had become paranoiacally suspicious of his relationships with women like Virginia Woolf and Ottoline Morrell – and the fact that some of her fantasies were pornographic in character[40] suggests the presence of a thwarted sexuality rather like that of her husband, as exhibited in his 'Bolo' verses.

But it seems likely that, on a deeper and much less easily negotiable level, Vivien felt that she did not really know her husband at all: 'Why? Why?' is the query Geoffrey Grigson remembered, and it sounds as if she were pleading with him to unravel something of his complexity and reveal himself to her. But by degrees the importunity of her behaviour made him withdraw from her even more, causing redoubled anger and suspicion. There is another aspect of Eliot's character, however, which bears upon this unhappy marriage. 'What is wrong, what is missing?' had been the question of Sibylla in Vivien's story, 'Fête Galante', when faced by the American financier-poet. For despite the gaiety and good humour which were a large part of Eliot's social character – he was 'nice to be with'[41] – there was also a detachment which indeed suggested something 'missing'. Frank Morley has recalled how kind he was with Morley's children but he was unsure whether he 'ever *saw* them or not'.[42] And Stephen Spender has described how he seemed 'blinded to the existence of people outside himself'.[43] It is this lack of connection, or of what is called 'empathy', which characterised the latter years of his marriage with Vivien. He could see her suffering, but he could do nothing but look on helplessly.

His detachment can also be measured by his exasperation with other people. In a curious essay on Pascal, published in 1931, he described the experience of a man of great intellect who 'sees through' human beings and recognises their insincerity, cowardice, pettiness, dishonesty and vanity. It is a damning list, and couched with a force which signals the presence of his own attitudes only barely disguised by his apparent theme. That he did on occasions consider other human beings in this light is adduced by what Aldington called a 'formidable sarcasm' and his sometimes savage reactions to other people. In a memoir of Charles Whibley, published in 1931, Eliot recalled his own description of a contemporary as an 'insignificant insect'; as one journalist put it many years later, he had a mind like a steel trap, 'all tensile and teeth'.[44] The teeth were visible in an exchange in this year, 1930, with E. M. Forster. On D. H. Lawrence's death, Forster wrote a tribute in the *Nation and Athenaeum* calling him 'the greatest imaginative novelist of our generation'. Eliot then wrote a letter to the periodical, asking Forster to explain what he meant exactly by 'greatest', 'imaginative' and 'novelist'. Forster replied that Eliot had entangled him in a web but, on occasions such as Lawrence's death, he would rather be a fly than a spider. Eliot's coldness was not even withheld from his friends: after Virginia Woolf's death in 1941 he wrote an obituary which, according to Herbert Read, 'shocked us all by its chilly detachment'.[45] And this chilliness, together with the sudden shafts of ferocity, has to be remembered if his marriage is to be seen clearly.

He himself knew well enough what that marriage had become. In August he explained to Paul Elmer More that there were certain decisions which instigated a lifetime of torment.[46] Such a decision he had made fifteen years before, when he married Vivien, and now he was living with a sick and perhaps deranged woman. At the end of an essay on Thomas Heywood, published in the following year, he quoted some lines as a valedictory:

> O God! O God! that it were possible
> To undo things done; to call back yesterday . . .

He was pondering upon the nature of choice and damnation not only in painful retrospection, but also because he was close to making another and equally significant decision. If he continued to live with his wife, there would be no end to her sufferings and no end to his own. But if he left her, he would be abandoning the one human being who relied upon and needed him. He could not evade the unhappy consequences of either choice. And Eliot was a Christian with a profound sense of sin: it is not too much to say that his own soul was in peril. But he was caught in a trap, and the need for release was the one that finally triumphed: he would leave Vivien. In March 1931, he told Stephen Spender that he had been listening to Beethoven's A Minor Quartet, and had heard in that music a kind of non-human gaiety which had emerged from the other side of extraordinary suffering.[47] There was no release for Vivien, however: in December of that year she was describing to Ottoline Morrell the unpleasant time she had had with her husband[48] and, two weeks later, complained that their Christmas had been a most unhappy one.[49]

Perhaps some measure of Eliot's own distress might be taken from the fact that, after the publication of *Ash-Wednesday* in 1930, he was not able to engage in sustained poetic composition for five years. He continued with the occasional work which appeared in the 'Ariel' sequence – and indeed 'Marina' of this year is suffused with a subtle but powerful lyricism which had not been given such free expression since 'La Figlia Che Piange' fifteen years before. He had also finished by 1930 his translation of St John Perse's *Anabase*, on which he had been working intermittently for four years. He was pleased with it, and speculated about doing more work of a similar kind – he contemplated turning some of Hugo von Hofmannsthal's plays into English, for example, but the idea came to nothing.

Anabase itself is a richly decorative and sometimes gaudy 'prose poem' in which Eliot was able to deploy his gifts for linguistic play – the nearest equivalent in English would be Oscar Wilde's 'The Sphinx'. In spite of its length it is thematically somewhat obscure, but he justified the lack of connectedness within the poem by describing it as 'the logic of the imagination'. He believed, also, that the influence of the poem was visible in some of his work that succeeded it – there are traces of its vocabulary and imagery in 'Journey of the Magi', 'Marina' and *Ash-Wednesday* – and that students of his later work would perhaps note its presence in all his work.[50] In fact the single most important effect of the French poem upon Eliot is what he described in the preface as 'the declamation' inherent in it.

The declamatory tone, in which the emphases of ordinary speech are controlled and heightened by a strong rhythmic pattern, was one he had explored in *Sweeney Agonistes* and he was to refine it further in the project which he now wished to complete. After *Ash-Wednesday*, he had been casting about for a new theme and a new structure – part of his constant effort never to repeat himself, always to attempt something quite different. Late in 1930 he told G. Wilson Knight that he was planning to write a poem which would be inspired by Beethoven's 'Coriolan Overture', and by the following year he had outlined its structure. He wanted to write a poem in four sections, of which one feature would be political satire.[51] He expanded on his plans in a letter to Middleton Murry. Murry had already seen the first poem in the projected sequence, 'Triumphal March', since it had been published at the beginning of October in the 'Ariel' series. The second poem of the sequence was already written – this was 'Difficulties of a Statesman', eventually published in the winter 1931–2 issue of *Commerce* – and Eliot thought he was capable of writing the third part; he was not so convinced about the fourth, however, which he wished to derive from St John of the Cross.[52] The project was serious enough for Eliot to have discussed it with Hugh Ross Williamson who, in a little book on his poetry published in 1932, explained that 'At the moment, the first two sections of this projected work (which is to be slightly longer than *The Waste Land*) are in print'. Williamson suggested that where *The Waste Land* had concerned the 'post-War world', the new poem was to address itself to the 'post-Peace world', and that the sequence would centre 'on the matters of government rather than on individual reactions to chaos'.

Even in spite of these hints, it is difficult to imagine what the poem would have contained if it had ever been completed, but the fact that Eliot wished to include aspects of St John of the Cross suggests that its political nature would be of the surface only. The two central protagonists were to be Young Cyril, a representative of the common people, and a leader of men based upon the figure of Coriolanus (the two sections actually written have the general title of 'Coriolan'). Coriolanus was a figure, in fact, who exercised a peculiar fascination for Eliot and he mentioned him often in his published criticism: it should be remembered that, in Shakespeare's play, the First Citizen accounts for Coriolanus's achievements on the grounds that ' . . . he did it to please his mother and to be partly proud'. Coriolanus is a man raised and then destroyed by his mother, as he becomes impaled upon the emotions which spring from his devotion to her; and, in 'Difficulties of a Statesman', the cry of 'Mother mother' returns with hopeless longing.

But it is impossible to speculate upon a poem which was not finished; what we do see, in the two fragments which Eliot published, is a quite new thing in English poetry – exuberant, funny, sharp, with a montage of poetry and prose and a conflation of voices or tones:

> The natural wakeful life of our Ego is a perceiving.
> We can wait with our stools and our sausages.

Eliot had written, in a preface to Harry Crosby's *Transit of Venus*, published in 1931, that it was necessary for poets to take chances, to go too far and 'risk complete failure'. He was taking just such a risk here. But, as had happened previously in *Sweeney Agonistes*, the novelty of the enterprise proved too much for him – he could not find an existing literary model from which he could draw strength and inspiration.

And so he abandoned the poem, and began to doubt once again whether he had any more poetry to write;[53] it is significant that his next major work was to be a verse drama on a religious theme, commissioned by the Church of England. The end of the 'Coriolan' experiment marked a decisive change in the direction of his creative life: if he had been able to complete it, we may speculate that his own art would have taken an entirely different shape. What is clear, at any rate, is that his succeeding work is less startling and more conventional, less innovative and more accessible – more 'public' work. The pages in *The Complete Poems and Plays* devoted to his 'Unfinished Poems', 'Sweeney Agonistes' and 'Coriolan', are the most poignant, in the sense of promise unfulfilled, of that volume. Everything after them would be more measured and more certain; and it is perhaps not inapposite to note that, in this period of transition, his private life was also drawing towards some kind of resolution.

10

Separate Lives
1932–1934

THE DECISION TO LEAVE his wife had come slowly and painfully.
He had consulted among others Vivien's brother, Maurice, and his
spiritual counsellor, Father Underhill, who had advised a separation. The problem remained of how and when to do so, but this
dilemma was resolved for him when he was invited to accept the
Charles Eliot Norton professorship at Harvard for the academic
year 1932–3. The extended period in America would give him the
opportunity both to accustom Vivien to his absence and cleanly to
break his marital ties with her. He was also eager to take up the
appointment because he needed the money: the Harvard authorities in fact offered him ten thousand dollars, although he was forced
to forgo his salary from Faber and Faber for the duration of his stay.
The extra income would be needed, of course, to finance what on his
return would become an independent existence.

And so in 1932, the final year of his marriage, he strove to
maintain the familiar pattern of life until the end. He was more than
usually busy in any case, having both to prepare for his visit and to
complete as much work as he could in advance to cover his ten
months away. In the spring he was attempting to collect as many
articles as possible for the three issues of the *Criterion* which would
appear in his absence and, in addition, he gave a series of talks on
the radio. They were entitled 'The Modern Dilemma', and were
concerned with the place and importance of Christianity in the
modern world, in which he emphasized the need for 'holy living and
holy dying . . . sanctity, chastity, humility, austerity'.

For the last time the Eliots appeared together as a married
couple. There were the usual visits to friends like the Schiffs and
Morrells – on one occasion, in June, they visited Ottoline Morrell in
Gower Street to meet Alberto Moravia. And there were familiar

trips to the country, to stay with the Morleys and the Woolfs – although Virginia Woolf was so unnerved and horrified by Vivien that she vowed never to see them together again.[1] Although Vivien had no idea that her husband was actively planning to leave her, the shock of his decision to go away for such a long time seems to have rendered her even more desperate. She told Ottoline Morrell in July that it was only due to Ottoline's efforts that she felt able to keep going.[2] When Vivien visited Edith Sitwell in March, the latter's maid – who had worked as an attendant in a mental hospital – smelt Vivien's drugs and told her employer, 'If she starts anything, Miss, get her by the wrists, sit on her face and don't let her bite you. Don't let her get near a looking glass or near a window'. Conversation on this occasion was difficult. When another guest offered Vivien a cigarette she replied that she *never* accepted anything from strangers: it was too dangerous. And when Edith Sitwell met her by chance in Oxford Street during the summer, she greeted her by name and Vivien replied, 'No, no, you don't know me. You have mistaken me *again* for that *terrible* woman who is so like me. . . . She is always getting me into trouble'.[3] Elizabeth Bowen visited the Eliots in Clarence Gate Gardens in the same period, and described it as 'sinister and depressing' since there were 'two highly nervous people shut up together in grinding proximity'.[4] That proximity was almost at an end, however. On Thursday, 15 September, two days before her husband's departure, Vivien held a farewell party for him at Clarence Gate Gardens. Then on the Saturday he and Vivien, together with Maurice, drove down to Southampton: he was to sail to Montreal, and then travel down to Boston. According to one account, it transpired that Vivien had deliberately locked some important papers in the bathroom and a taxi had to be despatched to the flat in order to retrieve them;[5] if true, it was a sure sign of that which he already knew: Vivien did not wish him to go. The Eliots walked on the deck of the ship before its departure, and then she returned alone to Maurice on the shore. When the ship left harbour, it was taking away her husband for ever. It was a decisive moment in Eliot's life, and one which would continue to torment him. He wrote in a foreword to Harold Monro's *Collected Poems*, published eight months later, while he was still in America, 'There is no way out. There never is'. He described the solitude of the poet, and how as the years passed it was something that became more and more difficult to bear; he ended with a quotation, 'Sleep, and if life was bitter to thee, pardon'.

When he arrived in Boston, it was his first visit to the United States for seventeen years. His last journey had been made in order to explain to his parents why he had decided to stay in England with Vivien, and now he had returned so that he might leave her. And yet it is one of the strange ironies of Eliot's fate that out of the ruins of his private life he had been able to construct a public monument: his years in England had transformed him into an authoritative figure, and an American edition of *Poems, 1909–1925* and *Selected Essays, 1917–1932* (together with a small book, *John Dryden: The Poet, The Dramatist, The Critic*, taken from some radio broadcasts) were published to coincide with his arrival. *The Bookman* declared it to be 'The Return of the Native' and their essayist was at pains to discern the essential Americanness of Eliot and his work. He described his virtues as those of the Puritan: 'the toughness, the patience, the conscientiousness, the acceptance of the new, the personal fidelity, the pioneering energy, the preciseness . . . an *American* Victorian'. Since the writer here was a New Zealander, Gordon George, otherwise known as Robert Sencourt, he may not have noticed the distrust among some Americans for their own native son. A reporter from the *Boston Herald* diagnosed at once the nature of Eliot's cultural unease: 'His accent is an obvious pose. But it is not half-baked . . .it goes the whole hog, and he nearly gets away with it . . . Personally Eliot seems to be all water. His manner is all a superimposed form and pose, which his special type of readers swallow with joy. But sometimes when he is silent he seems to enjoy watching them swallow'.[6] It was a pose, however, which one more obviously American poet, Robert Frost, refused to accept. He attended a dinner in honour of Eliot in November, at the St Botolph Club in Boston, and was enraged by his condescending attitude towards the young men who clustered around him: he was 'taking himself so seriously'. Somehow the conversation turned to Scottish poetry, and Eliot declared that no good poetry had been written in Scotland except William Dunbar's 'The Lament for the Makaris'. Frost asked if an exception might be made for Robert Burns. No, Eliot replied. But was he not at least a good song-writer? 'One might grant,' he said, 'that modest claim'.[7] It was not, for Frost, a pleasant occasion.

While at Harvard, Eliot stayed at B 11 Eliot House, by the River Charles, and in his rooms there he gave weekly tea parties for his students – a sufficiently English custom with which to begin. One of the students remembered his 'helpful benignity' on these occasions, and also 'his stateliness mitigated by shyness'.[8] While staying at the university he also saw a great deal of his relatives – sisters and brother, as well as one aunt, two uncles, two nieces, and various assorted Eliots and their scions. But in spite of the presence of his family, he did not feel at ease. He suffered from home-sickness, and there was also a resurgence of his old feeling that the atmosphere of Boston and Harvard stifled him. Almost at once he was sending long letters to his friends in England: in one letter to Mary Hutchinson, written soon after his arrival, he speculated in a somewhat objective manner about the course of Vivien's affairs, as if already trying to confirm the distance between himself and her.[9]

In spite of the marital problems which were still far from resolved, his most urgent task was to write the lectures which he had been commissioned to give. He had not had the opportunity in England to prepare them; in fact, he had not made up his mind, before he arrived in America, on what precisely he was going to lecture. And so in order to save time, and to spare himself the necessity of too much research, he was compelled to deal with subjects that were already familiar to him. He chose as his broad theme the history of criticism in England, as exemplified by poet-critics such as Dryden and Coleridge (and of course, by extension, himself). There were to be eight lectures, starting on 4 November and finishing on 31 March; in addition, he had undertaken to teach in the spring a course on contemporary English literature, 26b, for selected students.

The lectures were published in the following year in volume form, *The Use of Poetry and The Use of Criticism.* Although on this occasion they had to be published within a certain time as part of Eliot's agreement with the university, this was in fact the form in which most of his later criticism emerged: spoken addresses were printed as pamphlets or as books. He was economical both in time and effort, and one of his principal pieces of advice to colleagues like Herbert Read was to take on lecturing tasks because there would also be a book to construct from them. Nevertheless Eliot always felt surer of himself behind a typewriter rather than in front of an audience, and he often confessed that he was not a particularly good lecturer; although he had had by now a great deal of practice, he found it a difficult task, and his nervousness about such a perform-ance would affect him some days in advance.

He was nervous, also, about the public reception of his work: in his preface to the published version of the Harvard lectures, he apologized in advance for 'another unnecessary book'. But it was characteristic of him to make such a disclaimer, both publicly and privately – often, when he sent books to friends, he would add a note saying that he might be completely wrong, that he had yet to know his own mind on such matters, and so on. He vanishes in front of one's eyes, as it were, by deprecating in advance an inadequate performance or suggesting that he was not wholly in earnest about what he had said. When Stephen Spender reviewed *The Use of Poetry and The Use of Criticism*, Eliot told him that his strictures were just and that his only mistake had been to take the lectures too seriously – at times he was simply being ironic.[10] There is an element of native caution and self-protectiveness in such a manoeuvre, of course; he was, he once said, rather like Marianne Moore's 'jerboa' who could be in two places at once.[11] It was in this spirit that he attacked his own book in a letter to the *New English Weekly*. Pound had reviewed it somewhat acerbically but Eliot was just as capable of doing that himself and, in his letter to the magazine, Eliot proceeded to accuse himself of ignorance, inattention and haste; he had over-rated Dryden, misunderstood Coleridge and written a superfluous piece on Arnold, and Pound 'might have said that I spent eight hours in coming to no conclusion. . . .'[12]

He was at least right in that, although the essential point of his Harvard lectures was that no conclusions were really possible. Indeed *The Use of Poetry and The Use of Criticism* demonstrated once again, if any more demonstration were needed, what a relativ-ist and sceptic he was in literary matters. His examinations of Coleridge, Arnold and others are memorable for their brief but apposite remarks *ad hominem* – Coleridge was a 'ruined man', and Arnold unlike the 'riff-raff' who preceded him was one 'qui fait se [sic] conduire' – but the general context of his remarks is the 'historical process'. No final definition of poetry can be offered since 'every effort to formulate the common element is limited by the limitations of particular men in particular places and at particular times', and in the same way 'our criticism, from age to age, will reflect the things that the age demands . . .'. And what did the age demand of Eliot? In the first place, precisely the kind of attention to critical theory which he exhibited here; this was a period in which literary criticism, as an intellectual and sometimes even a moral discipline, had been established in the English departments of many American and British universities. Eliot, himself part of that 'historical process', emphasized the inevitability of criticism as an intellectual activity and also affirmed a strong connection between the 'critical' and the 'creative' mind – just as the allusive literariness of his own poetry, and his creation of a 'tradition' in which that poetry could be placed, offered to academics and students precisely what they needed for their own labours.

Despite the rushed conditions under which he wrote these lectures, as well as his scepticism about the permanent value of any one form of criticism, their tone of assurance is their most remarkable single characteristic. What Eliot provided, at a time when, as he said, 'never were there fewer settled assumptions as to what poetry is', was a certainty of judgment combined with an ability so to arrange various literary texts that they seem to form a coherent order among themselves. So it is that in one paragraph he mentions Elizabethan blank verse, Milton, Spenser, Pope and Dryden – and makes sense of them in terms of their relationship to each other. Classification and comparison are his devices, although his genius for organization sometimes conceals a peculiar lack of content in his own critical opinions – when he seeks for matter, he tends to quote someone else. But what the age demanded was the assumption of authority and the assertion of significance; and this Eliot was able to provide, employing that rhetoric which, as he said on more than one occasion, he had inherited from ancestors involved in the church, law and politics.[13]

But beneath his assurance there is in the lectures a more ambiguous note, which in itself may explain his intellectual scepticism. He suggests that poetry itself is inexplicable, a fusion of elements that remain obscure, deriving from sources that cannot be examined; it may be the remnant of a 'pre-logical mentality' and have begun 'with a savage beating a drum in the jungle'. A poet's imagery comes 'from the whole of his sensitive life since early childhood' and represents 'the depths of feeling into which we cannot peer'. As a result, he was later to adopt an attitude of wariness and even dislike towards poetry. His characteristic stance, in his prose, is found in his attempt to raise everything to a higher and more organized level of consciousness: from the despised 'inner voice' to spiritual authority, from personality to impersonality, from individual feelings to the 'emotion' of art. But his sense of poetry was of an activity or process that actively subverted such a hierarchy. It may have been this, together with his familial puritanism, that prompted him to assert in these lectures that poetry was not a 'career' but a 'mug's game'. No poet can know if his work has any permanent value: ' . . . he may have wasted his time and messed up his life for nothing.'

But if his scorn and weariness are here in part directed against himself, contemplating the 'mess' in which he now found himself, there are also intimations in these lectures of the work that was to come. In Harvard, where he had once been an undergraduate and where the shades of the Eliots were heavy around him, he confessed that poets would like to possess some kind of 'social utility' and 'the most direct means of social "usefulness" for poetry is the theatre'. He had returned to the environment in which such values had been inculcated into him; the presence of his grandfather's example can be sensed here, as well as his family's adoption of social responsibility and communal leadership. And the fact that, for Eliot, the demands of 'social utility' are implicated in the idea of the poet as dramatist was to become most important in the development of his own career.

The lectures at Harvard were not his only employment in America since, in order to earn as much money as possible, he had committed himself to a variety of engagements. There was a break in the lectures for the Christmas vacation, and Eliot went on a rapid tour of California. He spoke at UCLA, to a large and crowded auditorium, and then a few nights later gave an address at the University of Southern California on Swinburne, Lear and Lewis Carroll as nonsense poets. He intensely disliked California, although its more vulgar aspects seem to have been a source of some amusement: in one letter to Virginia Woolf, written in the style of an innocent abroad, he described to her some of the more ridiculous, or at least, more garish, aspects of Los Angeles life. The Brown Derby restaurant, in the shape of that hat, particularly caught his attention.[14] In January he was in his birthplace, St Louis, where he gave an address on 'The Study of Shakespeare Criticism', and spent some time in Buffalo; he went on to Baltimore where he lectured at Johns Hopkins University on the Metaphysicals and gave a reading at the Poetry Society. While he was staying there, he met Scott Fitzgerald – they had been in communication with each other some years before, since Eliot had tried unsuccessfully to acquire the English rights to *The Great Gatsby* after he had first arrived at Faber and Gwyer. Fitzgerald told Edmund Wilson that he seemed 'very broken and sad and shrunk inside'.[15] Others found him more attractive: while he was at Providence, on another engagement, a woman made eyes at him throughout dinner and whenever he talked would murmur, 'My what a line you've got!'[16]

He had returned to Harvard by the beginning of February, in order to deliver the remaining lectures. He was suffering from exhaustion (he had wanted to do some *Criterion* work, but had found no time for it) and had caught a cold, but that did not prevent him from fulfilling other engagements. He was at Yale University on 23 February lecturing on 'English Poets as Letter Writers' – a subject of which he himself had had considerable experience, although he sensed that the more earnest members of the academic community there suspected him of frivolity. In March he was in Princeton where he lectured on 'The Bible and English Literature'. He also travelled down to New York from time to time, and was in the city in both April and June; Edmund Wilson heard him read there, and wrote to John Dos Passos, 'He is an actor and really put on a better show than Shaw. . . . He gives you the creeps a little at first because he is such a completely artificial, or, rather, self-invented character . . . but he has done such a perfect job with himself that you end up by admiring him.'[17] In another letter, Wilson explained that the contradictions within Eliot became quite apparent on meeting him; that although his opinions were judicious, his personality was 'really rather incoherent'. He had to feed him quantities of gin in order to get him to talk (as a result, Eliot had a ferocious hangover the next morning), but Wilson could not help feeling rather in awe of him as 'the most highly refined and attuned and chiselled human being' he had ever encountered.[18]

By the time he had concluded his lectures at Harvard, Eliot had visited New York, Buffalo, Pasadena, Minneapolis, Princeton, Los Angeles, St Louis, Haverford, Yale, Smith, Mount Holyoke and

Bryn Mawr. In May he went to Vassar in order to attend a performance of *Sweeney Agonistes* by the girls there – a bizarre choice, even for that enlightened establishment, although he explained to the audience that he was not the type 'to do a girl in'. He had fulfilled a more important engagement the month before, however, when he travelled down to the University of Virginia to deliver the Page-Barbour lectures.

He was obliged to publish the lectures as part of his contractual agreement, and they duly appeared as *After Strange Gods: A Primer of Modern Heresy*. Although he was later to disavow the book, and never allowed any part to be reprinted, he was not entirely dissatisfied with it at the time. He said, in a letter to the *New English Weekly*, that although *The Use of Poetry and The Use of Criticism* was an attempt to say things which were not on the whole worth saying, *After Strange Gods* was an unsatisfactory attempt to elucidate an important subject.[19] What he wished to attack was the absence of moral, and therefore religious, criteria in the criticism of contemporary literature. Having at Harvard rebuked the dogmatism of those critics who considered literature (and especially poetry) to be some kind of substitute for religion, he was now reversing the equation: he wished to introduce into the appreciation of modern literature those concepts of good and evil which were part of the religious comprehension. He ascended the lecture platform, he said, not as an artist but 'only in the role of a moralist'. It was a justifiable position, although perhaps a difficult one for a man in his particular circumstances to assume. His cleverness and scepticism had allowed him to see through the critical principles which exercised his contemporaries, but the problem with the Virginia lectures is that Eliot treats his own concerns in such a sketchy and polemical way that they are rendered unconvincing. His dramatic manner was often akin to that of a preacher, but on occasions such as this he forgot that preaching is only really suitable for the converted.

His major purpose was to change the terms of critical debate, and to introduce into its vocabulary a scale of moral values; in his own account of his contemporaries, he talks of 'evil' and 'the diabolic' (although, interestingly enough, never of 'goodness' or 'the saintly'), and discards the polarities of 'classicism' and 'romanticism' in favour of 'orthodoxy' and 'heresy'. He had been preoccupied with such ideas for a long time; four years before, he had announced that he was about to write a book called *The Principles of Modern Heresy*, but the continuity of his concerns runs deeper than that. When in these lectures he attacks the notion of 'individuality' and of 'personality' in modern literature, he is reverting to arguments which he had rehearsed almost fifteen years before in 'Tradition and the Individual Talent'. His ideas remain the same – George Santayana once described them as 'subterranean without being profound' – and only their context has changed.

Eliot's tone was often savage and contemptuous, but in the Virginia lectures the savagery has lost its wit. He attacked Pound (and was still apologizing to him for it twenty-five years later) and he called D. H. Lawrence a 'sick man' (an opinion which he was willing publicly to repudiate in his old age). He also widens the scope of his polemic in a general diatribe against contemporary American civilization – its society was 'worm-eaten by Liberalism', and some parts of the United States had been 'invaded by foreign races'. A population should, ideally, be 'homogeneous' – linked by ties of 'blood kinship' and not 'adulterated' by other races. Specifically, he deprecates the presence of 'free-thinking Jews'. They are 'undesirable' in large numbers. The philosopher George Boas, who had previously been on friendly terms with Eliot, wrote to him that, 'I can at least rid you of the company of one';[20] Eliot did not reply. In fact, he was never to live down these remarks about the Jews, although afterwards he attempted to excuse himself on the grounds that he, too, was 'a very sick man'[21] when he gave the lectures: that, in other words, they reflected his own emotional condition.

He was, after all, about to leave his wife and thereby perhaps push her further into madness – perhaps it was his own fear of having no moral sense which prompted him into making moral formulations in this obsessive way. Certainly there is the presence of a private but barely hidden self-communing within the lectures which gives a worried, almost hysterical, edge to his attack on Lawrence for possessing neither conscience nor social morality, as well as to his affirmation of the reality of 'moral and spiritual struggle'. Where before his notions of 'order' and 'tradition' had been convincingly presented (if not argued), here they become obsessive – to be defended against subversion by 'free-thinking Jews' or 'foreign races'. They were obsessive because his own order was under threat: the unity, stability and purity which he invoked were the qualities which he was in danger of losing from his own life. On a more mundane level, he could not have been unaware that his role as an Englishman provoked doubt and unease among some of his American contemporaries, and here again he tried to defend himself by equivocation. He described himself to the Virginian audience as 'a stranger to your country' – 'I speak as a New Englander' – although, of course, he was born and raised in Missouri. It is a small thing, perhaps, but representative of what Edmund Wilson saw as his 'incoherence' of personality – and it was this incoherence which, I suspect, animated his fierce need for order and his equally fierce attacks upon those who might threaten it.

Throughout the American visit, Eliot, a self-confessed 'Yankee' for his Virginian audience, kept in contact with the other culture with which he identified himself. He continued to write to his friends in England, and read the *Manchester Guardian Weekly* (two weeks late). His main preoccupation was his wife's condition, of course. Ottoline Morrell had told him that she had not been seeing Vivien, and he wrote back saying that he regretted this, since he wished to have reliable accounts of her.[22] Clearly Vivien was waiting anxiously for his return: she decorated the flat in preparation for it, and held one party where all the guests drank to Eliot's health. In fact it seems that Vivien wrote to her husband and asked him if she could come and join him in the United States – when he read the letter, he told Robert Sencourt, it was as if he had received an electric shock.[23] And Vivien was also writing to Ottoline Morrell: in March she told her that she had hardly bathed, washed her hair or even changed her clothes since her husband's departure.[24] But it was in this month that Eliot confided to Paul Elmer More that, having sought both practical and religious counsel, he was planning some form of separation from his wife.[25] He also told his relatives that he was not going back to her – a decision which pleased them.[26] Only a few days before his letter to More, he had written to Ottoline Morrell once more in order to tell her that he would rather not see Vivien again.[27] Ottoline had already suggested to him that Vivien would be better off without him, and naturally he agreed with her.

And so the decision was made. Eliot wrote to his solicitors from America, instructing them to prepare a Deed of Separation and enclosing a letter which the solicitor was to take personally to

Vivien. The contents of this letter are not known but he realized, by this stage, that it was pointless trying to give her any precise reasons for his decision, apart from the fact that it would be in the interests of both of them eventually.[28] He told Robert Sencourt that as he dropped the letter and its enclosure into the postbox, he remembered the lines from *Julius Caesar*:[29]

> Between the acting of a dreadful thing
> And the first motion, all the interim is
> Like a phantasma, or a hideous dream

Sencourt also says that the letter was sent in February 1933, although it seems from the testimony of Virginia Woolf and others that Vivien herself was not aware of his decision until early July; she described to Ottoline Morrell the terrible shock which she received 'in the summer'.[30] It is possible, however, that Eliot asked his solicitor to prepare a Deed of Separation and hold it ready, but not to inform Vivien or present her with his letter until the time that he had found a place to stay in England where she could not find him.

On 17 June, just before he was preparing to sail home, he went to Milton Academy, his old school, in order to give a graduation address.[31] In this speech he talks in minatory terms to the ghost of the seventeen-year-old boy he had once been, and berates him for the 'mess' which he had created – much the same sentiments as his Harvard address, where he explained how a poet might 'mess up his life' for nothing. He then warned the boys to avoid writing poetry if they could possibly do so, since it would only get them into trouble. He said that he regretted that his younger self had not known certain things which he had since had to learn through hard experience: that it was important to be sure that you knew what you really thought and felt, since there would come a time when you had to stand 'quite alone'. There were also occasions in life when an irrevocable choice had to be made, and the consequences of that choice had to be faced. That was what he was now steeling himself to do.

But his American visit was by no means one of unrelieved or gloomy self-communing. His letters give the impression of a man who was, for once, reasonably happy, and Virginia Woolf had gathered the same impression.[32] It was freedom of a kind, and a reminder of the life he had once known. He had been able to see once more the beauty of the New England landscape in autumn, and had been particularly entranced by the bird life of that region which he had watched as a child.[33] He was also free of the burden of his wife, and was able to renew his acquaintance with old friends from the days of Smith Academy and Harvard. He saw a great deal of Emily Hale, for example, the girl to whom he had sent roses in the weeks before he had met Vivien in England. They resumed their close and sympathetic relationship, and it seems that Miss Hale offered him the attentive but respectful affection of which he had experienced so little with his wife. But the primary reason for his happiness was that he was once again near his family (three sisters lived in Cambridge itself), who provided the kind of domestic affection he had not had in England. For eighteen years, he told Ottoline Morrell, he had simply been himself but now he was part of a family once again, among people who were attached to him before he became a poet.[34] He spent a week with his brother, Henry, in Randolph, New Hampshire, before his departure: 'A most lovable person,' Henry wrote, and added that he was very different from the reviewers' conception of him.[35]

But he had to leave this domestic warmth and return to a life in England which, at least for the immediate future, promised nothing but anxiety and trouble: he was not looking forward to the summer there.[36] It is almost as if there were two incompatible images of life offered to him – familial affection in America and a career in England – which were all the more starkly outlined because there was no longer any possibility of a choice between them. He had to return to England even though, as he explained to More,[37] the past eighteen years there – the period of time he had spent with Vivien – had been terrible. He employed an image, in this letter, which he often used to describe his first marriage – Valerie Eliot remembers his saying, also, that it had been like a Dostoyevsky novel written by Middleton Murry.[38] But the decision had been made a long time before and he believed, in any case, that he had received more or less his just deserts.[39] Eliot's life was governed by such choices; to deny choice, after all, is to exist without definition and he was perhaps the most rigorously defined of all his contemporaries: 'chiselled', as Edmund Wilson had put it. In the same letter to More, he compared himself half-fancifully to Prometheus, whose liver was perpetually gnawed by vultures. But he needed that vulture and indeed in some ways he became his own, perpetually feeding upon himself and watching his own torments.

His plans to return to England were carefully laid, the primary aim being to keep away from Vivien until she had accepted his decision to leave her. His departure was shrouded in secrecy: he did not even want his friends in England to know on what date he sailed and on what boat he travelled, although he expected to spend a night or two at the Oxford and Cambridge Club in London before travelling to stay with friends in the country. On 24 June he sailed on the *Tuscania* to Greenock; he rested one night at his club when he arrived in London, and then travelled down to Pikes Farm in Surrey where his friend and colleague, Frank Morley, lived. Here he stayed at the house of Mrs Eames, the wife of the foreman of an adjacent brickworks, which became known to the Morley children as 'Uncle Tom's Cabin'. He worked and had his breakfast and lunch there, but walked a few yards to the Morleys' farmhouse for dinner. According to Mrs Morley he did not talk a great deal about his separation from Vivien,[40] but Frank Morley remembers his saying on one occasion several years later that there are times when 'a man may feel as if he had come to pieces, and at the same time is standing in the road inspecting the parts, and wondering what sort of machine it will make if he can put it together again'.[41] Somewhat more cheerfully, he told Virginia Woolf that he was observing the birds, playing patience and writing nonsense verses.[42] James Eames remembers that 'he was very quiet . . . he was so engrossed in what he was doing that you could almost touch him and he wouldn't realize you were there. He was a funny man, really'.[43]

Although he wanted to remain outside ordinary social life,[44] (no doubt because he wanted neither intrusive questioning nor bland sympathy), he was not entirely in seclusion. He did see some friends, although always under conditions of complete secrecy: when he was about to visit the Woolfs at Monks House, he asked Virginia Woolf to conceal his address and also the date of his arrival.[45] When later Ottoline Morrell asked to see him, he explained that he wanted to visit her but could not do so if other people were present.[46] Clearly, his primary object was to keep Vivien away from him. She had heard by cable that he had left America and, when he did not return to Clarence Gate Gardens, she became distraught. She took to her bed, and a nurse was called.

Virginia Woolf described how she feared that her husband had been drowned,[47] and to Ottoline Morrell Vivien wrote, on 7 July, that she was convinced he was in danger – the word 'danger' being underlined three times.[48] Friends were called in; St John Hutchinson telephoned Faber and Faber who, according to Virginia Woolf, told him that the matter could not be discussed on the telephone but reassured Mrs Eliot that there was no cause for alarm. Hutchinson had also seen one of Eliot's last letters to her – a 'very cold and brutal' document, he said.[49] By the second week of July, at the latest, Vivien must have been informed of the true nature of the situation. In that month a formal meeting between her and her husband was held in the presence of solicitors: 'He sat near me and I held his hand, but he never looked at me'.[50] Eliot knew his wife well enough to realize that it would take a great deal of time before she was convinced that he would not change his mind about the separation.[51] In her highly anxious state her paranoiac fears came once more to the surface, and she accused both Virginia Woolf and Ottoline Morrell of having affairs with her husband[52] – it was rumoured that she was going around looking for both of them with a carving knife in her handbag but, in fact, according to her brother, Maurice, she had only a 'joke' retractable knife, made of rubber, which she carried for effect.[53] Her behaviour was bizarre, but it was that of a desperate rather than a dangerous woman.

The whole business of separation was, as Eliot had feared, going to be protracted but when he visited Virginia Woolf at Monks House in September he appeared to be enjoying himself: he looked ten years younger and seemed to her to be eager for life, the life of which he had been deprived for so long. He spoke about Vivien with some bitterness, and was resentful of the time and labour he had wasted: he thought that she dramatized or exaggerated her insanity, in part to deceive herself;[54] no doubt he was right about that, although the primary reason was to display her own loneliness and unhappiness, and thus obliquely to appeal for help. The decision to leave his wife was justified – and it is significant that no one, not even the members of Vivien's own family, criticized him for it at the time. The manner of his doing so might leave something to be desired, but when Maurice Haigh-Wood asked him if there were any other, less cruel, way than that of writing through solicitors, he replied, 'What other way *can* I find?'[55] It is a difficult question to answer: the only alternative would have been a private confrontation, and of that both parties seem to have been incapable. He had followed what seemed to him to be the wisest and best course, by separating from his wife physically while superintending her through the proxy of friends and relatives – Hope Mirrlees, Mary Hutchinson and Maurice Haigh-Wood, as well as others, acted in that role; in addition, the Eliots' servant, Janes, performed various tasks for Vivien and reported back on her state to her husband. Eliot also supervised her finances: he was joint trustee, with Maurice, of the Haigh-Wood Estate and an allowance was paid to Vivien through her bank; according to Maurice, Eliot kept her cheque book in his briefcase, so that she would not be tempted to spend her income extravagantly.

He was not at the Morleys' farm continuously during this period. In July he attended the Anglo-Catholic summer school of theology at Keble College, Oxford, where he spoke on 'Catholicism and International Order'; in this address he emphasized the need for absolute ideals in political and social behaviour – contemporary circumstances were such that the virtues of tolerance were greatly overestimated and 'I have no objection to being called a bigot myself'.[56] In August he visited the Fabers at their home in Cardiganshire, and in the following month he stayed at the Anglican theological college at Kelham. He returned there again in January 1934 (in fact he went on retreat to the college two or three times a year until the Second World War), when he gave a talk on the moral purpose of criticism – essentially an abbreviated version of the theme which he had adumbrated in his Virginia lectures, although he added a rather severe attack upon Virginia Woolf and ended with an exhortation to the theological students of the college that it was their 'duty' to criticize modern literature. (Since in the following year he wrote an essay in which he claimed that ' . . . the whole of modern literature is corrupted by what I call Secularism . . .'[57] it is clear that he believed himself to be on the right track in his attempt to reformulate the vocabulary of criticism.)

In spite of Eliot's resolve never to see her again, Vivien meanwhile waited in 68 Clarence Gate Gardens, convinced that her husband would sooner or later return to her: she seems to have persuaded herself that he had left for no apparent reason[58] and would no doubt come back to her when he had thought better of it.

In September her solicitors told him that 'to induce her to regard the separation as final is quite impossible . . . she asks that her husband shall return to her and manage her affairs, and is ready to accept any conditions he may impose. She writes that she is staying at the flat until she has had another and more satisfactory interview with her husband and that this interview should be at the flat . . . if only Mrs Eliot could be given some hope, however faint, of occasional visits by her husband and of eventual reunion it would help enormously'. Eliot quoted this letter to Mary Hutchinson, and then confirmed that he would not go back to a wasteful and doomed relationship.[59] Vivien herself was adamant; a Deed of Separation had been drawn up, but she continued to refuse to agree to it. She declared that she would not sign any 'blackmailing paper' and abandon all rights to her husband.[60] In a letter to Ottoline Morrell on 26 December, she signed herself as Vivien Haigh-Eliot with the 'Eliot' underlined three times.

Although Eliot told Paul Elmer More that it had been the most happy summer he could recall – a strange remark until one remembers the exhilaration of freedom which Virginia Woolf noted – he nevertheless admitted that he had been suffering from great anxiety;[61] for a man of such agonizing complexity, 'peace of mind', in any conventional sense, was clearly impossible. Joseph Chiari, who knew him in later years, said that he was 'tormented by remorse and the weight of the past'.[62] His own faith could not lift this burden from him and, when S.S. Koteliansky accused him of seeking comfort in Christianity, he replied that it had, in fact, 'forced him to face the full dangers of the human predicament, not just in this life but for eternity; and it had burdened his soul with a terrible and hitherto unrealized weight of moral responsibility'.[63] Other friends noticed how, even many years after these events, he could not bring himself to mention Vivien by name and, at the end of his life, he confessed that there were certain things in his past which he could not endure contemplating for long.[64] But they emerge, nevertheless, in his own writing. The image of the man who believes himself to have committed a crime, and the notion of a secret which leads to guilt and feelings of worthlessness, are significant aspects of his later drama.

For a nature such as his, the only salvation lay in work and, as soon as he returned to England, he started again upon his own writing. His first task was to revise for publication the two sets of American lectures and, as it were, make the best of two bad jobs. He worked first on *The Use of Poetry and The Use of Criticism*, which was published in November, and then turned his attention to *After Strange Gods* which was published in February of the following year – the latter causing him rather more anxiety, since he expected it to provoke a certain amount of unwelcome controversy. He had wanted to get these obligatory tasks out of the way as soon as possible, so that he could concentrate upon some work for which he had been commissioned two months after returning to England – that of writing the choruses of a religious pageant. It may seem curious that he was willing to write verse 'to order' in this manner, but after the completion of *Ash-Wednesday* he had not been at all sure that he would ever again be able to write 'pure poetry'. His attempt at another poetic sequence, 'Coriolan', had failed, as we have seen, and the only work he had been able to finish in the last three years had been the short stanzas of 'Five-Finger Exercises' and 'Landscapes' – the former were published in the *Criterion* of January 1933, the latter were still being written.

But these poems are not as inconsiderable as their diminutive size and occasional nature might suggest. 'Five-Finger Exercises', despite the dismissive title, is a most attractive sequence. The last two, on Ralph Hodgson and Eliot himself, are sufficiently well known, but the first three of these short lyrics – addressed to a cat, a terrier and a duck – evince the power of his music which is here linked to odd and discomfiting themes. 'Landscapes', some composed in America and some on his return, display again the fineness of his 'ear'. These are wonderfully plangent poems which are only 'exercises' in the sense that Eliot has not cared to work them up into a larger thing – has not, in other words, imposed his formal will upon them. He has 'let go', and his own music emerges unscathed – the music of his being, slow, mournful and incantatory.

But this was still for him only 'occasional' verse, and he had reached a point where 'I seemed to myself to have exhausted my meagre poetic gifts, and to have nothing more to say'.[65] He believed *The Hollow Men* to mark the completion of one period of his work, and he did not wish to publish an expanded version of his collected poems until the second period (of which *Ash-Wednesday* was the only major exemplar) could equal it in weight[66] – but that, at the moment, seemed a doubtful prospect. The commission for choral verse came, then, as a welcome opportunity to spur himself into creative life. E. Martin Browne, whom Eliot had met with Bishop Bell in December 1930, first suggested the idea. Browne, himself an actor who had been appointed by Bell to be Director of Religious Drama for Chichester, had agreed to write the scenario for a pageant to raise money for forty-five churches in the 'New London' area – the fast developing suburbs north of the city – and in September he asked Eliot if he would provide the dialogue and verse choruses for the work. Eliot accepted the invitation promptly:[67] he felt a certain obligation to the Church in the matter, but the idea also appealed to him after labouring on the revision of his lectures.[68] Only a few months before, he had spoken at Harvard of the possible 'social utility' of the poet working in the theatre; now, on a small scale, he had a chance to demonstrate it. He was about to enter what might fairly be called the second phase of his creative life.

In November he went with Frank Morley on a brief visit to Scotland, and later in the same month he travelled to Paris in order to consult James Joyce about a new edition of *Ulysses*. After that excursion, he planned to settle permanently once again in London. His idea was to take a room in a boarding house for a few weeks while he looked for a small flat; he needed no more than a furnished bedroom and sittingroom, not too far from his work. He could not afford anything larger until he was sure what his financial resources would be, if and when Vivien agreed to a separation; his own prudence in monetary matters would, in any case, have prevented him from renting anything too lavish. The areas in which he was most interested were Islington and Clerkenwell Green, although he asked Virginia Woolf to look out for a flat in what he called 'East Bloomsbury'[69] by which he meant the area between Southampton Row and Gray's Inn Road. He had, in the meantime, found a room in a boarding house at 33 Courtfield Road, down the street from Gloucester Road tube station. This establishment was run by William Edward Scott-Hall, a rather eccentric figure who had once been ordained as a bishop in the 'Old Catholic' Church, but most of the proprietorial duties seem to have devolved upon his friend, Miss Freda Bevan. Miss Bevan has recalled how melancholy Eliot seemed at this time: 'He would come in and sit in the garden listlessly. "I wonder," he would keep repeating, "I wonder." [70] Perhaps he was affected by the drab anonymity of that part of Kensington, also, since he had already told Virginia Woolf that it was an area he did not like. [71]

That district, however, was to be his home for the next seven years. One evening Father Eric Cheetham came to dinner at Courtfield Road; he was the vicar of St Stephen's, nearby, as well as being a friend of Miss Bevan. Eliot was already in the habit of attending early morning mass at that church, and soon after the dinner Father Cheetham offered him rooms in his presbytery at 9 Grenville Place. It was an ideal arrangement: inexpensive accommodation, and the company of priests which had become congenial to him. He was also afforded a measure of privacy and protection – although even so he tended to keep his new address secret, even from his friends, in case Vivien should discover it. Father Cheetham himself was a flamboyant man, in the manner of certain Anglo-Catholic clergy, and Eliot clearly appreciated his company. Under the aegis of Cheetham, the services of St Stephen's were as 'high' as possible without bearing the taint of Romanism, and this also seems to have suited Eliot's tastes. In fact, in 1934 he became a Warden of the church, remaining in that post until 1959; his duties included those of administering the financial affairs of the church, and regularly supervising the collection during Mass. One friend has said that 'in church he looked very much like a businessman, and in business he looked very much like a cleric'. [72] But if he was a prominent member of the congregation, he was also a faithful one: 'It was a spiritual experience,' one priest who was at St Stephen's has said, 'To administer the Bread and Wine to so devout a worshipper'. [73] He also went on regular retreat to St Simon's in Kentish Town, where his spiritual counsellors were Father Bacon and Father Hillier. Here he would discuss with them the progress of his spiritual life, confess and receive absolution, and perform the acts of penance. He was now for the first time alone in the world, and had begun his life of public action and private devotion.

11

Beginning Again
1934–1935

ELIOT HAD LEFT his old, disordered life, but at first he seemed to
have entered a kind of limbo. He adopted an almost monastic style
of life and when, some months after his arrival at Grenville Place,
Virginia Woolf came for tea, she was surprised and a little depressed
by the barrenness of his rooms. His bedroom was over a railway
track leading to Gloucester Road tube station; the walls of his rooms
were papered dark green, the furniture was not his own, and the
bookcases had shelves missing.[1] This sounds like the habitation of a
man who does not pay much attention to his surroundings, and who
finds the ordinary comforts of domestic life unnecessary. It also
suggests the life of a man who does not really conceive of himself as a
social being: but he had also just passed middle age, and for the first
time was living alone; it is no wonder that he was growing more
aware of his isolation.[2] He was accustomed to it in his intellectual
and emotional life – now he had to become reconciled to ordinary
physical, and human, loneliness.

If he had any affection at all it came from that domestic life which
he had experienced in America, and he kept in close touch with his
relatives there. His sister, Marian, and a niece came to visit him in
the summer of 1934, and in the same year Emily Hale made the first
of a series of journeys to England in order to be with him. He wrote
frequently to the other members of his family, and had a particular
respect for the intelligence of his eldest sister, Ada. It was Ada who,
according to Frank Morley, saw her brother's character most
clearly. She was worried about him – not his physical state ('Tom
not only says he is tough, but is tough') but rather his psychological
health. She feared that he might withdraw from ' "human relationships" ' and enter a 'shadow world of "dramatism", into increasing
tendencies of outward "acting" and inward "mysticism" '.[3] By

which she meant, no doubt, that the outward world, and the part which he played in it, were to Eliot in some sense unreal – reality lay only within himself, to be explored in prayer, meditation and in his own creative work.

Even before he had moved to Courtfield Road, he had begun working on the pageant (which was eventually given the title of *The Rock*), which offered him the opportunity of writing in a quite different manner. He was trying to compose dramatic verse which would be both simple and direct, qualities which in their most inspiring form he found in Isaiah and Ezekiel.[4] He was still working on the text in the middle of March, with the deadline set for the end of that month. This was not the first time that he had written under such conditions – he had, after all, had a great deal of experience as a journalist and editor – and there was an urgency to this mode of production which appealed to him. He sometimes told his authors that, in order to complete any work, it was necessary to think about nothing else until it was finished – or to be in such a position that failure to complete the task would create problems with other people. The latter was, of course, true for his writing of *The Rock*, although there were specific problems of his own with which he had to deal. He was working in what for him was an unfamiliar medium, explicitly for a popular audience, and he had to learn the appropriate skills as he went along. His was essentially the role of a craftsman: he had once said of John Dryden that it was only by close application of his extraordinary intelligence that he was able to turn himself into a great dramatist,[5] and Eliot had now embarked upon a similar process.

There were difficulties, however, which Dryden had been spared. The pageant was to be performed by an amateur cast drawn from several parochial congregations, and the rehearsals in May rather demoralized Eliot: just three days before the first performance, the cast seemed to lack energy and the production was in chaos. He himself was not one to intervene, of course; Browne described him as a 'very silent witness' during the final rehearsals,[6] and one teacher who was working with the choruses remembered that he was 'shy and difficult to draw out if one wanted to know anything'.[7] In fact he seems to have been despondent about the whole venture: a few days before the pageant opened, he was pessimistic about the kind of audience such work would attract.[8]

The Rock was performed at Sadler's Wells between 28 May and 9 June. It is an account of the building of a church into which are introduced certain of the then fashionable 'experiments in time' which display the general history of the London Churches. In Eliot's hands, however, this unpromising subject is treated in a spirited manner; his fascination with the music hall still provoked some of his best writing, and the 'pageant' was turned into a combination of comic revue and expressionist theatre – in tone, if not in content, a populist version of *Sweeney Agonistes*. He explored the resources of spectacle and the 'stock type': a chorus of Blackshirts in military formation, and the appearance of the Plutocrat, the Agitator and the Unemployed testify to his attempts to grapple with contemporary social problems in a dramatic context. And, in spite of some difficulties with the 'cockney' dialogue, his composition of songs and comic 'patter' is very skilful – it is a gift of which he should have made more use. But within the conventions of a public spectacle he is still able to smuggle in some of his own preoccupations: the idea of ceaseless labour, the absurdity of most activities, the deceitfulness of human affections, and the palpable presence of evil in human affairs. On the page at least, the choruses on these themes retain their dramatic effectiveness:

> . . . The desert is squeezed in the tube-train next to you,
> The desert is in the heart of your brother.

As in *Ash-Wednesday*, he has borrowed the tone and cadence of the Bible and the liturgy, but these are robes he has put on here to play the part of a preacher – although such an atavistic role fitted oddly with his undoubted comic and theatrical skills. Nevertheless the rhetoric of judgment and of condemnation still came easily to him, and it may be related to that 'dramatism' which his sister recognized in his character.

When Leonard Woolf asked him the reason why he was writing *The Rock*, he simply chuckled.[9] But clearly there were those who considered his apparent abandonment of poetry, in favour of what was tantamount to preaching, as a diminution of his gifts: Conrad Aiken noticed 'a contraction both of interest and of power'.[10] Another critic quoted the funeral oration upon Rabbi Hilliel: 'Alas the humble and pious man, the disciple of Ezra'.[11] It was noticed how the devotees of Eliot sat uneasily at Sadler's Wells with the charabanc parties from the various London churches – 'the public' who at the end joined in singing his choruses.[12] He had in fact anticipated a reaction of this sort from his erstwhile admirers, and realized that he had reached that point in his creative life where his new work would be compared disadvantageously with the old.[13] He was quite sanguine about the prospect, however, and it ought not to be forgotten that he had already described poetry as a 'mug's game'. He had reached a definite decision – as much as any decision of such a kind can ever be definite – that he could not, and would not, work in the same way again. He wanted to move forward from the 'pure' poetry of the first part of his life, and the composition of *The Rock* had offered him a wider area to explore. But he was still uncertain of the precise direction which he wished to take – he did not think the poetry of the pageant, for example, had been very successful.[14]

It could be said that *The Rock* really finds its place in the context of the Thirties fashion for verse drama – Sean O'Casey had already written *Within The Gates* and Auden had completed *The Dance of Death* for the Group Theatre (Faber and Faber published the play in November 1933, and Eliot had borrowed incidental effects from it for *The Rock*). In fact the Group Theatre itself, with Rupert Doone as its guiding spirit, was planning to stage the first public performance of *Sweeney Agonistes*, the play which Eliot had abandoned some ten years before. It was given at the Group's headquarters in Great Newport Street in November 1934; the actors wore masks, and the entire performance lasted for a little over half an hour. 'The American accents,' the programme notes stated, 'are meant to be impressionistic and not authentic'. Eliot attended the performance but was rather puzzled by the fact that it had been conceived in a manner quite different from his own understanding of the play.[15] The problem seems to have been, according to another member of the audience, that the Group production emphasized the farcical aspects of the action and neglected its tragic quality.[16] The published version of the text, which had appeared in 1932, had met with some hostile criticism and the public production fared little better. When the Group Theatre gave performances of it in October of the following year, the audience reception was again 'mixed and somewhat muted'.[17]

However, Eliot's surprise at the Group Theatre's interpretation of his work did not prevent him from associating himself with

Rupert Doone's attempts to establish a theatrical home for verse drama in London, at the Mercury Theatre in Notting Hill Gate. A committee was formed of Eliot, Ashley Dukes, Auden and Yeats; discussions dragged on through 1934 and into 1935, without the plans advancing beyond a theoretical stage. There was no one who seemed able to combine the time, patience and influence properly to promote and supervise the scheme and, in addition, Yeats was often not in London at the times of the meetings: according to Robert Medley, the painter who worked with the Group Theatre, Eliot told Doone that he felt like kicking Yeats down the stairs.[18] Nevertheless, despite these distractions and disappointments, the Mercury Theatre was to become the London home of his next play.

Wyndham Lewis has described how in the Thirties Eliot would arrive for dinner haggard and apparently at his last gasp; 'refreshment' (drink, in other words) would then get rid of the appearance of someone 'in flight from some Scourge of God'.[19] He was in fact being pursued in the middle years of that decade by a more human agency: Vivien was trying to find and confront him. That was one reason why he did not like to attend social functions – in case she might suddenly appear – but it seems that in any case he felt more at ease among strangers;[20] no doubt he disliked the idea of being 'known' and 'talked about'.

Vivien's diaries for this period[21] give an extraordinary picture of a woman who is tearing herself to pieces, and scattering those pieces in the sight of all those she had known. At first, as Eliot suspected, she could not bring herself to believe that her husband had in fact left her, and then she feared a plot engineered by the hatred and envy of others. She wrote letters to her husband, imploring him to come back and 'be protected', but he never replied to them. It is difficult to establish a precise account of her movements – no doubt she would have had difficulty in doing so herself. She was still seeing her own friends and relatives, some of whom, like her brother Maurice, reported back to Eliot on her condition; she kept up the flat at 68 Clarence Gate Gardens although sometimes she would decide to stay with friends like Jan Culpin, who lived in a lodging house at 20 Roland Gardens in South Kensington. Her overriding aim was to see or waylay her husband. She went to the first performance of *The Rock* in May 1934, and kept her eyes fixed on the entrances at Sadler's Wells in case he arrived. He had either suspected such a move, or he had been warned that she had a ticket: in any case, he did not appear. Then she went to the last performance, and once again returned alone to her flat, disappointed and somewhat bitter.[22] Diary entries of this kind are followed by pathetic memories of 'Tom' as he had once been: how gentle he was with her during her illnesses, how they used to go to Eastbourne together, how 'handy' he was around the house. In one passage she related how she had fallen into an artificial fury, performing her tasks and then sinking back exhausted: that, she said, was how Tom used to feel.[23] Page follows page of cramped and troubled handwriting; she was talking to herself because there was nobody else to talk to; she was lonely, muddled, not sure whom to trust or what to do, looking forward helplessly to that moment when her husband would open the door of the flat and return to her.

On 17 September, two years after he had left her in order to travel to America, she sent an advertisement to *The Times*: 'Will T. S. Eliot please return to his home 68 Clarence Gate Gardens which he abandoned Sept. 17th 1932. Keys with WLJ'. 'WLJ' was the servant, Janes. In the same month, she joined the British Union of Fascists, then a movement only two years old. In December of the same year, as a result of a court order which Eliot had obtained, his books and property (together with the back numbers of the *Criterion*) were removed from the flat; it was a sign of the irrevocability of their separation and on Christmas Day Vivien wrote in her diary that she wished she was dead. But then her moods altered, and she speculated about a possible future together. It is clear that she needed him – that he was, as Osbert Sitwell noticed, the real centre of her life.

She had already discovered, in March 1934, that he was going to Faber and Faber regularly and so this was the one place where she thought she might catch him. She had a habit of turning up at the offices unexpectedly and asking for him – but she was always told that he was out, or at a committee meeting (the secretary in *The Cocktail Party* is called Miss Barraway). His secretary at the time, Bridget O'Donovan, has left her own account of such visits: 'The telephone would inform me that Mrs Eliot was in the waiting room. I would ring TSE and he would thank me.' Then she 'would go down and explain that it was not possible for Mrs Eliot to see her husband

Vivien's advert

and that he was well. . . .' Meanwhile, Eliot 'would be slipping down and out of the building . . . For the rest of the day Eliot would be on edge, talking even more slowly and hesitantly than usual . . .' Of Vivien, Bridget O'Donovan wrote that, 'she was a slight, pathetic, worried figure, badly dressed and very unhappy, her hands screwing up her handkerchief as she wept'.[24] And Vivien herself must have guessed that her husband's absences were not fortuitous. When in March 1935 she arrived and demanded to see him the receptionist, Miss Swann, at first told her that he was there; then, after waiting for a while, she said that in fact she had not seen him come back from lunch. Bridget O'Donovan eventually came down, and told Vivien he was not in. Vivien replied, 'Of course you know I shall have to keep on coming here,' and Miss O'Donovan said, 'Of course it is for you to decide.' Then Vivien exclaimed, 'It is too *absurd*. I have been *frightened* away *for too long. I am his wife*'.[25]

In April 1935 Vivien wrote in her diary that it no longer mattered what she did. In June she was told that Eliot was attempting to stop her allowance from the Haigh-Wood Trust Fund, for reasons unspecified, and then some more papers and books belonging to him were removed from the flat in July. She was by now in such an hysterical state that a doctor was called in to minister to her. Vivien told him that all the bills should be sent to her husband since he was responsible for her condition, but Eliot passed them on to his solicitors who refused to pay. And then, at the end of the month, she went back to Oxford with the dog, Polly, and this lonely and forlorn figure wandered along the banks of the Isis where she remembered her husband, Lucy Thayer and herself punting together. She visited Merton, Eliot's old college, and looked up at the windows of the room where, twenty years before, she had seen him calmly reading his books.[26] In October she attended the production of *Sweeney Agonistes* by the Group Theatre at the Westminster. She was sitting in the front row of the stalls, and during the performance members of the cast, wearing masks, came down among the audience and chanted her husband's words of murder and nightmare. It was a terrible ordeal for her, she wrote, and she wondered how she had managed not to faint.[27] There would be more for her to endure.

In spite of Eliot's reservations about the poetry of *The Rock*, the pageant was both a critical and popular success: 1,500 people came each evening to see it. It was also successful in ecclesiastical circles and, when Eliot stayed with Bishop Bell at Chichester in the summer of 1934, it was suggested to him that he might care to write a play for next year's Canterbury Festival. Such a project would have the advantage, from his point of view, that he would be working once again with E. Martin Browne: indeed, it seems that Eliot would only accept the commission if he was able to do so.[28] But in any case he was now 'stage-struck' – for the first time in his life, he had seen a popular audience moved by something he had written. He took the commission promptly and began work on the play during the winter of 1934. This was his second ecclesiastical assignment, and the nature of his creative life had changed in a fundamental way.

Such changes are, of course, more apparent from the outside, and Eliot was always careful to emphasize what he saw as the continuity of his own development. Even in that area least susceptible to misinterpretation, his critical and religious opinions, he saw progress where others saw change: all that had happened, as far as he was concerned, was that his values had been modified as his interests had enlarged.[29] But there is no doubt that he wanted to clarify his position to those who were interested. That was one reason why he wished to disassociate his views from those of men like Herbert Read and I. A. Richards with whom he had been superficially linked.[30] He was in any case dissatisfied with the lack of values and beliefs in English life, and it was in this spirit that, in a letter to Paul Elmer More,[31] he criticized the type of English mind represented by Bruce Richmond, who was editor of *The Times Literary Supplement* from 1902 to 1938. It must be remembered that he was addressing here an American who would have been unsympathetic to the compromises and evasive pragmatism of English intellectual life, and Eliot was in a sense playing to a gallery of one: but there is no doubt that, even though he remained on the most friendly terms with the men whom privately he attacked, he had already 'placed' them in an intellectual context with which he was fundamentally at odds.

His transformation was certainly obvious enough to baffle and sometimes enrage his friends. Virginia Woolf had denounced *The Rock* and in April 1934 was arguing violently with him about his religious convictions;[32] three months later she told Stephen Spender that Eliot seemed to be turning into a priest.[33] Nevertheless she noticed that he had also acquired more self-confidence and authority, although he had become rather more didactic in the process. She compared his head to a rock against which many forces have smashed: he was in some ways a melancholy man, but still with the 'wild eyes' which she had noticed before.[34] Other friends went further and accused him publicly of a kind of betrayal. Wyndham Lewis, in *Men Without Art*, noticed that the reviewers of *The Use of Poetry and The Use of Criticism* were shocked at 'its lavish inconsistencies, its studied evasiveness'. Lewis himself compared Eliot unfavourably with Pound and described him as arrogant, sly and insincere: '. . . he has allowed himself to be robbed of his personality, such as it is, and he is condemned to an unreal position'. It was a strong attack, and exhibited just the kind of misinterpretation of which Eliot was fearful: Lewis referred to his supposed theory of 'art for art's sake' and associated him with I. A. Richards. If you were to ask Eliot what he meant by a passage of his poetry, he would reply, 'I am sorry, I am entirely unable to answer you. I have not the least idea. It is not to *me* you must address such questions. Go rather and address yourself to my partner, Mr I. A. Richards. He is not very reliable, but he probably knows more about it than I do'.[35] Eliot was too nervous to buy a copy of Lewis's book, according to Hugh Gordon Porteus, and borrowed one; later he returned it to Porteus 'gravely'.[36] Ezra Pound was equally stern, although less nasty, about his old friend and in his review of *After Strange Gods* wrote that he 'implies that we need more religion, but does not specify the nature of that religion; all the implications are such as to lead the reader's mind into a fog'.[37] There is no doubt that such reviews of his prose books, and the fact that *The Rock* had not found favour among the contemporaries whom he most admired, rather unnerved Eliot. He had been expecting a hostile reaction, but it is one thing to expect and another to receive. He described his depressed state to Bonamy Dobrée in July 1934: he no longer had anything to say, and was worried about the lectures which he had to give in the winter.[38]

He was not entirely alone in his social and religious preoccupations, however. In the spring of 1934, for example, he was helping to circulate a letter to be published in *The Times* which urged 'a thorough and public examination of some scheme of national credit'. This was another way of promulgating the merits of 'Social

Credit', an economic nostrum devised by Major Douglas (whom Eliot had met) and espoused by Ezra Pound and A. R. Orage, the editor of the *New English Weekly* whom Eliot also knew. It is a difficult doctrine to understand – indeed some of its adherents, like Pound, had only the vaguest grasp of it. But in its simplest form it suggests that money should cease to be a commodity manipulated by bankers and financiers – 'It's all profit what nobody gets and nobody knows 'ow they gets it,' as one of Eliot's 'cockney' characters puts it in *The Rock* – and should instead be established upon the needs and aspirations of those who create the wealth of the country. For many, it was a way of rearranging capital without introducing socialism, but it is likely that the theory appealed to Eliot because it was conceived on a moral rather than simply economic understanding of the nature of money.

His tentative enthusiasm for the scheme, and his acquaintance with Orage, brought him as a result into contact with a number of people who shared those assumptions which had already alienated many of his friends. Orage died in the latter half of 1934 and his assistant editor at the *New English Weekly*, Philip Mairet, together with one of the contributors, Maurice Reckitt, approached Eliot and asked if he would assist them in the continuation of the newspaper. He agreed to do so, and for the next ten years he played an active role on its editorial committee and contributed a number of articles. In the first days of the *Criterion*, he had been eager to form a 'phalanx' of the 'best minds' in Europe, but the civilization which he had then wished to represent now seemed to be collapsing around him. No longer interested in pure literary criticism, he wished to discuss contemporary work primarily as a 'moralist':[39] 'the study of ethics has priority over the study of politics', he wrote.[40] As a result his 'phalanx' was of a kind different from that he had originally envisaged and, although the group associated with the *New English Weekly* shared a set of values similar to his own, he must have been quite aware of the more parochial character of the men with whom he was now connected. Philip Mairet remembered that at editorial committees, 'He gave his complete attention to what was submitted to him; and you knew it, though his comments were usually brief, even laconic. His words were not subject to the usual discount for politeness or the desire to be encouraging'.[41]

It was through the *New English Weekly* that he became associated with another group of like-minded English intellectuals. It was known as the Chandos Group, and among its members were Mairet and Reckitt as well as men like Revd. V. A. Demant who later became Professor of Moral and Pastoral Theology at Oxford – the Group took its name from the fact that it used to meet fortnightly at the Chandos Restaurant. It had been established after the General Strike of 1926 in order to discover 'certain absolute and eternal principles of true sociology' – its aim, in other words, was to formulate a Christian sociology. Eliot's own sense of social responsibility and communal leadership prompted him in the first place to join the group, but in fact its discussions were materially to affect the expression of his own thought; what had been a solitary and defensive espousal of his own convictions was replaced by a more careful formulation of the social and political consequences of his Christianity. Mairet recorded how at these meetings he manifested 'a kind of detachment and reserve' which often emerged in irony: 'He once lampooned us all with clerihews'.[42] This of course was characteristic of him: he lacked the sense of certainty which gave others their proselytizing zeal; he associated with such people while in some sense always remaining apart.

A large measure of the eminence and authority which he began to acquire in the Thirties came not from public activities of this kind, however, but from his private role as mentor and publisher of two generations of writers: he became known, in fact, as 'the Pope of Russell Square'. Many people have described his office on the second floor of Faber and Faber (to be reached in a small and creaking lift, although he was sometimes to be seen bounding up the stairs): the brass nameplate of 'Thomas Stearns' upon the door (originally a possession of his maternal grandfather), the photographs of Paul Valéry, Virginia Woolf and others on the mantelpiece, books piled upon the floor, and the view from his window of the trees of Woburn Square.

Although he made mistakes – he was one of those at Faber and Faber who decided to turn down George Orwell's *Animal Farm*, for example – he usually knew the 'genuine' article when he found it and his sustained support and encouragement helped to establish the literary careers of writers as different as W. H. Auden and Charles Williams, Lawrence Durrell and Marianne Moore. There were those like Pound whom it was a matter of course for Eliot to publish – Faber and Faber had a standing order for the *Cantos* – although this was not simply a benevolent duty on his part. When Pound was attacked, he would characteristically spring to his defence and describe him as the major poet of his time writing in English. But there were other writers who, although he did not exactly 'discover' them, owed the development of their reputation to his quiet but persistent 'boosting'. Such a writer was the American, Djuna Barnes, whose *Nightwood* he published in 1937; they first corresponded in that year and by the late Thirties he was addressing her in his letters as 'Darling Djuna' and 'Dearest Djuna', continually encouraging, advising and cajoling her about her work. His help could also be of a most practical kind, and when in 1934 he began to publish the poetry of George Barker he adopted an almost paternal attitude towards him. He organized an income of 25 shillings a week for him from anonymous contributors, and also sent money out of his own pocket (his quiet generosity to fellow poets was extraordinary); he advised Barker on the poems he ought to publish, and on the order in which they should appear in volume form; he wrote testimonials for him and, when he had not heard from him for a while, he would write asking for news. Ronald Duncan, the dramatist and prolific autobiographer, recalled how Eliot brought an author's understanding to his writers – he did not mind how much they altered their galley proofs, and was sympathetic to those who were late in delivering manuscripts.[43] Lawrence Durrell remembers him as a painstaking and punctilious editor who would listen carefully to the most trivial question and reply in his characteristically exact manner.[44]

His method of editing manuscripts was to pencil alterations or suggestions in the margin; with poetry, these were generally corrections of syntax or of sense: such as, 'I have not come across this word before . . . does this not need to be made clearer . . . you have used the same word twice . . .' and so on. In his letters he would deal in a detailed and carefully pondered manner with the arguments of, for example, a theoretical or philosophical work; although he would on occasions outline his own attitudes or opinions, his general procedure was to take the author's premises for granted and then help to clarify them, or to work out their implications in a cogent manner. Apart from anything else, he was a clever man, able to spot inconsistencies or confusions and to formulate his objections in a precise way. It was typical of him, however, that he disliked discussing poetry (especially his own) in any terms other than those of technique: he detested general statements on the subject.

His manner in conversation was slow and hesitant – in recordings, one hears the ponderous quality of his voice diminished only by the suspicion of a drawl – with the marked pauses in his delivery which everybody seems to have noticed. When talking with an author in his office, he would tend to look down at the carpet, or away from his interlocutor, as he spoke, only occasionally glancing up. Raymond Preston records that in his conversation there was 'a sense of inadequacy and inarticulacy that was even painful'.[45] F. T. Prince similarly remembers a kind of bleakness in his presence, a 'lowering of the temperature' which was compounded by the 'remoteness and withdrawnness' of his personality;[46] he had a habit, Prince has said, of uttering the most 'chilling' or 'discomfiting' things: 'You are not a very *prolific* poet,' he remarked on one occasion and then on another, 'Not everything you write is very *interesting*'. It was a severe truthfulness which is evident in one letter which he wrote to George Barker, in which he told him that he must be prepared to receive adequate recognition as a poet late in life, if indeed he received it at all.[47] Lawrence Durrell has also remembered remarks of Eliot which suggest this 'lowering of the temperature': 'One should write as little as one can' or 'I always try to make the whole business seem as unimportant as I can'.[48]

Anne Ridler, who became his secretary in the late Thirties, has described how he would compose his book reports and sometimes his letters standing upright in front of his typewriter. When he did give dictation, he was 'measured and fluent: as with his normal speech, the sentences were perfectly formed – there might be a pause but no humming and ha'ing'.[49] She describes how fond he was of teasing people: 'He certainly took pleasure in what we might now call oneupmanship; on the other hand, he liked people to defend themselves vigorously, and once said as much to me.' But again the quality of bleakness can be sensed in her account: ' "What must I bear?" I remember his saying, not with a smile,' after her over-tentative approach with some publishing business, and once he returned some poetry manuscripts she had given him 'with a blank look and the monosyllable "*Why*?" ' 'Sometimes,' he said to her, 'I feel I loathe poetry.' (His loathing, expressed more than once, may have had something to do with the fact that many aspiring poets, especially in the Thirties, were writing pastiches of his own style.) And yet there were times when he would attempt to console an author by describing his own experiences. He told F. T. Prince of the occasions when his critical faculty just 'went dead', and of the moment of 'despair' which always hit him when engaged upon his work. And to George Barker he spoke of the periods of 'dryness' in his own life.[50] In these exchanges he put himself on terms of absolute equality with those to whom he was proffering advice, and the bleakness others noticed was also one which he directed against himself.

By 1935 one interval of dryness had come to an end, however, and this year was to mark the most sustained and successful period of creative writing in his life. He was working very hard, in one sense, because he needed the income – apart from his ordinary duties for the *Criterion*, he was contributing regularly to *Time and Tide* and the *New English Weekly*. He was not particularly enthusiastic about this journalistic work: it was easy enough to agree to write something when asked to, but he often had great difficulty in finding anything to say.[51] His attention was being distracted by more important matters, in any case, and at the beginning of the year he was fully engaged on the drama which Bishop Bell had commissioned the previous summer. The only stipulation was that the play must have some connection with Canterbury, and Eliot had chosen the theme of Thomas Becket's return from exile and his murder in Canterbury Cathedral at the hands of Henry II's knights. He was not at first at all confident about his ability successfully to write such a play: his experience with *The Rock* had convinced him that he knew how to write choral verse, but he was less sure about dialogue or speech. Since the plot consisted only of Becket's martyrdom, he was also afraid that he would have to place too much emphasis on the choral sections in order to cover up the deficiencies of the story[52] and, in later years, he believed that he had in fact succumbed to that danger.

He began constructing the play in his usual deliberate and meticulous manner: he wrote a scenario, made prose notes for each scene, and devised a timetable for each segment of dramatic action. In the early stages of composition he sent drafts of certain passages to Rupert Doone for his comments: they were in prose, and Doone suggested that they be recast in verse;[53] Doone later conceived the idea of the Four Tempters embodying Becket's mental conflicts. Partly in order to discuss the play Eliot had stayed with E. Martin Browne and his wife just before the Christmas of 1934: it was Mrs Browne who persuaded him to change the title of the play from *Fear In The Way* to *Murder in the Cathedral*. Browne had already noticed his silence when four years before he had been with him in Chichester and now, with the problem of Vivien still not resolved, Eliot was equally taciturn. 'Of such things he hardly spoke to his most intimate friends, and no indication of his distress reached us,' Browne wrote, 'But conversation did not flow easily and we were aware of his weariness.[54] But he worked on; he sent part of the first act to Browne at the beginning of February 1935, and then a revised version of the whole act at the end of that month. Browne was not happy with the result, and told him that it seemed too abstract and that as a result it lacked dramatic momentum. At the beginning of March Eliot took note of some of these criticisms and, for example, added specific detail to the speeches of the Four Tempters. A complete script was ready by April, and rehearsals began at the beginning of May. Although they continued over a period of weeks Eliot, perhaps rendered nervous by his experience during *The Rock*, only attended the final dress rehearsal – he did, however, go to some of the separate rehearsals for the chorus of the 'Women of Canterbury'. He was not particularly forthcoming on such occasions, although once he went up to the choral director and 'murmured very confidentially, "That should be a colon, not a semi-colon" '.[55]

Murder in the Cathedral was first performed in the Chapter House of Canterbury Cathedral on 19 June, with Robert Speaight in the role of Becket. It was a success with the first-night audience of some seven hundred, and the reviewers – who were working from a printed version of the text which Faber and Faber had published just before the first night – were almost uniformly favourable. It seemed that Eliot had at last found his great theme, by discovering a way in which to combine his poetry and his faith in a satisfying formal unity. The narrative could hardly fail to elicit an imaginative response from him: he had, after all, been preoccupied with the theme of the martyr since the poetry of his Harvard days. Browne has recounted how moved Eliot was by the fact that his narrative of Becket's murder would take place within fifty yards of the location of the actual death,[56] and in this coincidence of event and representation he was coming very close to the religious origins of drama. In Old Tragedy, as in *Murder in the Cathedral*, the dramatic focus is upon the consciousness of one man: he does not change but, as the action proceeds, more and more of his character is revealed.

The play is typical of Eliot's work in the sense that it is concerned with a figure, not unconnected with the author himself, who has some special awareness of which others are deprived and yet whose great strengths are allied with serious weaknesses. Becket towers above ordinary men but, in the drama of his temptation and death, he is a passive and ambiguous figure. 'Old Tom, gay Tom' has been forgotten and instead there stands revealed a man who sees nothing but suffering ahead of him. This may seem to be the condition of a holy blissful martyr, but it fits uneasily with the first description of Becket as Chancellor:

> Despised and despising, always isolated.
> Never one among them, always insecure;
> His pride always feeding upon his own virtues . . .

Is 'Tom' vain or holy, a martyr or a self-deluded man, a pariah to be avoided as the Chorus suggests ('. . . you come bringing death into Canterbury') or a saint to be venerated? Eliot was deeply preoccupied with the nature of this solitary and ambivalent figure but, as in some of his earlier poetry, he seems too close to that character to be able to objectify him in dramatic terms. As a result, the verse is pervaded by a vague unease. The thematic centre of the play is Becket's murder and the knights' prose apologies to the audience for their action, but its imaginative centre lies in an obsessive presentation of guilt, uncleanness and the 'void'. The most powerful writing springs from this: 'I have tasted/The savour of putrid flesh in the spoon,' is a mild example of Eliot's choral rhetoric. The blood of Christ and of the martyrs is then invoked, like some shower bath for the spirit; it is altogether a most peculiar work, with all its blood and fear only just kept in check by the deliberate formality of its presentation.

Although Eliot thought of the play as only a successful *tour de force*,[57] it became a popular as well as a critical success. Ashley

Dukes, the owner of the Mercury Theatre, had gone to Canterbury to see it and quickly came to an arrangement with Eliot and Browne that the play should be transferred to his theatre and inaugurate the season of poetic drama which Dukes planned there. At the end of the Canterbury Festival, Browne and Dukes picked up the costumes and scenery and took them to the Mercury. The play opened on 1 November and for weeks it was impossible to get a ticket, since the combined appeal to churchgoers and to Eliot's admirers was such that the little theatre in Notting Hill Gate was full. Eliot himself approved of the production, although he felt that the knights tried to extract too much comedy from their roles.[58] After 225 performances it was taken on a provincial run; in October of the following year it was transferred to the Duchess Theatre and then later to the Old Vic. It was also broadcast by the BBC in January 1936 – 'oh them cawkney woices . . .' Pound complained to James Laughlin after he had heard it.[59] He had not been impressed. Everyone else seemed to be, however, and soon Eliot received a number of invitations to write other religious and historical dramas. But he had a horror of repeating himself – a poet ought to be 'disgusted' with what he has done before, he once wrote[60] – and turned down all such propositions. Nevertheless success had been good for him: he seemed to be more at ease, and his at least temporary self-assurance lent him a certain charm.[61] Virginia Woolf received the impression that he was at last beginning to work in the way he wanted, and that he was determined to write plays about contemporary life.[62] That had, of course, been his ambition since the early Twenties, although one constantly frustrated; now that he had engineered his first theatrical 'hit', however, as well as completing his first major work since the separation from his wife, he felt able to go on with a certain amount of confidence.

Although he was actively making plans for a new play, various distractions were to plague his work upon it; and, in any case, the success of *Murder in the Cathedral* at first afforded him a different kind of creative energy. After finishing the drama, he began work on what was to become his first major poem since *Ash-Wednesday*. During the production of *Murder in the Cathedral* Browne had told him that some spoken lines held up the action too much. 'He would say, "They are very nice lines here, but they're nothing to do with what's going on on stage".'[63] Some of them were discarded from the play but stayed in Eliot's mind, and a poem which was eventually to be called 'Burnt Norton' shaped itself around them.

Burnt Norton itself is a manor house and garden in Gloucestershire, which derives its name from the fact that it is built upon the site of another house which had been burned down in the seventeenth century. It is not particularly memorable, and Eliot said some years later that the house and garden would be rather a disappointment to visitors.[64] The circumstances of his own visit, however, had been more congenial. He had gone there, in the summer of 1934, with his American friend, Emily Hale, who was staying with her aunt and uncle in the nearby village of Chipping Campden. Miss Hale came to England each summer between 1934 and 1938 (except in 1936), and Eliot stayed with her and her relatives, the Perkins, on at least three or four occasions in each year. He would go for long strolls with Emily – one of them commemorated in a poem, 'The Country Walk' where he expressed his fear of cows and the way in which they stared at him; indeed his fear of large animals seems to have sprung from personal experience since on one of these visits to Gloucestershire, in September 1935, he ran from a bull and fell into some blackberry bushes. With Emily and her relatives he was able to relax and, in a letter to Mrs Perkins, he said that he had never felt quite so 'at home' with anyone for twenty-one years.[65] This would take him back to 1914, to the time when he was still in the United States with his own family. The Perkins were themselves American, and his remarks suggest once more how much he missed the domesticity he had known in his native country, and perhaps how much Emily Hale represented that life for him. He was certainly very close to her and in the one year when she did not travel to England, 1936, he himself returned to America; when they were apart, he wrote often to her and would send her draft copies of his work which she would then return with her own suggestions (she was a lecturer in drama at Smith College). And so for the six years after his separation from Vivien, they maintained an intimacy which only the war severed. Emily's own friends in America have explained that she felt herself to be unofficially 'engaged' to him,[66] but his own intentions or feelings towards her will not become clear until their correspondence is published – and perhaps not even then. Certainly when she was in England he would take her to meet his friends almost as if they were a recognizable 'couple'. He described her to Ottoline Morrell as an extraordinary person even though she might not seem so on first appearance;[67] Virginia Woolf found her rather dull,[68] but perhaps she did not appreciate the formal and somewhat repressed New England 'type' with whom Eliot himself felt quite at ease.

And so it was in the company of a woman he had known and admired before he met Vivien, and whom he might conceivably have married if his wife were not alive, that he visited Burnt Norton. The lines excised from *Murder in the Cathedral* which had been ringing in his head were on the nature of time and its irrecoverability; they had been spoken by the Second Priest, after the departure of the Second Tempter who had suggested that Becket might return to the days of 'Old Tom, gay Tom':

> Time present and time past
> Are both perhaps present in time future . . .

This is how the poem begins, and the tone of speculation or meditation is sustained throughout. 'Burnt Norton' has as a result been described as a religious or philosophical poem, like the three later works to which it was eventually joined as *Four Quartets*. But this is to obscure its connection with Eliot's drama: not just in the sense that its immediate origin lay in *Murder in the Cathedral* but, more importantly, in the fact that this was the first long poem in which he used the emphases and cadences of speech. It was part of his growing preoccupation with what he had called the 'social usefulness' of the poet that he should adopt the tone of someone addressing an audience, speaking out loud rather than to himself. In 'Burnt Norton' we see the poet as orator.

But in spite of the poem's air of formal deliberation, and the sense in which it appears to offer gnomic statements or injunctions, it would obviously be impossible to elicit a paraphrasable 'content'. Eliot's imagery is at once precise and non-specific, and the power of his abstractions is such that they float above the surface of the poem. We look down for a recognizable landscape, but find it concealed. 'Burnt Norton', in fact, gains its power and its effects from the modification, withdrawal or suspension of meaning and the only 'truth' to be discovered is the formal unity of the poem itself. We shall see how, in a similar manner, in Eliot's later criticism, the reader is given only a satisfying illusion that an argument has been

[margin handwritten note:] Four Quartets Suspends Meaning But Is Aesthetic Unity

proved or a conclusion reached: Aldous Huxley compared it to a great operation, in which 'powerful lights are brought into focus, anaesthetists and assistants are posted, the instruments are prepared. Finally the surgeon arrives and opens his bag – but closes it again and goes off'.[69] The authority of 'Burnt Norton' and Eliot's later poetry does indeed depend primarily upon its organization and its tone, in the way that the dramatic entry of a hooded figure on a stage will compel the attention of an audience.

12

Out of the Storm
1935–1939

THROUGHOUT 1935 Vivien continued her lonely pursuit of her husband. It seems to have been her settled conviction that she had only to see and to speak to him, and he would agree to return to her. And, in November, she found him. She had discovered that he was to deliver an address at a *Sunday Times* book exhibition, and she arrived there with Polly. This was the confrontation Eliot most feared. Vivien went up to him and said 'Oh, Tom'; he seized her hand and said 'How do you *do*' in a loud voice. The dog recognized him and jumped up at him, but he seemed not to notice. When he spoke at the exhibition, Vivien stood the whole time, keeping her eyes fixed upon his face. After he had finished his address she went up to him again and said, 'Will you come back with me?' He replied, 'I cannot talk to you now.' She gave him three of his books: he signed them, and returned them to her. Then he walked away.[1] They were never to see each other again. In the following month, Vivien sent out Christmas cards signed 'From Mr and Mrs T. S. Eliot'.

Eliot's own reactions to this meeting are not known, although it must have profoundly embarrassed and unnerved him – not least because further public encounters of that kind were always possible. His fears were no doubt compounded by the fact that Vivien's behaviour was becoming more and more erratic. As if to lure her husband into a false sense of security, she pretended in the following year that she had gone to America and had hired a secretary, called Daisy Miller, to answer her correspondence in her absence: but she herself was Daisy Miller. It is perhaps interesting that she gave her forwarding address in America as 83 Brattle Street which was, in fact, where Emily Hale lived. In the spring and summer of 1936, she went to the Mercury Theatre on at least seven occasions in order to see *Murder in the Cathedral*. And then she disappears from sight; the diary entries stopped, and the next written record is her death certificate eleven years later.

She died in Northumberland House, a private mental hospital in Finsbury Park, north London. The records of that hospital seem to have been long since destroyed, but Vivien's brother, Maurice Haigh-Wood, has explained what happened to her: a 'reception order' was drawn up for her committal. Her personal physician, Dr Miller, seems to have instigated the move in the summer of 1938 since it was his belief that 'she was in need of professional care'.[2] The procedure, if it followed the usual course, would have been this: two doctors would be taken to see her and would ask her a few questions. If her answers were unsatisfactory, their report would be taken to a magistrates' court the next morning and a petition for her 'reception order' drawn up and signed by two people – preferably near relatives or representatives of the family. Maurice suggested that an attempt had already been made, after Eliot's separation from her, to have her committed but that Vivien, having been warned about, or suspecting, such a move, went to Paris – certainly she recorded on 19 June 1935, some plan to have her 'arrested' but nothing happened; then, six days later, she is writing from Paris to a friend, Louise Purdon. But on this later occasion she did not escape, and the reception order was drawn up against her. It is not clear who signed it – her mother, Rose, was still alive but was now in her seventies. When Maurice was asked if he had done so, he replied, 'I don't think I did. If I did, I can't remember'.[3] Eliot himself could not legally have signed such a document since he was separated from her. But since he was the one most involved with Vivien's welfare, he must have either approved of, or acquiesced in, her committal; he was also a trustee of the Haigh-Wood Estate, and was responsible with Maurice for Vivien's financial affairs – they must, for example, have paid her bills at Northumberland House until the time of her death. The mystery of who signed the reception order remains: two people who were either relatives or close friends of Vivien, and who were asked to do so.

By August 1938 she had become a resident of the mental hospital, and Maurice reported to Eliot that she seemed 'fairly cheerful, had slept well and eaten well, and had sat out in the garden and read a certain amount.'[4] But the long-term effect on Vivien must have

233

been profound; already a lonely woman, she was dispatched into a mental asylum by people whom she knew and trusted. The paranoia which is evinced in the diaries of her last years at Clarence Gate Gardens is then partly justified, if she knew that such a course was being taken against her. There are reports that she attempted to leave Northumberland House: it seems that she stayed on one occasion with Louise Purdon, who was a 'night-nurse' with her own flat above a chemist's, until she was found and taken back. But these reports cannot now be substantiated; we are left with the bare fact that she spent the rest of her life in confinement.

Even before Vivien's committal, Eliot had been much more free than in the days of his marriage; in the summer of 1935 he was with Emily Hale in Gloucestershire, and also visited the Fabers in Wales. At a party given by John Hayward for the Herbert Reads in June, he came with fireworks and some items bought at the joke shop opposite the British Museum: sugar which when immersed let out little fish, and chocolates which he thought to be filled with sawdust but were in fact made of soap; the guests, he said, 'set on me'.[5] In October, in a similarly light-hearted vein, he recounted to Virginia Woolf how he had been sitting in the wings of the Westminster Theatre (where *Sweeney Agonistes* was playing) and, on another occasion, lighting fireworks in the company of John Hayward and W. H. Auden.[6]

Certainly the grave demeanour which made such an impression upon others – the 'sad eyes'[7] and the 'deep, sad voice'[8] – was lifted in the company of friends to reveal a playful and often funny man. He was fond of alcohol – he was a consistent, if not a heavy, drinker. He liked to recite from memory music-hall routines – one friend remembers him, much later in life, repeating a music-hall patter entitled 'Two Black Crows' which lasted three minutes.[9] At the offices of Faber and Faber, also, there seems to have been a succession of jokes (firecrackers in the coal scuttle on the Fourth of July) and spoof letters. As he wrote in his Harvard Class Report in this year, 'I like very simple and humane kinds of practical joke, which reminds me that I am also, at the moment, a Church Warden'. It was no doubt in this jocular spirit that he wrote a letter to *The Times* on 29 November suggesting the need of a Society for the Preservation of Ancient Cheeses. Mock solemnity of this kind may seem rather tiresome, just as practical jokes are often not funny to those on whom they are played (they may often appear to be lightly camouflaged forms of aggression), but such jokes were characteristic of the society in which he now moved: it is difficult to imagine him playing tricks on Pound or Lewis, for example.

In a nonsense poem addressed to Virginia Woolf he described himself as 'upper-middle', a class distinction which immediately associated him with the kind of solid and respectable Englishmen amongst whom he passed his business life and to whom he went for – to use one of the characteristic words – 'convivial' social life. John Hayward, for example, was by now a close friend: he was a bibliophile and editor of precocious talent, who in 1926, at the age of twenty-one, had published an edition of Rochester's poems. Two years later he had started writing for the *Criterion*, since he wished to fashion for himself a career as a 'man of letters'. He suffered from muscular dystrophy, however, and the creeping paralysis of that wasting and mortal disease had, by the time Eliot grew to know him well, consigned him to a wheelchair. In 1931, according to Helen Gardner, Eliot had written him 'an unusually intimate letter on suffering'.[10] It was at Hayward's flat at 22 Bina Gardens (only a short walk from Eliot's lodgings in Grenville Place) that Eliot, Geoffrey Faber and Frank Morley used regularly to meet in the late Thirties. They gave each other nicknames – Hayward was known as 'Tarantula' because of his sometimes acidulous wit, Morley as 'Whale', Faber as 'Coot', and Eliot as 'Elephant' (because he never forgot) or of course 'Possum'. It sounds sufficiently tedious in an English public school fashion, an effect compounded by a little book of mock verses, *Noctes Binanianae*, composed mainly in the summer and autumn of 1937; it was privately printed and announced as 'Certain Voluntary and Satyrical Verses and Compliments as were lately Exchang'd between some of the Choicest Wits of the Age'. It does not make particularly amusing reading, and at first glance it may seem odd that Eliot was willing to enter the spirit of such occasions.

But the fact is that, like most people, he reserved a special kind of behaviour or language for whomever he was with; in his correspondence with Ezra Pound in the same period, for example, he became an egregious Yankee addressing another. Pound called him 'my little marsupial', 'yew old Wombat' and so on, while Eliot replied in kind to 'Ezzumpo', 'Dear Doc', 'Rabbit My Rabbit'.

What is most apparent about the correspondence – apart from Pound's tendency to lecture Eliot on whom he should publish and what cause to support – is Eliot's extraordinary ability to mimic Pound's verbal mannerisms, as if he were willingly immersing himself in his personality. He even goes so far as to fabricate his signature in a way similar to Pound's, so that it forms a kind of hieroglyph. After a while, however, Pound's constant and insistent proselytizing began to annoy him, and he reverts to his usual more careful and elaborate prose while explaining (as so many of Pound's correspondents did) that he did not at all understand what Pound was talking about. He also became disenchanted with the amount of the correspondence; his replies become shorter and shorter until, in September 1937, his secretary wrote, 'Mr Eliot also asked me to say that he is intending to write to you as soon as he has several consecutive free hours'.[11]

Eliot was, then, a master of disguise or protective camouflage – an 'upper-middle' Englishman with his publishing colleagues, a Yankee with Yankees and indeed a pillar of the Church with other such pillars. This may help to explain the suspicion entertained by many of his friends that they were being placed in special compartments, never to mingle with those in other compartments, like cells in the honeycomb of his private life. Ronald Duncan recalled how he met Eliot and Pound together on one of Pound's rare trips to London; when he arrived, Eliot was 'singing a bawdy ballad most energetically'. But when Duncan reminded him of this incident some years later, he 'not only denied knowing the ballad but singing it. . . .'[12] In the same way, when Conrad Aiken sent him a copy of *Ushant* in which he described two incidents which displayed a 'streak of sadism' in Eliot's nature, Eliot denied any recollection of such events.[13] He had the curious ability to erase, or at least pretend to erase, from his memory that which did not suit his idea of himself at the time.

But if these were all roles he played, they were necessary ones; they protected a man who could be extremely shy and nervous in the company of other people.[14] He suffered from the kind of hypersensitivity which, unchecked or unguarded, would have incapacitated him. On one occasion in this period he was unusually self-revealing in a conversation with Virginia Woolf; she sensed an agonized and lonely man, filled with 'self-torture, doubt, conceit, desire for warmth and intimacy'.[15] This was a man who needed all the help and support from others he could get.

Early in 1938 two summations of his work were published: *Essays Ancient and Modern* in March and, a month later, *Collected Poems 1909–1935* which included the first publication of 'Burnt Norton'. He was clearing the ground, dispatching his previous writing to the putative immortality of volume form before he began seriously to concentrate on the work to come. *Essays Ancient and Modern*, as its title indicates, reflects Eliot in his more pious mood; here we are entering the church of his concerns. Half of the essays were reprinted, with slight alterations, from *For Lancelot Andrewes*, while the more recent of them, 'Religion and Literature', 'Catholicism and International Order' and 'Modern Education and the Classics', continue the theme which he had inaugurated in *After Strange Gods*; he assaults the dominant position of secularism in contemporary culture, and anticipates in lugubrious fashion the barbarism which will descend. (The two other new essays in the collection, 'The *Pensées* of Pascal' and '*In Memoriam*' are related to this mood but are more singular in conception.) His was by now a familiar position, and the critical reactions to it had also become predictable: praise at his critical acumen in the examination of individual authors was mixed with scorn or bafflement at the general principles he espoused. Eliot was perceptive enough about his own work to share this attitude in part; he realized, for example, that his essays on individual poets would probably be of more lasting worth than his more generalized pieces.[16] And in later life, he was less than satisfied with much of his prose work.[17]

His most interesting essays during this period are, in fact, on specific poets, and are quite unencumbered by the theoretical baggage which he felt compelled to carry with him on other occasions; as a result, they show his criticism at its best – witty, cogent, perceptive. In these occasional pieces, he is revealed as a psychological critic whose apparent ability to immerse himself in another poet's personality comes close to an act of clairvoyance. Tennyson was a poet whose emotions were so deeply suppressed, even from himself, that they emerged as 'the blackest melancholia'.[18] Milton was one whose sensual capacities 'had been withered early by book learning'.[19] Byron was a 'touring tragedian' whose preoccupation with his own performance made everything outside himself seem unreal, an actor 'who devoted immense trouble to *becoming* a role that he adopted'.[20] In his preface to Djuna Barnes's *Nightwood*, he introduced a passage of autobiography couched in a similar tone: 'In the Puritan morality that I remember . . . Failure was due to some weakness or perversity peculiar to the individual'.[21]

Collected Poems 1909–1935 provoked a respectful response from the critics, although there was a sense in which Eliot was now being taken for granted; he had been assimilated, after something of a struggle against him by the purveyors of contemporary taste, and could quietly become a monument standing unnoticed by the roadside. But he was aware of the stage in his career which he had reached, and work on the preparation of *Collected Poems* had made him feel that he was about to retire.[22] It would have been a public retirement, however – the first printing of the book was 6,000 copies, and it went through eleven impressions in as many years. But in spite of the immense authority which he now possessed, his poetry had ceased to be fashionable or 'chic' in the way that *The Waste Land* or even *Ash-Wednesday* had originally been: the new, or at least young, poets were no longer particularly interested in what he had to show them. It was not a situation which worried him; as he told George Baker, the best position for any poet was to have enough financial security to view in a detached and unenvious way the temporary reputations of more fashionable writers.[23] But there was a sense in which his critics were right: he had become a quite different poet.

In 'Inside the Whale' George Orwell described how the post-war group of writers, Pound, Joyce, Eliot and Lewis (who have since been described as the 'modernists') were united by their pessimism: unlike men such as George Bernard Shaw and H. G. Wells, they had seen through the ideals and systems of the late nineteenth century which had come to such a smash in the early decades of the twentieth. Orwell's point can be extended, since these writers recognized not only the dissolution of public or social values but also the bankruptcy of private ones: it ought to be remembered that the notion of 'personality' reached its apogee in Oscar Wilde during the same period of scientific and social optimism. With the collapse of private and public values – or, more specifically, the collapse of the language which had sustained them – the 'modernists' thought to construct a new order out of literature and art. Instead of simply proclaiming 'art for art's sake' they attempted to create a body of work which was on its own terms self-sufficient, with its own order and tradition, capable of embodying and communicating its own values. All of them were in that sense authoritarians. But it was Eliot who in the end loosened the hold of the 'modernists' on English culture – not only did he assert the public role and 'social usefulness' of the writer in an almost nineteenth-century manner, but he also announced that the principles he derived from his religious belief were more enduring than literary or critical ones. He helped to create the idea of a modern movement with his own 'difficult' poetry, and then assisted at its burial. This is the essential genius of the man: his private choices and obsessions became emblematic, and in some sense determined our understanding, of the twentieth-century tradition.

These are generalities which describe a culture only now properly coming into view. Eliot himself might not have recognized them, just as he might have considered negligible the surface of his life which is apparent to biographers. Biography is in that sense a convenient fiction since no one can probe, without the risk of farcical failure, those hidden perceptions or experiences which run alongside the observable life but may not necessarily touch it. On a clear spring day in May 1936 he visited Little Gidding, once the home of Nicholas Ferrar, and entered the small chapel there. In August of the following year he travelled to East Coker, the village from which his ancestors had journeyed more than two centuries before. Just as the events themselves can be known but not the experiences which they provoked, so we cannot hope to understand Eliot as he knelt in that chapel or in the presence of his God. It was at such times, he said, that he was divested of all those characteristics of family, personality and reputation which identified him to the outside world.[24] We cannot reach into the mystery of Eliot's solitude.

And yet the mundane circumference beyond which he stepped at such times was also necessary to him: it was the circle in which he could stand and be safe. He wrote in an essay published in 1937 that an artist must lead a 'commonplace life' if he is properly to do his work.[25] And in the two or three years before the Second World War that is precisely what he did. His daily existence was taken up with a routine of duties: ecclesiastical responsibilities, the membership of various committees, the *Criterion* dinners, his engagements at various Tory dining clubs, and of course primarily his publishing work with its endless round of letters and meetings. And then, in the evening, he would return to the priests of St Stephen's – first at Grenville Place and, from 1937, at Emperor's Gate across the road. This was the shape which his life had taken.

In the course of explaining his various duties to Virginia Woolf he confessed that he seemed to be turning into an 'Old Buffer' and wondered if he might not also be guilty of humbug.[26] Mrs Woolf explained his acquaintance with various dignitaries, however, as a way of practising society dialogue for his new play.[27] Certainly he gave the impression to some of being almost too respectable: 'He has grown such a crust on him . . .' Henry Miller wrote.[28] But he was, in any case, close to becoming a smiling public man – a man who gave speeches at school prizedays, who would answer the toast to 'poetry' at dinners, who collected the occasional doctorate or honorary fellowship. In January 1936 he lectured in Dublin and when in June of the same year he agreed to read poetry at Sylvia Beach's bookshop in Paris (he was in that city for a four-day visit) she described it as an 'historic event'[29] – although one member of the audience on that occasion remembered how he did not once glance at his listeners, but seemed 'fiercely defensive' and turned the pages with a 'look very near distaste': his profile was 'like a bird of prey of some sort'.[30] His reputation was such, however, that a photographer from the *New York Times* arrived and another member of the audience was so overwhelmed by the occasion that she described Eliot's face as 'that of an archangel who has too much work to do, and so does only half of it, leaving the rest to the North Wind'.[31] Bird of prey or archangel? This is precisely the question which Eliot was to ask himself in his drama.

In November of the same year he talked on 'The Idiom of Modern Verse' to the Cambridge English Club, where he had for one auditor the appearance of 'a very shy, neurotic man'.[32] In 1937 he gave an address to the Friends of Rochester Cathedral on religious drama, and lectured on Shakespeare at Edinburgh University – he told Lawrence Durrell, however, that he seemed to have spoken about what he himself was interested in doing in the theatre and not about Shakespeare at all.[33] In April 1938 he travelled to Lisbon in order to sit on the jury for the Camoens Prize; when he came back, he had to address the Friends of Salisbury Cathedral on the poetry of George Herbert and then, two months later, talk on 'The Future of Poetic Drama' at an International Theatre Congress in Stratford-upon-Avon. These are some of the public events in an already crowded life, but there were also a myriad of smaller but no less official duties which he felt obliged to perform. Here are his engagements for three successive days in January 1937, for example; on Thursday, 7 January, he visited a community centre in North Kensington in order to prepare a five-minute radio speech on it as a 'good cause'; on Friday, 8 January, he attended a meeting of the British Council of Churches and, on Saturday, 9 January, he went to Chelmsford in order to speak on behalf of a mystery play by Charles Williams which was being performed there.

The breaks from this routine of work were themselves predictable. Once or twice a year he would join the Fabers during their family holidays in Wales. Tom Faber has recalled how Eliot would characteristically dress in immaculate plus-fours; they would picnic in deserted coves, although 'Uncle Tom' would often be overcome by vertigo on the perilous descent to them. He was, in a sense, a member of the family: he would entertain spinsters to tea with Enid Faber and in the evening might read aloud from *The Pickwick Papers* or another suitable volume.[34] He also became a familiar weekend guest with friends like the Morleys, the Reads and the Richmonds, although his other duties were such that he was careful to ration the amount of time spent in this way: two weekends a month tended to be enough for him. Nevertheless on such occasions he gave the impression to friends and acquaintances that in some ways he had mellowed. When in November 1937 he stayed with Conrad Aiken he was 'very good company' – 'he played ping pong, went to church, drank his beer like a man'.[35] And when a fellow American expatriate, Ethel Sands, saw him at the Richmonds' in Wiltshire, he seemed 'peaceful and happy now, after his stormy life . . .'.[36]

He had found one protection from those 'storms' in the Anglican communion (although he indignantly denied that it was any kind of comfortable haven), and during these years his role as one of the most prominent laymen in that communion was increasing; as one biographical note in 1937 described him, Eliot had done much 'to interpret literature to the theologian and theology to the men of letters'.[37] Whether or not he was altogether comfortable in such a role is another matter; when Lawrence Durrell once suggested to him that he was not a Christian at all but more like a Buddhist or a primitive he replied only with a question, 'Perhaps they haven't found me out yet?'[38] The religion which he espoused was singularly his own, and when in February 1937 he gave a radio talk on 'The Church's Message to the World' he returned to a subject which was close to the centre of his concerns: the failure of Western civilization, and in particular the signal inability of liberal democracy to sustain moral or intellectual values which might effectively confront the ideologies of fascism or communism. Unless our own society renounced 'many wrong ambitions and wrong desires' and maintained its allegiance to God, it would certainly become no better and perhaps much worse than other régimes 'which are popularly execrated'. His doubts about the nature and value of contemporary society were frequently expressed also in the *Criterion*; in the issue of October 1935, for example, he had talked about the plight of Papuan natives who had been corrupted by Western civilization. If our 'helping hands' were in fact the embrace of a leper, 'what hope have we of saving ourselves?'

This was the general, and rather bleak, attitude behind his specific attempts to reach a formula for what was in effect a new Christian activism. In 1936 he had been a member of the Archbishop's committee preparing for a conference to be held at Oxford on Church, Community and State. At that conference, in July of the following year, he read a paper on 'The Ecumenical Nature of the Church and Its Responsibility Towards the World' and became a member of a special section dealing with the 'economic order'. These activities led in turn to further meetings at Lambeth Palace in January and March 1938, to consider the formation of a British section of the World Council of Churches; in September, he was at a meeting of the Council on the Christian Faith and the Common Life. He was a natural server on such committees – it was part of that large inheritance from his busily engaged family – although his own general pessimism about the state of English society no doubt encouraged his native scepticism about the efficacy of what were essentially only institutionalized good intentions.

Perhaps an exception might be made for the one important and sustained collective activity in which he participated during these years. As a result of the Oxford Conference of 1937, J. H. Oldham established a group of Christian intellectuals with the purpose of discussing political and social problems within a Christian context – a more ambitious version of the Chandos Group; it was known as the Moot, and among its members were Karl Mannheim, Middleton Murry, Alec Vidler as well as Eliot himself. They first met in April 1938 at High Leigh in Hertfordshire and Eliot regularly attended further meetings until 1943. Here he continued his intellectual dialogue with men like Mairet and Oldham, but the discussions also brought him into contact with European intellectuals such as Mannheim himself. This was the closest he would come to that association of the best 'minds' sharing certain fundamental ideals which had been a preoccupation of his since the early Twenties; and indeed it was through such encounters that he began to formulate the ideas which he was to express in *The Idea of a Christian Society* and *Notes Towards The Definition of Culture*.

But although at every opportunity he was continuing to urge a role for the Church in both social and economic matter, his attitude towards specific political events was still a tentative one; there was always a gap between his theoretical pronouncements and his actual reactions to one 'crisis' or another. This was partly the result of sheer indecision: during the Abdication imbroglio of 1936, for example, he admitted to an acquaintance that 'he changed his mind on the subject several times a day'.[39] And when in 1937 a questionnaire was distributed to authors about their attitude towards the Spanish Civil War, he sent the reply (which he said that he never expected to be published) that, 'While I am naturally sympathetic I still feel convinced that it is best that at least a few men of letters remain silent'. This sentence has frequently been used as a stick with which to beat Eliot, generally to prove that his attitudes towards fascism were ambiguous at best. There is a more convincing explanation, however. He told the writer Constantine FitzGibbon some years later that he disliked the idea of poets 'cashing in' on other people's misery;[40] his scepticism about his own motives as well as those of others, and his general belief that one should not comment on any situation until one understood it thoroughly, made him refrain from making the kind of easy judgment or fashionable 'stand' in which others indulged. It may not be an entirely satisfactory position, but it is an intelligible one.

All of the multifarious social duties in which he was now involved constantly encroached upon the time and energy which he wished to devote to his own writing. In spite of the success of *Murder in the Cathedral*, and his desire to begin a new play in a modern setting, he was working on his next project rather slowly. He started on the play which was eventually known as *The Family Reunion* in early 1936, having first completed 'Burnt Norton'. As we have seen, he had declined commissions to write further historical or religious dramas on the lines of *Murder in the Cathedral*: as far as he was concerned, that play was a 'dead end'.[41] He wanted to make another attempt at the kind of theatrical work with which he had experimented in *Sweeney Agonistes* – a verse drama but one in which the verse seems the natural expression of modern life, and which is able in a heightened or symbolic context to employ the tones and inflections of ordinary, contemporary speech. In fact, this need to turn contemporary life into drama had been the defining characteristic of his work since 'Portrait of a Lady'. His major criticism of *Murder in the Cathedral* had been that it contained too much obvious 'poetry', and in the new play he wanted to create a more flexible and less ostensible verse line which could handle demotic or rarefied material equally well.

But he was making his way very cautiously. The first drafts of the play are concerned to set the pattern of action and feeling rather than with the exploration of individual characters – this formalistic approach to his task was demonstrated in the preparation of a later drama, when he used a blackboard to set out the play and used symbols to denote his characters. He always required an underlying form from which he could then depart, just as he tended to use a literary 'model' from which he could derive a manner and a tone. Aeschylus was the dominant inspiration behind *The Family Reunion* itself, although before writing it, 'I read Ibsen's plays consecutively to work myself up . . .'.[42] The first scene of the play came quickly, and remained practically unaltered from draft to draft: he wrote it when the fit was on him. But the rest was composed slowly and painfully, the verse undergoing major revisions all the time, partly on the suggestions of the various friends to whom he sent versions of the play. He knew what mood he wished to create – in March 1937 he explained that it would be a melancholy play, and perhaps the most pessimistic thing he had ever written.[43] But it was a new development for him, and he was certain of nothing else. In November 1937 he read the script aloud to Martin Browne and his wife, and their reaction was one of 'fascination and doubt':[44] there was too much description and not enough action, they felt, and so he began once again the struggle to elucidate plot and characters. By February 1938 he sent a complete script to Browne, but major changes were still necessary and he was seeking advice until the end of the year. The process of revision continued at rehearsals, which began in February 1939; according to Michael Redgrave, who played the central role, Eliot kept his head buried in his text throughout them:[45] he still seemed ill at ease with actors, although responsive to their demands. When Redgrave suggested that an extra line was needed in order to clarify a crucial point in the action, Eliot said in a surprised voice, 'Do you really need one?' According to Redgrave's biographer, he returned the next day with twenty-five new lines,[46] although Martin Browne denied this.[47]

The Family Reunion opened at the Westminster Theatre on 21 March 1939. It was not an auspicious time for a new play to open, in any case, and the reaction of the critics was decidedly mixed – in spite, or perhaps because, of Eliot's labours the meaning of the play remained elusive and its symbolism jarred with the realism of its setting. The play closed after five weeks.

As in much of Eliot's drama, the issue of *The Family Reunion* lies in the revelation of a secret: his world is one in which disclosure is the thing most needed and also most feared. Harry, Lord Monchensey, has returned after an absence of eight years to the family home of Wishwood where his mother and other relatives are waiting for him. But he has brought with him the Furies who appear at key moments of the action – the spectral creatures whose gaze he cannot endure but whose presence he understands, since he believes he has murdered his wife. His sense of 'filthiness', of unreality and degradation, pervades the play. As it turns out, his 'crime' is an ambiguous one and, in any event, his actions are determined by a family curse: his father had wanted to kill his mother but had been dissuaded from doing so. Harry's sense of his own especial destiny is now strengthened, and he leaves the stage as one 'elected'. The shock of his departure, and abandonment of his family, kills his mother.

It has been suggested that Harry's guilt at apparently murdering his wife is a reflection of Eliot's own feelings after separating from Vivien. The play was in fact being written during the period which led to her committal in Northumberland House: 'You would never imagine anyone could sink so quickly' is Harry's comment on the death by drowning of his wife. And the description of her – 'A restless shivering painted shadow' – is very close to contemporary accounts of Vivien herself. But such an identification is at best hypothetical, since it implies that Eliot was unconsciously propelled towards some instinctive revelation of his own guilt and horror. But the fact that in this year he attended a party dressed as Dr Crippen[48] suggests that there was a large element of conscious display and theatrical bravura in his creation of a character such as Harry. Although such theatricality does not preclude self-examination – in some circumstances, it may actively encourage it – it does hinder the kind of self-revelation which a banal identification of author and character assumes. In any event, Eliot explained that the character closest to himself was that of Charles, Harry's uncle, a civilized 'club man' who nevertheless understands Harry's feelings.[49] But the game of 'hunt the author' is a barren one, since there are elements of Eliot in every character: in the powerful mother, the light-brained aunts, the boringly respectable uncles. These voices were all inside him, waiting to be freed, and the significant point is the formal pattern which he creates out of these disparate personalities.

There is no doubt that in *The Family Reunion* he was attempting that re-integration of religious and secular drama which he dis-cussed at the time he was working on the play.[50] He had, for example, refused to allow John Gielgud to play the part of Harry because he 'wasn't religious enough finally to understand the motivation of the character'.[51] But the religious theme is yoked here to the 'upper-middle' stereotype of country house drama, with its retinue of cheerful cockney servants and bumbling policemen. He had an idea of what 'Shaftesbury Avenue' drama consisted, and he had an idea of what his play should suggest; but ideas are not enough. The essential problem was that he could not visualize action or dynamic behaviour upon the stage; he understood only words and the power of rhetorical statement. As a result, *The*

Family Reunion becomes a static drama of explication in which symbols of guilt and fear are the most significant elements.

The failure of the play suggested to him that he should abandon symbolism altogether in favour of realism; this was a fatal mistake, based, I believe, upon an accidental misreading of the situation. A director other than Browne might have given more theatrical conviction to the Furies, as other more recent productions have done, and a more enthusiastic public response might then have persuaded Eliot to continue with his exploration of symbolist drama. This is hypothetical, of course, but *Sweeney Agonistes* had demonstrated that it was in such drama, rather than social realism, that his theatrical talents really lay. And, for all its deficiencies, *The Family Reunion* remains his most powerful play.

He knew it had been a failure with a contemporary audience, however, and he looked very sallow and melancholy a few days after its opening.[52] He believed it to work in scenes rather than in its entirety,[53] and in a lecture some years later he criticized himself for not properly developing the action and for failing to adapt the classical theme to a contemporary situation. Harry seemed to him, also, to be a 'prig'.[54]

But his depression at the failure of the play was only part of a pervasive depression from which he was now suffering. The pact between Hitler and Chamberlain at Munich in September 1938 had confirmed Eliot's sense that the civilization of which he was a part was a worthless and immoral one: 'I felt a deep personal guilt and shame for my country and for myself as part of that country,' he wrote a few months later. 'Our whole national life seemed fraudulent.'[55] The weeks which followed only increased his depression. That sense of disintegration which he always feared was now all around him; earlier in 1938, he had told Martin Browne that public events made him feel that he was working against time and that, in any case, the race might be lost.[56]

This pessimism was responsible for his decision to discontinue the publication of the *Criterion* in January 1939. In the editorial which he wrote for the last issue, he discussed the general political situation which had provoked in him a depression of spirit so different from anything he had experienced in the last fifty years as 'to be a new emotion'; but he also confessed to a feeling of staleness as editor. Three years before, he had told Bonamy Dobrée that he was reluctant to attend *Criterion* dinners,[57] and he was becoming slipshod in his editing – he printed a review, for example, which criticized John Lehmann for not including some choruses from *Murder in the Cathedral* in a new anthology, when he himself had forbade their inclusion. The magazine had been consuming too much of his time even though, ideally, he ought to have been devoting more to it.[58] But the exercise of editing had become for him a mechanical one, and he was glad to be rid of it. Even in its best days the circulation of the magazine had been limited to some eight hundred subscribers (most of whom were 'Eliot watchers', according to Stephen Spender,[59]) and by the time it had ceased publication that number had dropped to a couple of hundred. In a broadcast he made after the war, he described the journal as one 'which had clearly failed of its purpose several years before events brought it to an end'.[60] Nevertheless this lamentable epitaph should not obscure the fact that at least in part he achieved his purpose of 'bringing together the best in new thinking and new writing in its time'[61] and that, as he confessed in an interview, editing it had been 'one of the most important and rewarding' of all his activities.[62]

Part of his motive in undertaking to edit the *Criterion* had been to establish his own position within metropolitan culture and, since he had been a bank employee when he had begun the paper seventeen years before, in this he had triumphantly succeeded. But in the early years of his editorship he had also wanted to achieve something quite different from other contemporary periodicals – he was trying to express, if not create, a genuinely European consciousness which would subvert the characteristically insular nature of English cultural life. In this attempt he was only partially successful. Although the *Criterion* was the first English periodical to print the work of Cocteau, Valéry and Proust, it seems always to have been Eliot's fate to espouse causes just at the point when they are about to disappear or to disintegrate. His notion of a European intellectual and cultural order, for example, was being asserted at a time when political events began to destroy the illusion of a common European identity. And so although his early contributors had come from the European tradition which preceded the Great War, by the early Thirties he had come to rely more and more upon British contributors. The expression of his own opinions had also become more predictable, with an aloofness from the contemporary political debate only matched by his constant call for spiritual and ethical principles to be introduced into that debate. As he said in a radio broadcast in 1946, the *Criterion* in later years 'tended to reflect a particular point of view rather than to illustrate a variety of views on that plane'.[63] In its literary direction, also, the *Criterion* had lost its momentum. The magazine had started publication at a time when the work of Lewis, Joyce, Pound and Eliot himself was actively challenging the old standards and values of English literary culture. But it seemed, a generation later, that even the writers whom Eliot chose to publish – like W. H. Auden, George Barker or Vernon Watkins – had reverted to a more insular if not parochial tradition. All the ambitions and aspirations which had animated the *Criterion* in its first years had either been abandoned or destroyed. His own feeling of staleness as an editor had much to do with his disenchantment at the kind of culture with which he now had to deal.

That disenchantment prompted him into one further expression of his views before the beginning of the war. In March 1939 he gave the Boutwood Foundation lectures at Corpus Christi College, Cambridge, in which he outlined the kind of society which he wished to see established, a society which actively advanced the values and principles which he found so signally lacking in Neville Chamberlain's England. As always, he did not think the lectures successful[64] – although he had tried to avoid all social engagements in February when he was working on them, he had still been distracted by rehearsals for *The Family Reunion*. Nevertheless they were published later in the year under the title of *The Idea of a Christian Society*.

It was Eliot's belief that if Christianity disappeared our civilization would disappear with it, and in his letters to friends during this period he gave the impression that this process was already far advanced. By the beginning of 1939, he saw only the unpleasant alternatives of uninterrupted decay or some form of authoritarian political leadership which might arrest it artificially,[65] and exactly a year later he described the fatal weaknesses of Western democracy, and how the progress of industrialization was creating an apathetic citizenry[66] – the kind of people who could only be aroused by despots like Hitler. This was the prognosis which lay behind his description, in the first of the Boutwood lectures, of a contemporary 'negative' rather than 'pagan' society. He goes on to explain the nature of a specifically Christian order – a society which would construct a framework for the political acts of the state, which would realize the importance of a Christian education and in which a 'Community of Christians', an élite of both laity and clerisy, would influence the values of the ordinary citizens of the country. He suggests the importance of community 'units' like that of the parish, which have both a religious and social dimension. But his remarks are couched in a tentative and hypothetical form. He did not concern himself with the business of creating such a society, only with the description of what it ought to be like: the actual propositions in the book are not to be taken literally, in other words, since he was offering only the ideal model of a better civilization.

He makes some specific points, of course, and perhaps the most interesting are concerned with the need for a proper relationship with nature, in order to prevent 'the exploitation of the earth' – it has, if nothing else, a prophetic ring. But however admirable Eliot's aspirations are, his execution of them in this book is on occasions bizarre. His characteristic method is to make a statement so large or vague as to be practically meaningless, then to qualify that statement by explaining what he does not mean by it, and finally to outline the reasons why he does not propose to discuss matters arising from it; he apologizes, at this point, for wandering off course but, instead of clarifying or refining his original proposition, he classifies the arguments of those who might object to it and proceeds to deal with their objections. At the end his argument comes full circle. The first statement remains intact in its vagueness and generality, but the casual reader might assume from the wealth of clauses and subordinate clauses that it has been argued and proved. This is essentially a rhetorical technique. He had admitted some years before that his prose was that of a controversialist rather than a 'thinker'[67] and this is what emerges in *The Idea of a Christian Society*. He avoids any detailed account of his own position, and relies instead upon the denunciation of alternative arguments and a shrewd analysis of contemporary truisms. What sustains him throughout is his recourse to certain fundamental principles of order and authority which, although they may be tangentially related to his espousal of Christianity, have their roots much further back in his own past and particularly in his early study of Bradley and Maurras.

The combination of prophetic denunciation and broad generalization did not appeal to his contemporaries; as one of his colleagues in the Chandos Group (where Eliot had been discussing the matters contained in his book) wrote later, 'It is understandable that *The Idea of a Christian Society* should make little appeal to the large majority of the intelligentsia. But this volume received scarcely any warmer welcome from the Church'.[68] The point could be put differently by suggesting that in his notions of a 'community of Christians' and 'parochial units' he displayed little understanding of the nature of English life – his grasp of it was theoretical rather than actual; just as he adopted almost too perfectly the dress and manners of an Englishman, so he offered an idealized and therefore unconvincing account of English society. This does not affect the cogency of his criticism and prognostication – the cultural barbarism which he feared has perhaps descended, although not in a form which he could have envisaged. But he was so much part of his time, even in the very attempt to withdraw from it, that there was no possibility of his creating a viable alternative to the society in which he lived and worked. He was a prophet in the wilderness, perhaps, but one whom the wilderness had entered and upon which he depended for his terrible denunciations. After all, it was the wilderness that had helped to create him.

But even if the role of Jeremiah suited him, there were always others he could adopt. And, in the year in which he published *The Family Reunion* and *The Idea of a Christian Society*, *Old Possum's Book of Practical Cats* also emerged. A version of it had been announced by Faber and Faber, as 'Mr Eliot's Book of Pollicle Dogs and Jellicle Cats as Recited to Him by the Man in White Spats', in the spring of 1936; the blurb, written either by Frank Morley or by Eliot himself, explained that 'several of the poems, illustrated by the author, have been in private circulation in the Publishers' various families for a considerable time. . . .' Many of the verses on the subject of Growltiger or Macavity had in fact originally been written for the children of the Fabers and the Morleys; Eliot's own affection for small rather than large animals is sufficiently well known, and he was the owner (or patron) of a succession of cats with names like Pettipaws, Wiscus and George Pushdragon – he used the latter name when entering crossword competitions in *Time and Tide*.

The verses of *Practical Cats* revert to the 'thumping' rhythms which he had assimilated as a child, and perhaps they owe something of their inspiration, also, to the memory of Eliot's father who drew cats for recreation. They are essentially a form of nonsense verse for which Eliot had great affection and understanding; he had lectured on the subject while in America in 1933, and he once told Stravinsky that he considered Edward Lear to be a great poet and compared him with Mallarmé.[69] It was a kind of verse at which he himself excelled – there are those who say that it is to be found just under the surface of some of his apparently 'serious' poetry – and *Old Possum's Book of Practical Cats* has the spirit, if not the content, of the Bolovian stanzas which he had been writing since his early twenties. But the time and inspiration for such apparent frivolities were rapidly passing and he was soon explaining to Bonamy Dobrée that the Bolovian period had ended.[70]

13

The Years of War
1939–1945

GEORGE BARKER visited Eliot in his office at Faber and Faber two or three months before the declaration of war; it was late afternoon and Eliot stood by the window looking out. 'And, after a while, in a tired voice, he said, "We have so very little time" '.[1] This is the remark of an understandably anxious man, but one friend has observed that although he seemed as concerned as anyone about the advent of war he still retained his 'detachment of spirit'.[2] In fact, he had no great enthusiasm for the approaching conflict: he believed, as others did, that a short war would leave the essential problems unchanged while a long one would simply provoke unrest in the civilian population.

When war was finally declared, Eliot said in an interview, 'the conditions of one's life changed, and one was thrown in on oneself'.[3] He settled in for what seemed likely to be a long and gloomy winter: there was really nothing he could do except to carry on with his job and perhaps do some unpaid war work. In October 1939 he caught a feverish cold; he was altogether melancholy and restless, and when at the end of the year he was asked to make a radio broadcast, he refused because he could think of nothing to say.

Many of his acquaintances were already engaged in various forms of 'war effort' and he, too, wanted to feel 'useful' in some way. Indeed, the year before, he had spoken at the Moot of his hope, according to the minutes, 'for occupation in some form of national service without that official status which might shut his mouth, and that he would be free to take part in any work for the future that was possible.'[4] But such work did not seem to be forthcoming, and his sole immediate chance of usefulness was to become an air-raid warden for his area of Kensington: in this new role, he had to rehearse the procedure for marshalling people in the event of an air raid, and to practise his fire drill by putting out bonfires in Emperor's Gate. He was still living there with Father Cheetham, although conditions were by no means ideal for a man now in his fifties. The pipes had frozen during the severe weather, and the inhabitants of the street had to use a standing tap for their water: as a result, Eliot used to wash and shave at his club.

His feelings of restlessness were compounded by the fact that his own work seemed to be slipping away from him. In one letter to Virginia Woolf, he described the plight of an author anxious and dissatisfied with the work he is doing, and aware of the fact that he may never be able to write anything again.[5] In another, and ostensibly more jocular, letter to her he speculated about a future race which might come across the name of T. S. Eliot and wonder who he was.[6] These doubts about his work were directly related to his predicament in the last months of 1939. After the failure of *The Family Reunion* his first instinct was to start work at once on a new play which would avoid the failures of the earlier one.[7] No doubt he wanted to prove to himself, as much as to anyone else, that he could do better. But the outbreak of hostilities changed all of his plans; there would be no audience for a new play, and certainly no opportunity for it to be staged, while the conflict continued. And so he was stuck, his momentum stalled.

But his frustration was part of the larger crisis which now confronted him, as it did everyone else. The orderly life which he had adopted since his separation from Vivien, the routine in which he had seemed happier and more peaceful than before, had now been destroyed by external events, and everything was cast in doubt. As a result he was, as he said, forced in upon himself. In these uncertain and troubled circumstances he was called back to the one thing outside his faith in which he could place his trust. Although in September 1939 he did not seem sure whether he would be able to compose any more poetry – it was a time when any kind of 'plan' seemed futile – within three or four months he did start work upon another poem. At first, no doubt, it was in the nature of an exercise just to see if he could still write: he was working very closely to the structure of 'Burnt Norton' and seemed to be using the earlier poem as a model from which to draw inspiration. He even used a place name again as a title: it was called 'East Coker', the village from which Andrew Eliot had travelled more than two centuries before. He had visited the place in 1937 and it must have been on this occasion that he took photographs of the village and of St Michael's Church there (where later his ashes were to be interred). By February 1940 he had drafted two out of the five sections, and was describing the poem as a successor to 'Burnt Norton' – he was still not at all sure of its worth, however, since he seemed only to be imitating himself.[8] In spite of these reservations, he worked on the rest of the poem very quickly and its last three sections were drafted before the end of that month. Copies were sent to John Hayward, Herbert Read, and perhaps others – from earliest days, as we have seen, he had relied upon the advice and encouragement of friends.

'East Coker' was published in the Easter 1940 number of the *New English Weekly*, the journal for which he continued to write signed articles and anonymous editorials. Such was its popularity that two reprints were ready in May and June of the same year; Faber and Faber published the poem as a pamphlet in September, and it sold almost 12,000 copies. He told Anne Ridler some time later that such a success almost prompted him to believe that the poem was not very good,[9] although no doubt he was being partly ironic: he was, at least, demonstrating the 'usefulness' which a poet might possess in time of war. Just as *The Waste Land* had once been taken as the expression of a 'disillusioned' generation, in spite of Eliot's disavowals of any such intention, so 'East Coker' seemed to be an expression of historical continuity at a time when it was most threatened: the retreat from France in May of that year aroused fears of a German invasion of England itself. It was not, of course, a consciously propagandist poem, a poetic equivalent of *Mrs Miniver*; but, rather, it afforded consolation and the hope of release on a deeper level. Just as the poem reflects on the literary tradition of which it is a part – Eliot mentioned his own deliberate use of Cleveland and Benlowes as well as Blake and early Yeats[10] – it could also be read as a celebration of English history, of a tradition which would survive the betrayals of the contemporary generation:

There is only the fight to recover what has been lost
And found and lost again and again: and now, under conditions
That seem unpropitious.

The poem seemed to offer the possibility of regeneration ('In my end is my beginning' is its last line) from a false civilization, and is in that sense close in spirit to *The Idea of a Christian Society*, which also sold well during the war years. At any rate, a reader might find these themes in the poem if he wished to, and Eliot was always prepared to concede the possibility of such meanings when they were discovered. His own understanding of the poem, however, was a quite different thing and, as he explained to Anne Ridler, there was no central meaning, since he had attempted to find a method of uniting on an emotional level a variety of elements which were otherwise quite unrelated.[11]

The success of 'East Coker'emphasized what the critics had been saying since the publication of the *Collected Poems* four years before: Eliot was the most substantial, if no longer the most startling, poet writing in English. This position was confirmed by the death of Yeats in 1939, and it was an apt image of succession that Eliot was asked to give the first Yeats memorial lecture at Dublin in June 1940. He had become the representative voice of the nation under threat, and in the early months of 1940 he wrote a patriotic poem, 'Defence of the Islands', to accompany an exhibition of British war photographs at the New York World's Fair. John Hayward was already assiduously collecting Eliot's letters and drafts for inclusion in what he called the 'Archives' and Virginia Woolf noted in her diary that he had acquired a certain kind of writer's egotism and made remarks like, 'Coleridge and I. . . .'[12]

But the usefulness which he sought was not only that of a prominent poet, and in a postscript to *The Idea of a Christian Society* he had already discussed the need for 'constructive thinking' during the war. In February 1940 he had raised the possibility with Read of starting a group of 'Anglo-French' intellectuals, with headquarters both in London and Paris, but Hitler's invasion of France rendered the idea inoperable. The major forum for 'constructive' thought remained in the Christian organizations of which he was already a member, and throughout the war he played a prominent part in their deliberations. He regularly attended the fortnightly lunches, and sometimes all-day meetings, of the Chandos Group and joined most of the conferences of the Moot. At one such conference in July 1940, he affirmed the need for 'a re-education of the people's sense of values, from above',[13] and in April 1941 he talked about a 'Fraternity dedicated to action' – a 'revolution' led by people in certain key positions who would name the 'enemies'.[14] This is

T. S. Eliot by Cecil Beaton.

40. Above A scene from the original 1935 production of *Murder in the Cathedral* produced at the Chapter House of Canterbury Cathedral with Robert Speight in the role of Becket. **41. Below** T. S. Eliot talks to actors at a 1951 revival of *Murder in the Cathedral*.

Above left With Charles Victor during rehearsals for *The Family Reunion*.
Above right With Ruth Lodge and Helen Hayes who appeared in *The Family Reunion*.
Below *The Family Reunion* opened at the Westminster Theatre, London in March 1939.

45. Above Throughout the Second World War Eliot continued to give lectures, readings and radio talks. **46. Below** Here he addresses an audience at the Free Technical University in Berlin in 1949. **47. Opposite** *T. S. Eliot* by Wyndham Lewis, 1949.

8, 49, 50. At Faber and Faber T. S. Eliot became publisher to two generations of writers which included W. H. Auden, Charles Williams, Lawrence Durrell and George Barker.

51. Above Sir Geoffrey Faber, 1954.
52. Right Arriving in Hamburg to receive
the Hanseatic-Goethe prize, 1955.

Above T. S. Eliot after the presentation of the Nobel Prize for Literature from Crown nce Gustaf Adolf at the Concert Hall, Stockholm in 1948.
Below Giving his autograph to a student after the Nobel Prize ceremony.

5, 56. Left T. S. Eliot talks with director Martin Browne and actors Margaret Leighton, Rex Harrison and Ian Hunter at a rehearsal of *The Cocktail Party* which had the popular success which Eliot had always sought for his dramatic writings. **57. Below** On a blackboard Eliot transcribed diagrammatic models of the action of *The Cocktail Party*.

58. Above Eliot with the theatrical impresario Henry Sherek and the actress Margaret Leighton at the Lyceum Theatre, Edinburgh before a performance of *The Confidential Clerk*.

59. Left A scene from *The Confidential Clerk* which opened at the Lyric Theatre, London in September 1953.

60. Above right T. S. Eliot being mobbed by fans as he leaves the Lyceum Theatre, Edinburgh with Henry Sherek after the first night of *The Confidential Clerk*.

61. Below right With his second wife Valerie, Eliot arrives in Rome to receive an Honorary degree at the University of Rome. He was now greeted by large crowds wherever he travelled.

62. Above Eliot and his second wife arrive for the first night of *The Elder Statesman* at the Cambridge Theatre, London in September 1958. Later they attended a celebration for his seventieth birthday.   **63. Below** Alec McCowen and William Squire in a scene from the pla

64. Above With Igor Stravinsky and his wife at a Faber and Faber party in 1958. Eliot had always admired Stravinsky's music.
65. Left Wearing the Dante Gold medal awarded to him at the Italian Institute on behalf of the people of Florence, in 1959.

66. Above At a party at Faber and Faber in 1960 with (*left to right*) Stephen Spender, W. H. Auden, Ted Hughes and Louis MacNeice.   **67. Below** Eliot and his second wife on board the Queen Elizabeth at Southampton, 1961.

fighting talk, and suggests his fond memories of Maurras and the Action Française, but it was only talk – perhaps it was Eliot's way of enlivening what he thought to be the muted tone of discussion in England;[15] perhaps it was also a method of inspiring his colleagues at the Moot whom he called 'companions in affliction',[16] intellectuals or refugees who were on the periphery of events to which there was no foreseeable end. His polemical attitudes were somewhat softened when it seemed that he might have to act upon them, and he found it necessary to disavow the political and social activism which members of the Moot such as Karl Mannheim wished to pursue. As he explained to J. H. Oldham, the difficulty about 'Christian action' was that it depended on which side of the equation you wished to stress.[17] In fact just as he relied upon intuition and perception rather than sustained argument in his prose discourse, so his public attitudes were imaginative rather than practical. In a broadcast talk which he gave in the spring of 1941, 'Towards a Christian Britain', he talked about the sacrifices which would be necessary to bring about such a national conversion, and the need for Christian 'prophets' who would alter the social consciousness of the people. In this context, he described the life of Charles de Foucauld, a missionary who was killed in North Africa. Such an image had little real relevance to the situation he was ostensibly addressing, although its private significance was such that it reappeared in his later creative work.

A more practical aspect of his campaign to reintroduce the principles of a Christian society in the rubble of the old is apparent in his association with the *Christian News Letter*. This was established in 1939 by some of those involved in the Moot, and under the editorship of Oldham it consisted of a number of editorials combined with a long signed article from writers like Reinhold Niebuhr, Karl Barth and Dorothy L. Sayers. The newspaper's first editorial offices were in Belgrave Square but, because of the dangers of bombing, they were moved to Mansfield College at Oxford where Eliot would travel each fortnight to take part in the editorial conferences. There were occasions when he became 'guest editor' of the paper, as for example in August 1940, and he often wrote leaders in his best *Criterion* style on subjects such as 'Portugal' or 'The Channel Islands'. Although some years later he was to describe the kind of people with whom he now associated in a less than enthusiastic manner,[18] it was really only in such company that he could feel any sense of purposefulness.

There were, of course, various other schemes for social improvement, and at the beginning of 1940 Ezra Pound suggested to Eliot that they should combine forces with George Santayana and collaborate on a book which would describe the conditions for 'The Ideal University'. Eliot wrote back and discussed the matter; he was already formulating his own ideas on the general subject – he gave a paper on 'The Christian Concept of Education' at a conference in Malvern in January 1941 – but, since they were markedly different from those of Pound, it is probable that he was only humouring him. He did not, in any case, have a high opinion of Santayana – an animus which Santayana reciprocated towards Eliot. Of course the idea came to nothing; in fact, one gets the impression, throughout this period, that there were a great many ideas floating about whose sole value was to console, and occupy the time of, those who had them.

Eliot's unsettled and uncomfortable life at Emperor's Gate continued throughout the larger part of 1940. Although he had managed to complete 'East Coker' there, his duties as an air-raid warden were becoming too arduous for him – he had to sit up two nights each week, and his general loss of sleep made any kind of work more difficult. He was also anxious about the possibility of German attacks. Even during the period of the 'phoney war' he had fantasies of the house being bombed,[19] and in June 1940 he asked Herbert Read to store in the country some of his books and clothes in order to prevent them from being destroyed in an air-raid.[20] When on 7 September the 'blitz' against London did begin, he decided that he no longer wished to stay in the capital, and in October he moved down to Shamley Green, a village a few miles outside Guildford and within commuting distance of London. Here he became what he described as a kind of paying guest with the Mirrlees. He had known the writer Hope Mirrlees for some years, at first through her friendship with the Woolfs (the Hogarth Press had published her long poem, *Paris*, three years before *The Waste Land*), and she was now living with her mother and spinster aunt. The company of women was by no means disagreeable – he had, after all, been brought up in a similar household – and the Mirrlees family provided him with the kind of comfort and security which his life otherwise lacked.

Anthony Powell has recalled Eliot with the Mirrlees at the end of the period in which he was staying with them. It seems that the aunt used to cadge cigarettes from Eliot, and Powell remembers how he used to enjoy long solitary walks, wearing a cap and carrying a stick. Powell noticed, as others have, that he preferred to keep conversation to light topics – his manner was rather like that of a headmaster talking to the more intelligent boys. But although he was so sensitive to conversation that he picked up the slightest nuance, his combination of 'tea party cosiness and cold intellectuality' was 'if not exactly intimidating, at least restraining'.[21]

In spite of the predatory aunt, Shamley Green was to remain his home until the end of the war: he would engage in his ordinary business in London, and continue with his own writing in Surrey. In the first months he travelled up to London on Wednesday, sometimes by train but often one of his neighbours, Sir Philip Gibbs, would drive him. He would stay the night, and then return on Thursday evening with whatever correspondence there remained to deal with. But he soon realized that he was leaving himself too little time for all the work he had to complete, and a regular routine of three days in London (generally from Tuesday to Thursday) and four days at Shamley Green was established instead. When in London, he stayed with the Fabers; the capital was being bombed each night through the last months of 1940, but their house in Hampstead had the additional advantage of a reinforced basement shelter. It was quieter there than elsewhere, and he found it easier to sleep. His days in London were crowded with what were essentially business appointments – the regular book committee meeting at Faber and Faber on Wednesday itself took up the whole of the lunchtime and afternoon. On other days, he tended to have lunch either at the Reform or at the Oxford and Cambridge Club; to judge by his correspondence, there were few occasions when he happened to be 'free', and he was forced to arrange regular times in order to see close friends like Herbert Read.

In spite of his attempts to concentrate as much work as possible into his days in London, he still found he had to take a great deal of it back to Shamley Green. Since he had no typist or secretary in the country, this meant that much of the time which he wished to devote to his own work had to be spent on business correspondence. At first he found the increase of activity made him feel healthier, but soon the exhaustion of travelling – and the waste of time involved – began to affect him. The fact that he had very little free consecutive time for his own writing began to worry him a great deal, and he missed the familiar life of Kensington, with its public house and local shops.[22] But the old London was being destroyed around him, and on 29 December 1940, incendiary bombs set the City ablaze: life was peculiar now, he told Mary Hutchinson five days later,[23] and in the preface to an anthology published in the following year, he discussed the problems of a 'changing and bewildered world'.[24]

His exhaustion as the result of his new regime, and the strange world in which he found himself, was compounded by the fact that he felt obliged to take on other responsibilities. Not only was he engaged in his publishing work, his meetings of the Moot and the Chandos Group, and his visits to Oxford for the *Christian News Letter*, but also he set himself a punishing schedule of conferences, talks and lectures; in the first week of January 1941, for example, there were six full days of such conferences. And indeed it was from this time that he began to suffer the kind of serious ill health which was regularly to affect him for the rest of his life. Although his constitution was essentially a durable one (he was 'tough', his sister, Ada, had said), from the earliest days of his marriage he had in fact been prey to various kinds of viral infection. It ought to be remembered that he was still forced to wear a truss because of his congenital hernia – no one has speculated on the physiological origins of his need for order and control – and that he was a victim of tachycardia. In his later years, he was also to suffer from persistent bronchial trouble and emphysema exacerbated by his smoking.

In the winter of 1940–41, having moved to Shamley Green, he contracted influenza which he could not shake off: he spent half of January and most of February in bed, and was still recuperating at home in March. He felt well enough some of the time, but whenever he came under mental or physical strain, he contracted a cough and a high temperature.[25] The fact that he also became unwell after meeting strangers emphasizes the partly nervous origin of his condition: it suggests a peculiar mixture of shyness and aversion, the misanthropy of a nervous man. This impression is confirmed by a conversation Eliot had with George Seferis, the Greek poet, in which he explained how uncomfortable he felt when he was forced to take shelter in an underground station during the blitz: 'I would feel the need to get out as quickly as possible, to escape all those faces gathered there, to escape all that humanity'.[26] It is perhaps worth recalling the images of eyes which persist in his poetry – and 'Don't look at me like that!' is also Harry Monchensey's cry in *The Family Reunion*. 'Psychobiographical' accounts of Eliot have seized upon such references as evidence for his sense of guilt or unworthiness, but that is too deterministic. The evidence for it is very thinly spread, although there is one rather strange letter written in this year to Mary Hutchinson, in which he questioned the importance which anyone attached to his friendship.[27]

Whatever the causes, a pattern of illness was established in Eliot's now unsettled life, as it had been when he was living with Vivien. After the influenza of the early months, he contracted further feverish colds, with attendant bronchial trouble, right up to the early summer. When he spent the Whitsun weekend with John Hayward in Cambridge, he looked 'very haggard and washed out and dispirited' and simply went to sleep on Hayward's bed for two afternoons.[28] X-rays showed that his teeth were partly the source of the trouble, and in July those at the back were removed in stages and dental plates inserted in their place.

The only advantage of illness, as far as Eliot was concerned, was that it released him from the general round of works and days – it was, he used to say, his body's way of telling him to stop[29] – and during periods of ill health such as this one he seemed better able to write. The relationship between illness and creativity interested him, and he often emphasized it in his prose writings. In the conclusion to *The Use of Poetry and the Use of Criticism*, he had suggested that some forms of 'debility, ill health and anaemia may produce an efflux of poetry', and referred to the same phenomenon in his introduction to Pascal's *Pensées*, in which he declared that certain kinds of ill health may favour not only 'religious illumination' but also 'artistic and literary composition'. This was part of his belief that poetic composition was not an activity that could be consciously controlled, that it had its roots far down in the unconscious. The metaphors which he employs to describe this process are curiously disagreeable, however. He talks of the 'dark embryo' which gradually takes on the form of a poem,[30] of 'dark psychic material' with which the poet struggles;[31] it is a 'burden' to be relieved or a 'demon' to be exorcised.[32] This suggestion of a compulsive activity with which he wants as little to do as possible is confirmed by his description of poetry as a 'secretion' (he quotes Housman favourably on this[33]), an 'evacuation' and even a 'defecation'.[34] The impression given is of some sticky, viscous, unpleasant material which has to do with the satisfaction of obscure and uncontrollable personal needs. Perhaps Eliot's attitude is an aspect of his puritanism: the pleasure involved in the 'sudden relief' of producing the poem is itself considered by him to be suspect. Disgust with the body may be formulated as a disgust with the sheer materiality of words (the 'secretion'): hence the need to economize with them, to formalize them, to cut them down.

It was during the composition of 'East Coker' at Emperor's Gate that the idea of a quartet of poems occurred to him, a sequence which would be loosely based upon the scheme of the four seasons and the four elements.[35] The possibility of a long poem clearly inspired him and, almost as soon as he had settled himself with the Mirrlees, he began to work upon the next poem in the sequence. He was already feeling ill by Christmas, but nevertheless he was writing extraordinarily rapidly and by 1 January 1941 he sent a first draft of the poem, tentatively entitled 'Dry Salvages', to John Hayward. Queries and corrections passed between them throughout the month – a process in which Geoffrey Faber joined – and 'The Dry Salvages' was published in the *New English Weekly* in February.

The poem takes its title from a ledge of rock off Cape Ann which acted as a seamark when Eliot, as a boy, used to sail out of Gloucester Harbour, and its first lines evoke the presence of the Mississippi which he had felt as a child in St Louis. Many years before, he had contemplated writing a book of essays about his childhood experience to be entitled *The River and the Sea*[36] and in 'The Dry Salvages' these images of childhood return. There are other images, too: he mentions the 'ailanthus', one of which stood in the yard of the Mary Institute where he had once played, and the 'briar rose' by his father's house in Gloucester; in addition, he employs words like 'rote' or 'groaner' which he had heard as a child in New England. At a time when his life was unsettled and the future uncertain, he returns to the world of his childhood and, in the course of the poem, meditates upon the need for release from the wheel of time itself, 'the trailing/Consequence of further days and hours'.

Almost immediately after completing the poem, he began in the early months of 1941 to work on the fourth in the sequence; it was entitled 'Little Gidding'. This was the name of the place which he had visited five years before; he had gone almost in the role of a pilgrim, since it was there that Nicholas Ferrar established a small Anglican religious community in the seventeenth century – a familial life led in poverty, discipline and prayer which was extirpated by Parliamentary troops in 1646. Eliot recognized that this was not simply the last poem in his sequence but also its culmination, in which the themes and textures of the preceding three parts would be gathered together in a final statement. He had completed a first draft by July 1941, but he told Hayward that he was not pleased with the result because he was over-conscious of what he was attempting to do:[37] he was always aware of this problem in his work, and it had effectively led him to abandon much of the poetry he had been writing in his Harvard years. The difficulty was that he had started work on the poem before he had adequately prepared himself, although his haste was understandable. For the previous ten months London and provincial cities had been bombed night after night (on 10 May, three thousand Londoners were killed in the raids); although the worst of the blitz was now over, no one knew it then, and at this perilous juncture in the war Eliot had been anxiously writing against time.[38] As Mass Observation noted, 'One very vital effect of the air-raids is this blurring of the future. There is a tendency for people's whole outlook to be foreshortened, so that life exists from day to day'[39] – and Eliot was by no means immune from such general fears. These external pressures meant that he was writing 'Little Gidding' quickly but mechanically; the material was not properly seasoned[40] and the first version of the poem lacked the presence of concealed private memories which would make the language cohere.[41] Although he put the poem to one side it still continued to worry him, and in October he explained to Mary Hutchinson that the contemporary situation was such that only good work was appropriate;[42] bad writing, after all, would seem even more trivial or superfluous. The parlous state of England enters the poem, in fact, in a direct way: 'Dust in the air suspended/Marks the place where a story ended.' was an evocation of the debris which hung in the air after a bombing, and then 'would slowly descend and cover one's sleeves and coat with fine white ash'.[43] This is one of the few indications that Eliot gave of the fact that, in the periods between illness when he carried on with his ordinary duties in London (as much as anyone's life was 'ordinary' then), he experienced the horror of the German raids: the nightly bombings, the streets blocked with rubble, the glow in the evening as fires burned throughout the city, and the peculiarly dank smell of ruined buildings: it was this which provoked fear, precluded concentration on other things, and destroyed the will to work. Like everyone else's in this period, his life became one of monotony and anxiety, caught in a middle period when pre-war life seemed unreal and post-war life unimaginable. It was a time of physical and social constraints also, when more arduous duties and responsibilities had to be fulfilled in less and less time. His existence was swallowed up in the gloom and horror of the entire country – he did not, in other words, lead a private life in the sense in which that was true before the war. But he might at least be 'useful', as he had wanted, and part of that usefulness lay in the fact that, on one level at least, his poetry could have a public and national purpose – although, when the war had been won, he no longer cared to draw attention to those aspects of it. Some years later, in a draft version of 'The Three Voices of Poetry', he wrote that the last three quartets were patriotic poems; then he crossed out the remark.

Although the three earlier poems had been highly praised and widely read – their reception, Hayward told Frank Morley, had boosted Eliot's reputation at a time when it was in danger of being obscured by younger poets[44] – he was unable to finish the sequence. But the reasons were not entirely those of restlessness and imaginative deficiency. He had been anxious to finish 'Little Gidding' partly in order to get on with other jobs, particularly since he had spent so much of the early part of 1941 in seclusion in Shamley Green because of ill health, and these pre-empted his time and concentration. Even while he was working on the first draft of the poem, he was writing to Martin Browne about all the engagements ahead.[45] In September 1941, he had to be in Wales and Oxford, and in the following month he travelled to Bristol, Wells, Durham and New-castle – each appointment requiring the preparation of a lecture or talk. In addition he was having to select, and write an essay for, *A*

Choice of Kipling's Verse which was to be published at the end of the year – even this, given the nature of Kipling's poetry, might be described as 'war work'. Public activity of this kind was, he said, a kind of sedative[46] – no doubt to counteract feelings of uselessness – but it did mean that he was forced to postpone any creative work. His engagements in the early months of 1942 were equally arduous. In February he lectured on 'The Music of Poetry' at Glasgow University and in April gave an address to the Classical Association on 'The Classic and the Man of Letters'. At the end of this month he travelled to Sweden on a tour organized by the British Council; it lasted five weeks, and he gave a number of readings in Stockholm, Upsala, Lund and elsewhere. When he came back, he took his turn as 'guest editor' of the *Christian News Letter* and attended a conference at Wadham College for the Christian Frontier Council. These duties had to be fulfilled alongside those of his conventional publishing business, and he was also supposed to be writing a scene for inclusion in what was to be a filmed version of *Murder in the Cathedral*. He did not feel he could work on such a project, however, until 'Little Gidding' was finished.

But it was not until August 1942, after a year's delay, that he set to work on the poem again. It was by far the most laboriously produced of the sequence: there are some five drafts, and thirteen separate typescripts, extant. Some of it had come quickly; Eliot knew the verse was right, and left it alone. But the rest needed more attention. He composed a short preliminary scheme for the entire poem, as well as prose drafts for certain difficult passages. (For 'The Dry Salvages' he had even written out lists of rhyming words to assist him.) Like his pleasure in reading dictionaries or solving crosswords, this seemed to be the kind of soothing conscious activity which allowed the unconscious faculties an easier passage forward. Having constructed a working model, as it were, he left his conscious mind to one side and relied upon his ear – what he described as the interdependence of rhythm and diction,[47] or the recognition of meaning when it is embodied in cadence. In fact what he called the 'auditory imagination' was always his most powerful faculty, the most subtle and complex instrument at his disposal which he deserted at his peril. When in *Four Quartets* he was concerned to state or develop a theme, he frequently relapsed into flatness or banality. But in almost all instances he recovered himself in the process of revision, took out the passages which were rhythmically inert or altered words and images which did not sustain the underlying cadence and structure. Throughout August and early September he was engaged in this process, with drafts going between Hayward and himself, until on 19 September he sent Hayward the final version. With one or two minor changes, this was the poem published in the *New English Weekly* in October 1942. The sequence was now complete: although he had originally wanted to entitle it *Kensington Quartets*, in memory of his residence there, it was called *Four Quartets*.

The publication of his work generally provoked in Eliot a sense of release – he had evacuated something, to use one of his favourite expressions, and was left with an agreeable sensation of vacancy – and after the appearance of 'Little Gidding' in the autumn, he did not expect to do any serious intellectual work during the winter. In any case it seemed at this point that the war might be lost, and only a month after finishing the poem he was expressing to Martin Browne grave misgivings about the worth and value of his poetic activities, which often appeared to be futile.[48] Throughout the autumn and winter he suffered from feverish colds and attacks of bronchitis, and was often forced to take to his bed for a week or fortnight at a time. One observer who met him in November of this year at Lady Colefax recollected that 'he seemed to be holding himself together, almost as if he were a piece of riveted china'.[49]

He tried fitfully to proceed with a short prose book on the nature of culture which he had been contemplating for some time, but by the end of 1942 had produced only a first draft of two chapters: this must be the source of the four essays which appeared in the *New English Weekly* during January and February 1943 under the title, 'Notes toward a Definition of Culture'. In April he was still having difficulty in completing the book and in a letter to Henry Treece in September he was again expressing doubts about himself as a writer.[50] But the main reason for his slowness in composing it was that he felt obliged to take on what he called 'odd jobs'. He continued to give lectures, readings and radio talks. He was also working for the British Council, writing for foreign magazines and attending functions organized by the Anglo-Swedish Society or the Norwegian Institute, as well as seeing American G.I.s stationed in London – it seemed to him on occasions that every American sergeant wrote verse.[51] But he took such duties seriously; he often had to give his opinion on the work of young poets who were about to be dispatched into the war: and he knew that his comments might be the last they ever received.

He was now in London from Tuesday to Friday, and tended to stay in a flat at the office in Russell Square. This was principally because he had taken up fire-watching duties there, and once or twice a week he would go up on the roof: he would have heard the sound of the aircraft, and the bursts of shrapnel from the anti-aircraft guns, while all the time scrutinizing the 'blacked out' city for the evidence of fires. Since he suffered from vertigo, this was not a comfortable experience for him. From Friday evening to Tuesday, he was at Shamley Green, and although he tried to avoid visiting people or seeing his neighbours[52] his weekends were often occupied, which meant that a fortnight might elapse before he could get on with his own work. It is no wonder that in March 1943 he was suffering from fatigue which again brought on influenza.

He found the time and energy, however, to write a pamphlet attacking a scheme for Church Union in South India. It was called 'Reunion by Destruction' and in it Eliot set out his reasons for opposing the idea of uniting the Anglican, Presbyterian, Congregationalist and Methodist churches. He confessed that the model he had in mind was Pascal's letters,[53] but alas his pamphlet has not achieved a similar immortality. Although he was thus once more diverted from his book, he was nevertheless discussing the principles behind it in a variety of different contexts. He had become involved in the administration of St Anne's House in Soho, for example; it had been opened this year as a 'centre of Christian discourse', and in the autumn he and Philip Mairet conducted a discussion group, 'Toward the Definition of Culture', which met once a week until the middle of December.

In this year, he was appointed President of the English Circle of Books Across the Sea, and also became a member of the Apollo Society which was dedicated to reviving 'the neglected art of reading poetry and to show that poetry and music can be regarded as complementary'. Indeed in April he had proved that such reading was an art: the Sitwells had organized an evening for the Free French in the Aeolian Hall, and in front of the Queen he gave a memorable and dramatic performance of 'What the Thunder Said'.

That poetry had been written at Lausanne more than twenty years before, in a world which was now disappearing. James Joyce and Virginia Woolf were dead, Charles Maurras was a member of the Petain government and would soon be imprisoned for treason, Ezra Pound was about to be indicted on similar charges (although Eliot refused to assist the Federal Bureau of Investigation in their inquiries about him). In these last years of the war, he was simply continuing with his life, going on from day to day without much hope for the future. Certainly the lectures which he delivered in 1944 – 'Johnson as Critic and Poet' at University College, Bangor, 'What Is Minor Poetry?' to the Association of Bookmen in Swansea, 'What Is A Classic?' to the Virgil Society, of which he was president – are not among his best, the latter seeming particularly forced and mechanical.

The German blitz was resumed in the early months of this year and then a fresh terror, the 'flying bombs', was directed against London in the summer. No doubt Eliot's own fears and uncertainty were compounded when in June a bomb fell upon the offices of Faber and Faber (fortunately, he was not up on the roof at the time). The business was able to carry on but the flat he sometimes used was uninhabitable; he came up to London only on Tuesday nights and 'camped out' for the fire-watching while for the rest of the time he commuted between London and Surrey. In August he was again complaining of tiredness; there was no doubt that like most other Englishmen he was experiencing what he described in another context as a general weariness of war and desire for peace.[54]

Nevertheless his poetry, as he said in an interview some years later, had 'connected the wartime work very well' and 'fitted in very nicely to the conditions under which I was writing'.[55] The reviews of each separate quartet had on the whole been favourable and when the complete edition of *Four Quartets* was published at the end of October, there was general assent about his achievement. The volume had been published in the United States the year before, and the American critics had been more divided in their response. Although there was almost unanimous praise of Eliot's poetic or sheerly musical abilities (which in any case had their roots deep in his American experience), there was a certain distrust of the religious sensibility which seemed to be expressed in the sequence. These responses mark an important distinction in the later appreciation of Eliot. The respect afforded him in England had partly to do with the manner in which he had taken on the mantle of English culture; in the absence of any figure with equivalent influence, he was eventually to be invested with an almost shamanistic authority. The American critics, to whom it was rapidly becoming clear that the dominant culture was to be their own, were sceptical of his Anglicanism and Toryism. They were looking on things new born, it seemed, while he was preoccupied with that which was dying.

Four Quartets was recognized as an extraordinary *tour de force*, however, in which the balance between stylistic adaptation, lyric statement and dramatic narrative had been maintained throughout. In order to describe the sequence, we need only turn to the lectures which Eliot gave during and just after its composition: here he talked almost coyly of a poem which might develop themes instrumentally and arrange transitions 'comparable to the different movements of a symphony or a quartet',[56] of a poem elaborate enough to exercise the dramatic, descriptive and narrative talents of its maker.[57] All of which suggests what the drafts of the poems confirm – that he knew, or wanted to know, exactly what he was doing.

The context in which he was working was now a quite different one. Although he had had neither the time nor the opportunity to continue with his verse drama, the subject was never far from his mind. In the Yeats memorial lecture in Dublin, for example, he talked about the theatre as a medium for 'the expression of the consciousness of a people' and two years later he castigated the failure of most poetic drama to evoke the rhythms of 'colloquial speech';[58] he returned to this theme a year later when, in a preface to S. L. Bethell's *Shakespeare and the Popular Dramatic Tradition*, he described the language of poetic drama as the language which people 'would speak today if they could speak in poetry'. This is precisely what he had been attempting in 'The Dry Salvages', for example, and it is significant that he used much the same phrase in his demand that contemporary poetry should have such a strong relationship to current speech that 'the listener or reader can say "that is how I should talk if I could talk poetry" '[59] This identification of poetry and drama, and its connection with his own poetic practice, suggests the real direction of his concerns. Again and again in his wartime lectures, he stressed the need in poetry for a 'common style',[60] a 'common language of the people',[61] the attempt to reflect 'the changing language of common intercourse'.[62] Even his understanding of musical pattern and musical form, which in practice was for him a deeply instinctive activity, was discussed in terms of the musical pattern which is 'latent in common speech'.[63] This emphasis upon a common style is partly connected with that sense of national identity and community which the war provoked, but it was also intimately related to Eliot's preoccupation with what he termed 'The Social Function of Poetry' in both developing the language, and enriching the sensibility, of the culture. As the years passed, he was beginning to sound more and more like Matthew Arnold – although Arnold was never quite able to practise what he preached. However, Eliot was, and it is in this context that *Four Quartets* should be seen.

He was deliberately adapting his dramatic experience for use in poetic composition, since for the first time in his 'pure' poetry he was addressing an audience. His emphasis on the 'common style' suggests that he is no longer interested in talking to himself but to others, and *Four Quartets* is at one level an oratorical performance: it would not be too much to say that all of his previous work has led him to this point, where poetry is married with public exhortation. Certainly the sequence is the most elaborately and intricately shaped of all his poetry. Each of the four poems has five sections, and each of the sections reflects upon its counterparts in the other poems; just as each poem develops and resolves its theme, so 'Little Gidding' gathers up the three preceding ones in a magisterial synthesis. Eliot also introduces deliberate traces of his earlier writing from sources as disparate as 'La Figlia Che Piange' and *The Family Reunion*. No poet in the twentieth century has had such a conscious sense of his own work, or of the tradition in which he was operating.

For not only does he emphasize the continuity of his poetic development but he also introduces echoes and half-parodic reminiscences of the English and European literary inheritance of which he was a beneficiary. He had been doing that throughout his poetry – as he had said more than thirty years earlier, in 'Portrait of a Lady', 'And I must borrow every changing shape/To find expression . . .' – but the process reaches its culmination in 'Little Gidding' where he creates a replica of Dante's *terza rima*:

> In the uncertain hour before the morning
> Near the ending of interminable night
> At the recurrent end of the unending . . .

In a lecture which he delivered before completing the poem, he had described the 'unity' of 'English letters of the past' and related it to 'a recognizable entity called European literature'.[64] *Four Quartets* offers an image of that 'entity', and the figure who appears in the Dantesque passage is a 'familiar compound ghost' in whom Eliot suggested we might recognize Yeats, Mallarmé, Swift and Poe.[65] And yet in the same lecture he had expressed his belief that the tradition of which he spoke was drawing to a close; and, in the poem, the encounter with the familiar but only half-glimpsed figure is charged with a sense of transitoriness and loss:

> The day was breaking. In the disfigured street
> He left me, with a kind of valediction,
> And faded on the blowing of the horn.

In 'Little Gidding', and in *Four Quartets* as a whole, we see the outlines of a tradition, beautifully limned but shimmering like an hallucination before it disappears and the sirens of a catastrophic European war intrude. This ambivalence between the formal order of the poem and troubled intimations of its own fragility, between its eloquent directness and the presence of Eliot's private memories concealed beneath the surface of that eloquence, gives the poem its power.

As a result, any attempt to explicate the theme of the sequence is bound to run into peculiar difficulties, although there have been various attempts to interpret it in Christian, symbolist or political terms. Eliot once explained that, even if a poem meant different things to different readers, it was still necessary to assert its 'absolute' meaning.[66] This paradox is strongly reminiscent of Bradleyan idealism, and to understand the nature of *Four Quartets* it is appropriate to recall what Eliot as a student considered to be one of the central principles of Bradley's thought: that, for the sceptic faced with the possibility of acquiring only relative truth, coherence and comprehensiveness were important for their own sake. In *Four Quartets*, Eliot is providing a consummation of the European tradition, just as he is offering a coherent account of his own poetic development. At a late date in our cultural history, he had created a language both formal and authoritative. And yet we know the conditions under which the sequence was written and notice how fragile it is, how much a willed order, and how dependent upon a bravura performance – and suspect that it is from these elements that the permanent value of the poetry springs.

In March 1945, a few weeks before the German surrender, Eliot was expressing his pessimism about the future;[67] a few days later he wrote his last commentary for the *Christian News Letter* and used the pseudonym of 'Metoikos' or 'resident alien'. In May, just before VE Day, he travelled to Paris in order to lecture on 'The Social Function of Poetry' and took the opportunity to bring small presents of soap, China tea, and other commodities to old friends there like Sylvia Beach. But he felt no exhilaration, and he did not participate in the public celebrations after the surrender of the Japanese; the noise of the fireworks actually disturbed him more than the bombs of the blitz.[68] He was suffering from an infected throat as a result of another poisoned tooth, and in November he was feeling too ill to go out in the evenings.

His depression had been caused at first by what he considered to be the disturbing condition of the victors after the war: he was uneasy about the foreign policy of both England and the United States, as well as about the intentions of Russia. But his gloomy prognostications were also of a more general kind, and in January 1946 he described a public world which was becoming more 'incredible' and a private world which was more 'intolerable'. The world was a less 'moral' place than it had been before the war: Germany and Japan had brought to a crisis the sickness which infected civilization, but their collapse had not cured it but left it raging everywhere.[69]

In the late Thirties, in that period which he described as more 'moral', he had affirmed the need for something very like a Christian revolution which might alter the structure, and would certainly change the principles, of English society. The advent of a Labour government, and the dominance of America in post-war Europe, prompted a change of emphasis, and his abiding preoccupation came to be with the survival of European civilization itself. Even before the war was won, he had been afraid that peace might be associated only with the concept of 'efficiency',[70] and in radio talks in 1946 he spoke of the necessity for maintaining the 'spiritual organization' as well as the 'material organization' of Europe.[71] There was a prospect ahead of 'centuries of barbarism' which, in an interview the year before, he had already related to the coming dominance of technology.[72] The barbarians did not arrive in his lifetime, but there is no doubt that Eliot was aware that he was witnessing the end of that culture which, more than thirty years before, he had travelled to Europe to find. It is paradoxical, perhaps, that in these post-war years he came to enjoy his greatest fame and, in the end, happiness.

14

The Rigours of Life
1946–1949

AFTER THE CONCLUSION of hostilities, Eliot began the process of readjustment to the more settled but no less uncomfortable conditions of peace. He had already considered returning to London in the closing stages of the war, but had thought better of it. But, in the summer of 1945, he took a furnished room in Kensington and began to look for a suitable and convenient residence of his own. Most of the places he saw were uninhabitable, or required a permit from the Office of Works to make them less so, but a friend of John Hayward told him of some rooms in Carlyle Mansions,[1] a Victorian apartment building along the Chelsea Embankment which looks out over the Thames. In early 1946 he moved into 19 Carlyle Mansions, a large and comfortable flat on the third floor, beneath the one in which Henry James had once lived. Eliot had already agreed to share his new home with John Hayward who, having supervised its decoration, joined him a month after Eliot had 'settled in'; for the next eleven years this was to be their mutual address.

John Hayward had, in fact, first suggested in 1935 that they should set up together, but Eliot chose not to do so. He was then staying with Father Cheetham and, since Vivien was still in pursuit of him, he preferred the relative anonymity and seclusion of his status as a 'guest'. The two men knew each other much better now but, on the face of it, despite their joint passion for Sherlock Holmes and Eliot's reliance upon Hayward's editorial skills (not only did he inspect the poetry, but he also removed social malapropisms from the drama), they were an oddly matched pair. Hayward was gregarious, a great attender of dinners and parties, but he could also be a caustic and gossipy creature given to telling salacious stories. He was a man whose sexual energies had been forced inwards through his crippling disease, and had taken the form of mental passion which found relief in meticulous scholarship and mild prurience. His confinement to a wheelchair had made him defensively aware of his reliance upon other people, as well, and Anthony Powell has described him as 'at once nervous and dominating' with a manner which 'could at times approach the positively tyrannical'.[2]

And so what was the bond between the two men? Eliot certainly appreciated Hayward's caustic wit and was himself, according to Hayward, '. . . a connoisseur of the ridiculous, an ironical commentator on human folly, a lover of allusive quotation (particularly from the *dicta* of Sherlock Holmes and other eminent detectives), and a passionate observer of what may be called the *Bouvard et Pécuchet* way of life'.[3] But such a shared interest would scarcely be enough to form such a strong friendship. Of course Hayward's physical condition was such that he could no longer live alone – he had spent the war years as a guest of the Rothschilds in Cambridge – and there must have been an element of sympathy or even pity in Eliot's invitation to him; the presence of old-fashioned Yankee rectitude in his character, and the quiet acceptance of 'duty' in his role as Hayward's companion and helper, cannot be ignored. He would quite willingly lay aside his own business in order to take Hayward to a party, or wheel him in a park. But if he was a useful companion for Hayward, there were also ways in which Hayward could be of benefit to him. Eliot was a lonely man, and Hayward was the only single person he knew with whom he could share a flat. Solitude one can endure; mundane loneliness is more difficult to bear. Hayward was also a dutiful editor and keeper of the Eliot 'Archives', as his work on *Four Quartets* showed, and in addition his role was that of a social bulwark. There were times when Eliot seemed uncertain or ill at ease, suddenly very much the 'resident alien' – one has the impression, always, of a man invaded by inexplicable moods and anxieties which he did his best to conceal – and Hayward's own dominating and very English manner afforded him at such times a certain amount of confidence. Although Hayward might talk about his 'lodger' in a jocular fashion, he was proud of his association with the great man of letters and defended both his privacy and reputation. Sometimes he seemed to act almost as his 'representative on earth'; when Cecil Day Lewis was asked by *The Times* to compose Eliot's obituary, he suggested to Hayward that they collaborate upon it. It was clearly a delicate matter, with Eliot's wife in a mental hospital, and Day Lewis wrote to Hayward, 'I hope you feel my reference to his private tragedy is passable. . . .'⁴ Eliot, then, had a staunch defender.

There are many reminiscences of the two men together at Carlyle Mansions – Hayward talkative and Eliot silent, Hayward persuading Eliot to quote from memory long passages from the Sherlock Holmes stories (there was an element of putting his famous companion 'on show' in such circumstances, although his disease allowed him a certain immunity from conventional social niceties), Eliot on occasions reciting his poetry with 'an actor's pleasure',⁵ Eliot standing behind Hayward's wheelchair at literary parties – almost at attention, as one observer noticed. And then there were the weekend expeditions through Chelsea, generally in the afternoon, when Eliot would push Hayward across the bridge to Battersea Gardens or along Chelsea Embankment to the gardens of the Royal Hospital. They were often accompanied on such excursions by Christopher Sykes, who has recalled one wet Saturday afternoon when, in the Hospital gardens, they watched a football match between the Marylebone dustmen and the Chelsea Municipal Maintenance Staff: 'The forlorn scene fascinated Eliot and in spite of the cold and the drizzle he stayed and watched for several minutes'.⁶ Perhaps he was wearing his customary flat cap and voluminous raincoat, but there is in any case something highly appropriate about this scene of forlornness and dampness; the picture of Eliot in a prospect of drizzle evokes a quality in the man himself. There was indeed an element of almost willed despondency in his character in these post-war years. In Carlyle Mansions itself, Hayward's own rooms were at the front of the building and looked over the river and the gardens while Eliot satisfied himself with a study and bedroom down a dark passage at the back of the building. They were small and cheerless rooms. His bedroom was lit by a bare electric lightbulb, there was an ebony crucifix above his single bed, and the window looked out upon a brick wall. His study resembled that 'of a nineteenth-century pedagogue or parson'.⁷ In the same way he himself seemed to be acquiring a greater and greater starkness, and soon after settling into Carlyle Mansions the order of his new life emerged.

In the morning he would leave the flat at 6.30 and take the bus to St Stephen's at Gloucester Road, his familiar church, for early morning Mass. On his return home he would eat a large English breakfast and, before starting on his work, would play a hand or two of patience and begin *The Times* crossword. Then he would go to his study and attend to his own writing, characteristically composing straight onto the typewriter and standing at a kind of lectern. At about noon he would leave Carlyle Mansions for Faber and Faber, complete with battered briefcase, dark suit (with a white handkerchief in the breast pocket) and rolled umbrella. He would catch the bus to Piccadilly Circus – he sat on the top deck and worked on the crossword before turning to the company reports in *The Times*. He remained, as it were, invisible. When on one occasion a young Indian student approached him and asked if he was T. S. Eliot, he looked up at her in alarm, agreed that he was, and got off the bus. Generally, however, he travelled undisturbed; he would alight from the bus at Piccadilly Circus and then take the underground railway to Russell Square.

Even in the years of his greatest fame, he continued with the routine business of publishing. For a man who found it difficult to write for more than three hours a day it was one way of passing time but, more importantly, as he explained in an address in 1951, it was necessary for him to hold a job which other people considered useful; he had so little confidence in his own work that he did not want to risk wasting all of his time upon it.[8] (There is no doubt, however, that his fame was useful to the firm with which he was so closely associated.) His day at Faber and Faber was well regulated also. There was, of course, the usual business of a publisher – 'blurbs', reports, memos, correspondence with authors and negotiations with agents. Book committee day was Wednesday (later moved to Tuesday), when the board would lunch together and spend the afternoon discussing the week's business: considering written reports, commenting upon manuscripts received, arguing about the merits of ideas proposed for new books, and so on. Anne Ridler noticed how Eliot 'affected a certain detachment from the proceedings, and did *The Times* crossword during the meetings, but his business judgments were as shrewd as anyone's. . . .'[9] Having been involved in such proceedings since the Twenties he was now in fact finding them 'a bit tedious',[10] and 'Mr Eliot's list' was invented for a section of the agenda so that he did not have to attend the entire meeting. His main areas were those of poetry and theology;

sometimes, when discussing the manuscripts of poetry received, his laconic comment was 'All out'. On other days of the week he had fixed luncheon dates which, because of his crowded schedule and not infrequent trips abroad, were arranged well in advance. He would generally lunch in one of the clubs to which he belonged (by the end of his life, he was a member of the Athenaeum, the Garrick, and the Oxford and Cambridge) although there were occasions when he would take guests to his favourite restaurant, L'Etoile, in Charlotte Street.

After lunch he returned to his office where he would continue with his ordinary duties until the ritual of tea at four, when he would receive visitors. He would then work until approximately 6.00 or 6.30, and if there was no social or literary event he felt obliged to attend, would take a taxi back to Carlyle Mansions. (He was in every respect a most economical man, and, like many of his generation, continued to think of taxis as an expensive luxury long after he could easily afford them.) If he returned home in the evening he would sometimes dine with John Hayward but, since Hayward was an inveterate diner-out, he would often eat alone from a tray on his knees. After dinner he might finish some pressing publishing work, correcting manuscripts or writing blurbs; if not inveigled by Hayward into escorting him to a party, or sitting with guests in the shared 'living room', he would retire to his own rooms for study or contemplation. Wednesday night was the house-keeper's night 'off', and then Eliot might have dinner with friends at L'Etoile. Sometimes he and Hayward would invite friends to dinner at the Good Intent, a restaurant in the Kings Road, or entertain at home. Their neighbour, the writer Julia Strachey, found them 'congenial souls and seeing them *does* cheer one up',[11] although she recalled one evening when Eliot suddenly emerged in a dressing gown apparently 'utterly distraught and Strindbergian, with his at-all-times remarkable manner accentuated into something ghostly and weird. I wondered for a moment if he was dead drunk; but I fancy not.'[12] It is an unexplained incident, and in any case such moments were rarely visible to outsiders. The essential feature of the life which Eliot had constructed for himself is that it contained as few surprises as possible: it has been said that, for over thirty years, he patronized the same tailor, the same tobacconist and the same wine merchant. Such was the existence of the poet. There was a time for everything – a time for eating, a time for talking, a time for writing. It was all of a piece: his own conversation was unhurried and controlled and, when he spoke, he made few if any gestures. 'This is T. S. Eliot here,' he would say on the telephone; it was an instrument he detested and when using it his voice had 'a curiously strangled sound'.[13] One friend has described him checking his wristwatch with an almost deliberate thoroughness: 'He slowly and methodically raised his left hand and with his right hand carefully pushed back his coat sleeve and shirt sleeve at the same time and then painstakingly, at close range, studied the face of the dial.'[14] There is a sense of effort trying to vanquish inertia here, as though physical movements were difficult for him; but the prevailing impression is of a man who found comfort and relief in an ordered and disciplined life. Perhaps that is why one of his major recreations, apart from the reading of detective stories and the novels of P. G. Wodehouse, was playing the card game, patience. As his American publisher, Robert Giroux, put it, 'The typical image of the period was Eliot playing solitaire';[15] Eliot's first housekeeper, an Irish lady, had a similar impression. 'I've known many a writing man,' she told one of his friends, 'and he's no writing man, Mr Eliot. He's a very holy man . . . . It'll be playing patience I've only seen him doing'.[16] When W. H. Auden once found him playing that game and asked him why he seemed to relish it, he reflected gravely and then replied, 'Well, I suppose it's the nearest thing to being dead'.[17] This sounds like one of his more severe remarks, although perhaps an ironical inflection has not survived its reporting.

There was certainly a large element of irony in his demeanour and conversation, although it was a quality not immediately apparent when he was in the company of more sober or 'respectable' people; in those circumstances he could, as it were, give as good as he got. He gave the impression to some people of resembling a 'senior civil servant', as Lawrence Durrell put it,[18] emphasized by his 'impenetrable reserve' and 'inscrutable courtesy'.[19] But it has to be remembered that he was now being treated by many people with extreme deference, mixed with not a little nervousness, and it is very difficult to behave normally in such circumstances. When he was with close friends, he abandoned that somewhat starched public demeanour. One such friend has recalled how observant and amusing he could be, how quick to comment upon other people's expressions or appearance which he would 'associate with psychological traits'.[20] His fondness for practical jokes made him on occasions a 'tormenting tease', according to John Hayward, and he never lost his 'satirical wit'.[21] Instances of that wit are, at this late date, rather hard to obtain, although E. W. F. Tomlin has remembered two small examples. When Eliot heard that Wyndham Lewis had been travelling around North Africa in a thick English suit, he remarked, 'Lewis was always a heavily dressed man'; and of a lady who had acquired too many petrol coupons during the first year of the war, he said, 'There is always bound to be a certain element of iniquity in these matters'.[22] They are not perhaps the kind of remarks to be found in Christmas crackers, but they suggest that his humour was bound up with the idea of self-parody: he is mocking the pontifical manner which others associated with him.

His letters to friends are often funny in a less self-conscious way, and he will ramble in a high-spirited or nonsensical manner about nothing in particular. Such humour even stretched to the envelopes, and those addressed to friends such as Clive Bell often had on them verse instructions to the postman. One such friend with whom he could relax, and to whom he sent a great deal of comic correspondence, was Mary Trevelyan. He had first met her in 1938, when she invited him to give a reading at the Student Movement House of which she was Warden. During the war these readings were an annual event, and she became a close friend. In fact, it seems that only with women was Eliot ever fully at ease; Mary Trevelyan herself was funny, highly intelligent without being particularly 'literary', and socially astute – she was able to 'cope' with the world in a way that he was never quite able to. They would attend parties or receptions (often fortifying themselves with a drink or two in advance), and would frequently dine together. She was a good pianist, as well, and he enjoyed listening to her play. Their friendship was intimate but Platonic, and it was one in which Mary Trevelyan acted both as a confidante and social support. She helped him in other ways also – she was a chauffeuse on occasions, tended him when he was ill, and sometimes acted as a secretary. Certain drafts of *The Cocktail Party*, for example, are marked with Mary Trevelyan's handwritten alterations 'as dictated by T. S. E.' From the late Forties she kept a diary of their friendship, and in this it is possible to see how bewildering Eliot could appear, even to those who knew him best. It seems that she had fallen in love with him but she 'didn't know where I was at all' with him; he would be most affectionate towards her and then, for no apparent reason, seemed to avoid her for protracted periods.[23] This was not a novel characteristic, and other friends in the past had noticed the alterations between 'thaw' and 'freeze' in his relationships with them. He did not want anyone to get too close to him, especially after his years with Vivien, and there was a point at which he withdrew from those who expected too great an intimacy. This might simply be the expression of a natural *hauteur*, or even of a Puritan dislike for self-revelation; he also seemed to fear that other people would 'take advantage' of him but, more importantly, there is a sense in which he felt threatened by the personalities of others – as if he might be invaded by them.

If he was a difficult friend, he could also be a loyal one – the most notable example, of course, is that of Ezra Pound whom he continued to support and defend even though it meant that he became embroiled in the kind of public controversy which he detested. During the war Pound had broadcast over Rome Radio a number of bitter attacks on Roosevelt, Churchill and the Jews. In May 1945 he was arrested by the American forces and taken to a Disciplinary Training Centre near Pisa, before being flown back to Washington to stand trial for treason. Eliot must have heard of his arrest during or just after his visit to Paris at the beginning of that month since, on his return, he immediately sent a cable to Archibald MacLeish, the poet who was then Assistant Secretary of State, saying that he was eager to help Pound in any way he could. Pound did not reach Washington, however, until the middle of November 1945 and the first real chance Eliot had to acquaint himself with the situation was on the business trip to the United States which he planned for June and July of 1946. Two months before his departure he wrote to twelve or fifteen poets, requesting their public support for Pound and asking them to provide private testimonials in the event that he should be tried and sentenced for his crime: there was, at this stage, a strong possibility that Pound would be condemned to death.

In July, two or three weeks after arriving in the United States, Eliot travelled to Washington in order to visit Pound at St Elizabeth's, the asylum where he was being held. He told the

American poet, Allen Tate, after the meeting that Pound's character had not really altered: he had covered so many subjects during
their brief meeting, for example, that Eliot could not remember
much about them afterwards.[24] Robert Lowell has transcribed
Eliot's account of another such meeting in his *Notebook*: ' "*You
speak*," he said, when he'd talked two hours. By then I had
absolutely nothing to *say*.' After his return to England, he explained
to Dorothy Pound that her husband needed somehow to be calmed
down.[25] There was a reasonable chance that he might be released
from St Elizabeth's: Eliot himself suggested a private sanatorium,
to be followed by a retreat in California or New Mexico. He also
wanted to publish the next volume of the *Cantos* as soon as possible,
in order to bolster Pound's reputation, although he had expressed
private reservations that the most recent work was not of so high a
standard as the rest.[26] Pound was not to escape lightly, however, and
although he did not stand trial he was judged insane and spent the
next eleven years in confinement. Over those years Eliot would visit
him during what became regular trips to the United States; he also
wrote a number of letters to those in authority in order to ease his
conditions: he talks about the time Pound should be allowed to
spend alone, for example, and the condition of the buildings in
which he was confined. And, in concert with other friends, he
worked patiently but assiduously for Pound's eventual release.
Unlike some of those friends, however, he did not attempt to force
the pace and in this case at least his native caution was justified. He
always adopted a practical attitude in such affairs and, as Pound
remarked after one of their conversations, 'There is always a core of
solid sense in Mr Eliot's talk'.[27]

Although his trip to America in 1946 was partly of a business
nature, that business could be combined with pleasure in meeting
his 'authors', such as Auden and Djuna Barnes. He took an almost
paternal interest in them, and fretted about the fact that they did not
lead as settled a life as they needed in order to work properly: he
believed, for example, that Auden was wasting his talents.[28] Of
course, he saw his old friends too, Emily Hale in particular, but his
principal reason for making the journey was to visit his family. He
had not been with them since before the war and, as the youngest
son, he saw his older brother and sisters passing away from him:
Ada had died in 1943, and now Henry was seriously ill with

leukaemia. Having once been the protected member of the family, it was now upon him that responsibilities began to fall.

The fact that he had been able to make the journey across the Atlantic meant that life was at last reverting to its customary shape. There were great privations in post-war England, of course, and parcels of groceries and other rationed foods were dispatched to him by American friends well into the early Fifties. But it was a sign that those wartime conditions which had so much restricted him were being lifted when, in October 1946, *The Family Reunion* was revived at the Mercury Theatre. Martin Browne had suggested to him that he might like to revise certain scenes for this new production, but Eliot declined the opportunity – he did not want to tamper with the play, because he would have felt compelled to make further and extensive changes.[29] In any case, he was eager to start work upon another play and was trying to extricate himself from various official duties in order to give himself room for composition: he resigned from the board of the *Christian News Letter*, for example, on the grounds of lack of time. The omens were good for another dramatic venture. Not only had the reception of *The Family Reunion* been altogether more favourable than the ill-starred attempt in 1939, but both this play and *Murder in the Cathedral* were to be performed at the first Edinburgh Festival in the following year.

Although he had planned to start serious work in the autumn of 1946, he was not able to do so. Henry Eliot's condition had worsened, with a bout of pneumonia on top of his leukaemia, and in anticipation of another visit to America Eliot was trying to book his passage for spring 1947, although he was ready to fly out at once if there was a sudden crisis. Only a small amount of money could be taken out of the country because of post-war restrictions and, as this was a personal rather than a business trip, he was forced to prepare lectures from which he could earn income while he was away. To make matters worse, he was suffering from his usual bout of feverish colds and bronchial trouble during the late autumn and winter.

And then on 22 January 1947, Vivien Eliot died quite unexpectedly in Northumberland House; she was fifty-eight. On her death certificate the causes were listed as 'syncope' and 'cardio-vascular degeneration'. She had worn herself to death. It was so sudden that even her doctors were taken by surprise, and to her husband the news came as a profound shock. She had died during the night, and it seems that Maurice Haigh-Wood telephoned Carlyle Mansions very early in the morning; John Hayward received the call, and then passed on the news to Eliot who, according to one friend, 'buried his face in his hands, crying "Oh God! Oh God!" '.[30] Vivien Eliot was buried in a cemetery in Pinner, Middlesex; her husband and her brother were among the few mourners. Her life had been full of pain and perplexity; it is not too much to say that her emotional needs had been fastened on a man whom she never properly understood, and that he in turn was baffled and then enraged by her insistent and neurotic demands upon him. And so it was that she died alone in a mental hospital – as Eliot told Violet Schiff, one of the few who had known them both from their earliest days together, death could only have been a deliverance for her.[31]

He was, by one account, 'shattered by grief and almost despair' after Vivien's death and, if it had not been for John Hayward's help and encouragement, would have retired into complete seclusion.[32] Ronald Duncan offered a different account; a proposed lunch had been cancelled when Eliot sent a telegram explaining that he had to 'bury a woman'. When they did meet, Eliot was wearing a black tie but seemed 'unusually relaxed during the meal, almost gay at times'.[33] These accounts are contradictory but not incompatible: it is probable that he was indeed in a state of shock, since the nature of shock is to suspend ordinary or familiar reactions. The recognizable or permanent emotion comes after, and of that there is some evidence. One friend said that, in later life, Eliot could never bear to mention Vivien's name[34] and another has written of his feelings of 'guilt and horror, which haunted him daily' and how once he observed, 'I can never forget anything'.[35] During the period of his wife's death and funeral, he was ill again: his old feeling of 'numbness' in reaction to unpleasant events once again returned.[36] He had a bad attack of bronchitis during February and was forced to spend ten days in hospital. He had, in fact, been preparing for an operation to remove his hernia, which had been scheduled for the beginning of January, but because of his winter illnesses it was postponed until the summer. He was altogether in a parlous state: the weather was bad, there was no water in the flat; he did not care to go out at nights and was seeing fewer people.[37] But there was no chance for him to rest in seclusion, even if he wished to do so – by

April his brother was dying, and because of the urgency of the situation Eliot flew to New York on 22 April. Henry died twelve days later, and much of Eliot's time during the two months he stayed in the United States was spent in winding up his affairs. But, as he had anticipated, he was forced to lecture in order to finance his stay there. He had not had much time or energy to expend on such matters, and was quite happy to cover familiar, or at least already prepared, ground. On 3 May he gave an address on Milton at the Frick Museum in New York, in which he recanted his previously low opinion of the poet, and on this occasion he seemed to one observer 'incredibly refined, visibly aged'[38] – he had given the same address two months before to the British Academy, and thus had saved himself additional effort. On 23 May he read his poetry at the National Gallery in Washington, to an audience which included St John Perse, all the time 'keeping behind horn-rimmed spectacles an almost unchanging expression'.[39] In June he lectured 'On Poetry' at Concord University, in which he repeated his claim that the poet can never be a successful man. His address was part of a graduation ceremony, and he walked on stage with school officials and local dignitaries; he dutifully applauded as each student received a diploma, although 'One got the impression that it was an effort for him to look up'.[40] There were less important engagements as well: he had agreed to give a talk on behalf of the Episcopal Fellowship in Washington, but an announcement of his visit had appeared in the *Washington Post* and, much to his alarm, the little meeting hall was overflowing with people. One member of the audience made notes of his extemporaneous address, in which he admitted that he was unprepared 'for this specific situation or any situation in general'. Eliot was 'tall, gaunt, of pallid hue and tensely withdrawn from anything reminiscent of the flesh'.[41] He also received an honorary degree at Harvard University – it is a measure of his popularity, perhaps, that when he was at a reception there with E. M. Forster the students and teachers ignored the novelist and crowded around the poet.[42] Nevertheless, it had not been a happy visit. He returned to England in the latter half of June and hardly had time to catch up with outstanding work before going into hospital in July to undergo the postponed operation upon his hernia. He stayed in hospital for three-and-a-half weeks, and then spent several more convalescing in the country. He returned to work in September but, in the following month, was forced to have most of the remainder of his teeth extracted: he had now entered his sixtieth year, and was suffering some of the inconveniences of age. There was no sense in which he 'slowed down', however, and in fact he compared himself to a travelling Sherlock Holmes.[43] He was preparing himself for a British Council tour of France but it was cancelled at the last moment; he did, however, fly to Amsterdam and then on to Rome in December under the auspices of the same organization. He met poets like Ungharetti and Montale, and had an audience with Pope Pius XII – the Pontiff spoke to him on the theme of poetry and religion, although Eliot knew quite enough about that subject already. Pius XII also blessed a rosary and gave it to him – when he returned to London, he placed it on his mantelpiece with other *memorabilia*. He had been too rushed and busy in Rome to enjoy his stay there,[44] although it seems that the American writer, Frederic Prokosch, persuaded him to go on a pilgrimage one afternoon to find the legendary 'Golden Bough' on the shores of Lake Nemi; what they found was an old and dilapidated oak. ' "Never mind," said Eliot, "It has been a pleasant little journey" '.[45]

It had also been a difficult and painful year. When he was asked by the BBC in November to broadcast a 'personal anthology' of poems, he chose those, he said, which had remained in his memory for reasons which were mysterious to him: John Dryden's 'To the Memory of Mr Oldham', Samuel Johnson's 'On the Death of Dr. Robert Levet', Rudyard Kipling's 'Danny Deever', Edgar Allan Poe's 'For Annie' and the six lines from Shelley which begin 'Art thou pale for weariness . . .'. These are haunting and elegiac poems, in which expressions of sorrow and loss are given ceremonious form. They recall the occasion when, as a boy, he had read in an epigraph two lines from Henry King's 'Exequy' – and how he could not rest until he had found and read the poem entire. He was drawn to such slow, mournful music and he carried it with him everywhere.

It had been such an unsettled year altogether that he had had no opportunity for connected work of anything other than a temporary kind; at the beginning of November, faced with the prospect of the British Council tours to France and Italy, he did not believe that he would be able to begin serious composition until the new year. There were two projects on his mind: one was the little prose book which had been 'clogging his system', to employ another of his own phrases, since the mid-Forties, and the other was the new play which had been postponed effectively since 1939. He had been eager to start work upon the latter ever since the completion, and relative failure, of *The Family Reunion* – if only to correct the overt poeticizing and the unbalanced structure which he discerned in that drama. But since it was his habit to ease his mind of the burden of one job before taking on another, his first task was to finish the prose book. He had probably looked over the preparatory material which had already been published elsewhere, and sketched out the remaining chapters, during his period of convalescence in the late summer and autumn of 1947. He must have been working on it in January 1948 at the latest, since the book was sent to the printers in the second week of February. Certainly by 25 January he was discussing the prospect of a new play with Martin Browne, which he hoped to begin within two or three weeks. Browne had tentatively suggested the summer of that year as the 'deadline' for it, but Eliot was uncertain how quickly he could recover his dramatic skills and, since he often needed to work slowly, he believed the spring of 1949 to be a more appropriate date.[46] Throughout the spring and summer of 1948 he worked on it as consistently as he could, although there were egregious interruptions: in April, for example, he had to make the British Council trip to Aix-en-Provence which had been postponed the previous winter. Here he drank pastis with the mayors of the Basses-Alpes, and even found time to lecture on Edgar Allan Poe, although his new false teeth made it difficult for him to speak French.[47] By June, however, he had sent the first draft of three scenes to Browne and asked him if it was worth continuing. Browne affirmed that it was, and in July Eliot sent a draft of the first three acts; he had entitled the as yet incomplete play 'One-Eyed Reilly' but in a postscript explained that he had decided to change it to *The Cocktail Party*. He wanted to emphasize the new play's connection with *The Family Reunion*: once again he was to deal with characters who live in a worn-out society, and have lost their way. In August he joined the Fabers on holiday in Sussex, but he still wanted to complete a rough version of the whole play by late summer. Browne would then have time to look at it, before Eliot embarked for America in late September. He had been invited to become a visiting fellow at the Institute for Advanced Studies in Princeton: he would, in other words, have plenty of time on his hands and would there be able to consider Browne's suggestions.

In fact he was still working on a first version of the fourth act (which eventually became Act III) when he sailed for New York on 24 September. He noted with satisfaction that he would be in mid-Atlantic on his sixtieth birthday:[48] an apt metaphor, perhaps, for his own condition. He contracted a feverish cold on the boat, however, and after he arrived in New York at the beginning of October he went into virtual seclusion at the home of McKnight Kauffer and Marion Dorn before going on to Princeton. The Institute itself was a place where men of proven ability (most of them elderly) were paid to continue their work. He stayed in a small colonial-style house, and was given an office where he could pursue his own tasks undisturbed. Lunch was provided in a cafeteria and tea in a common room – an environment which sounds uncomfortably similar to that of more youthful days, and in fact he signed himself in one letter as 'Advanced Student'. At first, as always, he felt lonely and homesick; he suffered from the fate of many famous men: according to one observer, most people were afraid to talk to him and he ate dinner alone at the Nassau Club.[49] But Princeton seemed more agreeable than most university towns[50] and after he had met some old friends, like the Maritains and the Niebuhrs, he began to relax. After a while, too, some of the more literary residents of Princeton plucked up the courage to speak to him. Eileen Simpson, who was then married to the poet John Berryman, was introduced to him and recalled his elaborate courteousness: 'His manner was as formal as his dress. . . . On being introduced he made an effort not to avert his eyes, as one felt he would have done as a young man. Instead he faced one directly, and took a moment longer over the exchange of greetings than was usual even with people whose graciousness is studied'.[51] She also noticed that he drank five martinis, although they had no noticeable effect upon him. While he was staying at Princeton he went down to Washington – he had to give a lecture at the Library of Congress, and wanted to see his cousin, Martha, there as well as Ezra Pound; he also made two or three trips to Cambridge to visit his family. Work on *The Cocktail Party* was proceeding, however, as he incorporated some of Browne's suggestions and revisions – Browne believed the play to contain too much 'argument, hypothesis, generalized philosophical reflection'.[52]

Eliot's main task, then, was to bring it more fully alive in terms of character and action, in order to avoid the mistakes of *The Family Reunion*. In his office he had a blackboard, on which he transcribed diagrammatic models of the action, with letters of the ordinary alphabet for characters already invented and letters of the Greek alphabet for those whom he might need to invent; he was contemplating a further six months of composition.[53]

But he was informed in November, while still at Princeton, that he had won the Nobel Prize for Literature. For some time he had ignored rumours to that effect but now, he told reporters, he was 'immensely pleased'. This was indeed his year for honours since in January he had been awarded the Order of Merit by George VI; some have said that this gratified him more than the Nobel, and certainly he seemed to enjoy wearing the medal and ribbon on ceremonial occasions. This may, however, have simply been part of his lifelong preoccupation with correct dress: one friend remarked that his clothes were English, his underclothes American.[54]

He left Princeton at the end of November, having decided to cancel his sailing and fly back to London before attending the Nobel ceremonies in Stockholm. He was the sixth Briton to receive the award – Kipling, Tagore, Yeats, Shaw and Galsworthy were his predecessors. Before he left America he told a reporter that 'One seems to become a myth, a fabulous creature that doesn't exist. One doesn't feel any different. It isn't that you get any bigger to fit the world, the world gets smaller to fit you. You remain exactly the same'.[55] At a later interview he was asked for what the Nobel had been awarded; Eliot replied that he assumed it was for 'the entire corpus' and the reporter asked, 'When did you publish *that*?' He flew from London to Sweden at the beginning of December, and at the ceremony on 10 December he was described as 'a leader and champion of a new period in the long history of the world's poetry'. Then, at an after-dinner speech in the town hall of Stockholm, Eliot said that he had experienced on learning of the award, '. . . all the normal emotions of exaltation and vanity . . . with enjoyment of the flattery, and exasperation at the inconvenience of being turned overnight into a public figure'. Apart from predictable duties, like that of sitting through a performance of *The Family Reunion* (a play for which he now had little affection), he was asked to crown the Swedish snow queen at the winter festival: he told Robert Giroux that he had hoped this might be combined with the Nobel ceremony itself, so that he could wear ice-skates with his tails.[56] When he returned to London, Cyril Connolly gave a party to celebrate the prize and during the course of the evening Eliot sang 'Under the bamboo tree' from *Sweeney Agonistes*. The 'drunken helot', Arthur Waugh's description of the incomprehensible poet of thirty years before, now had good cause to drink.

Those who had known him from that earlier period, however, were less than enthusiastic about his elevation. Both Lewis and Pound hoped that the Nobel would free him of that cautiousness which had smoothed his ascent. Lewis was more bitter since he felt – as so many of his contemporaries did – that he had been forced all his life to live in Eliot's shadow. He told one correspondent that Eliot owed his best poetry to Pound – he was convinced that there would eventually be a vogue in favour of Pound which would take the form of a reaction against Eliot (in that he was to be proved right). In another letter, he described Eliot as sly, and the deliberate instigator of a 'cult' around himself.[57] In fact Lewis took some pride in his severe, no-nonsense attitude towards Eliot – 'He doesn't come *in here* disguised like Westminster Abbey!' he told one friend.[58]

Eliot, however, was himself less than sanguine about his monumental reputation, and although he was pleased about the Nobel he was worried about its effects. When John Berryman congratulated him after the news was first received in America, he replied, 'The Nobel is a ticket to one's funeral. No one has ever done anything after he got it';[59] and he described the prize in the same terms to Geoffrey Faber.[60] There is a similar air of gloom in a conversation which Ronald Duncan has recorded; Duncan suggested that he might use some of the prize money to go abroad and escape from the London winter. 'Where?' Eliot asked. 'Spain or the West Indies?' Duncan suggested. 'I couldn't bear the company'.[61] Part of his apparently subdued reaction to the Nobel no doubt sprang from a genuine lack of confidence in his ability to continue writing (it was not, for him, a novel feeling) but he also found it difficult in conversation to react to praise or flattery – like Coriolanus, he did not like to hear his 'nothings monster'd'. Although, as Robert Lowell remarked, 'He knew how good he was. It would come out, in flashes,'[62] there were also many occasions when he evinced modesty or self-effacement. In this year a collection of essays in his honour was published (edited by Richard March and Tambimuttu), and he told Mary Hutchinson that he had not begun to read some of the contributions.[63] It was this casualness that led him, as Edmund Wilson reported, to be humorous in private about his own reputation, and 'offhand and vague' about matters he had once taken seriously.[64] He had a habit, also, of putting disparaging comments like 'coo!' and 'double talk!' in the margins of his own published essays. Edmund Wilson explained this behaviour by suggesting that within Eliot there were a number of different characters – there was an 'idealist' as well as an 'operator', a serious man as well as a 'scoundrel'[65] – just as V. S. Pritchett had described him as 'a company of actors inside one suit'.[66] There is truth in this but it is also likely that, in a period which Eliot considered to be one of cultural decay before the onset of 'barbarism', he was genuinely sceptical about the importance or permanence of his work. Although he might on one level enjoy his fame and success, his own tendency to withdraw from the world turned such fame into a kind of game which he was happy to play but which he did not take altogether seriously. It was only after his second marriage, when he was able to share his life with another human being, that he began to take any real satisfaction in his life's work. Before this marriage, his own solitariness and his claustral Christianity made such an achievement seem partly unreal.

In November of this year, while he was still in America, *Notes towards the Definition of Culture* was published. It was to be his last substantial prose work, the final fruit of the project which he had been contemplating since the middle of the Second World War. Its somewhat sketchy character suggests, in fact, that his main purpose was simply to finish what he had begun rather than to give urgent or forceful expression to his views. He takes the idea of 'culture' and disassembles it into its constituent parts; he then goes on to argue, or assert, that it depends upon a class system, upon a variety of regionalism and upon the family. Although he describes religion as the 'incarnation' of a culture he does not fully elucidate the point – at this level of abstraction, elucidation is perhaps impossible – but goes on to discuss the relation of politics and education to this larger whole. By the end of the book, 'culture' has become a metaphor for some kind of Bradleyan unity to which we may aspire but which we can never reach; idealism consorts oddly with Eliot's sociology, however, and it is not at all clear if 'culture' is a neutral term used to describe the whole way of life of a people or if it is being employed as a diagnostic tool to evaluate the various standards and aspirations of a society. He affirms once again his belief that 'our period is one of decline' but then mutters his exequies in a curiously dispassionate manner, as if he were engaged in an intellectual exercise of no particular consequence. The paradox is, of course, that this little book has achieved a fortuitous permanence because of Eliot's fame.

In fact he seemed to have lost interest in the book before he had completed it – the last two chapters are haphazardly constructed – and he padded it out with three radio talks on 'The Unity of European Culture' which he had given two years before. It was not a critical success: as Philip Mairet, to whom the book was dedicated, put it, 'Nobody seemed to like this book very much. It is decidedly astringent and has been described as "prim" '.[67] Not that Eliot harboured any illusions about the efficacy of his work – although *Notes* . . . was selling well, he did not expect it to have much influence.[68] It was this constant strain of pessimism, both about his own writing and about the civilization of which he was a part, that Wyndham Lewis tried to evoke in a portrait of Eliot which he was painting in the spring of 1949: 'The body slightly tilted,' he explained, '. . . in resigned anticipation of the worst.'[69] The Nobel had afforded only a temporary alleviation of this condition: indeed, the abbreviated stay in Princeton, the rush back to England, and the trip to Stockholm made him feel worse rather than better.[70] And, after his return to England at the beginning of the year, he was forced to catch up with all the work he had neglected. There were letters to write, interviews to give, meetings with eminent writers whose work he might never have read or of whom he had no very high opinion, and of course the official round of duties: a speech at the Alliance Française on 19 January, and another at a lunch of the Anglo-Swedish society two weeks later. In January also he had to speak at Pusey House in Oxford on 'The Lambeth Conference and Education', but one student's disappointment at his performance on this occasion suggests the strain and lack of preparedness which were forced on him during this period: 'In questions Mr Eliot was most feeble and hesitant, humming and hawing much and throwing back the questions with "Is that not what I said?" or "Does it not prove my point?'' This may be temporarily quashing but it does not satisfy. . . .'[71] And he was also very tired: when sitting to Wyndham Lewis in the spring, he had a tendency to drowsiness and sometimes slumber.

The problem was that engagements like that at Pusey House were a distraction from what he considered to be his main business – that of finishing *The Cocktail Party*. He calculated that he would be able to meet all his daily and official duties if he devoted his entire time to them, and abandoned any attempt at his own writing,[72] but this he was determined not to do. He had to find all the time he could to write the play, even if it meant neglecting other matters, not least because it would be his first composition since the award of the Nobel Prize.[73] He spent each morning working on it and was, in addition, trying to keep down his evening engagements to only two a week, seeing no one at all on Fridays and Saturdays. He was working against time; he had promised Browne that he would complete the play by the summer, and already Browne had been negotiating with Rudolf Bing, the director of the Edinburgh Festival, to have *The Cocktail Party* performed as part of that year's event. After certain difficulties with the manager of the Old Vic, who did not want to commit himself to the play on the basis of the bare outline which had been shown to him, Browne approached the theatrical impresario, Henry Sherek, and asked him if he would care to produce the play – with Browne as director – at Edinburgh. Although Sherek saw only the drafts of the first two acts, he agreed at once to do so. The first meeting between producer and playwright was not a success, however – Sherek found Eliot difficult and withdrawn; he had heard of his reputation as a 'recluse' and noticed a look of 'horrified distress' when he was introduced to the plump and ebullient Sherek.[74] There were in fact periods of awkwardness throughout their association – 'What on earth can we do?' Eliot once muttered when they were left alone together, which Sherek took as a sign that he was uneasy in his company[75] – but, over the next ten years and three dramas, the partnership proved a fruitful one.

Eliot had already told Browne that he could not promise to deliver the play until June at the earliest. He worked on it consistently – drafts exist outlining the ideas of the play, as well as the mechanics of its production. Under the scrutiny of Hayward and

Browne, he began to revise and concentrate his verse – after the problems with *The Family Reunion*, he wished to use only poetry which met the test of 'strict dramatic utility'[76] although at a later date he was to worry in case he had strayed too close to the drama of Frederick Lonsdale.[77] By May the play was almost complete – all that was necessary was the process of readjustment which would necessarily take place in consultation with director and actors. Eliot had a bad attack of bronchitis in June, which forced him to stay in bed for a week, but in July his sister, Marian, and a niece arrived from America and he went with them to Suffolk for ten days – the first holiday he had been able to take all year. At the beginning of August he returned to London in order to attend rehearsals. At the first of these, according to Henry Sherek, he announced to the actors (among whom were Alec Guinness and Irene Worth), 'I will now read the play to you to show how I want my lines spoken':[78] as a poet, he did not want his own 'voice' to be lost. He stayed at the back of the theatre, silent but smoking constantly and scribbling notes. There was only one occasion when he intervened during the rehearsals, according to Irene Worth. Lavinia and Edward, the only married couple in the play, are quarrelling (he had once again delineated the woes of marriage): 'Eliot bolted up to the stage looking quite unsettled. "The wife," he insisted, "must be fierce. *Much more fierce*. The audience must understand that she is impossible" '.[79]

Eliot, together with his sister and niece, travelled up to Edinburgh on 20 August. He was nervous and unsettled before the opening, and suffered from chills and fever,[80] but, in spite of his aversion to conventional 'publicity', he was persuaded to give interviews to the press, although he was never at his best on such occasions. One extract may suggest the tone of his replies; 'Question: Do you intend the play to be a criticism of society without form? Answer: I intend to produce characters whose drawingroom behaviour was generally correct'.[81] His fears of failure were unjustified, and the play was enthusiastically received. Alec Guinness introduced him to the audience after the first night, although such was his nervousness that Sherek had to push him onto the stage[82] and, when a photographer blew a flash bulb in his face just as he was about to speak, he muttered 'Oh my God'. The first night reception was sustained throughout the Edinburgh run of a week, and the reviewers generally praised the play. Eliot himself was delighted with the production.[83]

The Cocktail Party has an elaborate, although not complicated, structure. It opens with the eponymous party in progress; Edward Chamberlayne is the sole host since his wife, Lavinia, has suddenly and unaccountably left him. He explains his situation to a mysterious guest, who promises to return his wife to him as long as he agrees to ask her no questions about where she has been (Eliot later located his source for this in *Alcestis*, although that is really only of importance to him). The guest turns out to be Sir Henry Harcourt-Reilly, 'a very great doctor', who in a role half-priestly and half-analytical reconciles Edward and Lavinia even though their marriage has already been described by him as that of

> A man who finds himself incapable of loving
> And a woman who finds that no man can love her.

He also intervenes in the life of another guest at the party, Celia Coplestone, a young woman who comes to him filled with a sense '. . . of emptiness, of failure'. Harcourt-Reilly takes her out of her conventional life, and leads her towards a spiritual quest and eventual martyrdom. He is a 'guardian', one of three who in *The Cocktail Party* adopt a benign role in curing or assuaging human misery. The play ends as another party is about to begin.

Here, as in *The Family Reunion*, the ordinary human world is presented as one of paltry illusion. But since *The Cocktail Party* is on one level a comedy, this mundane life is delineated as a form of charade – one which only the enlightened, the 'guardians', know how to control. The others are tormented by a sense of their own unreality – 'What are we to talk about?' is one refrain and, when they do talk, they misunderstand and confuse each other. 'Hell is oneself,' Edward exclaims because he, like the others, cannot escape from the small circle of his selfhood. Racine has entered the drawingroom, and these protagonists engage either in anguished self-revelation or in disillusioning judgments about each other. It is a bleak and somewhat chilly world which Eliot has constructed, an effect emphasized by the dispassionate way in which human emotion and human suffering are described. It has often been said that his characters are 'puppets' of his grand design, but his own vision necessarily makes them so. Since the significance of life is to be found outside the claims of the usual world, the 'ordinary' characters who inhabit that world are bound to seem unreal or flimsy.

But what of this other world, into which Celia Coplestone is dispatched and of which only the 'guardians' have any inkling? It is a world of 'visions' and of 'devils', of 'voices' and of 'shadows', and the fact that it is described throughout in vague and melodramatic terms suggests that it is fundamentally ill-suited to presentation in the kind of drama which Eliot wished to write. This had been the problem with *The Family Reunion* as well, and it was one which he attempted to solve in his next play. But he never did: the vision which can be intimated in his poetry could not be embodied upon the stage.

He continued to try, however. When he was engaged in writing *The Cocktail Party*, he was asked how long he would devote himself to the theatre rather than to poetry; he replied, 'Until I can convince people that I know how to write a popular play'.[84] There is an element of bravado here – having conquered the academic and 'literary' worlds, he wanted to move on – but it suggests also the extraordinary and self-conscious determination with which he worked. While writing *The Cocktail Party* he had admitted that he had no natural talent for dramatic composition[85] and yet he laboured to acquire the necessary skills. His idea of the 'popular play' is important, since his devotion to the music hall and his belief that the poet can only be socially useful in the theatre spurred him on to achieve what was for him the unachievable: the plays bear all the marks of their deliberate and laborious composition. He was working against the natural grain of his genius, and the fact that he went on to write two more plays suggests the triumph of will over natural capacity, of idea over sensibility.

Because of problems in finding a theatre in the West End, Henry Sherek had decided to take *The Cocktail Party* to New York rather than to London; this was a calculated gamble on Eliot's fame – to see, as it were, if the Nobel Prize would run on Broadway. Eliot was at first furious with him about the decision. There were various reasons for this, not least among them that the fame upon which Sherek was gambling had its disadvantages. He was accustomed to conventional envy from some of his contemporaries (although it could still distress him – Joseph Chiari recalls him leaving a party in Edinburgh because of the atmosphere of jealousy which he sensed there[86]). But abuse was another matter and he was extremely nervous about the treatment he was then receiving in America over the award of the Bollingen Prize to Ezra Pound. Eliot had been on the jury of the Fellows of the Library of Congress which had, in February 1949, awarded the prize to Pound's *Pisan Cantos* as 'the highest achievement of American poetry in 1948'. Since Pound was in confinement, not legally a 'traitor' but branded as a fascist and an anti-semite, this honour provoked controversy and anger among certain sections of the American public and press. And although Eliot was only one member of a jury which included among others Robert Lowell, W. H. Auden, Conrad Aiken and Katherine Anne Porter, he was singled out for abuse: in fact, he seemed to receive more than Pound himself.[87] It was a perfect opportunity for some writers to express the resentment which they had harboured against him for many years, and he himself was convinced that such people detested him because he had acquired British citizenship. The *Saturday Review* was particularly hostile, accusing him of anti-semitism and, among other things, of being 'a disciple of Dr Jung' (an author whom he had never read). Its attack was then enlarged into a general diatribe against the 'intellectual neo-fascism' which Eliot had encouraged among American critics. It suggested that 'this rootless expatriate' be at once dropped from the jury of the Library of Congress.[88] The charge of anti-semitism, and implied neo-fascism, was particularly serious just four years after the war, and Eliot seems to have been thoroughly discomfited by the affair. At first he thought of resigning from the jury but then decided not to do so. He refused to give any interviews to the press about the matter and in September, three months before the opening of *The Cocktail Party* in New York, he asked Sherek to try to ensure that there would be no attempt to obstruct the production.[89]

He hardly had time to dwell on such matters, however. He had returned to London from Edinburgh in a state of exhaustion. He was able to snatch one long weekend in the country, but almost at once he had to start work on the preparation of lectures for a three-week tour of Germany. He left England on 27 October and two days later he lectured at Hamburg on 'The Idea of a Christian Society'; the tour, which he made with Arnold Toynbee, included visits to nine cities, but he complained later that not the least exhausting part of it had been the expectation from his hosts that he was some kind of oracle as well as a poet.[90] On his return on 19 November, he hardly had time to catch up with his unfinished business before he was off to Brussels to deliver yet another lecture. But for once he had planned to escape the worst excesses of the English winter, and at the beginning of 1950 he embarked with the Fabers on a six-week cruise to South Africa: two weeks getting there, two weeks on the beach at St James near Cape Town, and two weeks back.

He left behind him at Faber and Faber a most efficient young secretary, Miss Valerie Fletcher, who had been appointed at the end of August. She had become obsessed with Eliot and his work at the age of fourteen, after she had heard a recording of 'The Journey of the Magi': 'It was extraordinary,' she said later, 'that I felt I just *had* to get to Tom, to work with him.'[91] After she left school she came to London from her home in Yorkshire in order to attend a secretarial college, but abandoned that and enrolled with a secretarial agency. She spent a year working for the writer Charles Morgan, but all the time her real purpose was somehow to work with Eliot himself. At last her opportunity arose when Collin Brooks, a friend of both Eliot and her own family, suggested that she apply for the post of Eliot's secretary which had fallen vacant. At the interview, 'he smoked hard and was obviously as nervous as I was'.[92] But she got the job, with consequences which neither she nor Eliot could then have foreseen.

15

The Public Man
1950–1956

ELIOT HAD ARRIVED in South Africa by the time *The Cocktail Party* opened in New York on 21 January 1950, at the Henry Miller Theatre. There were none of the demonstrations or obstructions which he had feared, and in fact such was the success of the play that he was featured on the cover of *Time* magazine on 6 March. His words, already being quoted in the pulpit, were also being used on Madison Avenue: an Esso advertisement in 1948 had had as its message 'Time future contained in time past'. A cartoon in the *New York Times* in April 1950 showed a sailor in a tattooing parlour, saying 'I have in mind a couple of lines by T. S. Eliot'. He was now a celebrity. When he arrived in South Africa, a crowd was waiting at the dock to greet him,[1] and on later visits to the United States he was besieged by autograph hunters and press photographers waiting for him after readings. When he lectured at Harvard in this year, policemen had to control the crowds who came out to see him, and loudspeakers were set up for those who could not get into the auditorium. Katherine Ann Porter has described how, at one New York party, the guests were 'swarming around him, grabbing him, patting him, *owning* him, trying to claw each other away from him'.[2] Fame is a less brilliant commodity in England, but nevertheless he had to keep his address secret, to protect himself not only from letters and telephone calls but also from undesirable visitors who might arrive at Carlyle Mansions.

There seems to be a law in human behaviour that people, in the end, get what they want, and there can be little doubt that Eliot would not have acquired the eminence which he now enjoyed unless on one level he had sought it: he said, in an address delivered during this period, that '. . . things sometimes become possible if we want them enough'.[3] Many observers noticed the force and weight of his presence; it might be called dedication, or ambition, or it might have been something below the level of consciousness which propelled him forward. Nevertheless, if we examine the pattern of his life, it reveals a programmatic aspect, and the steeliness of his resolve is not to be doubted. But there was also a sense in which he despised fame even as he obtained it, and when in this year he described Mark Twain as a man who wanted success or reputation and yet at the same time 'resented their violation of his integrity',[4] there can be little doubt that once again he was expressing his own feelings through the agency of another's. Already he was wondering if his fame meant that his writing had only a contemporary appeal,[5] and he complained that people now thought of him as a celebrity rather than as a poet.[6] In retrospect, of course, it is clear that his creative powers were beginning to wane and that his real work had been done. But there was also a growing disaffection among the younger poets and critics: he had ceased to be a poet and had become an institution, and the only thing to do with an institution is to attempt to pull it down. He was compared with Aristides the Just, and there were those who wished a similar fate for him. One phrase was repeated as a joke, 'The Blessed Thomas Eliot Considered as the Air We Breathe'; in the Fifties and Sixties there would be many attempts to dispel that air and to 'place' Eliot as some great, dim figure from the past.

He was a relatively wealthy man; his annual income, from both his publishing salary and his royalties, was approximately £4,000, and in the early months of this year his income from the New York production of *The Cocktail Party* was estimated at about £570 per week:[7] this was no doubt why, in June, he was looking for an accountant.[8] (At his death, he left £105,272.) Wealth did not make him lavish, however; he had always been careful about money – indeed, he was economical in all areas of life, even in small matters such as ensuring that all the tea in a tea-pot had actually been drunk – and Joseph Chiari has remembered how he kept a regular account of his expenses in a pocket notebook.[9] One friend has explained how, in a conversation in which she was lamenting the cost of electricity, Eliot asked her in a confidential manner, 'Are you on the *domestic* tariff?'[10] He was nothing if not practical in his dealings with the world – he insisted on proper fees for the republication of his essays, for example, and used to advise friends like Herbert Read on the amount they should charge for a lecture tour.

But if he was scrupulously careful about his own expenditure, he was generous to other poets and writers. He underwrote a loss of £1,500 on Ronald Duncan's play, *Stratton*, but only on condition that Duncan was not told.[11] And when in 1949 Wyndham Lewis completed his portrait of him, Eliot quietly paid Lewis £50 more than the agreed price. (He later made it clear that he did not wish the letters revealing his generosity to be published.) Then in the following year he gave Lewis £200, to finance a trip to Sweden where he was to receive X-ray treatment for his deteriorating eyesight. His secrecy abut his own generosity makes it very difficult to document in full; certainly, during the years of the Second World War, he gave money to Dylan Thomas and Roy Campbell, but many other such instances may have gone unrecorded.

After a spring and summer during which he was so busy with his ordinary duties that he had no time to himself at all – not even his evenings – he returned again to America in the late autumn of 1950. These trips to the United States were to become a regular event, part of his routine as it were, and there was a sense in which he was returning home. He spent one night in New York and then, nursing a cold which he had contracted on the boat, he went straight to Boston – with his relatives, in particular his two sisters and his late brother's family, and with old friends like Emily Hale and Djuna Barnes, he could still enjoy an affectionate intimacy which he seemed to lack in England. Willa Muir saw him in America and observed, 'Tom Eliot is much more human here than in England. He was less cautious, smiling more easily, spontaneous in repartee, enjoying the teasing he was getting from Djuna. . . . In her company he seemed to have shed some English drilling and become more American.'[12] And yet even to his relatives he must have seemed still in part a 'foreigner', with his accent and his clothes; that was an aspect of his loneliness, never to be completely at home anywhere. In a preface to *The Adventures of Huckleberry Finn*, published in this year, he described the landscape of his childhood and speculated about the boy who remained within the adult and successful figure of Mark Twain – the boy who was called 'Huck' and whom Eliot saw as a symbol of freedom like the Mississippi itself; it was impossible for that boy or that river 'to have a beginning or end – a *career*'.[13] In America, and in his memories of a life still to be wished for although lost and gone for ever, that boy could be glimpsed in Eliot also.

But he was still very much a public man, and to pay for his visit he had agreed to give a limited number of addresses and readings. At the University of Chicago, he gave four lectures in November on 'The Aims of Education' and in the same month talked on 'Poetry and Drama' at Harvard. At the beginning of the previous month, he had given a reading in New York where one observer described him as a 'hot ticket'.[14] Lecturing was now easier for him than it once had been – he had, after all, accumulated a great deal of experience – but the readings of his own poetry frequently left him exhausted.[15] Robert Giroux has recalled how, in advance of such occasions, Eliot was as 'nervous as a cat' but that, when he had begun, a 'great calm' descended upon him.[16] He was now a very effective reader of his own work – his theatrical instincts were here most valuable and, as Edmund Wilson noted, he could communicate a feeling of intense excitement to his audiences.

The lectures which he delivered in America on this visit are not of crucial critical significance and, like other addresses of the same period, they are chiefly remarkable for the fact that he felt able to talk at some length about himself and his work – as if he realized that audiences came to see him, rather than hear anything he might care to say. He described his childhood in America,[17] his experiences as a teacher,[18] his work as a publisher,[19] his poetic development,[20] and his progress in the drama.[21] He also admitted the faults in his writing – something which the Eliot of earlier years would never have been able to do, in public at least. In his Chicago lectures, for example, he described how certain passages of *Notes towards the Definition of Culture* had been exposed as a 'mass of contradictions' and, at the end, he also made a rueful disclaimer – 'I am quite aware that I have been trying to persuade, although I may not be quite sure of what'. In fact these lectures offered an elegant and lucid exposition of educational theories and assumptions (he had been exercised by this topic since the early forties) and although he failed to arrive at any conclusions he suggested that none could in any case be reached. He told George Seferis that, in his prose writings, the need for honesty and clarity entailed the kind of elaborate elucidation which audiences found dull;[22] but this was now the manner that Eliot adopted, and it is possible to see the equivocations and hesitations of his later prose work as aspects of what was essentially a Socratic method of inquiry rather than an expression of caution or indecision.

When he returned to England in the middle of December, the winter again affected him; he contracted bronchitis ten days after his arrival and suffered a further three attacks during January 1951. He stayed at home for part of that month, and his doctor advised him to restrict his engagements as much as possible. He was well enough in February, however, to attend a poetry reading at the Institute of Contemporary Arts; but it was not a pleasant occasion. Apparently without Eliot having been warned, the poet Emmanuel Litvinoff read a poem which attacked his attitude towards the Jews. At the end of the reading there was some consternation but Eliot, who was sitting at the back of the room, was heard to mutter, 'It's a good poem, it's a very good poem'. The incident was reported in the press, however, and his secretary was quoted in one newspaper as saying, 'Many Jewish people have written to him accusing him of anti-semitism. It is not true'.

Since it is the charge still most frequently levelled against him, it is perhaps worth examining the evidence for it. In his published writings there are two egregious instances: the line 'The Jew is underneath the lot,' in 'Burbank with a Baedeker: Bleistein with a Cigar' and the reference to the undesirability of a large number of 'free-thinking Jews' in *After Strange Gods*. In his unpublished correspondence there are four references. On two occasions he used the word 'Jew' as a perjorative adjective – once in a letter to John Quinn, dated 12 March 1923, and once in a letter to Ezra Pound, dated 31 October 1917. In a letter to Herbert Read, dated '16 February' (probably written in 1925) he described a racial prejudice from which he was not immune – although he did not specify that prejudice, its nature is clear from the context, in which he offered Disraeli as an example of what he meant. Finally in a letter to Bonamy Dobrée – dated by Dobrée 'about March 1929' – he made a number of supercilious remarks about the Jews. All the available evidence suggests, then, that on occasions he made what were then fashionably anti-semitic remarks to his close friends. Leonard

Woolf, himself a Jew, has said, 'I think T. S. Eliot was slightly anti-semitic in the sort of vague way which is not uncommon. He would have denied it quite genuinely',[23] which suggests Eliot's ability to seem quite different to different people. But there is one further distinction which needs to be made. He was drawn to the traditions of Sephardism, he had once explained;[24] that rigorous and secluded tradition appealed to his own sensibility, in the same way that 'free-thinking' Jews seemed to him to come too close to the rational Unitarianism which he despised. On a less theoretical level, it is also true that his expressions of anti-semitism occur in the Twenties or just before, when he was inclined to make misogynistic remarks also; it was a period when his own personality threatened to break apart, and it seems likely that his distrust of Jews and women was the sign of an uneasy and vulnerable temperament in which aggression and insecurity were compounded. This is an explanation, however, and not a justification.

At the end of February, he was admitted to the London Clinic for an operation to remove piles. He came out of the clinic on 19 March having stayed there for a week longer than he had anticipated, and was once again forced to rest. He took a walk each morning, and went to bed between lunch and tea. It was a most painful period altogether, and Ronald Duncan has described how Eliot, on his return from hospital, recounted in vivid detail the operation and its consequences. Duncan said that, like Luther, he had a 'gut obsession': 'Whatever you do, Ronnie,' he told him, 'avoid piles.'[25] But he recuperated steadily, and at the beginning of April he travelled to Granada for a month's vacation. He was not entirely happy there, however – he complained to some friends afterwards that dinner was served very late in Spain – and returned to London on 7 May with a sore throat, cold and catarrh. These illnesses – bronchitis and then emphysema being the most prominent – recurred throughout the Fifties and were provoked by a number of causes, not the least of which was the fact that Eliot was still a heavy smoker. He did apparently display signs of hypochondria, however – Herbert Read remembered how he was 'addicted to pills and potions'[26] and, according to another friend, he kept a variety of pills in his lower waistcoat pocket[27] – but hypochondria, if such it was, was only one aspect of a larger nervous disposition. By this period he was seriously addicted to the tranquillizer, nembutal, and there seem to

have been a number of objects to which he attached his fears – lifts
and large animals among them. He was often nervous before
meeting strangers, which was why at receptions, for example, he
found the company of a friend like Mary Trevelyan so reassuring.
He was anxious about travelling, and worried that he might miss his
train or enter by accident the wrong one:[28] this was a fear that seems
to have lingered since his youth when, as he said, 'I found a variety
of calamities to worry about. And I haven't changed'.[29] Many years
before he had described, as we have seen, the acute but generalized
sense of apprehension which invaded him at times of stress or
exhaustion and one recognizes in his temperament a permanent
sense of impending doom and disaster – as if the world were always
threatening to fall in upon him.

One reporter who came to interview him in this period noticed
how he looked as if he might collapse from 'lack of nourishment,
insomnia and fatigue',[30] and an acquaintance described him thus:
'His face was pale as baker's bread . . . he smoked and between
exhalations he hacked a dry, deathly smoker's hack . . . Eliot was
cadaverous.'[31] But there is no doubt that personal unhappiness
contributed to his ill health. E. W. F. Tomlin has recalled his
'stricken' look and the occasion when he inquired, 'How does one
set about *dying*?'[32] When he was told of a young man who wished to
become a poet, Eliot replied, 'He's getting ready for a sad life',[33]
and Ronald Duncan said that during this period he looked 'miserable and unwell' and 'began to affect many signs of premature old
age'.[34] Duncan's account is, in fact, a not unsympathetic one of Eliot
punishing himself, denying himself the small pleasures or luxuries
which someone of his wealth and distinction could have enjoyed:
'He always took his wine flavoured with guilt'.[35] Certainly the
picture of him during this period is of a man haunted by guilt and
remorse; it seems that he felt he had no right to happiness, and the
death of his wife had only served to convince him that he had done
some irreparable harm to another human being, for which he must
undergo a period of punishment. In an address on Virgil which he
gave in September of this year, he talked of certain men, like
Aeneas, who are elected to a special destiny. He suggested that
Aeneas left Dido in obedience to his fate but he was not thereby
relieved of feelings of shame or unhappiness – he felt 'a worm'. Such
a destiny does not make life easier but rather 'it is a very heavy cross

to bear'.[36] It is significant, perhaps, that he says 'is' rather than 'was' or 'must be'.

There is clearly an element of dramatic self-consciousness here, just as there is in Duncan's account of his affecting the symptoms of old age – ' . . . he even started to cup his hands at remarks he could hear perfectly well'.[37] Ever since the Twenties, in fact, Eliot had manifested so many visible signs of melancholy and weariness that 'poor Tom' had become the constant refrain of his friends. But such stylized behaviour does not affect the genuineness of his pain during this period, or of the loneliness which it seemed to impose upon him. After Mary de Rachewiltz, Ezra Pound's daughter, visited him in his gloomy study in Carlyle Mansions she wrote, 'I had met a great man, and Loneliness'[38] and one friend has remarked that 'I knew he was intensely – even wretchedly – lonely'.[39] Of course, his own eminence contributed to his isolation, but he also chose solitude as his appropriate fate. When in April 1949 Mary Trevelyan had written a letter in which she explained her feelings for him, and in fact suggested marriage, he explained in his reply that although he valued her friendship he was no longer capable of reciprocating such feelings for anyone. And then, in the following year, prompted by his frequent descriptions of his own loneliness – his fear of becoming ill, his dislike of attending receptions alone – she again wrote to him in similar terms. In a long letter, he then explained that his past affection for someone else (no doubt Emily Hale) rendered any new relationship impossible for him.[40] And so he hugged his loneliness to himself even as he bemoaned it. Herbert Read, in a conversation with Stephen Spender during this period, suggested that Eliot was lacking in affection for 'perhaps everyone' and that he wished 'to slink away into some corner and die'.[41] Allen Tate remembered one luncheon when he was silent and 'withdrawn into himself'.[42] And in a conversation with William Turner Levy, a young American who was about to become an Episcopalian minister, Eliot raised the possibility that he might eventually enter retirement in an abbey – such a life suited him, he said.[43] No doubt this seemed to be the natural course for him, since in that retreat he would complete the process which had begun with his conversion almost thirty years before.

Such solitariness was a condition and not a mood, however; it lay beneath those moments of inexplicable high spirits when Eliot seemed, as Sherek put it, 'as gay as a cricket',[44] just as it could be combined with apparent activity and 'busyness' in the world. When in May 1951 he returned from his holiday in Spain, for example, he had at once to prepare for three different public engagements in the following month – the first weekend was to be spent at Brighton for the annual meeting of the Alliance Française, occasions which he now found appallingly dull;[45] then he was obliged to make a speech on behalf of the Cecil Houses Trust for old people, and give an address at Chichester Cathedral. Quite apart from Faber business, he had to settle down and write prefaces for three books as well (one of them for his own selection of Pound's literary essays). All of these activities meant that he could not get on with his new play, of which the first two scenes were already drafted and which he had planned, tentatively, to finish in time for the Edinburgh Festival of 1952.

He was able to get away for a two week holiday in Switzerland at the end of August, where he relaxed and swam in Lake Geneva: it was the one European country which he found not to have changed out of all recognition, and he took an annual holiday there. He was involved in the same heavy round of duties as soon as he returned to London, however, and honorary positions were becoming increasingly a burden. Just as he was about to travel to Paris in November, to open a book exhibition and make a speech at the Bibliothèque Nationale, he caught a heavy cold which turned to bronchitis with congestion of the lungs; a nurse was called in and he took a course of penicillin, but he still managed to make the journey. He came back to England and seemed about to succumb to pneumonia but, ten days after his return, he went on another visit to Paris, on this occasion to receive an honorary degree from the University there. He did not like the city now – in fact he used to say that he disliked any place he had known before 1914.[46] He was in France again in the spring of 1952, and this was followed by a trip to the United States and then one to Scotland. He was now in his sixty-fourth year but, for all his ill health, he still had a surprisingly tough constitution – as tough as his will.

Throughout 1952 his major task was to finish the play which he had already begun. He was dissatisfied, as always, with his previous work, and he had detected flaws in *The Cocktail Party* which he wished to remove from the new play. The last act had been unsatisfactory and he wanted to provide a more effective resolution;

he was also concerned that he might have gone too far in removing the 'poetry' from his dramatic verse.[47] And so he set to work: despite the usual interruptions, by the end of the year he managed to complete drafts of two acts which he dispatched to Martin Browne. The play could now be tentatively scheduled for the Edinburgh Festival of 1953, one year later than Eliot had originally planned. Browne has noted that the early drafts he received, together with a synopsis of the action, already suggested the shape of the complete play – quite unlike the false starts and extensive rewriting which had been Eliot's procedure in his earlier work; Browne explained this in terms of his 'greater self-confidence as a playwright'.[48] That self-confidence had been acquired from the success of *The Cocktail Party*: it had opened in London in May 1950, just a few months after the New York opening, and, although the audiences began to fall off in November, Sherek did not feel it necessary to close the play until February 1951. But it was in the following year, 1952, that Eliot reached the largest audience he had known: *The Cocktail Party* was broadcast on television, and was watched by an estimated three-and-a-half million people. He was not particularly pleased with the result, however: when *The Family Reunion* had been televised two years before, he confessed that it was the first television play he had seen and that he found the medium deficient.[49] He had even written a letter to *The Times* (one of his favourite pastimes), deprecating 'The Television Habit'. But he had become, in one sense, a 'star' of both stage and screen since, the year before, *Murder in the Cathedral* had been released in its cinematic version. He told the American writer, John Malcolm Brinnin, that he had learned, from working on the film production, more about writing for the theatre than he had learned in the theatre itself,[50] but that did not prevent him from vetoing the idea, proposed by Sherek, that *The Cocktail Party* should also be filmed.[51] Similarly he rejected what was admittedly a bizarre offer to film 'The Love Song of J. Alfred Prufrock' – although it might have had its moments.

And so it was that Eliot was immersed in what he called ironically 'show business', and although he had reached an age where he performed his tasks more slowly, now more than ever his life was being conducted under pressure. Throughout January he worked upon the third act of the play and, on doctor's orders as much as anything else, he restricted his evening engagements to the Tuesday and Thursday of each week (those were now the evenings when his housekeeper was 'off'). But in February of this year a most unwelcome event claimed his attention. In the July 1952 issue of *Essays in Criticism* a young academic, John Peter, offered 'A New Interpretation of the Waste Land', the gist of which he summarized thus: 'At some previous time the speaker has fallen completely – perhaps the right word is irretrievably – in love. The object of this love was a young man who soon afterwards met his death, it would seem by drowning.' The inference which might be drawn from this analysis was that Eliot himself had conceived a homosexual passion for just such a young man and, when the article was reprinted four years after Eliot's death, it was suggested to be Jean Verdenal, the Frenchman whom Eliot had met in Paris when he was a student there and to whom, after his death in the First World War, he dedicated *Prufrock and Other Observations*.[52] John Peter's analysis described the elements of sexual guilt and misogyny in the poem, and pointed to a variety of literary allusions to pederasty and sodomy.

In the past, Eliot's reaction to the multiple interpretations of *The Waste Land* had been one of benign neglect – it was his apparently settled belief that the author's interpretation of his work is no more pertinent than that of the reader. On *The Waste Land* specifically, he told one inquirer that the real meaning of the poem is that which it holds for whoever is reading it.[53] His reaction to John Peter's interpretation was somewhat different, however. He seems to have come across the article in the early weeks of 1953, since in February he threatened a libel action if copies of the offending issue were not immediately destroyed. When John Peter, no doubt in a state of some alarm that his scholarship had provoked such a response, offered to publish a retraction, Eliot's solicitors wrote in March that their client considered it 'neither necessary nor desirable' for any such retraction to appear; their client would take the very gravest view of any 'further dissemination' of the article or its contents, which he had read 'with amazement and disgust'.[54] Clearly, Eliot was seriously perturbed.

There have been other attempts to imply that he had homosexual tendencies. Robert Sencourt's memoir contained a number of insinuations of this sort, and one academic study has traced the theme of homosexuality within Eliot's work.[55] The point generally made in corroboration of this theory is that his poetry is marked by images of sterility and mechanical lust, and that the excised passages of *The Waste Land* which have now been published contain evidence of pervasive and sometimes bitter misogyny. Certainly this is one aspect of the poetry he wrote during his marriage to Vivien, at least up to *Ash-Wednesday*, and also of the early poetry he wrote as a young man in Paris. For a long period he seems to have been disturbed or disgusted by female sexuality, particularly as it was embodied in his wife, and to have established relationships with women in which the dominant note was one of camaraderie not unmixed with his desire for comfort or protection. But it would be the tritest form of reductionism to assume that Eliot, because he could not adequately deal with female sexuality, was therefore homosexual. The essential point is that sexuality as such disturbed him – even in his early letters to Conrad Aiken we see his sexual impulses towards women engaged in an unequal struggle with his own need for self-possession (or self-preservation) and control. These letters themselves, with their references to women and his dependence upon them, should be taken with the facts of his first impulsive marriage and his second happy one: all the available evidence suggests that when he allowed his sexuality free access, when he was not struggling with his own demons, it was of a heterosexual kind.

The suggestions of homosexuality are, however, only one aspect of the attempt to discover some 'mystery' which he wished to conceal; and, in fact, the belief that there is such a secret has been largely provoked by the innate secretiveness of his own temperament. The paradox is that his sometimes self-dramatizing manner, both in his life and in his work, has provoked the interest and curiosity which apparently he wished to forestall. The fact that he forbade an official biography – as early as 1925, he had decided that he did not want one[56] – has suggested to many people that such a biography would necessarily be of a scandalous nature. We expect to find a guilty incident or relationship because he writes continually of guilt; we expect to find sin because he speaks of atonement and expiation. His own horror of self-revelation has led to the assumption that there are such revelations to be made. This obscures the true nature of Eliot's life, just as it diminishes his poetry.

By the end of February 1953, the third act of the new play, which Eliot had entitled *The Confidential Clerk*, was ready for typing. The casting was completed by May and rehearsals were scheduled for July. Before they were due to begin, Eliot travelled once again to America – first to his birthplace St Louis, where a heatwave affected him disagreeably, and then on to Cambridge where he spent two weeks with his relatives before travelling to Connecticut and New York. As always, he felt it necessary because of exchange controls to earn money while he was there and, while at St Louis in the beginning of June, he gave an address at Washington University on 'American Language and American Literature' (he received a doctorate on this occasion, as on so many others). When he had started to prepare his notes for this occasion, he was overwhelmed by private memories:[57] St Louis was the place of his birth, and Washington University itself owed its foundation to his grandfather; and when in the lecture he spoke of the characteristics of a national literature, and American literature in particular, as 'a strong local flavour combined with an unconscious universality' it is clear to what locale he belongs. In a later interview he was to say of his poetry that ' . . . in its sources, in its emotional springs, it comes from America'.[58] The wheel has come full circle. These were confessions he could not make earlier, when the disavowal of his origins and his deliberate acquisition of Englishness helped to form the remarkable character with which he confronted the world. Now there was no need for such disguises.

As soon as he returned to England in mid-July, he became involved in preparations for the play. He had great hopes for it, and told an American friend that he thought it his best to date.[59] Rehearsals started on 27 July, and Martin Browne had taken the precaution of advising the cast not to ask the author to elucidate any of the dialogue; one actress disregarded the advice and asked Eliot what one of her lines meant. 'My dear child, don't ask me,' he replied, 'I don't know!'.[60] At the end of the fourth week the players moved to Edinburgh where *The Confidential Clerk* was to open at the Lyceum on 25 August. There was, of course, now a great deal more interest in Eliot than in the play, but he had stipulated in advance that he was not to be subjected to any form of publicity: no press conferences, no interviews, no speeches; as a result, he was much more relaxed at the first night and was even able to laugh at his own jokes.[61] The reaction of the audience was enthusiastic, and the play continued to be a popular success after it had opened at the Lyric Theatre in London on 16 September, (Henry Sherek had again wanted to take the play first to New York, but Eliot vetoed the idea). The critics were less sure, however, and there were some doubts whether he had been able to combine his apparent religious intentions with the format of a conventional Shaftesbury Avenue entertainment. He himself thought *The Confidential Clerk* to be his most profound play,[62] but it is difficult now to see this.

Its central theme concerns a young man, Colby Simpkins, who has entered the service of Sir Claude Mulhammer as a 'confidential clerk'; Mulhammer in fact believes Colby to be his illegitimate son, raised by a Mrs Guzzard in Teddington, but his paternity is thrown in doubt when Sir Claude's wife, Lady Elizabeth Mulhammer, claims Colby as her own illegitimate son who had also been dispatched to Mrs Guzzard. Clearly only Mrs Guzzard can resolve the mystery, and arrives on stage to reveal that Colby is her own son and that his father, like Colby himself, was a 'disappointed musician'. At once Colby makes plans to become an organist in a small church in the strikingly named district of 'Joshua Park' outside London. This is greatly to simplify an already schematic plot, but the pattern of action is clear enough: it is essentially a comedy of identity, in the manner of late Victorian melodrama, upon which Eliot has grafted his characteristic exposition of the religious sensibility. Colby Simpkins is one of the elect, above familial ties or mundane circumstances, like Harry in *The Family Reunion* and Celia in *The Cocktail Party* – although Eliot has on this occasion eschewed the Furies or martyrdom as a way of emphasizing Colby's difference from those who are content with a secular existence. His essential vision remains the same, however: in a world which is unreal, inhabited by foolish or isolated people, only those with an especial destiny can escape its constrictions.

But the *Confidential Clerk* is also self-consciously theatrical, complete with exits, entrances and sudden recognitions. Eliot had already discussed the possibility of introducing more poetry into his drama, after the rigorous starkness of *The Cocktail Party*,[63] but once more in this play his reliance upon form and formal manipulation has taken precedence. The major difficulty with *The Confidential Clerk*, however, is that its techniques of stage action are so thoroughly and obviously conventional that anything Eliot cares to place within them is diminished. At best, it is a *tour de force*, a piece of self-conscious 'theatre' manipulated for his own purpose. But he had wished for more than that. In an interview which he gave in this year, he expressed his disappointment at the recent development of English poetry and suggested that any 'creative advance' would come in prose fiction or in poetic drama:[64] this is clearly what he himself was aiming at, as if he felt he could achieve in drama what he had already achieved in poetry. Certainly the ambition was in both cases the same: in a lecture which he gave soon after finishing *The Cocktail Party* he declared that he only wished to write plays 'of *contemporary* life'.[65] As a young man, it had been his recognition of the need for contemporary diction and contemporary imagery in poetry that had drawn him to sources as disparate as Baudelaire and John Davidson. But in spite of the insistent use of demotic speech in *The Confidential Clerk*, the very quality which seems to be missing from it is contemporaneity – it is worth remembering, in contrast, that John Osborne's *Look Back in Anger* was produced only three years later. In his social criticism Eliot assumes an idea of England which never existed and proposes an England which could not exist: in the same way, his own vision of the world was too singular for him to be able to invest his social dramas with the emblematic or representative significance to which he aspired. His was too literary, and now too deliberate, a talent to flourish in the public realm of the theatre. Perhaps he guessed as much: certainly he seems to have been surprised by the success of the play.[66] But that success was more or less assured: his reputation and authority were such that those who went to the theatre went, as a matter of course, to see Eliot. When Edmund Wilson attended a performance of *The Confidential Clerk*, however, he found it 'rudimentary'; everyone in London seemed to agree with him but, he said, 'respect for Eliot had made it impossible for anyone to commit himself by printing a sincere opinion'.[67] It is possible, then, that Eliot no longer knew what others really thought of his work.

A few weeks after the opening of the play, he once more began to suffer from bronchitis. In November he was able to lecture at Central Hall, Westminster, on 'The Three Voices of Poetry' – in the recording of that address, his clipped and precise speech, almost professorial in character, can be heard – but it was to be his last major engagement for many months. He had been urged by his doctor to escape the English winter and at the end of the year he went once more to South Africa for a ten-week holiday, sailing to Durban and then proceeding in a leisurely fashion to Cape Town. Although this cruise was to be in the nature of a 'rest cure', almost immediately after his return in early March 1954, he suffered an attack of tachycardia, marked by an acceleration of the pulse. He went into the London Clinic for three weeks and after X-rays, blood tests and cardiographic treatment it was discovered that the disorder had no organic origin – its source was essentially a nervous one and seemed likely to have been the result of over-exertion and worry. There was a risk that he might overstrain and enlarge his heart: he told one visitor that the sensation was like that of 'harbouring some runaway machine'.[68] But his pulse returned to normal by the end of April, and at the beginning of May he returned home to Carlyle Mansions. He was told by his doctor to cancel all engagements for two months, and was ordered to give up smoking; he was allowed, instead, one cigar a day. He had, of course, given up cigarettes by the time he had gone into the clinic, but as a result he had abandoned the puritanical principles inculcated into him in youth and had started eating sweets instead; and this meant that he was putting on weight.[69] He had been a heavy smoker all his life, however, and for a while he still felt the need for a cigarette before and after meals.[70]

In May he went to convalesce by the seaside, near Littlehampton, and on his return he stayed at home for another month, attempting only light work: all important social and public engagements were cancelled until the autumn. Under this enforced regimen of quiet and rest, he came to understand that it was necessary for him to retire a little from the active life in which he had previously been engaged; he told William Turner Levy that he would have to learn to concentrate his time and energy upon his real work.[71] It was in a similarly reflective vein that he wrote to Marion Dorn later in the year.[72] Her husband (and his old friend) McKnight Kauffer, had just died and Eliot speculated about the question of 'what might have been' in anyone's life – that crucial moment when a life is changed. Perhaps he was contemplating his own life with Vivien here just as, when he connected McKnight Kauffer's death with a sense of 'the void', he was once again returning to his own feeling of emptiness which had played so large a part in his religious conversion. He had known 'the void' himself and he knew, also, what it was not to love life.

As so often happens in the last years, his remaining family and oldest friends became of most importance to him. His sister came to England in July, and they went to the Isle of Wight together for a little over three weeks. Other American relatives came in August and then at the beginning of September he went to Switzerland again. He returned to England in mid-September but then, to add to his physical woes, he suffered an attack of arthritis: it required massage and he resented the time he had to spend travelling to and from the masseur. Time was now important to him: it had been a lazy year[73] and, as he had told Levy, there was still work for him to do. One of his last poems, 'The Cultivation of Christmas Trees', was published in the autumn as part of the Faber 'Ariel' series: it is a poem in which the memories of childhood Christmases are kept alive through the experience of age and weariness, both the beginning and end of life coming together in the fear and love of God.

Although his general health seemed more stable after his long recuperation, he was finding it more and more difficult to keep up with his daily obligations, let alone those of a more public nature. He had been awarded the Hanseatic-Goethe prize but was unable to make the trip to Germany in order to receive it, and even now was attempting to prepare an address for the following year. But these things were not easy for him. He had been asked to rewrite the words of *The Rock*, but he suggested to Ronald Duncan that he should do the job for him: 'Watching the time he took to write even his signature,' Duncan noted, 'it occurred to me that it must be a painful process for him to compose anything'.[74] And George Seferis saw also, when Eliot was inscribing a book, 'how nervously he grasped the pen'.[75] He was ill again with tachycardia in January 1955 and in the middle of the month returned to the London Clinic. He came out after two weeks and – despite a slight chill on the liver – he was recovering by the end of February. By March he was out again, and back at his office in Faber and Faber, although he was prudent enough to retire to bed early in the evening: with a complaint which had no organic cause, he could not be certain that he had been 'cured'. He flew to Hamburg at the beginning of May in order to attend the postponed ceremony for the Hanseatic-Goethe prize and to give an address on 'Goethe the Sage'. His problems in composing this lecture were no doubt compounded by the fact that he had had in the past expressed no great liking for Goethe's poetry – 'I can't stand his stuff,' he had once told Ronald Duncan – and in any case he now found public addresses a complete waste of time.[76] Immediately on his return from Germany, he travelled to the United States for a visit of two months. His primary purpose was to see his two sisters in Boston – one was now too old to travel, and the other was ailing. He had calculated, however, that he would need to give three poetry readings in order to cover his expenses on this visit: he did only the amount that was strictly necessary, since the Inland Revenue had a habit of taking much of any extra income he earned. He stayed first in New York with Robert Giroux, and then went down to Washington partly in order to see Ezra Pound. He did not enjoy such visits now, and would have been tempted to abandon them if it were not for the fact that people might gossip.[77] But although he found Pound's humourlessness and growing megalomania more and more distasteful, Eliot's activities on his behalf continued. He wrote regularly to Dorothy Pound, and his advice was always of a most practical nature. When in 1953 Wyndham Lewis suggested a further campaign to release Pound from confinement, Eliot at first advised against any precipitate step: a number of proposals were being considered – including a letter to President Eisenhower – but he was wary of doing anything from England without being sure that there was approval for such moves in America. He was also unhappy about Pound's own obstinacy and arrogance in the matter of his eventual release; he was raising objections to schemes that seemed perfectly sound and, as Eliot told his daughter, 'I fear your father does not want to accept freedom on any terms that are possible'.[78] Their relationship was further impaired when in 1954 Pound criticized Eliot's Christianity as 'lousy'; Eliot wrote a caustic letter back.[79] Their meeting in this year could have been chilly, then, but fortunately it was not: 'Possum more relaxed this year,' Pound wrote to Ernest Hemingway, 'last year rather edgy. . . .'[80]

On his return from America – with presents of nylons, and other goods still in short supply in England, for friends – he continued with his usual round of private and business engagements. In August he went again to Switzerland, and for a week in September he looked after his grandniece who had travelled to London to see him; but then he contracted athlete's foot and had once again to enter a nursing home. He expected to be there for only three or four days, but he was kept in for a fortnight. It was a miserable time; the winter proved too much for him, and at the beginning of 1956 he had a severe attack of bronchitis: his coughing and choking were so bad that it induced his tachycardia. He went back into hospital and stayed there for five weeks. He was now very weak and was forced to convalesce until March – after that, his doctor advised him, he would be able only to engage in part-time office work.

By April he had recovered sufficiently to travel to America once more, to see his sisters; this visit is perhaps most remarkable for the fact that he addressed the largest assembly ever gathered to attend a literary lecture (he also received what was then the largest fee for such an event, some two thousand dollars). On 30 April at the University of Minnesota, in Minneapolis, 14,000 people gathered in a baseball stadium to hear Eliot discourse on 'The Frontiers of Criticism': 'I felt,' he said, 'like a very small bull walking into an enormous arena.'[81] He spoke on the transformation of literary criticism over the previous thirty years and, no doubt with the memory of John Peter's interpretation of *The Waste Land* in mind, warned against too much psychological or biographical conjecture in the explication of poetry. But the subject of his lecture was not the reason so many thousands of young Americans had crowded into the stadium: they had come to see him. He had become a kind of totem; his extraordinary authority was based on that sense of a cultural order which he had once sought and which, by the strange alchemy of his career, he now embodied. He had become the representative of a tradition which, without his presence, might finally disappear, and the fact that he now had very little left to say only heightened the almost ritualistic sense of occasion which that presence provided.

He stayed with his relatives from the middle of May into June. Although his sister was now gravely ill he had to return to London but, on the voyage back, he was again afflicted with tachycardia and when the ship docked at Southampton he was rushed to hospital in London; while recovering there, he learned that his sister had died. Eliot himself was now in his sixty-eighth year. There remained one last work for him to complete; already he had begun writing a play

317

which was to concern a successful public man who, at the end of his life, is waiting for death. He had drafted two acts by January of this year, when ill health forestalled his plans to do further work upon it. But in August, just before setting off for a month in Switzerland, he still hoped to have finished a draft of the third act by the end of the year. There were other, smaller tasks which he wished to complete: when he had finished the play, he planned to revise for publication the lectures which he had given on education at the University of Chicago.

It was an exhausting schedule, and he was not able in the end to maintain it. He returned from a cold and rainy holiday in Switzerland to find himself faced with a mountain of correspondence and other business (he was receiving in this period something like fifty letters a day, although most of them were handled by Valerie Fletcher). He still tired easily, and disliked evening engagements. Igor Stravinsky met him for the first time in this year, and recalled how shy he seemed. Conversation was not easy: 'Eliot turned his head from speaker to speaker, with a slight jerk, emitting a nervous tic "yes" or "hmm" every few seconds. You felt he was registering unfavourable impressions'.[82] In the winter of 1956, he was further irritated by problems with his teeth: he was about to have X-rays for the three which remained to him. But personal troubles, he told Bonamy Dobrée, seemed trivial in comparison with public matters[83] – by which no doubt he meant the Soviet invasion of Hungary. Nevertheless there was one event of this year which seemed to lift such worries from him, and to help cure all his infirmities except that of age.

16

Happy at Last
1957–1965

TOWARDS THE END OF 1956 Eliot proposed to Valerie Fletcher, almost eight years after she had started working for him. The restrictions of office life might have formed a permanent barrier to any expression of their feelings for each other, but their relationship had grown appreciably closer when they had both stayed for part of one summer at the home of a friend, Margaret Behrens, in Mentone – although even here Valerie Fletcher still called him 'Mr Eliot'. He proposed to her at the offices of Faber and Faber; after she had accepted, he explained that he would have asked her much sooner if he had known her real feelings towards him, but she had been so formal with him that he was not even sure if she liked him[1] – which, after eight years, suggests an odd insecurity or impercipience. She was nervous that he might change his mind at the last minute, but he did not do so.

On 10 January 1957, at 6.15 in the morning when it was still dark, they were married at St Barnabas's Church in Addison Road, Kensington: she was thirty, and he now sixty-eight. The church had been chosen simply because its priest happened to be a friend of Eliot's solicitor, who was also 'best man'. Hardly anyone knew of the ceremony in advance: no banns were posted and no friends (except, perhaps, John Hayward) were informed. The only other witnesses present were Miss Fletcher's parents. Once again Eliot sought secrecy at one of the most important events of his life, although on this occasion his primary aim was to avoid the attentions of the newspapers. Quite by chance, he discovered just before the ceremony that Jules Laforgue, who had exercised such a decisive influence on his youthful poetry, had also been married at St Barnabas's. After the wedding, they were taken for breakfast to the house of the officiating priest which by curious coincidence

319

happened to be 10 Kensington Church Walk, where Ezra Pound had lived many years before. Past and present seemed to be animating each other in almost an Eliotic manner.

The marriage had come as a complete shock even to Eliot's closest friends, such as Emily Hale and Mary Trevelyan. Indeed it would not be too much to say that neither woman ever really got over it; a day before the wedding he had written to Mary Trevelyan, expressing the hope that she would remain on friendly terms both with him and his new wife, but the old intimacy had necessarily gone for ever. It vanished, too, from the friendship between Eliot and John Hayward. It is a matter of dispute how they parted; friends of Hayward suggest that Eliot left Carlyle Mansions on the morning of the marriage, leaving only a note of explanation behind – or, even, that he told Hayward as the taxi waited for him in the street below. Friends of Eliot suggest that he confronted his old friend with the news a day or two before the marriage. Whatever the exact circumstances, it is at least clear that Eliot vacated Carlyle Mansions quickly and deliberately – and that he left behind him a man to whom he had been a companion for ten years. There can be little doubt that Hayward had come to rely upon him over that period, and felt in some sense that he had been abandoned. In spite of the strangeness of Eliot's behaviour, however, few people begrudged him the happiness which in personal relations he had never experienced before: 'He obviously needed to have a happy marriage,' Valerie Eliot said on a later occasion, 'He couldn't die until he had had it'. 'There was,' she said, '. . . a little boy in him that had never been released.'[2]

After three weeks' honeymoon in Mentone, they returned to London where Eliot succumbed to bronchitis. They were staying in a hotel until they could find a flat, but his doctor insisted that they spend some days in Brighton so that he could properly recover. In April they were finally able to move into Kensington Court Gardens, off High Street Kensington. There were the usual problems of moving – Valerie Eliot, apart from having to scrub and prepare the flat, was also forced to continue with her old secretarial duties since her successor's father was ill. But by the beginning of May Eliot was safely ensconced: he had a typewriter, desk, table and chair and was looking forward to starting work again. Visitors noticed a quality of cosy impersonality about the new flat, with its watercolours and its piles of books, but Eliot never seemed much to care about his immediate physical surroundings. He was now, in any case, extremely happy; 'I'm the luckiest man in the world,' he told Robert Giroux,[3] and to Joseph Chiari he said that he did not think he deserved such happiness.[4] This was a quite remarkable transformation in a man who only two years before had talked of dying: neither fame nor literary achievement had brought him any contentment, and in the end it was human love, the love that he had dismissed in his writings as the consolation only of ordinary men, that rescued him from a lifetime of misery and isolation.

The Eliots were inseparable; they went to parties where they would stand arm in arm. He would often hold her hand when they were at large gatherings: it was, one friend wrote, 'very touching'.[5] Valerie Eliot was also his protector – as a secretary she had for a long time been organizing his daily life and guarding him from the world, and it was probably the calm assurance of her presence which first drew him towards her. His family had protected him when he was a child and youth, and the search for another such secure haven was one of the dominant notes of his life: both in its denial during his marriage to Vivien which rendered him so anxious and insecure, and in its triumphant restitution at the end of his life. He was now much more friendly and jaunty – 'I am thinking of taking up dancing lessons again,' he told a reporter from the *Daily Express*, 'as I have not danced at all for some years'. To his friends he seemed changed: the nervousness, the apparent decrepitude and the look of illness vanished. It is as if this had been the artificial carapace which had now dissolved and there emerged the smiling, bright-eyed figure of Eliot, with an expression close to that of the photographs taken of him in childhood. In an early draft of the play upon which he was working the elderly public man is compared to a silkworm who has chewed the bitter leaves of the mulberry all his life. It is time to leave off, his daughter tells him, it is time to burst forth like a butterfly.

Eliot's life, for the eight years still left to him, now took on a different pattern. He wrote at home in the morning and then, on free afternoons, he liked to walk with his wife in Kensington Gardens: particularly he enjoyed watching the boats which children brought to the Round Pond there. He spent three afternoons a week, from Tuesday to Thursday, at Russell Square; although he was still active as an editor, at least with the work of those authors who were now also old friends, age and reputation necessarily meant that he was now much more of a 'figurehead' than once he was. In what he called 'emphysema weather', he did not venture out at all and in his last years one member of the firm, Peter du Sautoy, would report to him on the business being conducted – what books had been accepted, for example. Sometimes he would vehemently disapprove of the choices, but du Sautoy remembered his 'mysterious smile' as well as 'his laughter, with a hint of mockery in it'.[6] In the evenings, if the Eliots did not go out to the cinema or theatre together, they would often listen to the gramophone – he had an especial affection for the music of Bartok, although sometimes he would play the songs of Edward Lear. He would also read to his wife at the end of the day – from Boswell's *Life of Johnson*, from Coleridge's *Letters*, from Rudyard Kipling's *Kim* (an especial favourite) and sometimes from his own work. Valerie Eliot now looked after his private correspondence, and would type out fair copies of his own work from his typewritten drafts. 'He usually asks me for my criticism,' she said to one interviewer. 'I'm often terrified to reply and I try to get out of saying anything. But he is a genuinely humble person.'[7] His domestic happiness meant that his desire to see other people waned somewhat, and there were certain friends who felt themselves to have been 'cut out' of his life. But those whom he had known longest remained close to him: he, Herbert Read, Bonamy Dobrée and Frank Morley would meet regularly once a fortnight or so, each in turn hosting the others at his club.

But if this state of comparative retirement owed much to his desire to experience as fully as possible the companionship of marriage, it was also imposed upon him by the demands of his still fragile health. His doctor constantly suggested to him the benefits of sun and sea air (not that he needed any encouragement to visit the sea, since it still evoked for him the happiest memories), and in July they travelled, with Eliot's sister who had come from America, to the Isle of Wight for two weeks. In September the Eliots were in Scarborough, again for a fortnight, but on his return he contracted Asiatic influenza. It was a protracted illness, accompanied by a high temperature, and it precipitated another bout of bronchitis. He was not properly well again until the end of October, although he was still extremely resilient. But when he had recovered sufficiently he wanted to resume work as quickly as possible on his play. He had already drafted two acts at the beginning of the previous year, and even before he had been taken ill this autumn he had begun the work of revising them. He worked consistently on the third act, and by the end of the year he had finished a draft of the entire play. The fact that he had written a large part of it after his marriage led him to think of it as a work quite different from the one he had originally envisaged.[8] It was while engaged on it at Kensington Court Gardens that he added the more tender love scenes which provide its real poetry. He had never written verse of this kind before, and it did not come easily to him: the drafts of these scenes underwent most revision. In December, while in the last stages of composition, he stayed at home because of the London fog, and at the beginning of the new year he took to his bed for a week with a slight chill. But he was in a sense revivified: his heart withstood the weakening effect of his illnesses much better than it had done in the same period of the previous year, and this was the first winter for some time when he had not been forced to seek treatment in a clinic.

He said in one interview that public honours meant nothing to him until his marriage[9] but, even so, the mist of respectability now clung about him always. He was part of a delegation that went to the BBC to complain about proposed cuts to the Third Programme, the 'cultural' channel of the broadcasting service; he was working on the Commission for the Revised Psalter; he was asked to give evidence to the Parliamentary Commission on Obscene Publications (he had had very little experience of pornographic literature, he told the members of that commission, and his own work was 'quite anodyne'). And in March 1958 he travelled with his wife to Rome where he was to receive an honorary degree: it is a mark of his extraordinary fame that students lined the route to the university and shouted 'Viva Eliot!' as they drove by. In the following month the Eliots travelled to the United States, primarily so that he could introduce his wife to his numerous relatives and friends. When they visited Texas he asked why the young men seemed so gloomy when there was so much to be happy about, and in Cambridge he publicly embraced his old friend, Conrad Aiken, moving Aiken almost to tears.[10] Everything had changed and, when he gave two readings at Columbia University and the University of Texas, on both occasions he made the same disclaimer – that he had almost lost contact with the young man who had written the earlier poetry. It might be more accurate to say that he had escaped from him. Just as he had the ability to compartmentalize his life, so he also seemed able to slough off the weight of the past and begin again. But there was so much of that past now that he could not easily do so: when in 1959 there were rumours that the original manuscripts of *The Waste Land* had been found (false rumours, as it turned out) the news, according to an acquaintance, 'depressed him'.[11]

The Eliots returned from America in May, and rehearsals began almost at once for the Edinburgh Festival production of his new play. It had originally been called *The Rest Cure* but Eliot discovered that the title had already been used and, after some hesitation, he replaced it with *The Elder Statesman*. Sherek recalled how nervous and agitated he seemed at the first reading with the actors – just as he had been when he had first shown the play to Sherek.[12] Even marriage could not cure him of all his anxieties, and it is salutary to remember that, in some situations, he was as frightened of other people as they were of him: he often seemed shy and hesitant in conversation still. When Stravinsky visited the Eliots in this year, his amanuensis, Robert Craft, recorded that 'he is a quiet man, slow in formulating his remarks, which trail off in *diminuendo. . . .* His long fidgety fingers fold and unfold, too, or touch tip to tip'.[13] And yet underneath this diffident and subdued exterior, there was a passionate temperament which he was generally at pains to control. When in July, for example, he was asked to testify for the London Library against a rating valuation, he was visibly nervous before giving his testimony (it seems, according to Rupert Hart-Davis, that he had been awake the whole night before[14]). At first he seemed fumbling and awkward when under cross-examination but the prosecuting counsel said something which annoyed him, and he responded fiercely and eloquently.

The rehearsals for *The Elder Statesman* proceeded although, because of Eliot's marriage, they were 'haunted by gossip writers'.[15] On 24 August the Eliots travelled to Edinburgh for the first night and, once again, the reaction of the audience was favourable. On this occasion, he did agree to make a speech on stage after the performance, although at first Sherek 'thought he was not going to say anything at all, because he just stood there trying to see his wife's face in the audience.'[16]

If it were not for the scenes written after his marriage, *The Elder Statesman* would have been by far the grimmest play he had ever written. Lord Claverton, in whom selfishness and ambition have combined to produce a 'public man', now in bad health and at the end of his career, contemplates the sterility of his life. His meditations are interrupted by two figures from his past, who remind him of separate acts of cowardice and inhumanity. Under the infliction of their memories, and prompted by a self-examination which is all the more rigorous for coming so tardily, his artificial, public self collapses and the real man, the ordinary human being, emerges. He confesses his past mistakes to his daughter who reaffirms her love for him and then, at the close of the play, he retires to the shade of a beech tree and dies. His daughter and her fiancé are left on stage, where they confirm their love for each other with a poetry that Eliot would have once found impossible to write:

> Not even death can dismay or amaze me
> Fixed in the certainty of love unchanging.

The critics seemed to approve of the poetry, although they emphasized the theatrical and 'dated' aspects of the play. Martin Browne himself believed that Eliot was too ready to rely upon outworn social and theatrical conventions, but suggested that they 'reflect an unconscious reversion to the drama that Eliot must have seen as a young theatregoer before 1914'.[17] It would perhaps make a poignant epitaph to Eliot's creative career that he should return to the literary associations and memories of his youth in America – the 'Victorian American' who even in his rebellion against that inheritance marked himself as its true heir. But the 'theatricality' of the play works beneath the purely formal level: Lord Claverton has always acted a role and it is only at the end of his life that he allows his true human self to emerge, although

> . . . the longer we pretend
> The harder it becomes to drop the pretence,
> Walk off the stage, change into our own clothes
> And speak as ourselves.

Theatrical images of this kind are apparent throughout Eliot's work and, as Browne has remarked, 'The image of the actor finding himself on stage in the wrong part comes to Eliot as the expression of a climax of disturbance'.[18] One character in *The Elder Statesman* remarks, 'Forgery . . . is a mug's game', which is precisely what Eliot had said of poetry twenty-five years before.[19] It is not necessary to conflate the two to recognize how artifice and expression are deeply implicated with each other in his work – how one can only speak freely by playing a part, like Cyrano in the shadows. But just as one theme of the play is that of artifice discarded, so Eliot produces here some of his simplest and most expressive poetry. There are passages of great beauty in the play, sustained by a perfectly adjusted theatrical cadence. The sudden transitions and complications have disappeared along with the irony and grandiloquence – and with them, too, the bitter distaste for the world and the yearnings for an elected fate as saint or martyr.

He returned to London with his wife on 2 September, and the London production of the play opened at the Cambridge Theatre three weeks later. A party was held at A L'Ecu de France to celebrate the first night, and on the following evening a small reception was held at Kensington Court Gardens to celebrate his seventieth birthday. There were only a few guests – among them Martin Browne and his wife, Rupert Hart-Davis and Jacob Epstein (whom Eliot had come to like and admire when he was sitting to him). Eliot's presents were laid out on the table, and there was champagne and a birthday cake: when Rupert Hart-Davis lit the candles on the cake, Eliot knelt down and blew them out. Epstein proposed a toast to him, to which he replied, 'This is the happiest birthday I've ever known'.[20]

Nothing could interfere with that happiness now. When *The Elder Statesman* received less than adulatory notices, and failed to succeed at the box office, he was noticeably calm in his reaction.[21] And the fact that he seemed to accept the failure of his play, which in previous years would have depressed and unnerved him, is further evidence that he was now a more sanguine man. In an interview which he gave in this year, the reporter noted how he seemed much 'heartier, more unworried and more unafraid of the world than he did . . . five years ago'.[22] 'Love reciprocated is always rejuvenating,' Eliot told him. 'Now I feel younger at seventy than I did at sixty. Any man if he is alone becomes more aware of being lonely as he ages. An experience like mine makes all the more difference because of its contrast with the past.'[23] In other interviews celebrat-

the impersonal mask

ing his seventieth birthday, he made similar confessions about his private experience – confessions which, in the past, he would have been too defensive to make. He was 'more reconciled and calm' than he had been at thirty;[24] age had not made him wiser 'but I have never been wise'.[25] There was also the prospect of more poetry although 'They would have to be new poems in a new idiom'.[26] He had written one poem since his marriage, dedicated to his wife, which is couched in a spirit quite different from any poetry he had written before – he had finally, he told Cyril Connolly, written a poem about love and happiness.[27] And he was looking forward again: 'I don't feel I've ever got to the point I aim at and I don't think I ever will, but I would like to feel that I was getting a little nearer to it each time.'[28] The future, it seemed, was all before him. But the truth is that he was never to publish poetry again: he had come to the end of his creative life. In his first schoolboy poetry the theme had been of love withered and decayed – practically the last lines he ever wrote were of 'the certainty of love unchanging'. He had come a long way.

The winter of 1958 again induced his emphysema; it was foggy, and he could not breathe without effort. He had had no holiday at all during the previous year, and the absence of sunshine and warmth affected him. And so in the middle of January 1959, the Eliots travelled to Nassau in the Bahamas, stopping at New York on the way there and on their return. Although Valerie Eliot did not like long sea voyages since she suffered from seasickness, and Eliot complained to friends like Marion Dorn about the expense involved, they travelled to the West Indies regularly over the next five years. There are photographs of him taken on this and other trips: Eliot smiling sleepily at the camera, wearing a white cap and sunglasses, smoking a cigar and wearing a pink shirt and blue pullover. In March they returned to England, and he attempted to catch up with all the work and correspondence he had left behind. Many of his public obligations were thoroughly familiar – on 12 May, for example, he gave an address at the University of Sheffield and then two weeks later received the Dante Gold Medal at the Italian Institute – but other duties were more painful to perform. He had reached the age when friends and companions were beginning to die around him, and in the spring of this year he composed memorial addresses for two of them: William Collin Brooks, who ten years before had encouraged Valerie Fletcher to apply for the post of Eliot's secretary, and Father Eric Cheetham, who had 'taken in' Eliot after the separation from Vivien. Two years later, Geoffrey Faber died also – the man who had taken pride in the fact that, many years before, he had 'rescued Eliot for poetry'.[29]

In the middle of May the Eliots went to Leeds to stay with Valerie Eliot's mother – her father had died in the year of her marriage. This visit, too, became an annual event – Eliot enjoyed the quiet of his mother-in-law's home, and Mrs Fletcher in turn was much taken by what she called the 'virginal' quality of her son-in-law.[30] The Northern air, in the countryside around Leeds, seemed to revive him and, in the company of his new family, he grew to love the area. On his return to London in June, however, he caught a cold which aggravated his emphysema and his doctor advised him to go once more to Brighton in order to recuperate. When Craft and Stravinsky visited him in the autumn of this year, Craft has recorded how he looked 'younger and livelier' than he had before, but that he seemed 'to think of himself as a hoary ancient with little time left'.[31] 'I cannot accept lectures,' he told his guests, 'because the people who pay for them expect me to attend cocktail parties at which I am caught between someone wanting to know what I think of existentialism and someone asking me what I really meant by such-and-such a line'. In spite of this disclaimer, he did continue to give lectures – in America especially, where he was paid very large fees for his performances. In fact the Eliots travelled across the Atlantic for the second time in October; when he stopped at Chicago to give a reading on his way to St Louis, a reporter noted that he 'looked rather tired and smiled in a vague, undirected way'. One journalist asked him about 'The Love Life of J. Alfred Prufrock' and he replied gravely, 'I'm afraid that J. Alfred Prufrock didn't have much of a love life'. What is most remarkable about the talks and lectures he gave on this trip is the extent to which America now revived in him the memories of his childhood. In November he gave an address at the Mary Institute; the ghosts of the past were all around him as he spoke of the door into the schoolyard, the corridors, the whisperings of his enclosed childhood world. And then, for the first time in his place of birth, he read 'The Dry Salvages' which opens with the Mississippi, the river which had so impressed his childish imagination. Before another reading of this poem on the same visit, he announced that it began where he had begun, and that it ended where he and his wife hoped to end – in the parish church of a Somerset village;[32] he could see now the pattern of his life completed.

The Eliots returned to England at the end of November, and as a precaution against catching bronchitis he was taking antibiotics. He was bearing the cold and damp better than he had in the previous year, but these winter months were a time when proper life had to give way to the struggle merely to exist. The fog exacerbated his emphysema: he was short of breath, found it difficult to walk very far, and had to stay at home in seclusion. On his doctor's orders the Eliots went to Worthing in January, but the weather there was almost as bad for his emphysema, and he could only manage short walks along the seafront. The only recourse was to get out of England altogether and so, with some hesitation, they travelled to Morocco at the end of the month. He caught a cold on his way to Tangiers which affected his left lung, but this was merely the prelude to what became an unfortunate trip. The weather inland was much too dry for him; there was an earthquake at Agadir; the heat and dust affected his lungs and he succumbed to a bout of bronchial asthma. The whole visit was something of a disaster, and he was still recovering from it months later. While in North Africa, however, he did manage to write out a fair copy of *The Waste Land*, in order to raise money for the London Library. As he did so, he remembered a line which almost forty years before he had struck out of the poem at Vivien's insistence. Now he put it back in. In spite of his ritual attempt to distance himself from the young man who had written that poem, he knew very well that even his contemporary reputation in large part rested on it: that, and the last three of the *Four Quartets*, he told Ezra Pound, had been worth writing.[33]

His letter to Pound was one of a series between the two old men. Pound had been released from confinement in April 1958, largely as a result of Eliot's collaboration with Robert Frost and Archibald MacLeish in petitioning the American government, but his exhilaration at his new freedom did not last very long. In the autumn of 1959 he wrote to Eliot from Italy, where he was staying with his daughter, expressing grave doubts about his worth as a poet. Eliot at once sent him a cablegram, saying that he was one to whom all contemporary poets owed a debt.[34] He followed this with a long letter two months later, in which he tried to convince Pound of his achievement and to sympathize with the despair and anxiety which now assailed him.[35] Pound was now also afflicted with guilt and remorse at the shape his life had taken, and Eliot did his best to comfort him. He was now 'Dear old Ez', and in a number of letters they commiserated about the problems of age.

It is a poignant correspondence. In many ways they had both been so much alike: the nervous, magpie-like intelligence, the pedagogical aspirations, the Yankee toughness combined with the shuddering sensitivity. They had both lived through the great period of modern literature and had survived its passing: they were in a sense foreigners, out of joint with their time. And yet Eliot had always been the subtler and more complicated man, shrewd enough to make his peace with an age to which he did not truly belong. Pound had noticed those qualities when, in 1915, he had written to Henry Ware Eliot in order to explain why his son should remain in London and not return to America – his course, he said, would be smoother than Pound's own. But he could not have guessed that, almost fifty years later, Eliot would be loaded with honours and with happiness while he himself would have retreated into a silence of guilt and despair. And yet, despite this, there was too much to separate the men; they exasperated each other and yet they needed each other. They knew what bound them together, and those bonds would be loosened only in death.

Eliot had in his early seventies became an historical figure, or one at least in whom the lineaments of history could be traced. He said in one interview that, whatever his final merit as a poet, he would perhaps have a 'certain historical place in the literary history of our period',[36] and Herbert Read recalled how he might on occasions say, 'Valéry, Yeats and I . . .'.[37] He was no longer particularly interested in the work of younger writers; this was partly because he no longer felt confident in his judgments about contemporary writing[38] but, at a more general level, he believed there had been a profound falling off in the standard of both literature and criticism since the Second World War. He told one interviewer that there was little, if any, worthwhile poetry being written in England;[39] of the poetry of 'the Movement', then a fashionable group, he said that it showed neither motion nor direction,[40] and he was also scornful of

the present generation of critics and reviewers.[41] He was resigned to
the thought of English culture sliding, as it were, into the abyss and
his major preoccupation was with the past and his own place in it.
That is perhaps why he was still sensitive about his public reputation
– an essay in *Twentieth Century* on him by Edward Dahlberg, and a
book by Northrop Frye, both incurred his displeasure; he insisted
also that certain lines about his alleged anti-semitism should be
removed from the preface to Wyndham Lewis's selected letters. He
was eager to put the past in order, and to make his peace with those
who had once been his contemporaries. He wrote a preface to David
Jones's *In Parenthesis* in which he noted the fact that Jones was of
the same generation as Pound and himself; he also wrote a preface
to Lewis's *One-Way Song* and described him as one of those who
had been falsely labelled by 'the *Messenmensch*' as a fascist but
nevertheless chose 'to walk alone'. He was also ready, during the
proceedings over *Lady Chatterley's Lover*, to go into the witness
box and publicly recant his previous attacks upon Lawrence. But the
opportunity did not arise: he waited in the corridors of the Old
Bailey, but was never summoned. Although he still expressed
private doubts about Lawrence, it was necessary for the public
gesture to be made: Lawrence was, after all, part of that same
generation of writers of which Eliot was now almost the sole
representative.

Four months after the Eliots returned from their disagreeable
holiday in North Africa, he contracted a virus and was forced to stay
in bed for two weeks; once more the rhythm of illness and flight from
illness established itself. In July he was in a nursing home where
Rupert Hart-Davis found him reading a detective story and studying
a Penguin book of crossword puzzles – he was 'in excellent spirits
but his breathing was bad'.[42] On his doctor's orders he went up to
Leeds and Scarborough in August, returning at the end of September. The late autumn and winter again aggravated his emphysema
and he looked tired and pale.[43] Although he preferred to stay where
he was, his doctor insisted that he travel once more to the sun for the
worst of the winter, and at the end of 1960 the Eliots went to
Jamaica. He took the precaution, however, of carrying a typewriter
and books among his luggage so that he could prepare for an address
at the University of Leeds which he was to give in the following year.

In Jamaica he sunbathed and swam in the sea (swimming always seemed to alleviate his disabilities), drank rum punch and slept very well. As a result his breathing was better and he had put on weight but, as he told Seferis, 'the spirit sleeps' in such places:[44] he became bored and restless.

In March they returned to England, and he was eager to get back to work at once. He was already contemplating a new play, but he had first to work on an essay on George Herbert which he had promised to Bonamy Dobrée. His affection and solicitude for Dobrée, as for other old friends like Herbert Read, Philip Mairet and Frank Morley, is very touching, and he seemed now almost a grandpaterfamilias for the men who had known him so well. In June he went up to Leeds for a three-week holiday: the air of the Yorkshire moors always did him good, and there were in the vicinity a doctor, an oculist and a radiologist to examine him periodically. But his wife was always his chief protector – he did not like her to leave his side for more than a day.[45] Towards the end of his stay in Yorkshire, he gave the Convocation Address at Leeds. In this lecture, 'To Criticize the Critic', he set his own prose writings in historical perspective – once more setting the past in order – but it is also notable for the manner in which he asserted the presence in his theoretical judgments of private feeling and experience; phrases like 'the objective correlative' and 'the disassociation of sensibility' were, for him, 'conceptual symbols for emotional preferences'. And, in the preface to David Jones's *In Parenthesis* written in this year, he declared that 'Understanding begins in the sensibility'. Can we not see in this new conviction of the importance of emotion and sensibility that awakening of feeling which his marriage had accomplished? 'The critics call me cold and learned,' he had said to Virginia Woolf many years before: and the truth was, that he was neither.

In the middle of November the Eliots travelled to America, where he made five public appearances in order to pay for their forthcoming holiday in Barbados after Christmas – as long as he could 'hobble up a stage', he could still pay for such trips.[46] But he did not like leaving England, even in the winter, and, among the American tourists of Barbados, they soon felt homesick: Eliot was convinced, too, that the manager of the hotel in which they were staying was trying to exploit his presence there.[47] They returned in

March 1962; he at last finished his essay on George Herbert but, before he could start work on a new play, he had to prepare for the press his early graduate thesis on the work of F. H. Bradley. His youth now seemed so distant that he was no longer particularly interested in such matters, and he confessed to his wife that he did not understand a word of that thesis. But it was, in fact, the last serious work he was ever able to do. In July the Eliots travelled up to Leeds, and although he had a mild infection in August he said that he felt in much better health. It was about this time, however, that friends began to notice a change in his physiognomy: he was much more hunched, leaning forward as he stood; his face was paler, and the lines more accentuated. In December he became ill after a four-day 'smog' and collapsed. He was rushed to Brompton Hospital where for five weeks he lay under continuous oxygen. At first his wife never left him, since the doctors had told her that it was vital that he should find her there when he came out of his coma, and then when the immediate danger had passed she visited him three times a day and gave him his meals. Although his situation was critical – and, for a man of his age almost hopeless – he pulled through. He came out of hospital in January 1963, and convalesced at home for the next few weeks. His wife washed and shaved him, and ensured that he swallowed the twenty-six pills each day which had been mainly prescribed for his heart. It was a cold and damp winter, but he recovered slowly and indeed seemed cheerful; he sat beside the open coal fire in the drawingroom and would sometimes sing music-hall ditties as his wife ministered to him – 'coddling', he used to call it. He had no visitors, although once or twice a week his secretary might come to deal with his correspondence. At the beginning of March his wife drove him to Regents Park, and he was able to take a few steps in the spring sunshine. In the same month they travelled to Bermuda for six weeks so that he might convalesce in the warmth: he responded well, and was walking more easily.

But he was now in the last stages of his infirmity. Allen Tate visited the Eliots in September, and saw how weak he was. When Tate took his leave, Eliot stood at the door of the drawingroom leaning on two canes; Tate waved goodbye, and although he was not able to raise himself from the canes he smiled and made a movement with one hand. At the end of November, however, he was able to make one last trip to his native land, and the Eliots stayed in New

York for the whole of December. Stravinsky had dinner with them there, and was concerned by Eliot's ashen complexion and faltering walk. During the meal, 'The poor man bent over his plate, drinking but not eating. . . . He raised himself bolt upright only at intervals'.[48] Eliot talked about Missouri and his childhood there and then, at the end of the meal, he proposed a toast to Stravinsky: 'Another ten years for both of us!' he said.[49] But the past, not the future, now claimed him: on this same trip to New York, he told William Turner Levy that he had dreamed of his family as it had been when he was a small child.[50]

From America they travelled on to Nassau. The swimming in the hotel pool benefited him, he told Herbert Read, but he was more and more conscious of the weight of the years.[51] They returned in April, and in June visited Leeds for the last time. And then in October he collapsed at home. Five doctors said that his condition was now so serious that he would not last the night: he was rushed to hospital, paralysed on his left side and in a deep coma. His wife sat with him for thirteen hours, and he clutched her hand as he struggled for life. In the morning, barely conscious, he turned to his wife 'and looked at me as if to say "I've done it" '.[52] He was sent home from hospital after a short period, since the doctors thought it more important that he should be there with his wife, and he shouted 'hurrah! hurrah! hurrah!' as he was carried over the threshold. He was now under continuous oxygen and too weak to take solid foods, but he would sit by the fire in his wheelchair for two hours each day while his wife read, or played music, to him. Until Christmas he seemed to be making progress, but then his heart began to fail. He relapsed into a coma again, returning to consciousness only once to speak his wife's name; and on 4 January 1965, he died.

After her husband's death Valerie Eliot declared, 'He felt he had paid too high a price to be a poet, that he had suffered too much.'[53] Two years before his death, he had told Herbert Read that the best of his poetry had cost him dearly in experience.[54] But the poetry which emerged from that experience is hard and clear, and it is as if his capacity for suffering existed with an immense ability to use and to order it. We are confronted with a number of paradoxes: Eliot proclaimed the impersonality of great poetry, and yet his own personality and experience are branded in letters of fire upon his work. He was a poet who insisted upon the nature and value of a tradition, and yet he had no real predecessors or successors. He was a writer who attempted to create order and coherence, and yet his central vision was of 'the Void'. His poetic voice is unmistakable, and yet it was composed from a number of other poets' voices which he adapted or borrowed. He was a strange, private and often bewildered man who was raised into a cultural guru, a representative of authority and stability.

Throughout his life Eliot brought the anguish of his difficult and divided nature to the surface of his poetry, just as in oblique form he analysed it in his prose. His predilection for order, as well as his susceptibility to disorder, were immense and in the jarring, crushing equilibrium between the two his life and work were formed. Both as a writer and a man, his genius lay in his ability to resist the subversive tendencies of his personality by fashioning them into something larger than himself. His work represents the brilliant efflorescence of a dying culture: he pushed that culture together by an act of will, giving it a shape and context which sprang out of his own obsessions, and the certainties which he established were rhetorical certainties. In so doing he became a symbol of the age, and his poetry became its echoing music – with its brooding grandeur as well as its bleakness, its plangency as well as its ellipses, its rhythmical strength as well as its theatrical equivocations.

He had left instructions for his body to be cremated and in April his ashes were taken, as he had wished, to the little church of St Michael's in East Coker, the village from which his ancestors had come. It was the final dramatic, but telling, gesture. On the memorial tablet to him in the church are the words, 'Remember Thomas Stearns Eliot, poet'. His dates of birth and death are added, together with two phrases: 'In my beginning is my end' and 'In my end is my beginning'. Both have been chronicled in this book, and perhaps we can say now of Eliot what he once said of another poet, 'We also understand the poetry better when we know more about the man.'[55]

Notes

IN ORDER to avoid unnecessary repetition, I have abbreviated the source references which are documented in full in the acknowledgments at the beginning of this book. The Humanities Research Centre at the University of Texas is here referred to as 'Texas'; the Department of Manuscripts at the British Library is referred to as 'British Library'; the Berg Collection of the New York Public Library is referred to as 'Berg'; and so on. I have denoted university libraries and special collections by a simple appellation – Cornell, Victoria, Beinecke, McMaster, Princeton, etc. In the first reference to a source book or thesis, I give the salient details of publication; in any further reference, I abbreviate that material. For example, all references, save the first, to H. W. H. Powel's *Notes on the Life of T. S. Eliot, 1888–1910* are as 'Powel'.

PRELUDE AND CHAPTER I

1 Eliot to Ezra Pound, 11 November 1961. Beinecke.
2 Eliot to Herbert Read, 1 August 1963. Victoria.
3 Charlotte Eliot to Bertrand Russell, 23 May 1916. Quoted in *The Tempering of T. S. Eliot, 1888–1915*, an unpublished Harvard dissertation by John Soldo, 1972. Hereinafter referred to as Soldo.
4 Abigail Eliot speaking in *The Mysterious Mr Eliot*, a BBC television documentary broadcast in January 1971.
5 In *Notes Towards The Definition of Culture*. London, 1948.
6 In an interview with V. S. Pritchett. *New York Times*, 21 September 1958.
7 In 'American Literature and the American Language'. Delivered at Washington University, 9 June 1953. Reprinted in *To Criticize The Critic*, London, 1965.
8 *William Greenleaf Eliot, minister, educator, philanthropist*. Boston, 1904.
9 *ibid.*
10 Quoted by Herbert Howarth in *Notes on Some Figures Behind T. S. Eliot*. London, 1965
11 Eliot to Bertrand Russell, 22 June 1927. McMaster.
12 *Criterion*, May 1927.
13 Eliot to William Force Stead, 7 February 1927. Beinecke.
14 In 'American Literature and the American Language'.
15 Eliot quoted in *Affectionately, T. S. Eliot. The Story of a Friendship* by William Turner Levy and Victor Scherle. London, 1968.
16 Quoted in Howarth.
17 Quoted in Soldo.
18 Valerie Eliot, quoted in *T. S. Eliot*

by Stephen Spender. London, 1975.

19 Henry Eliot, quoted in *Eliot's Early Years* by Lyndall Gordon. Oxford, 1977.

20 Quoted in Howarth.

21 Quoted in Soldo.

22 *ibid.*

23 Eliot quoted in *T. S. Eliot: a memoir* by Joseph Chiari. London, 1982.

24 Abigail Eliot in *The Mysterious Mr Eliot*, January 1971.

25 Quoted in Soldo.

26 Letter from Eliot in the *St Louis Post Dispatch*, 16 February 1964.

27 *Criterion*, August 1927.

28 *Dial*, May 1927.

29 From 'Virgil and The Christian World', BBC broadcast 9 September 1951.

30 Abigail Eliot in *The Mysterious Mr Eliot*, January 1971.

31 Thomas H. McKittrick to H. W. H. Powel, 19 June 1953. Brown.

32 Address to the Mary Institute, 1 November 1959.

33 Eliot to Herbert Read, 15 September 1932. Victoria.

34 In Soldo.

35 In H. W. H. Powel's unpublished master's essay, *Notes on the Life of T. S. Eliot, 1888–1910* (Brown University, 1954). Hereinafter referred to as Powel.

36 In *The Use of Poetry and The Use of Criticism*. London, 1933.

37 Quoted in Levy.

38 Quoted in Chiari.

39 *Daedalus*, spring 1960.

40 Quoted in *The Achievement of T. S. Eliot* by F. O. Matthiessen. London, 1935.

41 In *A Book About Myself* by Theodore Dreiser. London, 1929.

42 Eliot to Patricia Hutchins, undated. Department of Manuscripts, British Library.

43 Eliot to Herbert Read, 'St George's Day' 1928. Victoria.

44 From 'Indiscretions' by Ezra Pound, published in twelve issues of *The New Age* in 1920.

45 Thomas H. McKittrick to H. W. H. Powel, 19 June 1953. Brown.

46 Mr Hayward to H. W. H. Powel, 2 November 1953. Brown.

47 In 'American Literature and the American Language'.

48 In *T. S. Eliot: a symposium*, edited by Richard March and Tambimuttu. London, 1948.

49 In Soldo.

50 Eliot speaking in 'Personal Anthology', November 1943. BBC sound archives.

51 *The Use of Poetry and The Use of Criticism*. London, 1933.

52 Eliot speaking in 'Personal Choice', 30 December 1957. BBC sound archives.

53 *The Use of Poetry and The Use of Criticism*.

54 Interview with Eliot in the *Paris Review*, spring-summer, 1959.

55 Eliot quoted in the preface to *Poems Written In Early Youth*. London, 1967.

56 *ibid.*

57 Charlotte Eliot to Richard Cobb, March 1905. Quoted in Soldo.

58 *ibid.*

59 Eliot to Herbert Read, 'St George's Day', 1928. Victoria.

60 Preface to *This American World* by Edgar Ansel Mowrer. London, 1928.

61 Address to Milton Academy, 17 June 1933.

62 *The Listener*, 6 April 1932.

63 Quoted in Soldo.

64 *ibid.*

CHAPTER 2

1 Frederick May Eliot quoted in Powel.
2 *ibid*.
3 Conrad Aiken in March and Tambimuttu collection.
4 Phineas Henry to H. W. H. Powel, 20 January 1953. Brown.
5 Conrad Aiken in *Life*, 15 January 1965.
6 Eliot quoted in *The Composition of 'Four Quartets'* by Helen Gardner. London, 1978.
7 Dr Allen Gregg quoted in Powel.
8 Harvard *Advocate*, June 1938.
9 Quoted in Howarth.
10 Ezra Pound to Harriet Monroe, 30 September 1914. In *The Letters of Ezra Pound, 1907–1941*, edited by D. D. Paige. London, 1951.
11 Preface to *This American World* by Edgar Ansel Mowrer. London, 1928.
12 In *John Jay Chapman and his Letters* by M. A. DeWolfe Howe. Boston, 1937.
13 Quoted in *Copey of Harvard: a biography of Charles Townsend Copeland* by J. Donald Adams. Boston, 1960.
14 In *New English Weekly*, 31 October 1946.
15 Wireless talk by Eliot in April, 1947. BBC sound archives.
16 Preface to *John Davidson: A Selection of His Poems*. London, 1961.
17 From 'What Dante Means To Me', a talk delivered at the Italian Institute on 4 July, 1950.
18 *Criterion*, January 1930.
19 'What Dante Means To Me'.
20 Eliot quoted in *T. S. Eliot: a Memoir* by Robert Sencourt, edited by Donald Adamson. London, 1974.
21 Quoted in Powel.

22 Conrad Aiken in March and Tambimuttu collection.
23 *Criterion*, October 1933.
24 Stephen Spender in *T. S. Eliot: the Man and His Work*, edited by Allen Tate. London, 1967.
25 Stravinsky in *Esquire*, August 1965.
26 Eliot to Conrad Aiken, 25 February 1915. Huntington.
27 In *New England: Indian Summer*, by Van Wyck Brooks. New York, 1940.
28 *Athenaeum*, 23 May 1919.
29 *ibid*.
30 Quoted in *T. S. Eliot et La France* by E. J. H. Greene. Paris, 1951.
31 Charlotte Eliot quoted in *Eliot's Early Years* by Lyndall Gordon. Oxford, 1977.
32 *Paris Review* interview.
33 *Criterion*, April 1934.
34 A Sermon, preached in Magdalen College Chapel on 7 March 1948.
35 Eliot to Eudo Mason, 19 April 1945. Texas.
36 *Criterion*, October 1927.
37 Preface of *For Lancelot Andrewes*. London, 1928.
38 *Criterion*, April 1934.
39 Dr André Schlemmer, quoted in 'Quest For a Frenchman' by George Watson. *Sewanee Review*. Vol 84. 1976.
40 Eliot to Ottoline Morrell. Undated but on *Egoist* notepaper. Texas.
41 Gluyas Williams to H. W. H. Powel, 15 December. Brown.
42 Quoted in *Being Geniuses Together, 1920–1930*, by Robert McAlmon and Kay Boyle. London, 1970.
43 In *International Journal of Ethics*, October 1916.
44 Eliot to Conrad Aiken, 31 December 1914. Huntington.

45 Preface to *Bubu of Montparnasse*, by Charles-Louis Philippe. London, 1932.
46 Referred to in Lyndall Gordon.
47 Eliot to *The Times Literary Supplement*, 3 June 1960.
48 'Hamlet and His Problems' reprinted in *The Sacred Wood*. London, 1920.
49 Eliot to Conrad Aiken, 31 December 1914. Huntington.
50 Henry Ware Eliot to Thomas Lamb Eliot, 4 March 1914. Quoted in Soldo.
51 Conrad Aiken to Harriet Monroe, 4 September 1915. In the *Selected Letters of Conrad Aiken*, edited by Joseph Killorin. New Haven, 1978.
52 *Paris Review* interview.
53 Quoted in *Ushant, an essay* by Conrad Aiken. Boston, 1952.
54 Conrad Aiken quoting Eliot back at him, March 1913. In *Selected Letters*.
55 *Ushant, an essay*.
56 Conrad Aiken to Eliot, 23 February 1913. In *Selected Letters*.
57 Eliot to Conrad Aiken, 30 September 1914. Huntington.
58 In *After Strange Gods*. London, 1934.
59 Eliot to Rayner Heppenstall, 11 March 1935. Texas.
60 *Athenaeum*, 23 May 1919.
61 Quoted in *Josiah Royce's Seminar, 1913–1914*. Edited by Grover Smith. New Jersey, 1963.
62 *Essays on Truth and Reality*, by F. H. Bradley. Oxford, 1914.
63 *F. H. Bradley* by Richard Wollheim. London, 1959.
64 Quoted in *Poetry and Belief in The Work of T. S. Eliot*, by Kristian Smidt. London, 1961.
65 Bertrand Russell to Ottoline Morrell 27 March 1914. In *Autobiogra-phy* by Bertrand Russell, London 1968.
66 In *Autobiography* by Bertrand Russell.
67 *ibid*.
68 *The Diaries of Virginia Woolf*, 20 September 1920. Volume Two, London, 1978.
69 They are now in the Berg Collection of New York Public Library.
70 Eliot to Paul Elmer More, 'Shrove Tuesday' 1928. Princeton.

CHAPTER 3

1 Eliot to Conrad Aiken, 19 July 1914. Huntington.
2 *ibid*.
3 Eliot to Conrad Aiken, 25 July 1914. Huntington.
4 In *Ushant, an essay*.
5 Eliot to Conrad Aiken, 30 September 1914. Huntington.
6 In *Ushant, an essay*.
7 Ezra Pound to William Carlos Williams, 11 September 1920. In *Letters*.
8 *Paris Review* interview with Eliot.
9 Ezra Pound to Harriet Monroe, 30 September 1914. In *Letters*.
10 Eliot to Conrad Aiken, 30 September 1914. Huntington.
11 In *Blasting and Bombadiering* by Wyndham Lewis. London, 1937.
12 Eliot to Conrad Aiken, 30 September, 1914. Huntington.
13 Eliot to Conrad Aiken, 16 November 1914. Huntington.
14 In *Postmaster* (Merton College), December 1959.
15 Eliot to the Hon. Sec. of Merton College, 24 June 1963. Merton College Library.
16 *ibid*.
17 Eliot to Conrad Aiken, 31 December 1914. Huntington.

18 *ibid.*

19 *Yale Review*, Summer 1965.

20 Eliot to Conrad Aiken, 25 February 1915. Huntington.

21 Eliot to Ezra Pound, 2 February 1915. Beinecke.

22 Ezra Pound to Harriet Monroe, 10 April 1915. In *Letters*.

23 Ezra Pound to John Quinn, 24 March 1920. Quinn Collection, housed in the Manuscript Division of the New York Public Library. Hereinafter referred to as 'Quinn Collection'.

24 The diary of Vivien Eliot, 28 July 1935. Bodleian.

25 Unpublished memoir of T. S. Eliot, by Osbert Sitwell. Texas.

26 Maurice Haigh-Wood, in conversation with Michael Hastings. I am greatly indebted to Michael Hastings for showing me the records of these conversations.

27 Abigail Eliot in *The Mysterious Mr Eliot*. BBC.

28 Osbert Sitwell's memoir. Texas.

29 All Vivien Eliot's diaries and personal papers are held in the Bodleian.

30 Bertrand Russell to Ottoline Morrell, July 1915. *Autobiography*.

31 Maurice Haigh-Wood in conversation with Michael Hastings.

32 Eliot to Conrad Aiken, 25 February 1915. Huntington.

33 Eliot to Conrad Aiken, 21 November 1914. Huntington.

34 Aldous Huxley to Ottoline Morrell, 21 June 1917. Quoted in *Ottoline at Garsington*, edited by Robert Gathorne-Hardy.

35 Bertrand Russell to Ottoline Morrell, '1916'. *Autobiography*.

36 Maurice Haigh-Wood, in conversation with Michael Hastings.

37 Ezra Pound to Henry Ware Eliot, 28 June 1915. Beinecke.

38 Bertrand Russell to Ottoline Morrell, July 1915. *Autobiography*.

39 Charlotte Eliot to Thomas Lamb Eliot, 7 March 1923. Quoted in Soldo.

40 Charlotte Eliot to Henry Eliot, 10 November 1918. Missouri Historical Society.

41 Bertrand Russell's *Autobiography*.

42 Quoted by Stephen Spender in Tate collection.

43 Bertrand Russell's *Autobiography*.

44 Eliot to Bertrand Russell, 11 September 1915. McMaster.

45 Maurice Haigh-Wood in conversation with Michael Hastings.

46 Bertrand Russell's *Autobiography*.

47 Address to Milton Academy, 17 June 1933.

48 *ibid.*

49 Eliot to Henry Ware Eliot, 10 September 1915. Quoted in *The Waste Land: a facsimile and transcript of the original drafts*, edited by Valerie Eliot. London, 1971.

50 Eliot to Bertrand Russell, undated but 'January 11 1916' postmark. McMaster.

51 Bertrand Russell to Ottoline Morrell, 10 November 1915. *Autobiography*.

52 Eliot to Bertrand Russell. 'Friday'. McMaster.

53 Address to Milton Academy, 17 June 1933.

54 Eliot quoted in Levy and Scherle.

55 Sir John Betjeman recorded in BBC sound archives.

56 Eliot to Bertrand Russell, 11 October 1915. McMaster.

57 Eliot to Conrad Aiken, 21 August 1916. Huntington.

58 Quoted by Stephen Spender in Tate collection.
59 Charlotte Eliot to Bertrand Russell, 23 May 1916. *Autobiography*.
60 Vivien Eliot to Richard Aldington, undated but written from 9 Clarence Gate Gardens. Texas.
61 Eliot to Henry Ware Eliot, 1 March 1917. *The Waste Land* facsimile.
62 Eliot to Conrad Aiken, 10 January 1916. *The Waste Land* facsimile. And Eliot to Henry Eliot, 6 September 1916. *The Waste Land* facsimile.
63 William Tinckom-Fernandez to H. W. H. Powel, 28 November 1952. Brown.
64 Ezra Pound to Harriet Shaw Weaver, 4 April 1916. British Library.
65 Eliot to Henry Eliot, 6 September 1916. *The Waste Land* facsimile.
66 Maurice Haigh-Wood in conversation with Michael Hastings.
67 Extracts from letter quoted in Sotheby's 'Catalogue of Nineteenth Century and Modern Autograph Letters', for sale on 4 December 1973.
68 Ezra Pound to Henry Ware Eliot, 28 June 1915. Beinecke.
69 'March 1916', quoted in *Ottoline at Garsington*, edited by Robert Gathorne-Hardy.
70 Aldous Huxley to Julian Huxley, 19 December 1916. *Selected Letters of Aldous Huxley*, edited by Grover Smith. London, 1969.
71 Minutes of the Board To Promote the Extension of University Teaching. Palaeography Room, University of London Library.
72 Minutes of the Joint Committee for the Promotion of the Higher Education of Working People.

Palaeography Room, University of London Library.
73 Quoted in 'Eliot and Hulme in 1916' by Ronald Schuchard. *PMLA*, October 1973.
74 *Speculations: Essays in Humanism and the philosophy of art* by T. E. Hulme, edited by Herbert Read. London, 1924.
75 Eliot to Emily Hale, 6 October 1930. Princeton.
76 Eliot to Charles Maurras, 27 January 1928. Texas.

CHAPTER 4

1 Eliot to Charlotte Eliot, 11 April 1917. *The Waste Land* facsimile.
2 Eliot to J. C. Squire, 29 March 1917. Texas.
3 Eliot to Charlotte Eliot, 11 April 1917. *The Waste Land* facsimile.
4 Harvey Kershaw to J. R. Winton. Archives of Lloyds Bank.
5 L. W. Freeman to J. R. Winton. Archives of Lloyds Bank.
6 M. A. Evelyn Cotterell to J. R. Winton. Archives of Lloyds Bank.
7 *ibid*.
8 Referred to in *Criterion*, December 1928.
9 Eliot quoted in *Columbia University Forum*, 28 April 1958.
10 Conrad Aiken in the *Dial*, 8 November 1917.
11 *Paris Review* interview.
12 Eliot to Mary Hutchinson, 2 July 1917. Texas.
13 *Paris Review* interview.
14 Ezra Pound to Harriet Monroe, 21 August 1917. *Letters*.
15 Ezra Pound to Margaret Anderson, August (?) 1917. *Letters*.
16 Ezra Pound to Harriet Monroe, 26 August 1917. *Letters*.
17 Eliot quoted in Levy and Scherle.
18 Quoted in 'Bertrand Russell and

the Eliots' by Robert H. Bell. *The American Scholar*, summer 1983.

19 Vivien Eliot to Ottoline Morrell, undated. Texas.

20 Eliot to Ottoline Morrell, 14 March 1933. Texas.

21 Virginia Woolf Diaries, 22 March 1921. Volume Two.

22 Quoted in *Ottoline at Garsington*, edited by Robert Gathorne-Hardy.

23 Maurice Haigh-Wood in conversation with Michael Hastings.

24 Quoted in Osbert Sitwell's unpublished memoir. Texas.

25 *My Friends When Young: the memoirs of Brigit Patmore*, edited by Derek Patmore, London 1968.

26 Eliot to Henry Ware Eliot, 23 December 1917. *The Waste Land* facsimile.

27 Eliot to John Quinn, 4 March 1918. Quinn Collection.

28 Quoted in *Aldous Huxley: a Biography* by Sybille Bedford. London, 1973–4.

29 Eliot to John Quinn, 4 March 1918. Quinn Collection.

30 Eliot to John Quinn, 8 September 1918. Quinn Collection.

31 Eliot to Charlotte Eliot, 9 June 1918. *The Waste Land* facsimile.

32 Aldous Huxley to Julian Huxley, 28 June 1918. *Selected Letters*.

33 Eliot to John Quinn, 13 November 1918. Quinn Collection.

34 Eliot to John Quinn, 13 November 1918. Quinn Collection.

35 *Egoist*, January 1918.

36 *Egoist*, September, 1918.

37 Eliot to Sidney Schiff, undated. British Library.

38 *Athenaeum*, 25 April 1919.

39 *Criterion*, April 1923.

40 *Life Is My Song*, by John Gould Fletcher. New York, 1937.

41 *The Little Review*, August 1918.

42 *Egoist*, December 1917.

43 *Life for Life's Sake*, by Richard Aldington. New York, 1941.

44 Eliot to Ezra Pound, 31 October 1917. Beinecke.

45 Undated notes, now at the Humanities Research Centre, Texas.

46 *Laughter in The Next Room*, by Osbert Sitwell. Volume 4 of his memoirs. London, 1949.

47 Unpublished memoir by Osbert Sitwell, Texas.

48 *The Diaries of Virginia Woolf*, 15 November 1918. Volume One.

49 Virginia Woolf to Roger Fry, 18 November 1918. Volume Two of *The Letters of Virginia Woolf*. London, 1976.

50 *Beginning Again* and *Downhill All The Way* by Leonard Woolf. London, 1964 and 1967.

51 Eliot to Charlotte Eliot, 22 December 1918. *The Waste Land* facsimile.

52 Ezra Pound to John Quinn, 27 December 1918. Quinn Collection.

53 Eliot to Henry Ware Eliot, 23 December 1917. *The Waste Land* facsimile.

CHAPTER 5

1 Eliot to John Quinn, 6 January 1919. Quinn Collection.

2 Unpublished memoir by Osbert Sitwell, Texas.

3 John Lane to John Quinn, early August 1919. Quoted in *The Waste Land* facsimile.

4 Eliot to Mary Hutchinson, undated. Texas.

5 Eliot to Helen Gardner, 20 October 1956. Bodleian.

6 *The Monist*, October 1916.

7 *The Waste Land* facsimile.

8 Eliot to Mary Hutchinson, 4 April 1919. Texas.

9 Eliot to Virginia Woolf, 12 April 1919. Berg.

10 The unpublished memoir of Osbert Sitwell, Texas.

11 The unpublished memoir of Osbert Sitwell, Texas.

12 *Athenaeum*, 30 May 1919.

13 Correspondence between Eliot and Lytton Strachey quoted in *Lytton Strachey : a biography*, by Michael Holroyd. London, 1971.

14 Eliot to Charlotte Eliot, 29 March 1919. *The Waste Land* facsimile.

15 Quoted in *Lytton Strachey: a biography* by Michael Holroyd.

16 *Athenaeum*, 25 April 1919.

17 Virginia Woolf to Duncan Grant, 17 April 1919. Volume Two of *The Letters of Virginia Woolf*. London, 1976.

18 Eliot to Harriet Shaw Weaver, 5 June 1919. British Library.

19 Ezra Pound to John Quinn, August 1919. Quinn Collection.

20 Eliot to Mary Hutchinson, 6 August 1919. Texas.

21 Eliot to Henry Eliot, 14 September 1919. *The Waste Land* facsimile.

22 The diary of Vivien Eliot, 31 August 1919. Bodleian Library, Oxford

23 *Life for Life's Sake* by Richard Aldington.

24 Conrad Aiken to Jessie Aiken, 10 June 1920 in *Selected Letters*.

25 Eliot to Ezra Pound, '30 Maggio' 1920. Beinecke.

26 Eliot to Sidney Schiff, 12 January 1920. British Library.

27 Eliot to John Quinn, 26 March 1920. Quinn Collection.

28 I. A. Richards in Tate collection.

29 *ibid*.

30 Eliot to Charlotte Eliot, 15 February 1920. *The Waste Land* facsimile.

31 Eliot to John Quinn, 10 May 1920. Quinn Collection.

32 Eliot to John Quinn, 9 May 1921. Quinn Collection.

33 Ezra Pound to John Quinn, June 1920. Quinn Collection.

34 Eliot to John Quinn, 25 January 1920. Quinn Collection.

35 *ibid*.

36 Eliot to Wyndham Lewis, 'Saturday'. Cornell.

37 Eliot to Mary Hutchinson, 20 September 1920. Texas.

38 Eliot to Sidney Schiff, 22 August 1920. British Library.

39 *Blasting and Bombadiering*, by Wyndham Lewis.

40 Eliot to Sidney Schiff, 22 August 1920. British Library.

41 Eliot to Wyndham Lewis, 15 October 1920. Cornell.

42 Eliot to Wyndham Lewis, 18 October 1920. Cornell.

43 Among Vivien Eliot's papers in the Bodleian.

44 Wyndham Lewis to Sidney Schiff, 2 May 1922. British Library.

45 Eliot to Leonard Woolf, 23 October 1920. Berg.

46 Eliot to Mary Hutchinson, 28 September 1920. Texas.

47 Eliot to Sidney Schiff, 30 November 1920. British Library.

48 Eliot to Sidney Schiff, 6 December 1920. British Library.

49 Eliot to Sidney Schiff, 30 November 1920. British Library.

50 *The Diaries of Virginia Woolf*, 20 September 1920. Volume Two, London 1978.

51 *The Diaries of Virginia Woolf*, 5 December 1920. Volume Two, London 1978.

52 Eliot to Richard Aldington, 16 September 1921. Texas.

53 Eliot to Leonard Woolf, 26 December 1920. Berg.

54 Eliot to John Quinn, 9 May 1921. Quinn Collection.

55 Quoted in Lyndall Gordon.

56 *The Diaries of Virginia Woolf*, 16 February 1921. Volume Two.

57 Eliot to John Gould Fletcher, 23 September 1920. Arkansas.

58 Conrad Aiken to Jessie Aiken, 10 June 1920. *Selected Letters*.

59 *The Diaries of Virginia Woolf*, 5 December 1920. Volume Two.

60 Eliot to Mary Hutchinson, 20 September 1920. Texas.

61 *The Use of Poetry and The Use of Criticism*. London, 1933.

62 The diaries of Vivien Eliot, 25 December 1934. Bodleian.

63 In *Studies in Hand-Reading* by Charlotte Wolff. London, 1936.

64 Conrad Aiken in Tate collection. Aiken dates this incident to the winter of 1921–2, but it is more probable that it took place earlier in the year.

CHAPTER 6

1 *Being Geniuses Together*, by Robert McAlmon and Kay Boyle.

2 In *Lytton Strachey: a biography*, by Michael Holroyd.

3 Ezra Pound to Wyndham Lewis, 27 April 1921. *Selected Letters*.

4 Eliot to Richard Aldington, 7 April 1921. Texas.

5 Wyndham Lewis to Sidney Schiff, 7 February 1921. British Library.

6 *The Diaries of Virginia Woolf*, 22 March 1921. Volume Two.

7 Eliot to John Quinn, 9 May 1921. Quinn collection.

8 *Life for Life's Sake* by Richard Aldington.

9 Eliot to Henry Eliot, 15 February 1920. *The Waste Land* facsimile.

10 Osbert Sitwell's unpublished memoir, Texas.

11 Eliot to Richard Aldington, 6 July 1921. Texas.

12 Eliot to Ottoline Morrell, 14 July 1921. Texas.

13 Eliot to James Joyce, 12 May 1921. Texas.

14 *Dial*, November 1923.

15 *Dial*, August 1921.

16 Eliot to Sidney Schiff, 25 August 1921. British Library.

17 Eliot to Mary Hutchinson, 1 September 1921. Texas.

18 Eliot to John Quinn, 21 September 1922. Quinn Collection.

19 Eliot to Richard Aldington, possibly 3 October, 1921. Texas.

20 Vivien Eliot to Sidney Schiff, 26 October 1921. British Library.

21 Eliot to Sidney Schiff, early November 1921. British Library.

22 *ibid*.

23 *ibid*.

24 Eliot to Richard Aldington, 6 November 1921. Texas.

25 Eliot to Ottoline Morrell, 30 November 1921. Texas.

26 Eliot to Mary Hutchinson, 4 (?) December, 1921. Texas.

27 Eliot to Henry Eliot, 13 December 1921. *The Waste Land* facsimile.

28 Eliot to Ottoline Morrell, 30 November 1921. Texas.

29 *Paris Review* interview with Eliot.

30 Eliot to Ezra Pound, January 1922? *Selected Letters*.

31 *New York Times*, 21 September 1958.

32 'Andrew Marvell' in *The Times Literary Supplement*, 31 March 1921.

33 Entry for 30 March, 1922 in Siegfried Sassoon's *Diaries, 1920–*

1922, edited and introduced by Rupert Hart-Davis. London, 1981.

34 *The Diaries of Virginia Woolf*, 26 September 1922. Volume Two.

35 Eliot to Paul Elmer More, 20 July 1934. Princeton.

36 Paper to the Harvard Philosophical Club, 1913–14.

37 Ezra Pound to James Laughlin, 5 (?) January 1936. *Selected Letters*.

38 Eliot to John Quinn, 25 May 1922. Quinn Collection.

39 *The Diaries of Virginia Woolf*, 12 March 1922. Volume Two.

40 *The Diaries of Virginia Woolf*, 12 March 1922. Volume Two.

41 Eliot to Ezra Pound, January 1922? *Selected Letters*.

42 Eliot to Wyndham Lewis, 16 March 1922. Cornell.

43 Eliot to Sidney Schiff, 20 April 1922. British Library.

44 Richard Aldington to Ezra Pound, quoted in *The Waste Land* facsimile.

45 Ezra Pound to William Carlos Williams, 18 March 1922. *Selected Letters*.

46 The Bel Esprit prospectus quoted in Ezra Pound's *Selected Letters*.

47 Eliot to Richard Aldington, 30 June 1922. Texas.

48 Vivien Eliot to Richard Aldington, undated. Texas.

49 Eliot to Ottoline Morrell, undated. Texas.

50 Eliot to Richard Aldington, 17 May 1922. Texas.

51 Eliot to Virginia Woolf, 1 July 1922. Sussex.

52 Eliot to Sturge Moore, 3 April 1922. Texas.

53 Vivien Eliot to Ottoline Morrell, undated. Texas.

54 In *The Voyage Home* by Richard Church. London, 1964.

55 Eliot to Sturge Moore, 3 April 1922. Texas.

56 Eliot to Richard Aldington, 13 July 1922. Texas.

57 Vivien Eliot to Richard Aldington, undated. Texas.

58 Eliot to Richard Aldington, 13 July 1922. Texas.

59 Eliot to Ford Madox Ford, 2 February 1923. Cornell.

60 Entry for 6 May 1922 in Sassoon's *Diaries*.

61 Eliot to Wyndham Lewis, 26 September 1923. Cornell.

62 Charlotte Eliot to Thomas Lamb Eliot, 7 March 1923. Quoted in Soldo.

63 *ibid*.

64 In Eliot's contribution to *Freundesgabe für Ernst Robert Curtius*, edited by Max Rychner. Bern, 1956.

65 Eliot to Alfred Knopf, 3 April 1922. Texas.

66 Eliot to John Quinn, 21 September 1922. Quinn Collection.

67 'The Frontiers of Criticism', reprinted in *On Poetry and Poets*. London, 1957.

68 *The Autobiography of William Carlos Williams*. London, 1968.

69 *New Republic*, 7 February 1923.

70 Eliot to Ford Madox Ford, 4 October 1923. Cornell.

71 Edmund Wilson to John Peale Bishop, 22 September 1922. *Letters on Literature and Politics, 1912–72*, edited by Elena Wilson. London 1977.

72 Cyril Connolly in the *Sunday Times*, 10 January 1965.

73 *New Statesman* 8 November 1930.

74 I. A. Richards in *The Mysterious Mr Eliot*, BBC production.

75 Virginia Woolf to Ottoline Morrell, 6 August 1922. *The Letters*

of Virginia Woolf. Volume Two.

76 Virginia Woolf to Ottoline Morrell, 25 September 1922. *The Letters of Virginia Woolf.* Volume Two.

77 Virginia Woolf to Roger Fry, 22 October 1922. *The Letters of Virginia Woolf.* Volume Two.

78 Conrad Aiken to G. B. Wilbur, 26 September 1922. *Selected Letters.*

79 Eliot to Ottoline Morrell, undated. Texas.

80 Prefatory notes to *The Collected Poems of Harold Monro.* London, 1933.

81 Eliot to Virginia Woolf, 30 September 1922. Berg.

82 Ezra Pound to John Quinn, 4–5 July, 1922. Quinn Collection.

83 Vivien Eliot to Richard Aldington, undated. Texas.

84 Vivien Eliot to Sidney Schiff, October. British Library.

85 Eliot to Virginia Woolf, 4 December 1922. Berg.

86 Eliot to Wyndham Lewis, 8 December 1922. Cornell.

87 Eliot to Virginia Woolf, 4 December 1922. Berg.

88 Eliot to John Gould Fletcher, 29 January 1923. Arkansas.

89 In *festschrift* for Ernst Robert Curtius.

CHAPTER 7

1 Eliot to Ottoline Morrell, 5 January 1923. Texas.

2 Virginia Woolf to Maynard Keynes, 12 February 1923. *The Letters of Virginia Woolf.* Volume Three.

3 *The Diaries of Virginia Woolf,* 19 February 1923. Volume Two.

4 Vivien Eliot to Mary Hutchinson, 4 March 1923. Bodleian.

5 Described in *Façades: Edith,*

Osbert and Sacheverell Sitwell by John Pearson. London, 1978.

6 *The Diaries of Virginia Woolf,* 6 March 1923. Volume Two.

7 Address to Milton Academy, 17 June 1933.

8 Eliot to John Quinn, 4 October 1923. Quinn Collection.

9 Eliot to John Gould Fletcher, 29 January 1923. Arkansas.

10 *The Diaries of Virginia Woolf,* 17 March 1923. Volume Two.

11 Eliot to John Quinn, 26 April 1923. Quinn Collection.

12 Eliot to Mary Hutchinson, 27 April 1923. Texas.

13 Vivien Eliot to Virginia Woolf, 27 April 1923. Sussex.

14 Eliot to John Quinn, 26 April 1923. Quinn Collection.

15 *The Diaries of Virginia Woolf,* 17 July 1923. Volume Two.

16 Vivien Eliot to Virginia Woolf, 27 April 1923. Sussex.

17 Vivien Eliot to Virginia Woolf, 13 June 1923. Sussex.

18 Eliot to Mary Hutchinson, 27 April 1923. Texas.

19 Eliot to Leonard Woolf, 27 May 1923. Berg.

20 Eliot to Richard Aldington, 15 November 1922. *The Waste Land* facsimile.

21 Eliot to John Quinn, 26 April 1923. Quinn Collection.

22 Eliot to Wyndham Lewis, 26 September 1923. Cornell.

23 Virginia Woolf to Roger Fry, 18 May 1923. *The Letters of Virginia Woolf.* Volume Three.

24 Entry of 30 March, 1922 in Sassoon's *Diaries.*

25 Conrad Aiken to R. N. Linscott, 20 June 1923. *Selected Letters.*

26 Eliot to Mary Hutchinson, undated. Texas.

27 Osbert Sitwell's unpublished memoir, Texas.
28 Quoted in *Façades* by John Pearson.
29 *The Diaries of Virginia Woolf*, 27 September 1922. Volume Two.
30 Clive Bell to Vanessa Bell, 11 March 1922. I am indebted to Mr Richard Shone for this information.
31 'Rhetoric and Poetic Drama', in *The Sacred Wood*, London, 1920.
32 *The Diaries of Virginia Woolf*, 19 December 1923. Volume Two.
33 In *Elizabeth Bowen: Portrait of a Writer* by Victoria Glendinning. London, 1977.
34 *The Diaries of Virginia Woolf*, 19 December 1932. Volume Two.
35 William Force Stead in the *Alumnae Journal of Trinity College*, Winter 1965.
36 Eliot to Virginia Woolf, 7 April 1924. Berg.
37 *Athenaeum*, 28 November 1919.
38 *The Times Literary Supplement*, 31 March 1921.
39 *Criterion*, April 1924.
40 *Dial*, June 1921.
41 Anne Ridler in conversation with the present author.
42 'The Function of Criticism' in *Criterion*, October 1923.
43 Requiem Address for Eliot at Church of St Stephen, 17 February 1965.
44 Eliot to Wyndham Lewis, 24 February 1924. Cornell.
45 Eliot to Ottoline Morrell, undated. Texas.
46 Eliot to Leonard Woolf, 1 May 1924. Berg.
47 Vivien Eliot to Sidney Schiff, March 1924. British Library.
48 Eliot to Richard Aldington, undated. Texas.
49 Vivien Eliot to Sidney Schiff, 31 March 1924. British Library.
50 Held in the Bodleian.
51 The diaries of Vivien Eliot, 27 March 1935. Bodleian.
52 *Criterion*, January 1925.
53 Eliot to Virginia Woolf, 7 April 1924. Berg.
54 Quoted in *Hugh Walpole* by Rupert Hart-Davis. London, 1963.
55 Quoted in *The Third Rose* by John Malcolm Brinnin. London, 1960.
56 Eliot to Wyndham Lewis, undated. Cornell.
57 *Ushant, an essay* by Conrad Aiken.
58 Eliot to Richard Aldington, 18 February 1926 and undated. Texas.
59 Eliot to Herbert Read, 18 October 1924. Victoria.
60 Eliot to Herbert Read, undated but presumably October 1924. Victoria.
61 Eliot to Ford Madox Ford, 2 February 1923. Cornell.
62 In Howarth.
63 Virginia Woolf to Elizabeth Bowen, 29 January 1939. *The Letters of Virginia Woolf*. Volume Six.
64 Herbert Read in Tate collection.
65 Eliot to Herbert Read, undated but presumably October 1924. Cornell.
66 Eliot quoted by Read in Tate collection.
67 Charlotte Eliot to Thomas Lamb Eliot, 7 March 1923. Quoted in Soldo.
68 Eliot to Virginia Woolf, 27 August 1924. Texas.
69 *ibid*.
70 *ibid*.
71 *The Diaries of Virginia Woolf*, 5 May 1924. Volume Two.
72 Eliot to Virginia Woolf, 27 August 1924. Texas.

73 Entry of 10 September, from *The Journals of Arnold Bennett,* edited by Newman Flower. London, 1932-33.

74 *Nation and Athenaeum,* 6 October 1923.

75 Eliot in *Columbia University Forum,* 28 April, 1958.

76 Eliot to Paul Elmer More, 28 April 1936. Princeton.

77 Letter from F. T. Prince to the present author.

78 Eliot to Virginia Woolf, 22 May 1924. Berg.

79 Eliot to Ottoline Morrell, 30 November 1924. Texas.

80 Interview in the *New York Times,* 29 November 1953.

81 Ezra Pound to Simon Guggenheim, 24 February 1925. *Selected Letters.*

82 Eliot to Virginia Woolf, 4 February 1925. Texas.

83 Eliot to Ottoline Morrell, 20 February 1925. Texas

CHAPTER 8

1 Eliot to Virginia Woolf, April 1925. Texas.

2 The diaries of Vivien Eliot, 24 November 1934. Bodleian.

3 Eliot to Mary Hutchinson, 3 April 1925. Texas.

4 Eliot in conversation with Virginia Woolf, quoted in *The Diaries of Virginia Woolf,* 29 April 1925. Volume Three.

5 Eliot to Leonard Woolf, April 1925. Berg

6 In *Autobiography* by Bertrand Russell.

7 Letter to 'Jack' [Hutchinson] placed in Vivien Eliot's diary entry for 8 December 1935. Bodleian.

8 Eliot to Ottoline Morrell, 1 May 1925. Texas.

9 Eliot to Leonard Woolf, May 1925. Berg.

10 Conrad Aiken to Robert Linscott, 4 January 1926. *Selected Letters.*

11 Entry on Geoffrey Faber, written by Charles Monteith, in *The Dictionary of National Biography, 1961–1970.* Oxford, 1981.

12 Frank Morley in March and Tambimuttu collection.

13 *The Diaries of Virginia Woolf,* 30 September 1925. Volume Three.

14 *The Diaries of Virginia Woolf,* 30 September 1925. Volume Three.

15 Eliot to Wyndham Lewis, 4 September 1925. Cornell.

16 Vivien Eliot to Ada Leverson, undated but written in 1926. Berg.

17 Eliot to Leonard Woolf, 17 December 1925. Berg.

18 *Criterion,* January 1939.

19 Eliot to Wyndham Lewis, 9 January 1926. Cornell.

20 *Adelphi,* February–March, 1926.

21 Eliot to Herbert Read, 11 December 1925. Victoria.

22 *ibid.*

23 James Reeves in March and Tambimuttu collection.

24 *The Autobiography of William Carlos Williams.*

25 Vivien Eliot to Ada Leverson, written in 1926. Berg.

26 Vivien Eliot to Ottoline Morrell, 16 April 1926. Texas.

27 *Stravinsky: Chronicle of a Friendship,* by Robert Craft. London, 1972.

28 Maurice Haigh-Wood in conversation with Michael Hastings.

29 In *Façades* by John Pearson.

30 In *T. S. Eliot: a memoir* by Robert Sencourt. Sencourt dates this encounter in June 1927, but Eliot specifically mentions seeing him

in a letter to Herbert Read in September 1926.

31 Eliot to Herbert Read, 11 August 1926. Victoria.

32 Vivien Eliot to Ottoline Morrell, 27 March 1926. Texas.

33 *The Times Literary Supplement*, 23 September 1926.

34 Quoted in Lyndall Gordon.

35 *Criterion*, April 1933.

36 The *Listener*, 9 January 1947.

37 Requiem address at the church of St Stephen, 17 February 1965.

38 *Criterion*, October 1926.

39 Letter to the present author.

40 Stephen Spender in Tate collection.

41 'Religion without Humanism' in *Religion Without Humanism*. New York, 1930.

42 Eliot to William Force Stead, January or February 1927. Beinecke.

43 Maurice Haigh-Wood in conversation with Michael Hastings.

44 Eliot to Virginia Woolf, 2 June 1927. Berg.

45 *Alumnae Journal of Trinity College*, Winter 1965.

46 *ibid*.

47 Introduction to *Savonarola* by Charlotte Eliot. London, 1926.

48 *Dial*, March 1927.

49 Eliot quoted by Hugh Sykes Davies in Tate collection.

50 Paul Elmer More to Austin Warren, 11 August 1929. Quoted in *Paul Elmer More* by Arthur Hazard Dakin.

51 Eliot to Bonamy Dobrée, 12 November 1927. Brotherton.

52 Quoted by Eliot in *The Use of Poetry and The Use of Criticism*. London, 1933.

53 *Time* magazine, 28 November 1927.

54 *The Diaries of Virginia Woolf*, 22 October 1927. Volume Three.

55 *Life and the Dream* by Mary Colum. London, 1947.

56 *Life for Life's Sake*.

57 Hope Mirrlees in 'The Mysterious Mr Eliot', BBC.

58 Eliot to Richard Aldington, 13 December 1927. Texas.

59 Frank Morley in Tate collection.

60 Eliot to Herbert Read, 'Wednesday'. Victoria.

61 Eliot to Herbert Read, 14 January 1928. Victoria.

62 'Wilkie Collins and Dickens' in *The Times Literary Supplement*, 4 August 1927.

63 Eliot to Bertrand Russell, 5 October 1927. McMaster.

64 Quoted in *Façades* by John Pearson.

65 Vivien Eliot to Ottoline Morrell, 31 January 1928. Texas.

66 Virginia Woolf to Vanessa Bell, 7 June 1928. *The Letters of Virginia Woolf*. Volume Three.

67 *ibid*.

68 *Faces in My Time*, by Anthony Powell. Volume Three of his memoirs, 'To Keep The Ball Rolling'. London, 1980.

69 Virginia Woolf to Vanessa Bell, 7 June 1928. *The Letters of Virginia Woolf*. Volume Three.

70 In *Ottoline: the Life of Lady Ottoline Morrell* by Sandra Darroch. London, 1976.

71 Eliot to William Force Stead, 15 March 1928. Beinecke.

72 Eliot to William Force Stead, 10 April 1928. Beinecke.

73 Eliot to Paul Elmer More, 'Shrove Tuesday' 1928. Princeton.

74 *Criterion*, June 1928.

75 Introduction to *The Sacred Wood*.

76 *Criterion*, April 1933.
77 *Criterion*, June 1928.
78 *Criterion*, December 1928.
79 *ibid*.
80 *Thoughts After Lambeth*.
81 Eliot to Paul Elmer More, 3 August 1929. Princeton.
82 Virginia Woolf to Vanessa Bell, 11 February 1928. *The Letters of Virginia Woolf*. Volume Six.
83 Quoted in *T. S. Eliot and Ezra Pound. Collaborators in Letters* by Donald Gallup. New Haven, 1970.
84 Eliot quoted in *Paul Elmer More* by Arthur Hazard Dakin.
85 *Princeton Alumni Weekly*, 5 February 1937
86 Paul Elmer More to Austin Warren, 11 August 1929. Quoted in Dakin.
87 Quoted in 'To Criticize the Critic', reprinted in *To Criticize The Critic and other writings*. London, 1965.
88 Eliot to Ottoline Morrell, 2 October 1928. Texas.
89 *Thoughts After Lambeth*.
90 Eliot to Paul Elmer More, 3 August 1929. Princeton.
91 Quoted by Eliot in *Thoughts After Lambeth*.
92 *Dial*, July 1929.
93 In Howarth.
94 Virginia Woolf to Roger Fry, 16 October 1928. *The Letters of Virginia Woolf*. Volume Six.
95 Eliot to John Gould Fletcher, 6 March 1928. Arkansas.
96 *Paris Review* interview.
97 Virginia Woolf to Roger Fry, 16 October 1928. *The Letters of Virginia Woolf*. Volume Six.
98 *Downhill All The Way* by Leonard Woolf.
99 *The Diaries of Virginia Woolf*, 29 April 1929. Volume Three.
100 Eliot to Virginia Woolf, 2 May 1929. Berg.

CHAPTER 9

1 The diaries of Vivien Eliot, October 1934. Bodleian.
2 *T. S. Eliot: A Memoir* by Joseph Chiari.
3 Eliot to Marianne Moore, 31 October 1934. Philadelphia.
4 Eliot to Paul Elmer More, 3 August 1929. Princeton.
5 Quoted in *A Student's Guide to the Selected Poems of T. S. Eliot* by B. C. Southam. London, 1968.
6 Eliot to Paul Elmer More, 2 June 1930. Princeton.
7 Eliot to William Force Stead, 9 August 1930. Beinecke.
8 The *Listener*, 4 January 1965.
9 Eliot to John Hayward, 27 April 1930. Quoted in Southam.
10 In *The Making of T. S. Eliot's Plays* by E. Martin Browne. London, 1969.
11 Eliot to Paul Elmer More, 2 June 1930. Princeton.
12 Introduction to Baudelaire's *Intimate Journals*, translated by Christopher Isherwood. London, 1930.
13 Eliot to Paul Elmer More, 10 August 1930. Princeton.
14 Paul Elmer More to T. S. Eliot, undated, quoted in Dakin.
15 Quoted in *T. S. Eliot* by Stephen Spender. London, 1975.
16 *ibid*.
17 *Criterion*, January 1932.
18 Frank Morley in March and Tambimuttu collection.
19 Quoted in *W. H. Auden : The Life of a Poet* by Charles Osborne. London, 1980.
20 Eliot to E. McKnight Kauffer, 6 January 1930. Pierpoint Morgan.

21 *The Listener*, 28 April 1977.
22 Quoted by Stephen Spender in Tate collection.
23 Quoted in *W. H. Auden: a Tribute*. London, 1974.
24 Conrad Aiken to Theodore Spencer, 31 October 1930. *Selected Letters*.
25 *The Diaries of Virginia Woolf*, 8 November 1930. Volume Three.
26 Maurice Haigh-Wood in conversation with Michael Hastings.
27 *ibid*.
28 *ibid*.
29 *The Diaries of Virginia Woolf*, 8 November 1930. Volume Three.
30 The Diaries of Harold Nicolson, 2 March 1932. Entry in *The Diaries and Letters* of Harold Nicolson, edited by Nigel Nicolson. London, 1966–68.
31 Eliot to Leonard Woolf, 22 September 1930. Sussex.
32 Quoted in *Façades*, by John Pearson.
33 Herbert Read in Tate collection.
34 In Sencourt.
35 *Dante*. London, 1929.
36 Eliot to George Barker, 24 January 1938. Texas.
37 Richard Aldington to Sidney Schiff, 9 December 1931. British Library.
38 Richard Aldington to Sidney Schiff, 6 August 1931. British Library.
39 In Sencourt.
40 Virginia Woolf to Ethel Smythe, 7 September 1932. *The Letters of Virginia Woolf*. Volume Five.
41 Elizabeth Bowen, quoted in *Elizabeth Bowen: Portrait of a Writer* by Victoria Glendinning.
42 Frank Morley in Tate collection.
43 Stephen Spender in *T. S. Eliot: A Selected Critique*, edited by Leonard Unger. New York, 1948.
44 Interview in *New York Times*, 7 February 1954.
45 Herbert Read in Tate collection.
46 Eliot to Paul Elmer More, 10 August 1930. Princeton.
47 Quoted by Stephen Spender in Tate collection.
48 Vivien Eliot to Ottoline Morrell, 11 December 1931. Texas.
49 Vivien Eliot to Ottoline Morrell, 28 December 1931. Texas.
50 Quoted in Southam.
51 Eliot to Mary Hutchinson, 28 October 1931. Texas.
52 Eliot to Middleton Murry, 29 October 1931. Berg.
53 Quoted in Howarth.

CHAPTER 10

1 Virginia Woolf to Ottoline Morrell, 22 June 1932. *The Letters of Virginia Woolf*. Volume Five.
2 Vivien Eliot to Ottoline Morrell, 4 July 1932. Texas.
3 Incidents quoted in *Façades* by John Pearson.
4 Quoted in *Elizabeth Bowen: Portrait of a Writer* by Victoria Glendinning.
5 In Sencourt.
6 Quoted in *Great Tom: Notes Toward The Definition of T. S. Eliot* by T. S. Matthews. London, 1974.
7 In *Robert Frost: The Years of Triumph* by Laurance Thompson. London, 1971.
8 Harry Levin at a symposium on T. S. Eliot at the University of Kent at Canterbury, 8 May 1983.
9 Eliot to Mary Hutchinson, 29 September 1932. Texas.
10 Quoted by Stephen Spender in Tate collection.

11 Eliot to Ezra Pound '23 Jugglio' 1934. Beinecke.

12 Eliot to the *New English Weekly*, 14 June 1934.

13 Eliot to Richard Aldington, '8 October'. Texas *et al*.

14 Eliot to Virginia Woolf, 5 March 1933. Berg.

15 Quoted in *Some Sort of Epic Grandeur: The Life of F. Scott Fitzgerald* by Matthew J. Bruccoli. London, 1981.

16 Quoted by Eliot to Virginia Woolf, 5 March 1933. Berg.

17 Edmund Wilson to John Dos Passos, 11 May 1933. *Letters in Literature and Politics*.

18 Edmund Wilson to Maxwell Geismar, 27 May 1942. *Letters in Literature and Politics*.

19 Eliot to *New English Weekly*, 14 June 1934.

20 Quoted in *Tributes* by E. H. Gombrich. London, 1984.

21 Quoted in *The Composition of 'Four Quartets'* by Helen Gardner. London, 1978.

22 Eliot to Ottoline Morrell, 9 February 1933. Texas.

23 Quoted in Sencourt.

24 Vivien Eliot to Ottoline Morrell, 9 February 1933. Texas.

25 Eliot to Paul Elmer More, 26 March 1933. Princeton.

26 Abigail Eliot in *The Mysterious Mr Eliot*, BBC.

27 Eliot to Ottoline Morrell, 14 March 1933. Texas.

28 Eliot to Mary Hutchinson, 20 September 1933. Texas.

29 In Sencourt.

30 Vivien Eliot to Ottoline Morrell, 26 December 1933. Texas.

31 Published in *Milton Graduates Bulletin*, 9 November 1933.

32 Virginia Woolf to Elizabeth Bowen, 16 May 1933. *The Letters of Virginia Woolf*. Volume Five.

33 Eliot to Bonamy Dobrée, 'SS Simon and Jude'. Brotherton.

34 Eliot to Ottoline Morrell, 14 March 1933. Texas.

35 Henry Eliot to Christopher Morley, 28 June 1933. Texas.

36 Eliot to Paul Elmer More, 26 March 1933. Princeton.

37 Eliot to Paul Elmer More, 18 May 1933. Princeton.

38 Interview with Valerie Eliot in the *Observer*, 20 February 1972.

39 Eliot to Paul Elmer More, 18 May 1933. Princeton.

40 In conversation with the present author.

41 Frank Morley in Tate collection.

42 Eliot to Virginia Woolf, 16 August 1933. Berg.

43 James Eames in *The Mysterious Mr Eliot*, BBC.

44 Eliot to Ottoline Morrell, 9 August 1933. Texas.

45 *The Diaries of Virginia Woolf*, 2 September 1933. Volume Four.

46 Eliot to Ottoline Morrell, 27 December 1933. Texas.

47 Virginia Woolf to Frances Birrell, 3 September 1933. *The Letters of Virginia Woolf*. Volume Five.

48 Vivien Eliot to Ottoline Morrell, 7 July 1933. Texas.

49 *The Diaries of Virginia Woolf*, 10 July 1933. Volume Four.

50 *The Diaries of Virginia Woolf*, 21 July 1933. Volume Four.

51 Eliot to Mary Hutchinson, 13 July 1933. Texas.

52 Virginia Woolf to Quentin Bell, 26 July 1933. *The Letters of Virginia Woolf*. Volume Five.

53 Maurice Haigh-Wood in conversation with Michael Hastings.

54 *The Diaries of Virginia Woolf*,

10 September 1933. Volume Four.
55 In Sencourt.
56 'Catholicism and International Order', in *Christendom*, September 1933.
57 'Religion and Literature' in *Faith That Illuminates*. London, 1935.
58 Eliot to Mary Hutchinson, 20 September 1933. Texas.
59 *ibid.*
60 The diaries of Vivien Eliot, 20 January 1934. Bodleian.
61 Eliot to Paul Elmer More, 7 November 1933. Princeton.
62 In Chiari.
63 Quoted by Lord David Cecil in *Lady Ottoline's Album*, edited by Carolyn G. Heilbrun. London, 1976.
64 Eliot to Ezra Pound, 29 January 1960. Beinecke.
65 'The Three Voices of Poetry' reprinted in *On Poetry and Poets*. London. 1957.
66 Eliot to Marianne Moore, 31 January 1934. Philadelphia.
67 In Browne.
68 Eliot to Paul Elmer More, 7 November 1933. Princeton.
69 Eliot to Virginia Woolf, 7 December 1933. Berg.
70 In Sencourt.
71 Eliot to Virginia Woolf, 31 October 1933. Berg.
72 E. W. F. Tomlin speaking at Canterbury symposium, 8 May 1983.
73 In Sencourt.

CHAPTER II

1 *The Diaries of Virginia Woolf*, 31 March 1935. Volume Four.
2 Eliot to Paul Elmer More, 26 March 1933. Princeton.
3 Frank Morley in Tate collection.
4 Eliot to Paul Elmer More, 7 November 1933. Princeton.
5 *John Dryden, the Poet, the Dramatist, the Critic*. New York, 1932.
6 In Browne.
7 *ibid.*
8 Eliot to Bonamy Dobrée, 10 May 1934. Brotherton.
9 Virginia Woolf to Quentin Bell, 3 December 1933. *The Letters of Virginia Woolf*. Volume Five.
10 *Poetry*, December 1934.
11 Michael Sayers in the *New English Weekly*, 21 June 1934.
12 Hugh Sykes Davies in Tate collection.
13 Eliot to Paul Elmer More, 8 December 1933. Princeton.
14 Eliot to Bonamy Dobrée, 11 July 1934. Brotherton.
15 Eliot to Mary Hutchinson, 22 November 1934. Texas.
16 In *An Assessment of Twentieth Century Literature* by J. Isaacs. London, 1951.
17 In *Drawn from The Life* by Robert Medley. London, 1983.
18 Robert Medley in the *London Magazine*, January 1981.
19 Wyndham Lewis in March and Tambimuttu collection.
20 Eliot to Ottoline Morrell, 2 March 1934. Texas.
21 Now held in the Bodleian Library, Oxford.
22 The diaries of Vivien Eliot, 9 June 1934. Bodleian.
23 The diaries of Vivien Eliot, 17 September 1935. Bodleian.
24 Bridget O'Donovan in *Confrontation*, fall-winter 1975.
25 The diaries of Vivien Eliot, 13 March 1935. Bodleian.
26 The diaries of Vivien Eliot, 28 July 1935. Bodleian.
27 The diaries of Vivien Eliot, 2 October 1935. Bodleian.
28 In Browne.

29 Eliot to Paul Elmer More, 27 March 1936. Princeton.

30 Eliot to Paul Elmer More, 8 December 1933. Princeton.

31 Eliot to Paul Elmer More, 20 June 1934. Princeton.

32 *The Diaries of Virginia Woolf*, 19 April 1934. Volume Four.

33 Virginia Woolf to Stephen Spender, 10 July 1934. *The Letters of Virginia Woolf*. Volume Five.

34 The *Diaries of Virginia Woolf*, 21 November 1934. Volume Four.

35 *Men Without Art* by Wyndham Lewis. London, 1934.

36 Unpublished memoir by Hugh Gordon Porteus, in the Beinecke Library.

37 Ezra Pound in the *New English Weekly*, March 1934.

38 Eliot to Bonamy Dobrée, 11 July 1934. Brotherton.

39 *Criterion*, October 1933.

40 *Criterion*, July 1933.

41 *Philbeach Quarterly*, summer 1965.

42 Philip Mairet in *T. S. Eliot: a Symposium for His Seventieth Birthday*, edited by Neville Braybrooke. London, 1958.

43 In *How To Make Enemies* by Ronald Duncan. London, 1968.

44 Lawrence Durrell in the *Atlantic Monthly*, May 1965.

45 Raymond Preston in Braybrooke collection.

46 F. T. Prince in letter to the present author.

47 Eliot to George Barker, 26 September 1937. Texas.

48 Lawrence Durrell in *Atlantic Monthly*, May 1965.

49 Anne Ridler in *Poetry Review*, spring 1983.

50 Eliot to George Barker, 24 January 1938. Texas.

51 Eliot to Virginia Woolf, 'Twelfth Night' 1935. Berg.

52 'Poetry and Drama' reprinted in *On Poetry and Poets*.

53 In *Drawn From The Life* by Robert Medley.

54 In Browne.

55 ibid.

56 ibid.

57 Eliot, quoted by Anne Ridler in *Poetry Review*, spring 1983.

58 Eliot to Henry Sherek, 8 April 1953. Texas.

59 Ezra Pound to James Laughlin, 5(?) January 1936. *Selected Letters*.

60 Preface to *Transit of Venus* by Harry Crosby. Paris, 1931.

61 *The Diaries of Virginia Woolf*, 20 June 1935. Volume Four.

62 Virginia Woolf to Julian Bell, 14 October 1935. *The Letters of Virginia Woolf*. Volume Five.

63 *Paris Review* interview.

64 Eliot to Helen Gardner, 2 December 1942. Bodleian.

65 Eliot to Mrs Perkins, 30 October 1935. Quoted in Gardner.

66 Quoted in Matthews.

67 Eliot to Ottoline Morrell, 29 October 1934. Texas.

68 Virginia Woolf to Ethel Smythe, 26 November 1935. *The Letters of Virginia Woolf*. Volume Five.

69 Aldous Huxley, quoted in Matthews.

CHAPTER 12

1 The diaries of Vivien Eliot, 18 November 1935. Bodleian.

2 Quoted by Valerie Eliot. The *Times Literary Supplement*, 10 February 1984.

3 Maurice Haigh-Wood in conversation with Michael Hastings.

4 Quoted by Valerie Eliot. *The*

Times Literary Supplement, 10 February 1984.

5 *The Diaries of Virginia Woolf*, 20 June 1935. Volume Four.

6 Eliot to Virginia Woolf, 3 October 1935. Berg.

7 In *How To Make Enemies* by Ronald Duncan.

8 William Empson in March and Tambimuttu collection.

9 In Levy and Scherle.

10 In Gardner.

11 Eliot to Ezra Pound, 9 September 1937. Beinecke.

12 In *How To Make Enemies* by Ronald Duncan.

13 Eliot to Conrad Aiken, 7 November 1952. Huntington.

14 Eliot to Djuna Barnes, 19 February 1951. McKeldin Library, University of Maryland.

15 *The Diaries of Virginia Woolf*, 5 February 1935. Volume Four.

16 Eliot to F. R. Leavis, 16 December 1935. Texas.

17 Eliot to Ezra Pound, 29 January 1960. Beinecke.

18 'In Memoriam', an introduction to *Poems of Tennyson*. London, 1936.

19 'A Note on The Verse of John Milton'. *Essays and Studies* by Members of the English Association. Oxford, 1936.

20 'Byron' in *From Anne to Victoria*, edited by Bonamy Dobrée. London, 1937.

21 Introduction to *Nightwood* by Djuna Barnes. New York, 1937.

22 Eliot to Paul Elmer More, 27 March 1936. Princeton.

23 Eliot to George Barker, 26 September 1937. Texas.

24 Eliot to Paul Elmer More, 11 January 1937. Princeton.

25 Essay in *Revelation*, edited by John Baillie and Hugh Martin. London, 1937.

26 Eliot to Virginia Woolf, 27 April 1937. Berg.

27 Virginia Woolf to Vanessa Bell, 28 December 1937. *The Letters of Virginia Woolf*. Volume Six.

28 Henry Miller to Lawrence Durrell, 6 December 1936. In *Lawrence Durrell-Henry Miller. A private correspondence*. London, 1963.

29 Sylvia Beach to Eliot, 24 April 1936. Princeton.

30 Katherine Anne Porter in *Southern Review*, summer 1965.

31 Quoted in *Sylvia Beach and the Lost Generation* by Noel Riley Fitch. London, 1984.

32 John Berryman quoted in *The Life of John Berryman* by John Haffenden. London, 1982.

33 Quoted by Lawrence Durrell in the *Atlantic Monthly*, May 1965.

34 Tom Faber speaking at the University of Canterbury symposium.

35 Conrad Aiken to Henry A. Murray, 14 November 1937. *Selected Letters*.

36 Quoted in *Miss Ethel Sands and Her Circle* by Wendy Baron. London, 1977.

37 In *Revelation*.

38 Eliot quoted by Lawrence Durrell in the *Atlantic Monthly*, May 1965.

39 Quoted in *Bound Upon A Course* by John Stewart Collis. London, 1971.

40 Quoted in a letter from Constantine FitzGibbon to the present author.

41 'Poetry and Drama' reprinted in *On Poetry and Poets*.

42 Eliot quoted in *The Importance of Recognition* by Kristian Smidt. Tromso, 1973.

43 Eliot to Geoffrey Faber, 20 March

1937. Quoted in *The Family Reunion*, with notes and commentary by Neville Coghill. London, 1969.

44 In Browne.

45 In *In My Mind's Eye* by Michael Redgrave. London, 1983.

46 In *Michael Redgrave, actor* by Richard Findlater. London, 1956.

47 In Browne.

48 Virginia Woolf to Elizabeth Bowen, 29 January 1939. *The Letters of Virginia Woolf*. Volume Six.

49 Quoted in Browne.

50 'Religious Drama: Medieval and Modern'. Address to the Friends of Rochester Cathedral, reprinted in *University of Edinburgh Journal*, autumn 1937.

51 Quoted in Levy and Scherle.

52 *The Diaries of Virginia Woolf*, 29 March 1939. Berg.

53 Eliot to Bonamy Dobrée, 12 April 1939. Brotherton.

54 'Poetry and Drama' reprinted in *On Poetry and Poets*.

55 *The Idea of a Christian Society*. London, 1939.

56 Eliot to E. Martin Browne, 19 March 1938. Quoted in Browne.

57 Eliot to Bonamy Dobrée, 30 November 1936. Brotherton.

58 Eliot to Bonamy Dobrée, 14 January 1939. Brotherton.

59 In *T. S. Eliot* by Stephen Spender. London, 1975.

60 'The Unity of European Culture', radio broadcast 1946. Reprinted as an appendix to *Notes Towards the Definition of Culture*. London, 1948.

61 *ibid*.

62 Interview with John Lehmann, *New York Times* 29 November 1953.

63 'The Unity of European Culture'.

64 Eliot to Conrad Aiken, 28 March 1939. Huntington.

65 Eliot to Bonamy Dobrée, 14 January 1939. Brotherton.

66 Eliot to Leonard Woolf, 13 January 1940. Sussex.

67 Eliot to Paul Elmer More, 20 June 1934. Princeton.

68 Maurice Reckitt in *Philbeach Quarterly*, summer 1965.

69 Stravinsky in *Esquire* magazine, August 1965.

70 Eliot to Bonamy Dobrée, 6 August 1941. Brotherton.

CHAPTER 13

1 George Barker in the *New English Review*, March 1949.

2 Philip Mairet in Braybrooke collection.

3 Interview with John Lehmann, *New York Times* 29 November 1953.

4 Minutes of Moot at Westfield College, London, September 1938. Quoted in *T. S. Eliot's Social Criticism* by R. Kojecky. London, 1971.

5 Eliot to Virginia Woolf, 'Holy Innocents Day' 1939. Berg.

6 Eliot to Virginia Woolf, 12 October 1939. Berg.

7 Interview with Leslie Paul, 8 July 1958. I am indebted to Mr Leslie Paul for playing to me a tape-recording of this interview.

8 Eliot quoted in a letter from John Hayward to Frank Morley, February 1940. Quoted in Gardner.

9 Eliot to Anne Ridler, 10 March 1941. Quoted in Gardner.

10 Eliot to Montgomery Belgion, 19 July 1940. Texas. And Eliot to Anne Ridler, 10 March 1941. Quoted in Gardner.

11 Eliot to Anne Ridler, 10 March 1941. Quoted in Gardner.

12 *The Diaries of Virginia Woolf*, 25 May 1940. Berg.

13 Minutes of Moot meeting, quoted in Kojecky.

14 *ibid.*

15 Eliot to Philip Mairet, 18 February 1941. Texas.

16 Quoted in Kojecky.

17 Eliot to Oldham, 9 August 1943. Quoted in Kojecky.

18 Eliot to Herbert Read, 24 February 1951. Victoria.

19 Eliot to E. McKnight Kauffer, 23 May 1940. Pierpoint Morgan.

20 Eliot to Herbert Read, 4 June 1940. Victoria.

21 Quoted in Powell.

22 Eliot to Djuna Barnes, 2 December 1940. Maryland.

23 Eliot to Mary Hutchinson, 3 January 1941. Texas.

24 Preface to *The Little Book of Modern Verse*, chosen by Anne Ridler. London, 1942.

25 Eliot to Philip Mairet, 15 February 1941. Texas.

26 Eliot, quoted by George Seferis in the *Quarterly Review of Literature*, 15 (1967).

27 Eliot to Mary Hutchinson, 26 September 1941. Texas.

28 John Hayward to Frank Morley, June 1941. Quoted in Gardner.

29 Anne Ridler in conversation with the present author.

30 Note on *The Collected Poems of Harold Monro*. London, 1933.

31 'The Three Voices of Poetry' reprinted in *On Poetry and Poets*.

32 *ibid.*

33 *The Use of Poetry and The Use of Criticism*.

34 Eliot to Herbert Read, 18 September 1942. Victoria.

35 Eliot quoted in *The Importance of Recognition* by Kristian Smidt.

36 Eliot to Herbert Read, 15 September 1932. Victoria.

37 Eliot to John Hayward, 14 July 1941. Quoted in Gardner.

38 Eliot to Bonamy Dobrée, 6 August 1941. Quoted by Dobrée in Tate collection.

39 Quoted in *Under Siege. Literary Life in London, 1939–1945* by Robert Hewison. London, 1977.

40 Eliot to Bonamy Dobrée, 6 August 1941. Quoted by Dobrée in Tate collection.

41 Eliot to John Hayward, 5 August 1941. Quoted in Gardner.

42 Eliot to Mary Hutchinson, 25 October 1941. Texas.

43 Eliot quoted in Levy and Scherle.

44 John Hayward to Frank Morley, July 1942. Quoted in Gardner.

45 Eliot to E. Martin Browne, 9 July 1941. Quoted in Browne.

46 Eliot to E. Martin Browne, 20 October 1942. Quoted in Browne.

47 'Johnson as Critic and Poet', reprinted in *On Poetry and Poets*. London, 1957.

48 Eliot to E. Martin Browne, 20 October 1942. In Browne.

49 In Matthews.

50 Eliot to Henry Treece, 8 September 1943. Texas.

51 Eliot to Djuna Barnes, 'Whit Monday' 1944. Maryland.

52 Eliot to Bonamy Dobrée, 10 March 1943. Brotherton. And Eliot to Sidney Schiff, 16 August 1943. British Library.

53 Eliot to Montgomery Belgion, 12 April 1943. Texas.

54 Report on Herbert Read's *Education for Peace*, 11 September 1948. Victoria.

55 *Paris Review* interview.

56 'The Music of Poetry' reprinted in *On Poetry and Poets*.

57 'Johnson as Critic and Poet', reprinted in *On Poetry and Poets*.

58 'The Music of Poetry', reprinted in *On Poetry and Poets*.

59 *ibid*.

60 'What Is A Classic?' reprinted in *On Poetry and Poets*.

61 'The Social Function of Poetry', reprinted in *On Poetry and Poets*.

62 'The Music of Poetry', reprinted in *On Poetry and Poets*.

63 *ibid*.

64 *The Classics and the Man of Letters*. London, 1942.

65 Eliot to Eudo Mason, 23 January 1946. Texas.

66 Eliot to Philip Mairet, 31 October 1956. The collection of Violet Welton.

67 Eliot to Allen Tate, 13 March 1945. Princeton.

68 Eliot to Philip Mairet, 24 August 1945. Texas.

69 Preface to *The Dark Side of the Moon*. London, 1946.

70 'The Responsibility of the Man of Letters in the Cultural Restoration of Europe', in *Norseman*, July/ August 1944.

71 'The Unity of European Culture'.

72 *Horizon*, August 1945.

CHAPTER 14

1 Anne Ridler in conversation with the present author.

2 In *Faces In My Time* by Anthony Powell.

3 Quoted by John Haffenden in *Quarto*, June 1981.

4 In *C. Day Lewis: An English Literary Life* by Sean Day Lewis. London, 1980.

5 Christopher Sykes in *The Book Collector*, winter 1965.

6 Christopher Sykes in *The Book Collector*, winter 1965.

7 In *Customs and Characters: Contemporary Portraits* by Peter Quennell. London, 1982.

8 'The Value and Use of Cathedrals in England Today'. An address given at Chichester Cathedral, 16 June 1951.

9 Anne Ridler in *Poetry Review*, spring 1983.

10 Peter du Sautoy speaking at Canterbury symposium.

11 In *Julia: A Portrait of Julia Strachey by Herself and Frances Partridge*. London, 1983.

12 *ibid*.

13 Anne Ridler in *Poetry Review*, spring 1983.

14 In Levy and Scherle.

15 Robert Giroux in Tate collection.

16 Quoted by Christopher Sykes in *The Book Collector*, winter 1965.

17 Quoted in *T. S. Eliot* by Stephen Spender.

18 Lawrence Durrell to Henry Miller, June 1947. In *Lawrence Durrell – Henry Miller. A private correspondence*.

19 G. S. Fraser in Braybrooke anthology.

20 In Chiari.

21 Quoted by John Haffenden, *Quarto* June 1981.

22 E. W. F. Tomlin speaking at Canterbury symposium.

23 This information about Mary Trevelyan has been communicated to me by Humphrey Carpenter.

24 Eliot to Allen Tate, 10 July 1946. Princeton.

25 Eliot to Dorothy Pound, 12 September 1946. Beinecke.

26 Eliot to Ronald Duncan, 23 January 1947. Texas.

27 Quoted in *Ezra Pound: The Last*

Rower by C. David Heymann. London, 1976.

28 Quoted in *W. H. Auden: The Life of a Poet* by Charles Osborne. London, 1980.

29 Eliot to E. Martin Browne, 27 August 1946. In Browne.

30 In Sencourt.

31 Eliot to Violet Schiff, 28 January 1947. British Library.

32 Christopher Sykes in *The Book Collector*, winter 1965.

33 In *How To Make Enemies*, by Ronald Duncan.

34 Reported in the *Observer*, 15 May 1983.

35 E. W. F. Tomlin in the *Listener*, 28 April 1977.

36 Eliot to Mary Hutchinson, 17 February 1947. Texas.

37 Eliot to Wyndham Lewis, 7 March 1947. Cornell.

38 William York Tindall in the *American Scholar*, autumn 1947.

39 Katherine Chapin in *Poetry*, September 1947.

40 Richard Chase in the *American Scholar*, autumn 1947.

41 Hans Meyerhoff in the *Partisan Review*, January 1948.

42 In *E. M. Forster: A Life* by P. N. Furbank. London, 1977–8.

43 Eliot to Philip Mairet, 23 December 1947. Texas.

44 Eliot to Herbert Read, 20 December 1947. Victoria.

45 From *Voices: A Memoir* by Frederic Prokosch. London, 1983.

46 Eliot to E. Martin Browne, 25 January 1948. In Browne.

47 Eliot to Djuna Barnes, 3 May 1948. Maryland.

48 Eliot to Marion Dorn, 28 July 1948. Texas.

49 In *Poets In Their Youth: A Memoir* by Eileen Simpson. London, 1982.

50 Eliot to Herbert Read, 15 October 1948. Victoria.

51 In *Poets In Their Youth* by Eileen Simpson.

52 In Browne.

53 Interview in the *New York Times*, 21 November 1948.

54 E. W. F. Tomlin at Canterbury symposium.

55 Interview in the *New York Times*, 21 November 1948.

56 Robert Giroux in Tate collection.

57 Wyndham Lewis to D. D. Paige, 25 October 1948. *The Letters of Wyndham Lewis*. And Wyndham Lewis to Felix Giovanelli, 1 November 1948. In *The Enemy* by Jeffrey Meyers. London, 1980.

58 Lewis quoted in *The Enemy* by Jeffrey Meyers.

59 Quoted in *Poets In Their Youth* by Eileen Simpson.

60 Quoted in *The Cocktail Party*, with notes and commentary by Neville Coghill. London, 1974.

61 Quoted in *How To Make Enemies* by Ronald Duncan.

62 Robert Lowell in *The Mysterious Mr Eliot*, BBC.

63 Eliot to Mary Hutchinson, 10 October 1948. Texas.

64 Edmund Wilson to Van Wyck Brooks, 6 October 1957. In *Letters on Literature and Politics 1912–72*, edited by Elena Wilson. London, 1977.

65 *ibid.*

66 *New York Times*, 21 September 1958.

67 *Philbeach Quarterly*, Summer 1965.

68 Eliot to Eudo Mason, 19 January 1949. Texas.

69 *Time* magazine, 30 May 1949.

70 Eliot to Violet Schiff, 14 January 1949. British Library.

71 Chanchal Sarkar in *T. S. Eliot:*

Homage from India, edited by P. Lal. Calcutta, 1965.

72 Eliot to Violet Schiff, 14 January 1949. British Library.

73 Eliot to Geoffrey Faber, 29 August 1949. Quoted in *The Cocktail Party*, with notes and commentary by Neville Coghill.

74 In *Not In Front of The Children* by Henry Sherek.

75 *ibid.*

76 'Poetry and Drama', reprinted in *On Poetry and Poets*.

77 In Browne.

78 In Sherek.

79 Irene Worth quoted in the *New York Times*, 21 November 1982.

80 Eliot to Henzie Raeburn, 28 August 1949. In Browne.

81 Interview in *World Review*, November 1949.

82 In Sherek.

83 Eliot to Mary Hutchinson, 1 September 1949. Texas.

84 Quoted in *The Importance of Recognition* by Kristian Smidt.

85 Eliot to Violet Schiff, 14 January 1949. British Library.

86 In Chiari.

87 Eliot to Wyndham Lewis, 21 July 1949. Cornell.

88 *The Saturday Review*, 11 June 1949.

89 Eliot to Henry Sherek, 20 September 1949. Texas.

90 Eliot to Eudo Mason, 3 January 1950. Texas.

91 Interview with Valerie Eliot in the *Observer*, 20 February 1972.

92 *ibid.*

CHAPTER 15

1 Reported to the present author by A. L. Rowse.

2 Katherine Anne Porter in *Shenandoah*, Spring 1961.

3 'The Value and the Use of Cathedrals in England Today', 1951.

4 Introduction to *The Adventures of Huckleberry Finn* by Mark Twain. London, 1950.

5 Eliot to Djuna Barnes, 4 April 1950. Maryland.

6 In Levy and Scherle.

7 *Time* magazine, 6 March 1950.

8 Eliot to Henry Sherek, 1 June 1950. Texas.

9 In Chiari.

10 Glur Dyson-Taylor in conversation with the present author.

11 In *How To Make Enemies* by Ronald Duncan.

12 In *Belonging* by Willa Muir. London, 1968.

13 Introduction to *The Adventures of Huckleberry Finn*.

14 In *Sextet* by John Malcolm Brinnin. New York, 1981.

15 In Levy and Scherle.

16 Robert Giroux in Tate collection.

17 'American Literature and the American Language', an address delivered at Washington University, 9 June 1953. Reprinted in *To Criticize The Critic*, London 1965.

18 'The Aims of Education', lectures delivered at the University of Chicago, November 1950. Reprinted in *To Criticize The Critic*.

19 'The Value and Use of Cathedrals in England Today', 1951.

20 'What Dante Means To Me', an address given at the Italian Institute 4 July 1950. Reprinted in *To Criticize The Critic*.

21 'Poetry and Drama', 1951. Reprinted in *On Poetry and Poets*.

22 George Seferis in *Quarterly Review of Literature*, 15 (1967).

23 Quoted in *A Marriage of True Minds: An Intimate Portrait of*

Leonard and Virginia Woolf by George Spater and Ian Parsons. London, 1977.

24 Eliot to Henry Sherek, 7 December 1955. Texas.
25 In *How To Make Enemies* by Ronald Duncan.
26 Herbert Read in Tate collection.
27 In Levy.
28 Eliot to Djuna Barnes, 4 January 1949. Maryland.
29 In Levy.
30 *New York Times*, 7 February 1954.
31 In *Remembering Poets* by Donald Hall. New York, 1978.
32 E. W. F. Tomlin in the *Listener*, 28 April 1977.
33 George Seferis in the *Quarterly Review of Literature*, 15 (1967).
34 In *How To Make Enemies* by Ronald Duncan.
35 *ibid*.
36 'Virgil and The Christian World', BBC radio broadcast, 9 September 1951.
37 In *How To Make Enemies* by Ronald Duncan.
38 In *Discretions* by Mary de Rachewiltz. London, 1971.
39 E. W. F. Tomlin in the *Listener*, 28 April 1977.
40 Information supplied to the present author by Humphrey Carpenter.
41 Quoted in *The Thirties and After* by Stephen Spender. London, 1978.
42 Allen Tate in Tate collection.
43 In Levy.
44 In *Not In Front of the Children* by Henry Sherek.
45 Eliot to Conrad Aiken, 13 May 1954. Huntington.
46 Eliot to Djuna Barnes, 26 December 1951. Maryland.
47 'Poetry and Drama', reprinted in *On Poetry and Poets*.

48 In Browne.
49 Eliot to Violet Schiff, 27 February 1950. British Library.
50 Quoted in *Sextet* by John Malcolm Brinnin.
51 Eliot to Henry Sherek, 23 July 1956. Texas.
52 *Essays in Criticism*, April 1969.
53 Eliot to C. C. Abbot, 13 October 1927. University Library, Durham.
54 Quoted in the postscript to *Essays in Criticism*, April 1969.
55 *T. S. Eliot's Personal Waste Land* by James Miller. Philadelphia, 1977.
56 Eliot to Alfred Kreymborg, 30 May 1925. Alderman Library, University of Virginia. Quoted in Gordon.
57 'American Literature and the American Language', reprinted in *To Criticize The Critic*.
58 *Paris Review* interview.
59 In Levy and Scherle.
60 Alison Leggatt in Braybrooke collection.
61 In *Not In Front of the Children* by Henry Sherek.
62 In Levy and Scherle.
63 'Poetry and Drama' reprinted in *On Poetry and Poets*.
64 Interview in *New York Times*, 29 November 1953.
65 *The Aims of Poetic Drama*. London, 1949.
66 Eliot to Mary Hutchinson, 12 October 1953. Texas.
67 In 'Miss Buttle and Mr Eliot', reprinted in *The Bit Between My Teeth* by Edmund Wilson. London, 1965.
68 In *Sextet* by John Malcolm Brinnin.
69 Eliot to Mrs Levy, 27 December 1954. Texas.
70 Eliot to Conrad Aiken, 27 August 1954. Huntington.

71 Eliot to William Turner Levy, 'Whitsunday' 1954. Texas.

72 Eliot to Marion Dorn, 7 November 1954. Texas.

73 Eliot to Conrad Aiken, 27 August 1954. Huntington.

74 In *How To Make Enemies* by Ronald Duncan.

75 George Seferis in the *Quarterly Review of Literature*, 15 (1967).

76 Eliot to Conrad Aiken, 13 May 1954. Huntington.

77 Eliot to Allen Tate, 10 March 1955. Princeton.

78 Quoted in *Discretions* by Mary de Rachewiltz.

79 Eliot to Ezra Pound, 13 August 1954. Beinecke.

80 Ezra Pound to Ernest Hemingway, 9 August 1955. Quoted in *The Life of Ezra Pound* by Noel Stock. London, 1970.

81 Quoted in *T. S. Eliot* by Bernard Bergonzi. London, 1972.

82 Igor Stravinsky in *Esquire*, August 1965.

83 Eliot to Bonamy Dobrée, 22 November 1956. Brotherton.

CHAPTER 16

1 Valerie Eliot quoted in the *Observer*, 20 February 1972.

2 Valerie Eliot in *The Mysterious Mr Eliot*, BBC.

3 Robert Giroux, quoting Eliot, in Tate collection.

4 In Chiari.

5 Rupert Hart-Davis to George Lyttleton, 2 June 1957. In *The Lyttleton Hart-Davis Letters*. Volume Two. London, 1979.

6 Peter du Sautoy speaking at the Canterbury symposium.

7 Interview with Valerie Eliot in the *Evening Standard*, 25 September 1958.

8 Eliot to William Turner Levy, 11 January 1958. Texas.

9 *New York Times*, 26 September 1958.

10 Edmund Wilson to Van Wyck Brooks, 8 June 1958. *Letters on Literature and Politics*.

11 In *Remembering Poets* by Donald Hall.

12 In *Not In Front of the Children* by Henry Sherek.

13 In *Stravinsky: Chronicle of a Friendship* by Robert Craft.

14 Rupert Hart-Davis to George Lyttleton, 5 July 1958. In *The Lyttleton Hart-Davis Letters*. Volume Three. London, 1981.

15 In Browne.

16 In Sherek.

17 In Browne.

18 *ibid*.

19 *The Use of Poetry and The Use of Criticism*.

20 Rupert Hart-Davis to George Lyttleton, 28 September 1958. In *The Lyttleton Hart-Davis Letters*. Volume Three.

21 Eliot to Henry Sherek, 26 November 1958. Texas.

22 Henry Hewes in the *Saturday Review*, 13 September 1958.

23 *ibid*.

24 *New York Times*, 26 September 1958.

25 *New York Times*, 21 September 1958.

26 *Sunday Times*, 21 September 1958.

27 Quoted by Cyril Connolly in the *Sunday Times*, 10 January 1965.

28 *Paris Review* interview.

29 Reported to the present author by A. L. Rowse.

30 Interview with Valerie Eliot in the *Observer*, 20 February 1972.

31 In *Stravinsky: Chronicle of a Friendship* by Robert Craft.

32 In *Daedalus*, spring 1960.
33 Eliot to Ezra Pound, 29 January 1960. Beinecke.
34 Eliot to Ezra Pound, 31 October 1959. Beinecke.
35 Eliot to Ezra Pound, 28 December 1959. Beinecke.
36 *Yorkshire Post*, 30 August 1961.
37 Herbert Read in Tate collection.
38 Eliot to Bonamy Dobrée, 28 May 1961. Brotherton. And George Seferis in the *Quarterly Review of Literature*, 15 (1967).
39 *Trace*, June/July 1959.
40 *ibid*.
41 Eliot to Owen Barfield, 25 March 1960. Bodleian.
42 Rupert Hart-Davis to George Lyttleton, 16 July 1960 and 24 July 1960. In *Lyttelton Hart-Davis Letters*. Volume Five.
43 George Seferis in the *Quarterly Review of Literature*, 15 (1967).
44 *ibid*.
45 Valerie Eliot to the Levys, 27 August 1961. Texas.
46 'T. S. Eliot: A Memoir and a Tribute' by Henry Rago, *Poetry*, March 1965.
47 Quoted in *Remembering Poets* by Donald Hall.
48 Igor Stravinsky in *Esquire*, August 1965.
49 *ibid*.
50 In Levy and Scherle.
51 Eliot to Herbert Read, 20 May 1964. Victoria.
52 Interview with Valerie Eliot in the *Observer*, 20 February 1972.
53 Interview with Valerie Eliot in the *Observer*, 20 February 1972.
54 Eliot to Herbert Read, 1 August 1963. Victoria.
55 Eliot on Edwin Muir, BBC broadcast 5 May 1959.

Bibliography

MAJOR WORKS BY T.S. ELIOT

Prufrock and Other Observations. London, 1917.
Ezra Pound, His Metric and His Poetry. New York, 1918.
Poems. London, 1919.
Ara Vos Prec. London, 1920.
Poems. New York, 1920.
The Sacred Wood. London, 1920.
The Waste Land. New York, 1922 (first English edition in 1923).
Homage to John Dryden. London, 1924.
Poems, 1909–1925. London, 1925.
For Lancelot Andrewes. London, 1928.
Dante. London, 1929.
Ash-Wednesday. London, 1930.
Anabasis, a Poem by St-J Perse. London, 1930.
Thoughts After Lambeth. London, 1931.
Triumphal March. London, 1931.
Selected Essays. London, 1932.
John Dryden: The Poet, the Dramatist, the Critic. New York, 1932.
Sweeney Agonistes. London, 1932.
The Use of Poetry and the Use of Criticism. London, 1933.
After Strange Gods. London, 1934.
The Rock. London, 1934.
Elizabethan Essays. London, 1934.
Murder in the Cathedral. London, 1935.
Essays Ancient and Modern. London, 1936.
Collected Poems, 1909–1935. London, 1936.
The Family Reunion. London 1939.
Old Possum's Book of Practical Cats. London, 1939.
The Idea of a Christian Society. London, 1939.
East Coker. London, 1940.
Burnt Norton. London, 1941.
The Dry Salvages. London, 1941.
Little Gidding. London, 1942.
Reunion By Destruction. London, 1943.
Four Quartets. London, 1944.
Notes Towards the Definition of Culture. London, 1948.
The Cocktail Party. London, 1950.
The Complete Poems and Plays, 1909–1950. London, 1952.
The Confidential Clerk. London, 1954.
On Poetry and Poets. London 1957.

MAJOR WORKS BY T.S. ELIOT (continued)

The Elder Statesman, London 1959.
Collected Plays. London, 1962.
George Herbert. London, 1962.
Collected Poems, 1909–1962. London, 1963.
Knowledge and Experience in the Philosophy of F. H. Bradley. London, 1964.
To Criticize the Critic, and other writings. London, 1965.
Poems Written in Early Youth. London, 1967.
The Complete Poems and Plays of T. S. Eliot, London 1969.
Selected Prose of T. S. Eliot, edited by Frank Kermode. London, 1975.

BOOKS ABOUT, OR RELATING TO, T.S. ELIOT

BIBLIOGRAPHIES

GALLUP, DONALD. *T. S. Eliot: A bibliography*. London, 1969.
MARTIN, MILDRED. *A half century of Eliot Criticism*. London, 1972.
RICKS, BEATRICE. *T. S. Eliot: a bibliography of secondary works*. New Jersey, 1980.

CRITICAL COLLECTIONS

GRANT, MICHAEL. (ed.) *T. S. Eliot: The Critical Heritage*. London, 1982.

CHRONOLOGIES

BEHR, CAROLINE. *T. S. Eliot. A Chronology of his Life and Works*. London, 1983.

MEMOIRS OR BIOGRAPHIES

CHIARI, JOSEPH. *T. S. Eliot: a memoir*. London, 1982.
GORDON, LYNDALL. *Eliot's Early Years*. Oxford, 1977.
LEVY, WILLIAM TURNER and SCHERLE, VICTOR. *Affectionately, T. S. Eliot. The Story of a Friendship, 1947–1965*. London, 1968.
MATTHEWS, T. S. *Great Tom: Notes Toward the Definition of T. S. Eliot*. London, 1974.
SENCOURT, ROBERT. *T. S. Eliot: A Memoir*, edited by Donald Adamson. London, 1974.

These three collections contain much biographical and anecdotal material:

BRAYBROOKE, NEVILLE (ed.). *T. S. Eliot: A Symposium*. London, 1958.
MARCH, RICHARD and TAMBIMUTTU (eds.). *T. S. Eliot: A Symposium*. London, 1948.
TATE, ALLEN (ed.). *T. S. Eliot: the Man and His Work*. London, 1967.

These critical studies also contain essential biographical information:

BERGONZI, BERNARD. *T. S. Eliot*. London, 1972.
BROWNE, E. MARTIN. *The Making of T. S. Eliot's Plays*. London, 1969.

COGHILL, NEVILLE (ed.). *The Family Reunion*, with notes and commentary by Neville Coghill. London, 1969.
The Cocktail Party, with notes and commentary by Neville Coghill. London, 1974.
ELIOT, VALERIE (ed.). *The Waste Land*: a facsimile and transcript of the original drafts, edited by Valerie Eliot. London, 1971.
GALLUP, DONALD. *T. S. Eliot and Ezra Pound. Collaborators in Letters*. New Haven, 1970.
GARDNER, HELEN. *The Composition of 'Four Quartets'*. London, 1978.
HOWARTH, HERBERT. *Notes on Some Figures Behind T. S. Eliot*. London, 1965.
SPENDER, STEPHEN. *T. S. Eliot*. London, 1975.

There were occasions when Eliot himself discussed episodes and scenes from his own life, and material of unusual interest is contained in the following of his prefaces and lectures:

Preface to E. A. Mowrer's *This American World*. London, 1928.
Preface to Baudelaire's *Intimate Journals*. London, 1930.
Preface to Pascal's *Pensées*. London, 1931.
Preface to Charles Louis Philippe's *Bubu of Montparnasse*. London, 1932.
Milton Graduate Bulletin. November, 1933.
Preface to Djuna Barnes's *Nightwood*. New York, 1936.
Preface to Mark Twain's *The Adventures of Huckleberry Finn*. London, 1950.
Preface to Joseph Pieper's *Leisure: The Basis of Culture*. London, 1952.
From Mary to You. St Louis, 1959.

CRITICAL STUDIES

There are many critical studies. These are ones which were of most value or interest in my research:

ALLAN, MOWBRAY. *T. S. Eliot's Impersonal Theory of Poetry*. Lewisburg, 1974.
ALLDRITT, KEITH. *Eliot's Four Quartets: poetry as chamber music*. London, 1978.
ANTRIM, HARRY. *T. S. Eliot's Concept of Language: a study of its development*. Gainesville, 1971.
BANTOCK, G. H. *T. S. Eliot and Education*. London 1970.
BERGONZI, BERNARD (ed.). *T. S. Eliot, Four Quartets. A casebook*. London, 1969.
BERGSTEN, STAFFAN. *Time and Eternity. A study in the structure and symbolism of T. S. Eliot's Four Quartets*. Stockholm, 1960.
BODKIN, MAUD. *The Quest for Salvation*. London, 1941.
BORNSTEIN, G. *Transformation of romanticism in Yeats, Eliot and Stevens*. Chicago, 1977.
BUCKLEY, VINCENT. *Poetry and Morality*. London, 1959.

CHACE, WILLIAM M. *The Political Identities of Ezra Pound and T. S. Eliot.* Stanford, 1973.

COX, C.B. and HINCHCLIFFE, A. P. (eds.). *The Waste Land: a casebook.* London, 1968.

CRAIG, CAIRNS. *Yeats, Eliot, Pound and the politics of poetry.* London, 1982.

DONOGHUE, DENIS. *The Third Voice. Modern British and American verse drama.* Princeton, 1959.

EDEL, LEON. *Stuff of Sleep and Dreams. Experiments in Literary Psychology.* London, 1982.

FABRICIUS, JOHANNES. *The Unconscious and Mr Eliot.* Copenhagen, 1967.

FRYE, NORTHROP. *T. S. Eliot.* London, 1963.

GARDNER, HELEN. *The Art of T. S. Eliot.* London, 1949.
T. S. Eliot and the English Poetic Tradition. Nottingham, 1966.

GEORGE, A. G. *T. S. Eliot: His Mind and Art.* London, 1963.

GRAY, PIERS. *T. S. Eliot's Intellectual and Poetic Development, 1909–1922.* Sussex, 1982.

GREENE, E. J. H. *T. S. Eliot et La France.* Paris, 1951.

GUNTER, BRADLEY (ed.). *The Merrill Studies in The Waste Land.* Ohio, 1971.

HARGROVE, NANCY. *Landscape as Symbol in the Poetry of T. S. Eliot.* Jackson, 1978.

HOLDER, ALAN. *Three Voyagers in Search of Europe.* Philadelphia, 1966.

JONES, D. E. *The Plays of T. S. Eliot.* London, 1960.

KENNER, HUGH. *The Invisible Poet.* London, 1960.
T. S. Eliot, a collection of critical essays ed. Hugh Kenner. Englewood Cliffs, 1962.

KNOLL, ROBERT. (ed.). *Storm Over The Waste Land.* Chicago, 1964.

KOJECKY, R. *T. S. Eliot's Social Criticism.* London, 1971.

LEAVIS, F. R. *New Bearings in English Poetry.* London, 1932.
English Literature in our Time and the University. London, 1969.
The Living Principle. London, 1975.

LEE, BRIAN. *Theory and Personality: the Significance of T. S. Eliot's Criticism.* London, 1979.

LEVIN, HARRY. *Ezra Pound, T. S. Eliot and the European horizon.* Oxford, 1975.

LITZ, A.W. (ed.). *Eliot In His Time.* London, 1973.

LOBB, EDWARD. *T. S. Eliot and the Romantic Critical Tradition.* London, 1981.

MARGOLIS, J. D. *T. S. Eliot's Intellectual Development, 1922–1939.* London, 1972.

MARTIN, C. G. (ed.). *Eliot in Perspective. A Symposium.* London, 1970.

MATERER, TIMOTHY. *Vortex: Pound, Eliot and Lewis.* London, 1979.

MATTHIESSEN, F. O. *The Achievement of T. S. Eliot.* London, 1935.

MILLER, JAMES. *T. S. Eliot's Personal Waste Land.* Philadelphia, 1977.

MOODY, A. D. *Thomas Stearns Eliot: poet.* Cambridge, 1979.
The Waste Land in Different Voices, edited by A. D. Moody. London, 1974.

NEWTON-DE MOLINA, D. (ed.). *The Literary Criticism of T. S. Eliot.* London, 1977.

PATTERSON, GERTRUDE. *T. S. Eliot: poems in the making.* Manchester, 1971.

REES, THOMAS R. *The Technique of T. S. Eliot.* Paris, 1974.

SCHNEIDER, ELISABETH. *T. S. Eliot: the Pattern in the Carpet.* Berkeley, 1975.

SEYPPEL, JOACHIM. *T. S. Eliot.* New York, 1972.

SIMPSON, LOUIS. *Three on The Tower. The lives and works of Ezra Pound, T. S. Eliot and William Carlos Williams.* New York, 1975.

SMIDT, KRISTIAN. *Poetry and Belief in the work of T. S. Eliot.* London, 1961. *The Importance of Recognition.* Tromso, 1973.

SMITH, CAROL H. *T. S. Eliot's Dramatic Theory and Practice.* London, 1963.

SMITH, GROVER C. *T. S. Eliot's Poetry and Plays.* London, 1974. *The Waste Land.* London, 1984.

SOUTHAM, B. C. *The Student's Guide to the Selected Poems of T. S. Eliot.* London, 1968.

STEAD, C. K. *The New Poetic: Yeats to Eliot.* London, 1964.

SULLIVAN, SHEILA. (ed.). *Critics on T. S. Eliot.* London, 1973.

THOMPSON, ERIC. *T. S. Eliot, the Metaphysical Perspective.* Carbondale, 1963.

UNGER, LEONARD. *T. S. Eliot: Moments and Patterns.* London, 1966. *T. S. Eliot: A Selected Critique,* edited by Leonard Unger. New York, 1948.

WARD, GEORGE. *T. S. Eliot Between Two Worlds.* London, 1973.

WILLIAMSON, GEORGE. *A Reader's Guide to T. S. Eliot.* New York, 1966.

BIOGRAPHIES, REMINISCENCES AND CONTEMPORARY MEMOIRS

There are few accounts of the literary culture of this century which do not mention Eliot, and he appears in many memoirs by his contemporaries. The following list includes those books which I found most helpful:

ACKROYD, PETER. *Ezra Pound and His World.* London, 1980.

ADAMS, J. DONALD. *Copey of Harvard: a biography of Charles Townsend Copeland.* Boston, 1960.

AIKEN, CONRAD. *Ushant, an essay.* Boston, 1952. *The Clerk's Journal.* New York, 1971. *Selected Letters of Conrad Aiken,* edited by Joseph Killorin. New Haven, 1978.

ALDINGTON, RICHARD. *Stepping Heavenward. A Record.* London, 1931. *Life for Life's Sake.* New York, 1941. *Ezra Pound and T. S. Eliot.* Hurst, Berkshire, 1954.

BELL, QUENTIN. *Virginia Woolf: A biography.* London, 1972.

BENNETT, ARNOLD. *The Journals of Arnold Bennett,* edited by Newman Flower. In three volumes. London, 1932–3.

BRINNIN, JOHN MALCOLM. *Sextet.* New York, 1981.

CARPENTER, HUMPHREY. *W. H. Auden: a biography.* London, 1981.

CHURCH, RICHARD. *The Voyage Home.* London, 1964.

COLUM, MARY. *Life and the Dream.* London, 1947.

CRAFT, ROBERT. *Stravinsky: Chronicle of a Friendship.* London, 1972.

DAKIN, ARTHUR HAZARD. *Paul Elmer More.* Princeton, 1960.

DARROCH, SANDRA. *Ottoline. The Life of Lady Ottoline Morrell.* London, 1976.

DUNCAN, RONALD. *How To Make Enemies*. London, 1968.
Obsessed. London, 1977.

ELLMANN, RICHARD. *James Joyce*. Oxford, 1959.
Eminent Domain: Yeats among Wilde, Joyce, Pound, Eliot and Auden. Oxford, 1967.

FLETCHER, JOHN GOULD. *Life is My Song*. New York, 1937.

GLENDINNING, VICTORIA. *Edith Sitwell: a unicorn among lions*. London, 1981.

HALL, DONALD. *Remembering Poets*. New York, 1978.

HEYMANN, DAVID C. *Ezra Pound: The Last Rower*. London, 1976.

HOLROYD, MICHAEL. *Lytton Strachey: a biography*. London, 1971.

HUXLEY, ALDOUS. *Selected Letters of Aldous Huxley*, edited by Grover Smith. London, 1969.

KREYMBORG, ALFRED. *Troubadour*. New York, 1925.

LEWIS, WYNDHAM. *Men Without Art*. London, 1934.
Blasting and Bombadiering. London, 1937.
The Letters of Wyndham Lewis, edited by W. K. Rose. London, 1963.

The Lyttleton Hart-Davis Letters. Correspondence of George Lyttleton and Rupert Hart-Davis. Volumes 2–5. London, 1979, 1981, 1982, 1983.

McALMON, ROBERT and BOYLE, KAY. *Being Geniuses Together, 1920–1930*. London, 1970.

MARX, GROUCHO. *Letters from and to Groucho Marx*. New York, 1967.

MEYERS, JEFFREY. *The Enemy: a biography of Wyndham Lewis*. London, 1980.

MORRELL, OTTOLINE. *Ottoline at Garsington. Memoirs of Lady Ottoline Morrell, 1915–18*. Edited by Robert Gathorne-Hardy. London, 1974.

NORMAN, CHARLES. *Ezra Pound*. New York, 1960.

PATMORE, BRIGIT. *My Friends When Young: the memoirs of Brigit Patmore*, edited by Derek Patmore. London, 1968.

PEARSON, JOHN. *Façades: Edith, Osbert and Sacheverell Sitwell*. London, 1978.

POUND, EZRA. *The Letters of Ezra Pound. 1907–1941*, edited by D. D. Paige. London, 1951.

POWELL, ANTHONY. *To Keep the Ball Rolling: the memoirs of Anthony Powell*. Volumes 2 and 3, 'Messengers of Day' and 'Faces In My Time'. London, 1978 and 1980.

PROKOSCH, FREDERIC. *Voices*. London, 1983.

REID, B.L. *The Man from New York. John Quinn and His Friends*. New York, 1968.

Josiah Royce's Seminar, 1913–14: as recorded in the notebooks of Harry T. Costello. Edited by Grover Smith. New Jersey, 1963.

RUSSELL, BERTRAND. *The Autobiography of Bertrand Russell*. Volume 2. London, 1968.

SASSOON, SIEGFRIED. *Diaries, 1920–22*, edited and introduced by Rupert Hart-Davis. London, 1981.

SHEREK, HENRY. *Not In Front of the Children*. London, 1959.

SIMPSON, EILEEN. *Poets in Their Youth: a memoir* London, 1982.

SITWELL, OSBERT. *Left Hand, Right Hand. Memoirs of Osbert Sitwell*. Volume 4: 'Laughter in the Next Room'. London, 1949.

SPENDER, STEPHEN. *World Within World*. London, 1951.
  The Thirties and After. London, 1978.
STOCK, NOEL. *The Life of Ezra Pound*. London, 1970.
STRACHEY, JULIA. *Julia: A Portrait of Julia Strachey by Herself and Frances Partridge*. London, 1983.
WILSON, EDMUND. *Classics and Commercials. A literary chronicle of the Forties*. London, 1951.
  The Bit Between My Teeth. A literary chronicle of 1950–65. London, 1965.
  Letters on Literature and Politics: 1912–72, edited by Elena Wilson. London, 1977.
WILLIAMS, WILLIAM CARLOS. *The Autobiography of William Carlos Williams*. London, 1968.
WOOLF, LEONARD. *Beginning Again*. London, 1964.
  Downhill All The Way. London, 1967.
WOOLF, VIRGINIA. *The Diaries of Virginia Woolf*, edited by Anne Olivier Bell. Volumes 1–4. London, 1977, 1978, 1980 and 1982.
  The Letters of Virginia Woolf, edited by Nigel Nicolson and Joanna Trautmann. Volumes 1–6. London, 1975, 1976, 1977, 1978, 1979 and 1980.

MAGAZINE ARTICLES

There are innumerable vignettes of Eliot buried in the files of scholarly and literary magazines. I have simply included here the more interesting ones; others are referred to in my notes.

Harvard Advocate: June 1938. A festschrift.
Paris Review: Spring-Summer, 1959. An interview with Eliot.
Atlantic Monthly, May 1965. A memoir by Stravinsky.
Yale Review: June 1965. A festschrift.
Esquire, August 1965. A memoir by Lawrence Durrell.
The Book Collector, Winter, 1965. Accounts of T. S. Eliot and John Hayward.
Quarterly Review of Literature: 15, 1967. A memoir by George Seferis.
The Observer, 20 February 1972. An interview with Valerie Eliot.
The Listener, 28 April 1977. A memoir by E. W. F. Tomlin.

THESES

POWEL, JR, H. W. H. *Notes on the Life of T. S. Eliot, 1888–1910* (Brown University, 1954).
SOLDO, JOHN. The Tempering of T. S. Eliot, 1888–1915 (Harvard University, 1972).

Illustration
Acknowledgments

The publishers would like to thank the following for permission to use their photographs:

1 Missouri Historical Society
2 By permission of the Houghton Library, Harvard University
3 Missouri Historical Society
4 Missouri Historical Society
5 By permission of the Houghton Library, Harvard University
6 By permission of the Houghton Library, Harvard University
7 Missouri Historical Society
8 By permission of the Houghton Library, Harvard University
9 By permission of the Houghton Library, Harvard University
10 Missouri Historical Society
11 Missouri Historical Society
12 By permission of the Houghton Library, Harvard University
13 By permission of the Houghton Library, Harvard University
14 By permission of the Houghton Library, Harvard University
15 By permission of the Houghton Library, Harvard University
16 By permission of the Houghton Library, Harvard University
17 Photography Collection, Humanities Research Center, The University of Texas, Austin
18 Photography Collection, Humanities Research Center, The University of Texas, Austin
19 Photography Collection, Humanities Research Center, The University of Texas, Austin
20 By permission of the Houghton Library, Harvard University
21 National Portrait Gallery, London
22 National Portrait Gallery, London

23 By permission of the Houghton Library, Harvard University
24 Jane/Ann Haigh Wood
25 Jane/Ann Haigh Wood
26 By permission of the Houghton Library, Harvard University
27 By permission of the Houghton Library, Harvard University
28 By permission of the Houghton Library, Harvard University
29 Cecil Beaton photograph. Courtesy of Sotheby's London
30 National Portrait Gallery, London
31 National Portrait Gallery, London
32 Cecil Beaton photograph. Courtesy of Sotheby's London
33 By permission of the Houghton Library, Harvard University
34 By permission of the Houghton Library, Harvard University
35 By permission of the Houghton Library, Harvard University
36 By permission of the Houghton Library, Harvard University
37 Jane/Ann Haigh Wood
38 Missouri Historical Society
39 Cecil Beaton photograph. Courtesy of Sotheby's London
40 Fisk-Moore, Canterbury
41 BBC Hulton Picture Library
42 BBC Hulton Picture Library
43 BBC Hulton Picture Library
44 Theatre Museum. Photo Angus McBean
45 BBC Hulton Picture Library
46 Popperfoto
47 John Topham Picture Library
48 Popperfoto
49 The Bettmann Archive
50 The Bettmann Archive
51 National Portrait Gallery, London
52 Popperfoto
53 John Topham Picture Library
54 Popperfoto
55 Popperfoto
56 John Topham Picture Library
57 The Bettmann Archive
58 Popperfoto
59 Mander and Mitchenson Collection
60 Popperfoto
61 Popperfoto

62   John Topham Picture Library
63   Mander and Mitchenson Collection
64   Mark Gerson
65   Popperfoto
66   Mark Gerson
67   BBC Hulton Picture Library

Index

growing religious belief 137–8, 159–61; writes *Sweeney Agonistes* 145–8; writes *The Hollow Men* 147, 148; considers separation from Vivien 149, 159, 188–9, 192; joins Faber and Gwyer 151–2; first plans at Faber's 153; rift with Virginia Woolf 154; putative conversion 155–6; increasing academic respectability 156; joins Vivien at sanatoria 158; baptized and confirmed into Church of England 162; adopts British Citizenship 165, 178; makes first confession 169; meets Paul Elmer More 173; first published book on him 176; rumours about Eliots 186–7; lack of empathy with Vivien 187; 'Coriolan' experiment 189–91; offered Charles Eliot Norton professorship, Harvard 192; leaves Vivien 193; other American lectures 198–9, 199–202; *After Strange Gods* published 200; Deed of Separation 202–3, 208; happy interlude in New England 204; involvement in *The Rock* 209–10, 213–15; stays with Father Cheetham 211; first public performance of *Sweeney Agonistes* 215; and *The Cocktail Party* 217, 280, 286–7, 288, 293–6, 297; hostile reaction to his transformation 219–20; support of 'Social Credit' scheme 220–21; assists with *New English Weekly* 221; and Chandos Group 222; success as publisher 222–5; first performance of *Murder in the Cathedral* 226; writes 'Burnt Norton' 228, 230–31; and 'modernists' 238–9; increasing public engagements 239–41; increasing involvement in Anglican communion 241–3; and *The Family Reunion* 244–7; decides to discontinue *Criterion* 247–9; war effort (1939–45) 253–4, 258, 267, 268; writes 'East Coker' 254–6; increasing illness 260–61; and *Four Quartets* 262–6, 268–72; supports arrested Pound 268, 281–2; depression over post-war foreign policy 272–3; shares flat with Hayward 274–6, 278; routine in late 1940s 276–8; reaction to Vivien's death 283–4, 305; goes to America on death of brother 284–5; awarded Nobel Prize for Literature 289–90, 292, Pl.53; receives Order of Merit 289; abusive treatment over award of Bollingen Prize to Pound 296–7; appoints Valerie Fletcher as his secretary 298; becomes a celebrity 299–300; lecturing in America, 1950 299, 302–3; tranquillizer addiction 304; increasing hypochondria and phobias 304–5; allegations of homosexuality 309–10; completes *The Confidential Clerk* 311; awarded Hanseatic-Goethe prize 315, Pl.52; marries Valerie Fletcher 319–20; receives honorary degree in Rome 323, Pl.61; completes *The Elder Statesman* 323; seventieth birthday reception 326; receives Dante Gold Medal 327; trip to Morocco 329; late correspondence with Pound 329–30; recovers from coma 333; last trip to America 333–4; last visit to Leeds 334; death 334; ashes taken to East Coker 335